SUCH IS THE POWER OF LOVE
Saint Francis As Seen by Bonaventure

The Morning and Evening Sermons, October 4, 1255

The Major Legend of Saint Francis
(1260–1263)

The Minor Legend of Saint Francis
(1260–1266)

The Evening Sermon, October 4, 1262

A Sermon, October 4, 1266

A Sermon on the Feast of the Transferal of the Body of Saint Francis, May 25, 1267

The Morning and Evening Sermons, October 4, 1267

SUCH IS THE POWER OF LOVE
Saint Francis As Seen by Bonaventure

The Morning and Evening Sermons, October 4, 1255
The Major Legend of Saint Francis (1260-1263)
The Minor Legend of Saint Francis (1260-1266)
The Evening Sermon, October 4, 1262
A Sermon, October 4, 1266
A Sermon on the Feast of the Transferal of the Body of Saint Francis, May 25, 1267
The Morning and Evening Sermons, October 4, 1267

Edited by
Regis J. Armstrong, O.F.M. Cap.
J. A. Wayne Hellmann, O.F.M. Conv.
William J. Short, O.F.M.

New City Press
Hyde Park, New York

Published in the United States by
New City Press, 202 Cardinal Rd., Hyde Park, New York 12538
©2007 Franciscan Institute of St. Bonaventure University, St. Bonaventure, NY

Cover design by Durvanorte Correia

Translations taken from Francis of Assisi: Early Documents (vol. 2: *The Founder*),
Hyde Park, NY: New City Press, 2000.

Library of Congress Cataloging-in-Publication Data:

Bonaventure, Saint, Cardinal, ca. 1217-1274
    Such is the power of love : the life of Saint Francis as seen by Bonaventure /
Regis J. Armstrong, Wayne Hellmann, William J. Short (eds.).
        p. cm.
    Includes bibliographical references.
    Contents: Introduction -- Minor legend -- Major legend -- Sermons on Saint Francis.
    ISBN-13: 978-1-56548-257-9 (pbk. : alk. paper)
    1. Bonaventure, Saint, Cardinal, ca. 1217-1274. Legenda maior S. Francisci.
2. Bonaventure, Saint, Cardinal, ca. 1217-1274 Legenda minor S. Francisci. 3. Francis,
of Assisi, Saint, 1182-1226--Legends. 4. Francis, of Assisi, Saint, 1182-1226--Sermons.
5. Bonaventure, Saint, Cardinal, ca. 1217-1274.   I. Armstrong, Regis J.   II. Hellmann,
J. A. Wayne.   III. Short, William J.   IV. Title.
BX4700 . F65S83 2007
271' .302--dc22
[B]   2006025939

Printed in the United States of America

Contents

Foreword

Three years after Bonaventure's election as Minister General, the Lesser Brothers gathered for the Chapter of Narbonne, France, which became famous for the fact that the brothers commissioned him to compile "one good" legend of Saint Francis based on those already in existence.[1] Even a cursory glance at *The Major Legend* reveals how faithful Bonaventure was to his mandate to compile one good legend from all the existing ones. The largest number of episodes contained in the first fifteen chapters of *The Major Legend* come from *The Life of Saint Francis* by Thomas of Celano, refined by the writings of Julian of Speyer, and from *The Remembrance of the Desire of a Soul.* The influence of *The Legend of the Three Companions* and *The Assisi Compilation* are evident, although it is difficult to determine whether or not these influences were transmitted by way of Thomas's *Remembrance of the Desire of a Soul.* For the most part, Bonaventure contributes little to the biographical data provided by his predecessors. In fact, in the second section of *The Major Legend,* the consideration of Francis's miracles, the texts come almost entirely from Thomas's *Treatise on the Miracles of Saint Francis.*[2]

Bonaventure crafted his portrait according to the overall structure of his theology. Francis had become for him a symbol of the workings of grace. To understand the unfolding of his life was to perceive the inner dynamics of the gift of the Holy Spirit. Thus Bonaventure developed the first fifteen chapters of *The Major Legend,* those that treat of Francis's life, virtues, death and canonization, in a carefully thought out manner, maintaining that the human mind works from the visible to the invisible. At the same time, however, each chapter has a structure of its own as Bonaventure articulates through the use of stories the theologies of different virtues. As a result Bonaventure crafts a brilliant synthesis of Thomas's trilogy, *The Life of Saint Francis, The Remembrance of the Desire of a Soul,* and *The Treatise on the Miracles,* with the refinements of Julian of Speyer's liturgical pieces and *Life of Saint Francis.*

While *The Major Legend* was read during the brothers' meals, a shorter text, *The Minor Legend,* was written at the same time. It was meant primarily for chapel and church choirs for liturgical celebrations, often in the company of the faithful. *The Minor Legend* offers a testimony to a life uniquely paradigmatic of the journey into God. Celebrative and spiritual in nature, *The Minor Legend* played a major role in diffusing this image and message of Francis as it became a salient element of the brothers' celebration of their founder.

In 1263 Bonaventure presented both of these completed works to the brothers at the General Chapter of Pisa. Three years later, the brothers gathered again at the General Chapter of Paris and, in the following words, established *The Major* and *The Minor Legends* as the definitive portraits of Francis:

The General Chapter likewise orders under obedience that all the legends of the Blessed Francis that have been made should be removed. Wherever they find these outside the Order, let the brothers strive to remove them. For this Legend made by the General Minister has been compiled as he received it from the mouth of those who were always with blessed Francis and had certain knowledge of everything, and proven facts have been diligently placed in it.[3]

Controversial as this degree may be, it suggests that the brothers recognized the genius of Bonaventure's theological approach, one that would guarantee a more universal acceptance of Francis of Assisi. At the same time, although the critics might argue about lacuna or emphasis, *The Major Legend,* in particular, clearly reveals the brilliant mind of a theologian profoundly aware of the spiritual traditions of the Middle Ages. As in his earlier *Soul's Journey into God,* in *The Major Legend* Bonaventure identifies Francis's unique place among those traditions.[4] In both instances, he does so with his ministry of guiding his brothers, that is, of aiding them in discovering the wonder of their Founder and his vision of the world, themselves, and the God Who calls them.

As the last texts of Bonaventure in this volume indicate, the sermons on Saint Francis that he later preached to his brothers suggest that he saw them as opportunities to explain and further many of the images in his portraits. In 1276, shortly after Bonaventure's death, the General Chapter of Padua initiated a search for new information pertaining to Francis's life, some of which later found its way into *The Major Legend.*[5] The texts that appear in the third volume of *Francis of Assisi: Early Documents* (*The Prophet*) attest to the fact that Bonaventure did not resolve fundamental questions about the spirit of the Founder. He did, however, place Francis of Assisi in the larger framework of history and, in doing so, provided future writers with the image of the prophet, one sent by God with a message to tell.

Notes

1. Cesare Cenci, "De Fratrum Minorum constitutionibus praenarbonensibus," *Archivum Franciscanum Historicum* 83 (1990): 50-95 (hereafter AFH); "The Constitutions of Narbonne" (1260), in *Writings Concerning the Franciscan Order,* Works of Saint Bonaventure V, introduction and translation by Dominic Monti (St. Bonaventure, NY: Franciscan Institute Publications, 1994), 71-135.

2. The source of this mandate is obscure. It cannot be found in either the *Constitutions of Narbonne* nor in its *Definitiones.*

3. Bonaventure intersperses thirty-five of the miracles described in 3C in LMj. Bonaventure adds five new episodes to his own *Treatise on the Miracles,* the second part of LMj.

4. Cf. *Miscellanea Franciscana* 72 (1972): 247.

5. Ewert H. Cousins described Bonaventure's *Soul's Journey into God* as " a *summa,* comparable in its own sphere to the *Summa theologicae* of Thomas Aquinas, for he draws together in a comprehensive synthesis major strands of Christian spirituality." Cf. *Bonaventure: The Soul's Journey into God, the Tree of Life, The Life of Saint Francis,* translation and introduction by Ewert H. Cousins, preface by Ignatius C. Brady (New York, Ramsey, Toronto: Paulist Press, 1978), 20.

Abbreviations

Writings of Saint Francis

Adm	The Admonitions	LtL	A Letter to Brother Leo
BlL	A Blessing for Brother Leo	LtMin	A Letter to a Minister
CtC	The Canticle of the Creatures	LtOrd	A Letter to the Entire Order
CtExh	The Canticle of Exhortation	LtR	A Letter to Rulers of the Peoples
1Frg	Fragments of Worchester Manuscript	ExhP	Exhortation to the Praise of God
2Frg	Fragments of Thomas of Celano	PrOF	A Prayer Inspired by the Our Father
3Frg	Fragments from Hugh of Digne	PrsG	The Praises of God
LtAnt	A Letter to Brother Anthony of Padua	OfP	The Office of the Passion
1LtCl	First Letter to the Clergy (Earlier Edition)	PrCr	The Prayer before the Crucifix
		ER	The Earlier Rule (*Regula non bullata*)
2LtCl	Second Letter to the Clergy (Later Edition)	LR	The Later Rule (*Regula bullata*)
		RH	A Rule for Hermitages
1LtCus	The First Letter to the Custodians	SalBV	A Salutation of the Blessed Virgin Mary
2LtCus	The Second Letter to the Custodians	SalV	A Salutation of Virtues
1LtF	The First Letter to the Faithful	Test	The Testament
2LtF	The Second Letter to the Faithful	TPJ	True and Perfect Joy

Franciscan Sources

1C	The Life of Saint Francis by Thomas of Celano	ScEx	The Sacred Exchange between Saint Francis and Lady Poverty
2C	The Remembrance of the Desire of a Soul	AP	The Anonymous of Perugia
		L3C	The Legend of the Three Companions
3C	The Treatise on the Miracles by Thomas of Celano	LP	The Legend of Perugia
		AC	The Assisi Compilation
LCh	The Legend for Use in the Choir	UChL	An Umbrian Choir Legend
Off	The Divine Office of Saint Francis by Julian of Speyer	1-4Srm	The Sermons of Bonaventure
		LMj	The Major Legend by Bonaventure
LJS	The Life of Saint Francis by Julian of Speyer	LMn	The Minor Legend by Bonaventure
		BPr	The Book of Praises by Bernard of Besse
VL	The Versified Life of Saint Francis by Henri d'Avranches	IntR	The Intention of the Rule
1-3JT	The Praises by Jacopone da Todi	OL	An Old Legend
DCom	The Divine Comedy by Dante Alighieri	WSF	The Words of Saint Francis
		WBC	The Words of Brother Conrad
TL	Tree of Life by Ubertino da Casale	DBF	The Deeds of Blessed Francis and His Companions
1MP	The Mirror of Perfection, Smaller Version	LFl	The Little Flowers of Saint Francis
2MP	The Mirror of Perfection, Larger Version	KnSF	The Kinship of Saint Francis
		ChrTE	The Chronicle of Thomas of Eccleston
HTrb	The Book of Chronicles or of the Tribulations of the Order of Lesser Ones by Angelo of Clareno	ChrJG	The Chronicle of Jordan of Giano

Other Sources

AF	Analecta Franciscana	DEC	Decrees of the Ecumenical Councils
AFH	Archivum Franciscanum Historicum	DMA	Dictionary of the Middle Ages
AM	Annales Minorum	GR	Greyfriars Review
BFr	Bullarium Franciscanum	PL	Patrologia Latina
CCSL	Corpus Christianorum, Series Latina	PG	Patrologia Graeca
CSEL	Corpus Scriptorum Eccles. Latinorum	TM	Testimonia Minora Saeculi

Scripture abbreviations are from *The New American Bible*; the Psalms follow the modern numbering sequence. Scripture references accompanying non-italicized text imply *confer*, or cf. References to the volumes in *Francis of Assisi: Early Documents* will be abbreviated FA:ED I, II.

THE LEGENDS AND SERMONS

ABOUT SAINT FRANCIS

BY

BONAVENTURE OF BAGNOREGIO

(1255–1267)

Introduction

In 1260 the Lesser Brothers gathered for a General Chapter in Narbonne, France. An important item on their agenda was the codification of the decisions made at the eleven previous general chapters. This resulted in a legal document that became known as the *Constitutions of Narbonne*.[1] The Chapter became famous, however, for another reason: the brothers mandated Bonaventure of Bagnoregio, the general minister whom they had elected three years earlier, to compile a new legend of Saint Francis based on those already in existence. Nothing in the *Definitiones* or decisions of the Chapter record indicates the reasons for this mandate. Only the brothers' decision to correct the liturgical antiphon *Hic vir in vanitatibus nutritus indecenter* suggests the need to bring uniformity to the voluminous material forming around the Founder.[2]

According to his own testimony, Bonaventure was hesitant. "I feel," he writes in the Prologue to the *Major Legend*, "that I am unworthy and unequal to the task of writing the life of a man so venerable and worthy of imitation. I would never have attempted it if the fervent desire of the brothers had not aroused me, the unanimous urging of the General Chapter had not induced me, and the devotion which I am obliged to have toward our holy father had not compelled me."[3] History confirms the legitimacy of the brothers' intuition. Six years later, the decision of the brothers at the Chapter of Paris effectively recognized Bonaventure's portraits of Francis as a "hagiographical and theological masterpiece."[4]

Bonaventure was born Giovanni di Fidanza, in the small town of Bagnoregio about 1221. Although he never claims to have met Francis, the devotion to which he felt obligated undoubtedly came from a cure he enjoyed because of the saint's intercession. "When I was just a child," he declares in the *Major Legend*, "and very seriously ill, my mother made a vow on my behalf to the blessed Father Francis. I was snatched from the very jaws of death and restored to the vigor of a healthy life."[5] That Francis's influence rested on the boy is verified in Bonaventure's entrance into the Order of Lesser Brothers in 1243, probably in Paris where, eight years earlier, he had gone to study.

As a young student brother in the Parisian Couvent des Cordeliers, the friary of the "Cord-bearers," as the brothers were known, established in 1231, Bonaventure's formation was strongly influenced by four great Franciscan "masters:" John de la Rochelle (+1245), Odo Rigaldus (+ 1275), William of Middleton (+1260), and, above all, Alexander of Hales (+ 1245). In 1250, now enjoying the title "Master of Arts," Bonaventure began his commentary on *The Sentences of Peter Lombard*, a mandatory exercise introduced by Alexander into the curriculum of the Parisian brothers. Four years later, the General Minister, John of Parma (+1272), granted him the license to teach theology. He immediately became engrossed in a dispute with William of Saint-Amour (+ 1272) of the University of Paris over the principles governing the Lesser Brothers and the Friars Preacher. The dispute brought such notoriety to Bonaventure and his Dominican colleague, Thomas of Aquino (+ 1274), that Pope Alexander IV urged the Parisian masters to incorporate both men into their ranks. This incorporation was achieved in August, 1257, six months after the brothers had elected Bonaventure their General Minister.

The Chapter of Ara Coeli, Rome lasted one day, February 2, 1257. Pope Alexander IV, the former Cardinal Rainaldo, the Cardinal Protector of the Order, had asked for and obtained the resignation of the General Minister, John of Parma. In his place, the brothers turned to Bonaventure. Their choice was understandable for the saintly John of Parma had been accused of being sympathetic to and of promoting certain tenets of Joachim of Fiore (+ 1202). Joachim, a Cistercian abbot, had proposed a theology in which an understanding of the Trinity, revelation and history were all entwined. His followers, including one of the Lesser Brothers, Gerardo of Borgo San Donnino, promoted his millenarian vision and his references to the coming age of the Holy Spirit heralded by the Angel of the Sixth Seal. In 1254 William of Saint-Amour and other Parisian masters condemned Gerardo, proposing him as another example of the distorted understanding of evangelical life expounded by the brothers. Alexander IV condemned Gerardo's *Introductorius in Evangelium Eternum* in 1255. The following year he condemned William of Saint-Amour's *Tractatus de periculis novissimorum temporum,* and, to cleanse the Lesser Brothers of any suggestion of Joachimite influences, urged John of Parma to resign.

Understandably the quickly developing Order, now grown to thirty thousand brothers spread throughout Europe, Africa and Asia, was in need of direction. The brothers were becoming gradually more divided in their interpretations of the Founder's ideals and their day-to-day expression.[6] Since the death of Francis, the brothers had seen a succession of General Ministers: Elias (1226-1227), John Parenti (1227-1232), Elias again (1232-1239), Albert of Pisa (1239), Haymo of Faversham (1239-1244), Crescentius of Iesi (1244-1247), and John of Parma (1247-1257).

No stranger to controversy, Bonaventure guided the brothers from February 2, 1257 until May 20, 1273 when Pope Gregory X made him Cardinal Bishop of Albano. While Bonaventure's earlier writings reveal his respect for tradition and suggest that he was conservative by temperament, they also indicate his perceptive mind as well as his ability to confront the issues threatening the Order. Above all, these early writings clearly show Bonaventure's profound grasp of the mystical tradition and his sensitivity to the unique place of Francis's vision within it.[7] Within the Order, therefore, Bonaventure strove to address various crises confronting the Order, to articulate the unique character of its Gospel ideals, and to re-enkindle it among the brothers. His first two letters, written ten years apart, show the intensity of his efforts, the depth of his comprehension, and the simplicity of his solution: a return to the rule and life of the Lesser Brothers, that is, to the *Later Rule*.[8]

Early Writings about Saint Francis

By the time he had begun to honor the request of the brothers assembled at the Chapter of Narbonne, Bonaventure had already written a considerable amount. Surprisingly, beyond the *Soul's Journey into God*, little is concerned with Francis of Assisi. Occasional references can be found in Bonaventure's commentaries on the *Sentences* of Peter Lombard and the Gospel of Luke. Were these his only references, the judgment of John H.R. Moorman may be justified: Bonaventure "never really understood the Franciscan ideal."[9] His letter to an unknown master, however, provides an insight into his understanding of his call to be Francis's follower.

> Do not be disturbed, that the brothers were simple and illiterate men in the beginning; this should confirm your faith in the Order even more. I confess before God that it is this that made me love the life of blessed Francis above all, because it is similar in its beginning and perfection to that of the Church, which began with simple fishermen and grew to include the most illustrious and learned doctors. And so you will see in the Order of blessed Francis, as God displays, that it was not invented by human discernment but by Christ.[10]

While it is difficult to date this letter, this passage suggests it was written during the same period as two sermons he delivered on the Feast of Saint Francis, October 4, 1255, five years before the brothers commissioned Bonaventure to compile the new legend. All three, the letter and the morning and evening sermons of October 4, touch on aspects of the same theme: "the essence of true discipleship of Jesus Christ, which was singularly realized and shone in Saint Francis."[11]

The sermons of 1255 are Bonaventure's first known writings dedicated principally to Saint Francis. Although they do not have the depth that can be found in his later Franciscan works, they nevertheless reveal seminal ideas that come to fruition in the *Major* and *Minor Legends*. Bonaventure reveals in the morning sermon his struggle with the meaning of "conversion" in the Christian life of the young Francis, his cultivation, even at an early age, of solitude, and the differing shades and meanings of his embrace of poverty. In a milieu in which Francis's stigmata were being challenged,[12] Bonaventure subtly crafts a theology of signs maintaining that the stigmata were "signs of consummate love." "Such is the power of love," Bonaventure reminds his listeners in the words of Hugh of St. Victor, "that it transforms the lover into the Beloved."[13] Throughout, Bonaventure displays his awareness of the literary heritage left by Thomas of Celano. His use of many of Thomas's images, undoubtedly controversial in the anti-Joachimite milieu of the University of Paris, indicate how sensitive Bonaventure was to their implications.

The evening sermon takes a somewhat different approach as Bonaventure explores the significance of his calling, and that of his brothers, to be a Lesser Brother. While the morning sermon was dedicated to Christ's words (Mt 11:29), "Learn from me," the evening sermon developed the remaining part of the verse, ". . . for I am meek and humble of heart." "To be meek is to be a brother to everybody," he declares, "to be humble is to be less than everybody. Therefore, to be meek and humble of heart is to be a true lesser brother."[14] Thus, in the evening sermon, Bonaventure lays the foundations of the universality of the fraternal relations he describes in the eighth chapter of *The Major Legend.*

Valuable as these insights into Bonaventure's Franciscan thought may be, those provided by his *Itinerarium mentis in Deum* [The Soul's Journey Into God] are even more so. The *Itinerarium* is the fruit of Bonaventure's stay on LaVerna where Francis had received the stigmata. At the opening of the work, the meditative General Minister writes:

> Inspired by the example of our most blessed father, Francis, I wanted to seek after this peace with yearning soul, sinner that I am and all unworthy, yet the seventh successor as Minister to all the brothers in the place of the blessed father after his death. It happened that, thirty-three years after the death of the saint, about the time of his passing, moved by a divine impulse, I withdrew to Mount La Verna, as to a place of quiet, there to satisfy the yearning of my soul for peace. While I dwelt there, pondering on certain spiritual ascents to God, I was struck among other things, by that miracle which in this very place had happened to the blessed Francis, that is, the vision he received of the winged seraph in the form of the Crucified. As I reflected on this marvel, it immediately seemed to me that this vision might suggest the rising of Saint Francis into contemplation and point out the way by which that state of contemplation may be reached.[15]

On the cliffs of La Verna, it became clear to him that Francis's mystical experience was not only the goal of his vocation and that of his brothers, but also the road to it. A sermon Bonaventure delivered on Holy Saturday reveals his reflections on three ways of ascending into God: that of Bernard of Clairvaux,[16] another of Richard of St. Victor,[17] and, finally, that of Giles of Assisi, the companion of Francis himself.[18] His first letter to the brothers, April 23, 1257, suggests that he may have returned to these reflections as a means recalling the Order from the paths onto which it had strayed and of finding consolation for his soul. On La Verna, however, Bonaventure, like Francis, seems himself to have had a mystical experience. His understanding of the saint deepened; his insight into the rapture of Francis's experience on La Verna and its result, the stigmata, left an indelible mark on Bonaventure's genius. The vision of a six-winged Seraph re-enforced his conviction that the crucified Christ was at the very heart of Christian life, the center around which all else revolved.

> The six wings of the Seraph, can be rightly understood as signi-
> fying the six levels of uplifting illuminations by which, as if by
> steps or stages, the soul is disposed to pass over to peace through
> ecstatic transport of Christian wisdom. The road to this peace is
> through nothing else than a most ardent love of the Crucified,
> the love of which so transformed Paul into Christ when he (2 Cor
> 12:2) *was carried up to the third heaven* that he could say: (Gal 2:20)
> *With Christ I am nailed to the cross. I live, now not I, but Christ lives in*
> *me.* And this love also so absorbed the soul of Francis that his
> spirit shone through his flesh the last two years before his death
> when he carried in his body the sacred marks of the passion.[19]

Bonaventure then proceeds to articulate his own understanding of the vision. In doing so, however, the figure of Francis becomes that of the Christian
soul, the one who enters through the Crucified, who washes in the blood of
the Lamb, who becomes inflamed with desire.

> The figure of the six wings of the Seraph, therefore, brings to
> mind the six steps of illumination which begin with creatures
> and lead up to God, Whom no one rightly enters save through
> the Crucified. (Jn 10:1) *For he who enters not by the door, but climbs*
> *up another way, is a thief and a robber* (Jn 10:9) *But if anyone enter* by
> this door, *he shall go in and out and shall find pastures.* For this rea-
> son Saint John says in the Apocalypse: (Rv 22:14) *Blessed are they*
> *who wash their robes in the blood of the Lamb, that they may have a right*
> *to the tree of life and that by the gates may enter into the city.* That is to
> say, no one can enter by contemplation into the heavenly Jeru-
> salem unless he enters through the blood of the Lamb as
> through a door. For no one is in any way disposed for divine con-
> templations that lead to spiritual transports unless, like Daniel
> he is also (Dn 9:23) *a man of desires.* Now, such desires are
> enkindled in us in two ways, to wit, through the outcry of
> prayer, which makes one sigh (Ps 37:9) from *anguish of heart,* and
> through *the refulgence of speculation* by which the mind most di-
> rectly and intently turns itself toward the rays of light.[20]

Those "signs of consummate love," as Bonaventure described the stigmata
in his 1255 sermon on Saint Francis, now provided for those who would follow Francis's lead on the path into God. And, as Bonaventure articulated in
his final work, *The Collations on the Six Days,* they provided one of the underly-
ing principles of the *Major Legend:* the *impressed* stigmata were *expressed* signs.[21]

The stigmatized Francis became for Bonaventure someone whose life provided a road map of perfection, one that could be followed not only because of internal evidence, but, more so, because of these external signs of God's approbation.

The Major Legend

Even a cursory glance at the *Major Legend* reveals how faithful Bonaventure was to his mandate to compile one good legend from all the existing ones.[22] The largest number of episodes contained in the first fifteen chapters of the *Major Legend* come from Thomas of Celano's *Life of Saint Francis*, refined by the writings of Julian of Speyer, and *The Remembrance of the Desire of a Soul*. The influence of the *Legend of the Three Companions* and the *Assisi Compilation* are certainly evident, although it is difficult to determine whether or not these influences were transmitted by way of Thomas's *Remembrance*. For the most part, Bonaventure contributes little to the biographical data provided by his predecessors. In fact, in the second section of the *Major Legend*, the consideration of Francis's miracles, the texts come almost entirely from Thomas's *Treatise on the Miracles*.[23]

Bonaventure's contribution consists in setting these earlier materials in a new framework. "From the visible to the invisible," he teaches in his *Commentary on John's Gospel*. Thus, the historical, observable events of Francis's life led Bonaventure to understand more concretely the mysterious, hidden designs of God. The opening lines of the Prologue reveal immediately this appreciation of Francis's life. "The grace of God our Savior," Bonaventure declares at the outset, "has appeared in his servant Francis . . ." The sanctity of Francis, as that of every Christian, consists in the unfolding of grace, that gift of the Holy Spirit that, according to the *Breviloquium*, purifies, illumines, and perfects.[24] In a rich mosaic of biblical passages, Bonaventure elegantly outlines his portrait of the "hierarchic man" in a framework that resonates with the threefold approach found throughout his writings.[25]

Undoubtedly Bonaventure was influenced in this approach by the writings of the Pseudo-Dionysius and Thomas Gallus (+1246), both of whom described growth in the spiritual life as growth through the successive stages of purgation, illumination, and unification.[26] For Francis's disciple, Bonaventure, however, growth in virtue consisted in more than this hierarchical progress. Francis's *Canticle of Brother Sun* opened a new horizon and showed that the saint had discovered God in the most simple gifts of creation. This dimension of the mystic Francis challenged Bonaventure, his follower, to re-think the hierarchical vision. The *ordo amoris* [the ordering of love], as he described virtue in the first of the *Disputed Questions on Evangelical Perfection*, demands a clear sense of direction. His view of creation sees a "twofold order of things, one within the universe, and another with regard to their end."[27] By the time of his compilation of Thomas and Julian, Bonaventure had produced a well-developed theology in which he envisioned God having written for humanity three books: the Book of Creation, the Book of Scripture, and the Book of Life. Had Adam not sinned, he maintains, the Book of Creation would have been efficacious in leading human beings to discover the power, wisdom, and goodness of God. Because of sin, that Book had become obscured prompting God to provide the Book of Scripture. In it, a human can discover the triune God and, enlightened by grace, a human can discover the Book of Life and in it the fullness of life.[28] Bonaventure's portrait of the "hierachic man" Francis is also that of the individual whom grace teaches to see correctly and to interact with the created world in which he lives.

At the very heart of this vision is the cross. As in all his other writings, Bonaventure places the mystery of the crucified Christ at the very center of his understanding. After the manner of John the Evangelist, he accentuates six manifestations or signs pointing to a seventh, that is, six apparitions of the cross, all of which are in the first four chapters, pointing to the reception of the stigmata in the thirteenth. Then, in Chapter Nine, at the very heart of the nine chapters treating the virtues of Francis, Bonaventure describes the saint's burning desire to be identified with Christ crucified. The evening sermon that he preached on October 4, 1262, while he was writing *The Major Legend*, focuses on Matthew 24:30: *Then will appear the sign of the Son of man in heaven*. Reading that sermon now, it is obvious that it was a key to Bonaventure's portrait of Francis. His reception of the stigmata was not only the supreme moment of contemplative ecstasy, it was the vindication of his entire life. "The cross of Christ is the sign of God's perfect works and of all his wonderful deeds," Bonaventure reminds his brothers in Paris. "And because Saint Francis can be likened to the heavens in all he did, we should expect to find the cross imprinted on him, so that by this sign he would be raised on high."[29]

While it is important to understand the overall structure of Bonaventure's portrait of Francis, the *Major Legend,* each chapter has a structure of its own. In some of these, the theology of the Parisian master is more obvious than in others. Linear in some, it is concentric in others. Chapter Six, for example, begins describing the foundations of Francis's humility before God and continues with its exercise before his brothers, especially in the practice of obedience. The second half of the chapter is dedicated to God's response to this practice of virtue, providing by way of examples a balanced picture of the pursuit of virtue. Chapter Eight, on the other hand, describes Francis's practice of piety through a pattern of concentric circles in which his devotion to God after the example of Christ is at its very heart. Bonaventure then continues with the saint's relations with his brothers, his fellow human beings, especially with the poor and the sick, and proceeds to his relations with animals. In each instance, Bonaventure respectfully uses the texts of Thomas of Celano and Julian of Speyer to craft his image of Saint Francis.

As he describes Francis's life in visible detail, Bonaventure underscores the invisible strokes of God's grace. The result is a remarkable piece of literature, written in much the same way as the artisans and craftsmen of those recently built Gothic structures that surrounded his Parisian friary.[30] To understand the aesthetics of his portrait of Francis, it is as important to comprehend the architectonic lines of his thought as to concentrate on the nuances of his delicately crafted tableaux. Like any gifted architect living in close contact with the sculptors, glass painters, and wood carvers, Bonaventure focused his attention on the details of Thomas of Celano, Julian of Speyer, and those who knew Francis, and studied their writings attentively that he might gracefully incorporate them into his own design.

The Minor Legend

The second commission Bonaventure received was to write a work similar to Thomas of Celano's Legend for the Use in Choir. *The Minor Legend* for official use during the Octave of the Feast of Saint Francis ensured the eradication of Thomas of Celano and Julian of Speyer's earlier liturgical-hagiographical memories of Francis. The possible insertion of this concise theological reflection on Francis's life into the portable breviaries[31] also encouraged the broad diffusion of Bonaventure's text throughout Europe.[32]

The Minor Legend emerged as the brothers promoted Francis's spirituality in the midst of an on-going interpretation of their identity and mission. Architects and artists assisted in these efforts as they designed and decorated the Basilica of Saint Francis in Assisi and other large urban churches.[33] In surprisingly spacious and stunningly beautiful liturgical environs,[34] men and women were reminded through paintings, preaching, and praying of God's incredible condescension in the Crucified Christ[35] and Francis's response to this divine initiative. Present in image and word, Francis's life revealed a paradigmatic conformity to Christ invoking and inviting people everywhere, regardless of social or ecclesial standing, to follow him, in union with the Crucified, into the mystery of God.[36] *The Minor Legend,* celebrative and spiritual in nature,[37] played a major role in diffusing this image and message of Francis as it became a salient element of the celebration of the Founder.[38]

The liturgical celebration of Francis's spiritual journey focused on the Feast of Saint Francis which was celebrated throughout the Roman Church on October 4th. The opening chapter of *The Minor Legend* was read during the solemn office on that day, and the remaining chapters throughout the Octave of the Feast of Saint Francis culminating on October 11th when the first chapter was repeated. The nine lessons of each chapter were divided among the nocturnal hours.[39]

The liturgical nature of *The Minor Legend* underscores the relationship between the text of Francis's story and the context of Bonaventure's personal dedication to prayer. It also offers a hermeneutic insight into how to read *The Major Legend*. As both theologian and General Minister, Bonaventure had urged his brothers to pray unceasingly with the entire Church and recognize, in prayer, the opportunity to encounter the Crucified Christ manifested in the stigmatized flesh of Francis.[40] An echo of Bonaventure's devotion is heard at the conclusion of *The Major Legend*. At the opening of *The Major Legend,* Bonaventure links the miracle of his childhood healing through Francis's intercession with a formal recognition of a literary debt owed to the saint. In *The Minor Legend* of Saint Francis, however, the memory of Francis's intercession evokes a prayer of gratitude and an accompanying plea for the Franciscan minor fraternity to come together in the prayerful remembrance of the Poor Man, now venerated as the saint from Assisi.

Approval

In 1263 Bonaventure presented his completed legends to the brothers at the General Chapter of Pisa. It is not difficult to imagine that, as Michael Bihl suggests, thirty-four manuscripts of the text were prepared, one for each Province of the Order.[41] There is no evidence of these manuscripts, nor is there any statement of the Chapter's approval of the work. The brothers gathered at the General Chapter of Paris in 1266 may well have mandated that each friary have a manuscript of the text, but their decision to establish the *Major Legend* as the definitive portrait of Francis remains its far more important contribution. "The General Chapter likewise orders under obedience that all the legends of the Blessed Francis that have been made should be removed. Wherever they find these outside the Order, let the brothers strive to remove them. For this Legend made by the General Minister has been compiled as he received it from the mouth of those who were always with blessed Francis and had certain knowledge of everything, and proven facts have been diligently placed in it."[42]

In light of Bonaventure's prologue to the *Constitutions of Narbonne* in which he states that "the highest governing authority of the Order resides in the general chapter,"[43] it is difficult to imagine that he would be so presumptuous as to mandate his portrait of Francis as definitive and to order the destruction of all others. In reaction to the autocratic administration of Elias and following the example of the Friars Preacher, the Lesser Brothers decided that the chapter determined policy; the responsibility of the general minister was to execute it.[44] Nevertheless, the results of the decree were drastic. The editors of the *Analecta Franciscana* discovered less than twenty manuscripts of Thomas's *Life of Saint Francis* and most of these were in the possession of the Cistercians. There were only two of Thomas's *Remembrance of the Desire of A Soul.*

Thus Bonaventure's work became the fundamental, primary portrait of Francis and, next to his *Rule* and *Testament,* the principal interpreter of his vision. By the middle of the next century, there were one thousand five hundred and thirty manuscripts of the *Major Legend* in friaries throughout Europe and at least another four hundred in the monasteries of the Poor Clares. Sadly, the Order had begun to fragment at this time and Bonaventure and his interpretation of Francis became a highly contested point. Nevertheless, Arnaud of Sarrant eloquently compared Bonaventure's portrait in terms of John's Gospel:

> The fourth author was like another John the Eagle, Brother Bonaventure. His knowledge was like that of an eagle lifted ever high. And when he was general minister, it was as if he were the king of all fowl. This man, more clearly than the others, de-

scribed the rapture and ecstasy of Francis, and recounted that vision and appearance of the Seraph more brilliantly than the rest.[45]

Undoubtedly, it was that mystical dimension of Bonaventure's work that made it such a reservoir of spirituality to the second generation of Francis's followers. As the spiritual climate changed at the end of the thirteenth century, so did the appeal of Bonaventure's portrait.

The final judgment of the scope of his portrait, however, is best left to Bonaventure himself. At the conclusion of his *Soul's Journey into God,* he wrote:

> . . . In a transport of contemplation on the mountain height, there appeared to Blessed Francis the six-winged Seraph fastened to a cross, as I and many others have heard from the companion who was then with him at that very place. Here he passed over into God in a transport of contemplation. He is set forth as an example of perfect contemplation, just as previously he had been of action, like a second Jacob-Israel. And thus, through him, more by example than by word, God would invite all truly spiritual persons to this passing over and this transport of soul.[46]

Later Writings

Bonaventure was to dedicate four more sermons to Saint Francis, all of which he preached to his brothers at the University of Paris. All of these, the sermon of October 4, 1266, that commemorating the transferral of Francis's body to the new basilica built in Assisi in his honor, that is, the sermon of May 27, 1267, and the morning and evening sermons of October 4, 1267, seem to be outlines. The first of these, in particular, is quite brief and proceeds in an orderly fashion, numbering each point that it might easily be remembered. Although it is somewhat longer, the same manner of presentation is obvious in the second of these sermons. Only the last two pieces show the same in-depth, carefully developed composition that can be seen in Bonaventure's first sermon on Saint Francis, October 4, 1255.

It is important to note, however, Bonaventure used these sermons to explain or deepen images or biblical passages present in his legends. The third sermon, for example, revolves around Haggai 2:23, I will take you, O Zerubbabel my servant . . . and make you like a seal. "For as Zerubbabel," Bonaventure explains, "whose name means 'leader of the exodus,' led the people out of Babylon and rebuilt the Temple, so Saint Francis brought many people from the disorder of sin to Christ and, he founded a religious Order." The sermon becomes a brilliant elaboration of the seal that Bonaventure's new Zerubbabel, Francis, had become: "refashioned, transformed, imprinted and declaratory."[47] In the Sermon on the Feast of the Transferral, Bonaventure elaborates on the images of Jacob and Moses, both present in the *Major Lege*nd, and offers a new one as he applies the image of Mordecai, the guardian of Esther, to Francis.

The final sermon, that of October 4, 1267, reveals Bonaventure at his biblical best. His theme is Isaiah 42:1, *Behold my servant whom I uphold . . .* Zerubbabel, Job, Elijah, Paul, the wise servant of Luke's Gospel, Jesus Himself: all become images of Francis and reminders of what it means to be a Lesser Brother. Bonaventure offers new insights into persons who appear in his legends, Gregory IX, Pacifico, Saint Clare and her Sisters: each of these reveals a dimension of Francis's story portrayed in passages from Scripture, and authors such as Augustine, Anselm, Bernard, and Francis himself. This final sermon is, in a sense of *tour-de-force,* a commentary on Bonaventure's developing appreciation for the saint he knew as a boy, Francis of Assisi.

Notes

1. Cesare Cenci, "De Fratrum Minorum constitutionibus praenarbonensibus," AFH 83 (1990): 50-95; The Constitutions of Narbonne (1260), in *Writings Concerning the Franciscan Order,* Works of Saint Bonaventure V, introduction and translation by Dominic Monti (St. Bonaventure, NY: Franciscan Institute Publications, 1994), 71-135.

2. Julian of Speyer, following the biographical material presented by Thomas of Celano, wrote *Hic vir in vanitatibus nutritus indecenter/Plus suis nutritoribus, Se gessit insolenter* [This man was raised in vanities/And shameful was his rearing;/Outstripping those that nurtured him,/His ways were overbearing.] The Chapter changed the last phrase of the antiphon to: *Divinis charismatibus/Praeventus est clementer* [Through divine gifts/He was mercifully delivered.] Cf. FA:ED I 332 c.

3. Cf. LM Prol 3, infra 46.

4. Bernard McGinn, *The Flowering of Mysticism: New Men and Women in the New Mysticism–1200-1350,* The Presence of God: A History of Western Christian Mysticism, Vol. III (New York: The Crossroad Publishing Company, 1998), 94-95. McGinn's judgment reflects that of contemporary scholarship and at odds with those of A.G. Little, "Guide to Franciscan Studies," in *Études franciscaines* 40 (1928): 517-533; (1929): 64-68; John H.R. Moorman, *The Sources of the Life of Saint Francis* (Manchester: University Press, 1940), 141; and Anthony Mockler, *Francis of Assisi: The Wandering Years* (Oxford: Phaedon, 1976).

5. LMn VII 8, infra 235.

6. For an understanding of these divisions, see Duncan Nimmo, *Reform and Division in the Franciscan Order (1226-1538),* (Rome: Capuchin Historical Institute, 1987), 51-108.

7. Bernard McGinn notes: "Bernard of Clairvaux and Bonaventure–the *doctor mellifluous* and the *doctor seraphicus*–may be justly described as the two premier mystical teachers of the Medieval West. Both were important ecclesiastical officials who were forced to be men of action, as well as of contemplation. Both wrote on a variety of theological and church-political topics, as well as on how the soul attains God in this life." Bernard McGinn, *The Presence of God: A History of Western Christian Mysticism,* The Flowering of Mysticism (New York: The Crossroad Publishing Company, 1998), 87.

8. Both of these letters can be found in Monti, *Writings,* 57-62, 225-229.

9. Moorman, *Sources,* 141.

10. Bonaventure of Bagnoregio, *Doctoris Seraphici S. Bonaventurase opera omnia.* 10 volumes, in folio. (Ad Claras Aquas, Quaracchi: Collegium S. Bonaventurae, 1882-1902), VIII, 336. This work is referred to by the traditional method, citing Roman numeral for volume, Arabic for page. A translation of the entire *Letter to an Unknown Master* can be found in Monti, *Writings,* 39-56.

11. Cf. Sermon 1 on Saint Francis by Bonaventure of Bagnoregio, 1 (hereafter 1-4 Srm).

12. Cf. André Vauchez, "The Stigmata of St. Francis and Its Medieval Detractors," GR 13 (1999): 61-89.

13. cf. 1Srm, infra 33a.

14. cf. 1Srm, infra 35.

15. Bonaventure, *The Journey of the Mind into God,* Prologue 2, translated by Philotheus Boehner, edited, with Introduction and notes by Stephen F. Brown (Indianapolis/Cambridge: Hackett Publishing Company, 1993), 1.

16. Cf. Bernard of Clairvaux, *Five Books on Consideration: Advice to a Pope,* V 14:32, translated by John D. Anderson and Elizabeth T. Kennan (Kalamazoo, MI: Cistercian Publications, 1976), 139.

17. Richard of St. Victor, *The Mystical Ark (Benjamin Major)*, III 6, in *Richard of St. Victor: The Twelve Patriarchs, The Mystical Ark, Book Three of The Trinity,* translation and introduction by Grover A. Zinn, preface by Jean Châtillon (New York, Ramsey, Toronto: Paulist Press, 1997), 231-232.

18. Cf. LMj III 4, infra 62 a.

19. Bonaventure, *Journey,* 2.

20. Bonaventure, *Journey,* 2.

21. Cf. Bonaventure, *Collationes in Hexaëmeron* XXII 23: *illa apparitio Seraph . . . quae fuit expressiva et impressa* [that apparition of the Seraph . . . that was expressed and impressed]; LMj XIII 10.

22. As noted in the text, the source of this mandate is obscure. It cannot be found in either the *Constitutions of Narbonne* nor in its *Definitiones.* Golubovich notes that the *Ceremoniale ordinis minorum vetutissimum* or *Ordinationes divini officii* issued in 1254 during the generalate of John of Parma contains this phrase: *Item ordinetur de legenda beati Francisci, ut de omnibus una bona compiletur* [Likewise it is ordained concerning the legend of blessed Francis, that one good one be compiled from all the others]. Golubovich and, later, Desbonnets maintained that the decision referred to the composition of LMn because of difficulties in reconciling the liturgical texts with the data provided by later texts. Michael Bihl, on the other hand, was convinced that the decree was appended to the *Ceremoniale* at a later date and, in reality, was directed at the composition of LMj. Cf. *Ceremoniale ordinis minorum vetutissimum* seu *"Ordinationes divini officii"* sub *Ioanne de Parma ministro generali emanatae an. 1254,* a cura di G. Golubovich, in AFH 3 (1910): 76.

23. In LMj Bonaventure intersperses thirty-five of the miracles described in 3C. Bonaventure adds five new episodes to his own *Treatise on the Miracles,* the second part of LMj.

24. Bonaventure, *Breviloquium* V 1:1 (V 222): "Grace is a gift that cleanses, enlightens, and perfects the soul; that vivifies, reforms, and strengthens it; that lifts it up, makes it like to God, and unites it with Him, thus rendering it acceptable to Him."

25. Bonaventure, *Commentary of Luke's Gospel* XIII 21: 47 (VII 349). Bonaventure develops this concept of the "hierarchical man" in his Prologue of his *De Triplici Via:* "This threefold understanding, moreover, corresponds to a threefold hierarchical activity, which is purgative, illuminative, and perfective. Purgation, in fact, leads to peace, illumination to truth, perfection to love. Once it has perfectly mastered these [activities], the soul becomes blessed and, as it behaves in these ways, grows in merit. The entire knowledge of Sacred Scripture as well, the reward of eternal life depends upon knowing these three activities." Cf. Also, *Itinrarium* IV 4-8; *Collationes in Hexaëmeron* XXII.

26. Cf. McGinn, *Flowering* 78-87.

27. Cf. *Questiones Disputatae de Perfectione Evangelica,* q. I, concl. (V 123); *Commentarius in Libros Sententiarum* I., dist. XLIV, a.1, q.3, ad 2 (I, 786).

28. See K. Foster, *"Liber Vitae* bei Bonaventura: Ein begriffsgeschichtlicher Aufriss," *Theologie in Geschichte und Gegenwart. Michael Schmaus, zum 60. Geburtstag dargebracht* (Munchen, 1957); W. Rauch, *Das Buch Gottes: Eine systematische Untersuching des Buchbegreffes bei Bonaventura* (Munchen: Hueber, 1961); Grover A. Zinn, Jr., "Book and Word. The Victorine Background of Bonaventure's Use of Symbols," *S. Bonaventura 1274-1974* (Sta. Maria degli Angeli: Tipografia Porziuncula, 1973): 143-169.

29. Cf. 2Srm, infra, 730. Cf. Noel Muscat, *The Life of Saint Francis in Light of Saint Bonaventure's Theology of the Verbum Crucifixum,* (Floriana, Malta: Edizzjoni Tau, 1989); Zachary Hayes, "The Theological Images of Saint Francis of Assisi in the Sermons of St. Bonaventure," *Bonaventuriana: Miscellanea in onore di Jacques Guy Bougerol, ofm,* edited by Francisco de Asis Chavero Blanco,. 2 Vols. (Rome: Edizioni Antonianum, 1288): 1:323-45

30. Cf. Edwin Panofsky, *Gothic Architecture and Scholasticism,* Wimmer Lecture, 1948 (Latrobe, PA: The Archabbey Press, 1951).

31. "Praefatio" in AF X, LXXIV. On the development of hagiographic texts, portable breviaries, and travel, see: Eric Palazzo, *A History of Liturgical Books from the Beginning to the Thirteenth Century,* trans. Madeleine Beaumont (Collegeville, Minnesota: The Liturgical Press, 1998): 156-158 and 169-172.

32. Stanislao da Campagnola, "La *Legenda maior* e la *Legenda minor sancti Francisco di Bonaventura da Bagnoregio"* in *Fontes Franciscani: Introduzioni critiche* (S. Maria degli Angeli: Edizioni Porziuncola, 1997) 64-65.

33. On this theme, see: Dieter Blume, *Wandmalerei als Ordenspropaganda. Bildprogramme im Chorbereich franziskanischer Konvente Italiens bis zur Mitte des 14. Jahrhunderts* (Worms: Werner'sche V.-G, 1983).

34. Franciscan churches offered a unique integration of theology, art, architecture, and social awareness to the medieval worshiper, see: Gennaro Bove, "Luogo" in *Dizionario Francescano* (Padua: Edizioni Messaggero, 1983) 914-918. Light, as the privileged metaphor for God's grace, was a theological concept germane to this architectronic-artistic synthesis. On light in Bonaventure's writings, see: Emma Thérèse Healy, *On the Reduction of the Acts to Theology* (St. Bonaventure, N.Y: The Franciscan Institute, 1955) 45-110; and with reference to Gothic architec-

ture, see: Remigus Boving, *Bonaventura und die französische Hochgotik* (Wel/Westfallen: Franziskus Drukerei, 1930) 85-96.

35. On the theological significance of divine condescension, see: Alexander Gerken, *Theologie des Wortes* (Düsseldor: Patmos Verlag, 1963) 328-329 and Zachary Hayes, *The Hidden Center: Spirituality and Speculative Christology in St. Bonaventure* (Ramsey, N.J.: Paulist Press, 1981): 136-137. On the image of the Crucified in Franciscan art and architecture, see: Pasquale Magro, "Il Cristo crocifisso dei minori" in *Città di Vita*, 35 (1980): 17-29.

36. The representation of Francis of Assisi in early Franciscan writings and art is delineated in Ruth Wolff, *Der heilige Franziskus in Schriften und Bildern des 13. Jahrhunderts* (Berlin: Gebr. Mann Verlag, 1996). On the relationship between the Giotto cycle in the Upper Basilica of Saint Francis and *The Minor Life of Saint Francis*, see: 224-225; 282.

37. Jacques Guy Bougerol, *Francesco e Bonaventura: La Legenda Major* (Vicenza: Edizioni L.I.E.F., 1984) 109.

38. Stanislao da Campagnola, "La *Legenda maior* e la *Legenda minor sancti Francisco di Bonaventura da Bagnoregio*" in *Fontes Franciscani: Introduzioni critiche*, 62-63.

39. Jacques Guy Bougerol, *Francesco e Bonaventura: La Legenda Major*, 109.

40. On prayer in Bonaventure's theology, see: Timothy Johnson, *Iste Pauper Clamavit: Bonaventure's Mendicant Theology of Prayer* (Frankfurt am Main: Peter Lang Verlag, 1990); especially 137-148 in regard to unceasing prayer and the Liturgy of the Hours.

41. Michael Bihl, "Praefatio," *AFH* X, lxxii.

42. Cf. *Miscellanea Franciscana* 72 (1972): 247. See discussion FA:ED I 18.

43. Cf. Monti, *Writings* 75.

44. Monti, *Writings* 29.

45. Arnald of Sarrant, *De cognatione S. Francisci*, in F. M. Delorme, "Pages Inédites sur S. François, Écrites vers 1365 par Arnaud de Sarrant Min. Prov. d'Aquitaine," *Miscellanea Franciscana* 126.

46. Bonaventure, *Journey* VII.

47. Cf. 3Srm, infra 249.

The Morning Sermon on Saint Francis
Preached at Paris, October 4, 1255

Scholars have traditionally considered this sermon coming not earlier than 1269.[a] However, there are no parallels with the *Major Legend* and there is no evidence in the sermon that Saint Bonaventure was acquainted with the papal document of Pope Alexander IV on the stigmata, *Benigna operatio,* published on October 19, 1255.[b] Rather than Gerard of Abbeville's attack on the mendicant way of life, this sermon is concerned especially in its first part to refute the onslaught of William of Saint Amour, made in 1255. The sermon is to be dated, therefore, October 4, 1255.[c]

Mt 11:29

Learn from me, for I am meek and humble of heart.

These words from Saint Matthew's Gospel were spoken by the greatest follower of Christ, Saint Francis, and they are taken from the gospel which is read on his feast day. But whether on the lips of Christ or Saint Francis, they are a short and succinct saying,[d] which Mass I in concise and plain terms expresses the sum total of gospel perfection. The saying is concise, so that nobody can claim ignorance of it because of scarcity of books, and plain, so that nobody may be excused from understanding it through lack of schooling.

The saying has two parts: a preliminary statement and a word of instruction. The first is to encourage the hearers, the second to inspire them. To encourage us he says: *Learn from me,* and to inspire us he adds: *for I am meek and humble of heart.* In other words, be meek and humble like me.

---

a. Sophronius Clasen, *Franziskus Engel des Sechsten Siegels. Sein Leben nach den Schriften des heligen Bonaventura* (Werl/West, 1962), 160.

b. Cf. FA:ED II 779-781

c. Ignatius C. Brady, "The Authenticity of Two Sermons of Saint Bonaventure," *Franciscan Studies* 28 (1968), 12; "The Writings of Saint Bonaventure Regarding the Franciscan Order," *San Bonaventura Maestro di vita francescana e di sapienza cristiana.* Atti del Congresso Internazionale per il VII Centenario di San Bonaventura I (Roma, 1976), 95; "Saint Bonaventure's Sermons on Saint Francis," *Franziskanische Studien* 58 (1976), 139-140.

d. The Latin reads: "*est verbum abbreviaturn et consummatum,*" *Opera Omnia* IX, 590. The Vulgate text of Romans 9:28: "*Verbum enim consummans, et abbrevians in aequitate, quia verbum breviatum faciet Dominus super terram* [For completing the word, and cutting it short in justice, the Lord made his word short while on earth]."

Learn from me . . .

The words *Learn from me* have two meanings, both of which can give encouragement: Take me as your model of discipleship and embrace my teaching. Both can be applied to Saint Francis, the first on account of the life he led as a result of his conversion, the second because he attained perfection. The former made him a true disciple, and the latter an excellent teacher.

Because of the life he embraced at his conversion, Saint Francis can say: *Learn from me,* that is, take me as your model of discipleship, for I am a true disciple. The essence of true discipleship of Jesus Christ, which was singularly realized and shone in Saint Francis, consists first of all in separating oneself from the company of evil people, as Proverbs says: *A friend of fools shall become like them.* This is the meaning of those words about Christ that *privately to his own disciples he explained everything* where "privately" signifies well removed from wicked people and away from the crowds. This shows that the disciple of Christ must keep away from evil and divisive company.

Realizing this, Saint Francis, under God's inspiration, immediately left the company of the young people who had been his comrades in sin, for it was evil company. He also stopped associating with merchants, which was worldly company, and went off alone to a secluded place, knowing that *Christ explained everything to his own disciples privately.* That is what anyone must do who desires to be a perfect disciple of Christ: he must withdraw from evil and worldly company. At the least one must withdraw from evil company, which the call to perfection demands, even if one has no desire to relinquish worldly company. We are told of the Israelites: *They mingled with the nations and learned to do as they did. They served their idols which became a snare to them.* "The nations" in this text refer to those who lead an ungodly life and "to mingle with them" means to associate with them in such a way as of necessity to copy their evil ways. The Book of Sirach tells us: *Whoever touches pitch will be defiled and whoever associates with a proud man will become like him.* Proverbs advises us: *Make no friendship with a man given to anger, nor go with a wrathful man, lest you learn his ways and entangle yourself in a snare;* and the Psalmist warns us: *With the perverse you will be perverted.*

Second, it is essential for true discipleship to free oneself from useless cares in the affairs of life. Anyone who is anxious about useless things cannot give attention to those that are profitable. As Saint Matthew's Gospel says: *the cares of the world and the delight in riches choke the word and it proves unfruitful.* Thus it is recorded by Saint Luke: *Whoever of you does not renounce all that he has cannot be my disciple.* The

Prv 13:20

Mk 4:34

1C 5; LJS 3

Ps 106:35-36

Sir 13:1

Prv 22:24-25

Ps 17:26

Mt 18:22

Lk 14:33

Lord says this not because there is sin in having possessions, but because it is sinful to be anxiously concerned about them. In any case, it is impossible, or at least very difficult, to have great possessions without being preoccupied with them. And so the Lord stipulates: *Whoever of you does not renounce all that he has cannot be my disciple.*

Taking this to heart, Saint Francis on hearing God's voice at once gave everything away to the extent that he did not even keep back a stitch to cover his nakedness. As in his heart he despised all possessions, so outwardly he gave away everything he had. This is what anyone must do who desires to be a perfect disciple of Christ: *he must go, sell everything he has and give to the poor.* If one does not have the will to do that, one must at least keep oneself from the cares, anxieties, and vanities that go with possessions; otherwise, one will be a disciple, not of Christ, but of the devil. It is impossible to serve God and mammon at the same time. As it says in the First Epistle to Timothy: *Those who desire to be rich fall into temptation, into many senseless and hurtful desires that plunge men into ruin and destruction.* Not all learn the teaching of Christ; some learn to catch prey as Ezechiel has it: *She brought up one of her whelps; he became a young lion, and he learned to catch prey; he devoured men.*

Third, the true disciple must rid himself of inordinate attachments to his loved ones. As Saint Paul teaches, the sensual or *unspiritual man does not receive the gifts of the Spirit of God,* and Saint Luke records: *If anyone comes to me and does not hate his own father and mother and wife and brothers and sisters, yes, and even his own life, he cannot be my disciple.* The Lord does not forbid us to love our father and mother, for the Decalogue commands that we honor them; what he does forbid is to be inordinately attached to our parents, because inordinate attachment rejects the teaching of Christ.

Understanding this, Saint Francis hated his father and mother, and having broken the ties of natural attachment, he abandoned them completely. Anyone who desires to attain perfect discipleship of Christ must *forget his father's house* and hate *his own life,* that is, his natural affections, in order to imitate Christ who gave *his dear soul into the hands of her enemies.* But if a man does not wish to hate or sacrifice natural affections for his parents altogether, he must at least sacrifice them in regard to women; otherwise, he will not be able to attain knowledge of the truth. As Saint Paul writes to Timothy: *For among them are those who make their way into households and capture weak women, burdened with sins and swayed by various impulses who will listen to anybody and can never arrive at a knowledge of the truth.*

Fourth, the true disciple of Christ must purify his heart of all that militates against the practice of virtue. As the Book of Wisdom says:

Mt 19:21

Mt 6:24

1 Tm 6:9

Ez 19:3

1 Cor 2:14

Lk 14:26

Ps 45:10

Jer 12:7

2 Tm 3:6-7

Wisdom will not enter a deceitful soul, nor dwell in a body enslaved to sin and as Isaiah admonishes: *Cease to do evil, learn to do good.* In other words, you will not be able to learn holiness from Christ unless you have resolved to eradicate its opposite, sinfulness, just as knowledge cannot be acquired unless satisfaction with its opposite, ignorance, has been uprooted. Wis 1:4 — Is 1:16

Acknowledging this, Saint Francis strove with constant sighs of sorrow to root out vice and sin totally from the field of his heart. Nor did he cease to lament up to the moment when he was found worthy to hear from God: *Your sins are forgiven.* In the same way, anyone who desires to be a perfect disciple of Christ, must *every night drench his couch with weeping,* just as Saint Francis did. If one cannot follow that advice which leads to perfection, then one must at least cease to do evil if one wishes to become Christ's disciple. Therefore, anyone who does not resolve to abandon his evil ways cannot learn virtue, as Jeremiah reflects: *Can the Ethiopian change his skin or the leopard his spots? Then also you can do good who are accustomed to do evil.* Here the Prophet is addressing those who from long habit have become stubborn in their malice so that it is well nigh impossible to root it out. They cannot learn virtue because they learned evil habits well enough in their youth.

Saint Francis, then, can rightly say: *Learn from me,* that is, take me as your model of discipleship, for I am a true disciple of Christ.

Likewise he can say to us *Learn from me* in the second sense, namely, embrace my teaching, because by being a true disciple, he became an authentic teacher. There are four grounds on which he can address these words to us.

First of all, he taught what he himself had learned without error because of the truth of God's revelation. As Scripture tells us: *God is true, and every man a liar.* Therefore, the teaching which anyone receives from revelation cannot be other than true. It is from having learned in this way that Saint Paul commends his teaching to the Galatians: *For I would have you know, brethren, that the gospel which was preached by me is not man's gospel. For I did not receive it from man, nor was I taught it, but it came through a revelation of Jesus Christ.*

Saint Francis learned his teaching in the same way. Indeed, one may well wonder at his teaching. How was he able to teach others what no human had taught him? Did he come by this knowledge of himself? Be assured he did not. The evidence of that is found in the account of his life. When he was instructed by another human or had to prepare something himself, he had absolutely nothing to say. In that, however, he is more to be praised and wondered at than imitated. Hence it is not without reason that his sons attend the schools.

Side notes:
Wis 1:4
Is 1:16
Lk 7:48
Ps 6:7
Jer 13:23
Rom 3:4
Gal 1:11-12
1C 73; LJS 58

To arrive at knowledge without a human teacher is not for everyone, but the privilege of a few. Though the Lord himself chose to teach Saint Paul and Saint Francis, it is his will that their disciples be taught by human teachers.

Second, he taught what he had learned without guile due to his fervent love, which directs the whole heart to grasp what is being taught. Speaking of wisdom Solomon glories that he himself learned in this way: *I learned without guile and impart without grudging; I do not hide her wealth.* That is to say, as ardent love brought me to learn without guile, so it moves me to share without jealousy or grudging envy what I have learned.

Wis 7:13

That is precisely how Saint Francis learned and taught. He so loved what he learned that he *accounted wealth as nothing in comparison with that; gold as but little sand and silver as clay; he gave up all the wealth of his house and scorned it as nothing.* He learned with such diligence that he became the teacher of many disciples whom he taught to *think of the Lord with uprightness and seek him with sincerity of heart, because he is found by those who do not put him to the test, and manifests himself to those who do not distrust him.* He manifested himself to Saint Francis who, because he had learned without guile, shared what he had learned without envy.

Wis 7:8-9; Sg 8:7

Wis 1:1

Third, he taught what he had learned without forgetting it, because he put it into practice *being no hearer that forgets but a doer that acts,* and because of that he was an excellent teacher. On observing the commandments Saint Matthew records: *He who does them and teaches them shall be called great in the kingdom of heaven.* Sirach praises this method of learning when he says: *A man who has much experience knows many things,* which he will think on with composure and without blame; *and one who has learned many things will speak with understanding,* because he did not acquire his knowledge by reflecting in general terms on a limited number of truths, but by individual experience over a wide range of life.

Jas 1:25

Mt 5:19

Sir 34:9

That is how Saint Francis learned, but by experiencing sufferings not joys. We can say of him what Saint Paul says of his own Teacher: *He learned obedience through what he suffered.* At the outset of his conversion Saint Francis experienced derision, beatings, fetters, imprisonment, destitution, nakedness, and adversity. Like Saint Paul he learned to be content in his sufferings: *For I have learned, in whatever state I am, to be content. I know how to be abased and I know how to abound; in any and all circumstances I have learned the secret of facing plenty and hunger, abundance and want.* And because the teaching of a true disciple is recognized by his patience, Saint Francis is to be praised and imitated in his teaching and we should learn from him.

Heb 5:8

Phil 4:11

Fourth, he taught what he had learned without doubting because of the trustworthy signs he was given. He knew by those signs with absolute certitude that the teaching he had learned was saving truth. Therefore, he held to it firmly as Saint Paul advised Timothy: *But as for you continue in what you have learned and have firmly believed, knowing from whom you learned it.* Saint Paul exhorted Timothy to remain steadfast in what he had learned because he knew and was certain through signs and miracles that the teaching he had learned was for salvation.

2 Tm 3:14, 39;
Mk 16:20

In the same way Saint Francis was established in what he had learned and so like the Apostles he *went forth and preached everywhere, while the Lord worked with him and confirmed the message by the signs that attended it.*

Mk 16:20

Moreover, it pleased the Lord to endorse and confirm the teaching and *Rule* of Saint Francis, not only by miraculous signs, but also by the marks of his own stigmata, so that no true believer could possibly call them into question on external or internal evidence.[a] It pleased God in his goodness to affix his own seal to the *Rule* and teaching of Saint Francis, for Saint Francis would never have dared to teach or write down other than what he received from the Lord. As he himself testifies, God revealed to him the entire *Rule.* As it is the Pope's practice to endorse documents with his seal, so Christ, having recognized the teaching of Saint Francis as his own, affixed the seal of his stigmata to his body, and thereby irrevocably confirmed his teaching.

Test 14

His teaching could not have had its lasting character, in the eyes of others, from Saint Francis himself, for he was an uneducated merchant and no learned doctor. Therefore, it was the Lord's good pleasure to confirm it by manifest signs in the form of an awe-inspiring seal from on high, so that none of the learned could dare despise his teaching and *Rule* as only the efforts of an uneducated man. This shows us clearly how we ought to marvel at the depth of God's judgments, which Christ indicates at the beginning of today's Gospel when he says: *I thank you, Father, Lord of heaven and earth, that you have hidden these things from the wise and understanding and revealed them to little ones.*

Mt 11:25

Consequently, anyone who doubts that the doctrine and *Rule* of Saint Francis are a most perfect way to reach eternal life, when these have been confirmed by such great signs, must be exceedingly hard of heart. And particularly so, when it is abundantly evident from the

---

a. Bonaventure is using an argument from Aristotle, one that he seems to have been taken from Boethius's translation of Aristotle's *Organon,* cf. *In Librum Aristotelis de Interpretatione, edtio secunda, seu majora commentaria, liber primus* (PL 64, 422), and in *I Sent.,* d. viii, p. I, a.viii, q. 2, (I, 155).

great number of witnesses, their authority, and their holiness, that God wondrously imprinted these signs on his body.

The great number of witnesses furnishes definite assurance. Many trustworthy lay people actually saw the stigmata of Saint Francis and more than a hundred clerics confirmed it by their own testimony. And if *every word is confirmed by the evidence of two or three witnesses,* how much more by the evidence of a hundred?

Mt 18:16

The authority of the witnesses strengthens the minds of believers with certainty. The fact of the stigmata was established and confirmed by the Roman Curia which possesses the highest authority on earth. Should any contradict this, they are by this same authority to be cut off from the communion of the faithful, as they have estranged themselves from the faith.

The holiness of the witnesses totally dispels all doubt. His companions are men of outstanding holiness, upright life, and manifest virtue. They affirm, not in timid defense, but unhesitatingly by steadfast oath, that they themselves saw those wonderful signs with their own eyes and touched them with their own hands.

The whole world, therefore, ought to give thanks to the Most High Creator for this sublime gift, that by the stigmata imprinted on Saint Francis, he deigned not only to reveal the way of truth, but to establish it in a wondrous way and for readily intelligible reasons.

It happened in a wondrous way indeed when considered in terms of natural causes. The stigmata were imprinted in a way outside usual experience, contrary to nature's laws and above human powers. They were outside usual experience, for whoever heard of such precious gems appearing on a human body? They were also contrary to nature's laws, for there was a wound in his side from which his holy blood flowed, yet without applying bandages to it, the saint of God went on living and continued untiringly in his works; and they were above human powers: for his hands had no open wounds nor were they injured, which would have been the case had iron or wooden instruments been used. On the contrary, the nails came up out of the flesh, the heads on one side and the points bent over on the other, quite above the surface of the skin and distinct from the rest of the flesh of his hands and feet. It was so remarkable that no believer could possibly doubt that these signs were imprinted other than by an unparalleled miracle.

If we raise our minds a little and consider the stigmata in terms of supernatural causes, we discover they were imprinted for readily understandable reasons. This miracle was made necessary under the law of divine providence, for the needs of the church in this final age and because of Saint Francis's eminent holiness.

The law of divine providence required it because God willed to make this cloth merchant a fisher of men, and the leader of those who imitate Christ perfectly. Therefore, he handed over to him his own ensign, namely, the marks of the Crucified Lord.

Further, it was made necessary by the needs of the church in these last times. At the beginning of the Church unbelief held sway; as it developed heresy reigned and at the end wickedness will prevail, for then *most men's love will grow cold.* So at the beginning of the church, the Lord granted powerful miracles to drive out idolatry. Later on he endowed learned men with proofs of wisdom to root out heresy. In these latter times, he bestowed the signs of goodness and mercy on Saint Francis to enkindle love, and what are the signs of consummate love except the marks of the passion which God chose to endure for us out of measureless love?   Mt 24:12

Third, this miracle was made necessary because of Saint Francis's eminent holiness which found expression in his most fervent love of the Crucified Lord. For the sake of that love he so weakened his eyes by tears of compassion that he lost his sight. Hugh of Saint Victor tells us: "Such is the power of love, that it transforms the lover into the Beloved."[a] Love of the Crucified Lord was supremely and gloriously aflame in his heart, and so the Crucified himself, in the form of the Seraph, an angelic spirit burning with the fire of love, appeared before his saintly eyes and imprinted the sacred stigmata on his body.

We should not consider this impossible to believe or less than reasonable, for it is recorded that something similar happened to Saint Ignatius of Antioch.[b] When he was ordered by the tyrant to deny Christ, he replied that Christ could not be taken from his lips. Then the tyrant threatened that he would cut off his head and so remove Christ from his lips. Saint Ignatius answered that though Christ might be taken from his lips, he could never be removed from his heart. Then consumed with fury to prove the Saint of God wrong, the tyrant had his head cut off and ordered his heart to be torn from his body. When it was done his heart was found to have written on it the name of Jesus Christ in gold letters. How fitting that was, for he had

---

a. *Ea vis amoris est, ut talem esse necesse sit, quae illus est quod amas, et qui per affectum conjungeris, in ipsius similitudinem ipsa quodammodo dilectionis societate transformaris* [This is the force of love, that it is necessary for you to be such as the one you cherish. Somehow by the association of love you are transformed to the likeness of the very one to whom you are joined by affection]. Hugh of St. Victor, *De arrha animae*, PL 176, 954; *Soliloquy on the Earnest Money of the Soul*, translated with introduction by Kevin Herbert (Marquette: Marquette University Press, 1956), 16.

b. Ignatius of Antioch (+c. 110) was martyred in Rome during the reign of Trajan. According to an ancient account of his death, the *Martyrium Ignatii*, the "tyrant" mentioned by Bonaventure is Trajan himself. Cf. PG V 37-473. B. Mombritius, *Sanctuarium seu vitae sanctorum* (Paris, 1910), 10:45, 46-53; *Acta Sanctorum*, die 1 Feb, Commentarium praevius (Antwerp, 1658), 14.

Sg 8:6   *set* Christ *as a seal upon his heart, as a seal upon his arm.* Because Saint

Sg 8:6   Francis *set* Christ crucified *as a seal upon his arm,* the precious gems of
the stigmata of Jesus Christ appeared visibly on his body. This took
place for understandable reasons by the glorious power of God.

Mt 20:15   Let no one begrudge God's generosity, but let everyone listen to
and learn the teaching of Christ, indeed, of Saint Francis, that good
teacher who taught others what he had learned without error, without guile, without forgetfulness, and without doubting. Saint Francis, therefore, can rightly say: *Learn from me,* to encourage others, and
equally, *for I am meek and humble of heart,* to inspire them.

The Evening Sermon on Saint Francis
Preached at Paris, October 4, 1255

Learn from me, that is, be meek and humble after my example. A person is meek by loving his brothers, humble by loving lowliness or "minority." To be meek is to be a brother to everybody; to be humble is to be less than everybody. Therefore, to be meek and humble of heart is to be a true lesser brother. Saint Francis can say to us: Learn from me to be meek and humble, that is, to be Lesser Brothers.[a] Although it is not for everyone to take the habit and profess the *Rule* of the Lesser Brothers, it is necessary for everyone who wants to be saved to be a lesser brother in the sense of being meek and humble. As the Lord himself teaches: *Unless you turn and become like children, you will never enter the kingdom of heaven.* Mt 18:3

As the easier of the two, he mentions meekness first. While it is no effort for a soul that is well-disposed, it is nevertheless both necessary and profitable to the spiritual life: to the pursuit of truth for beginners, in the practice of virtue for the advanced, to make right judgments by those in authority, and to attain eternal life by those tending toward it. Meekness, in fact, pertains to every form and state of life.

First, then, meekness is necessary to the pursuit of truth both in those learning and those who teach. Those learning have to be meek in order to grasp the truth, as Sirach says: *Be meek to hear the word, that you may understand.* As an image is reflected only in peaceful waters, Sir 5:13 so the word of doctrine is received only by meek minds. Also those who teach have to be meek because "anger hinders the mind from perceiving the truth."[b] As the *Gloss* on Matthew 5:4 explains: "He is meek whom neither anger nor spitefulness, harshness nor bitterness, disturbs."[c] Saint Paul writes to Timothy: *The Lord's servant must* 2 Tm 2:24 *not be quarrelsome but kindly to everyone, an apt teacher, forbearing, correcting his opponents with gentleness.* How much more gently ought he to listen to those who are seeking the truth.

---

a. The English rendering cannot have the impact of the Latin in which Bonaventure plays with words: *unde esse mitem, hoc est esse omnium fratrem; esse humilem, hoc est esse omnibus minorem: esse ergo mitem et humilem corde, hoc est esse vere fratrem minorem; discite igitur a me esse mites et humiles, hoc est esse fratres minores,* (IX, 594).

b. *Catonis disticha* II, 4 in *The Distichs of Cato: A Famous Medieval Textbook*, University of Wisconsin Studies in the Social Sciences, vol. 7, translated by Wayland Chase (Madison: University of Wisconsin Press, 1922).

c. *Glossa ordinaria* in Mt 5:4 in *Biblia sacra cum glossa ordinaria . . . et Postilia Nicolai Lirani . . .* vol. v (Antwerp, 1634), f. 1gr.

Second, meekness is necessary for the inward and outward practice of virtue so that one may remain serene in conscience and be well pleasing in the judgment and minds of one's neighbors. Sirach urges us to acquire interior meekness: *My son, keep your soul in meekness and give it honor according to its desert.* To keep one's soul in meekness and give it honor according to its desert is to let it not be troubled except on account of sin. He exhorts us to outward meekness with the words: *My son, perform your tasks in meekness, then you will be loved by those whom God accepts.* Everybody loves a meek man because he epitomizes natural human goodness and is naturally blessed with a fondness for company.

Third, meekness is necessary to make right judgments, for without it others are not corrected, but destroyed. Saint Paul asks the Corinthians: *What do you wish? Shall I come to you with a rod, or with love in a spirit of gentleness?* That is to say: I will come with both, because there can be no truly equitable judgment if meekness is not coupled with the rod and *vice versa.* Without the rod, meekness is a defect in a prelate, as it was in Eli. Zephaniah tells us: *Seek the Lord all you meek of the earth, you that have wrought his judgment.* Likewise, the rod without meekness destroys, it brings no correction. The Psalmist says: *For mildness is come upon us and we shall be corrected.* A good prelate does not rage against a subject as if he were an enemy, but corrects him as a friend and companion. As Sirach advises: *Do not be like a lion in your home, terrifying the members of your household, and oppressing those under you.*

Finally, meekness is necessary to attain eternal life. The Gospel tells us: *Blessed are the meek for they shall inherit the earth,* and the Psalm says: *the meek shall possess the land and shall delight in abundance of peace.* Because they lived on this earth in goodness and peace even when unjustly oppressed by harsh people, by God's just judgments *the meek shall inherit the land,* not this earthly land, but *the land of the living,* and the harsh will be rejected. The land of the living will be assigned and awarded to them in the future judgment, just as the kingdom of heaven will be awarded to the poor who, having set their hearts on heavenly treasures, willingly give up earthly possessions. We read in Isaiah: *With righteousness he shall judge the poor,* which means God will grant them the kingdom of heaven; the text continues: *and decide with equity for the meek of the earth,* which is to say, he will give them the land of the living.

We ought to learn meekness, which is utterly necessary, from Saint Francis. He cherished an extraordinary meekness not only toward other people, but also toward dumb animals. He called all animals by the name "brother" and we read in the account of his life

Sir 10:31

Sir 3:19

1 Cor 4:21

1 Sm 2:22-25; Zep 2:3

Ps 2:3

Sir 4:35

Mt 5:5
Ps 37:11

Ps 27:13

Is 11:4

1C 58; LJS 37

that even wild animals came running to him as their friend and companion. And so what is said of Moses in the Book of Numbers, may well be sung in praise of him: *The man Moses was very meek, more than* *all men that were on the face of the earth.* Like another Moses, Saint Francis can say: *Learn from me for I am meek of heart.*

He can also say to us: *Learn from me for I am humble of heart.* Learn, that is, to have true, not counterfeit, humility as hypocrites cunningly humble themselves. Of these Sirach says: *There is one who humbles himself wickedly and inwardly he is full of deceit,* and Saint Paul writes to the Colossians: *Let no one disqualify you, insisting on self-abasement* *and worship of angels, taking his stand on visions, puffed up without reason* *by his sensuous mind.* He is not encouraging us to that sort of humility, but to humility of heart on which Saint Bernard writes: "The truly humble man wants to be considered despicable rather than to be proclaimed a humble man."[a]

Saint Francis possessed this humility supremely. He loved and sought it, from the origin of his religious life until his death. For this he left the world, ordered that he be dragged naked through a city, ministered to lepers, told his own sins while preaching and even commanded others to pour scorn on him. We ought to learn this virtue especially from him.

That we may desire it let us look at the fruits which make it so attractive, the manner in which it is acquired and the means by which it is maintained.

The fruits of humility are manifold. First, it calms the anger of God, while moving him to suspend judgment due to guilt. This is well exemplified in the Book of Kings where the Lord says to Elijah: *Have* *you seen how Ahab has humbled himself before me? Because he has humbled* *himself before me, I will not bring the evil in his days.* What extraordinary power humility has, that it can contain the hand of God! The Psalmist tells us: *The Lord is the keeper of little ones: I was humbled, and he delivered me,* and Saint James says: *God opposes the proud, but gives grace to the* *humble.* He protects and guards them. *The haughty he knows from afar,* *but the lowly he* does not cease to regard from near at hand, nor can he despise them, as the Psalmist says: *The sacrifice acceptable to God is a broken spirit; a contrite and humbled heart, O God, you will not despise.*

The second fruit of humility is that it finds grace. Just as anyone looking for water must dig down into the earth, so anyone longing to

Num 12:3

Sir 19:23

Col 2:18

Wis 8:2

1 Kg 21:29

Ps 114:6

Jas 4:6

Ps 50:19

---

a. Bernard of Clairvaux, Sermon 16:10, *On the Song of Songs* I, The Works of Bernard of Clairvaux, vol. II, translated by Kilian Walsh and introduction by M. Corneille Halflants (Spencer, MA: Cistercian Publications, 1971), 121.

Jn 4:10

Sir 3:20; Jas 4:6

Lk 1:30

Lk 1:48

Sir 35:17

Ps 145:19

Mt 3:15

Prv 15:5

Sir 3:20

find *living water* has to dig a well of humility inside himself. As Sirach says: *The greater you are, the more you must humble yourself and you will find grace before God.* It was on account of her humility that the Blessed Virgin Mary *found grace with God,* as she herself testifies in Saint Luke's Gospel: *He has regarded the low estate of his handmaiden.* That is hardly to be wondered at because humility prepares a dwelling place for love and clears the mind of vanity. That is why Saint Augustine writes: "The more we rid ourselves of the canker of pride, so much the more are we filled with love."[a] As water flows into valleys, so the grace of the Holy Spirit comes down on the humble; or again, the higher water rises, the further it descends, so it is with prayer coming from a humble heart. It rises up to God and resounds in his ears to implore his grace. Thus Sirach tells us: *The prayer of the humble pierces the clouds and he will not be consoled until it reaches the Lord,* and the Psalmist says that the Lord *fulfills the desire of all who fear him, he also hears their cry and saves them.*

The third fruit of humility is that it brings righteousness to perfection. The Lord said to John the Baptist: *Let it be so now; for thus it is fitting for us to fulfill all righteousness,* "that is," according to the *Gloss* on this text, "perfect humility, which is perfect righteousness."[b] Total righteousness consists in perfect humility, and humility, the greatest virtue, in total righteousness, as we read in Proverbs: *In total righteousness there is the greatest virtue.* Perfect humility is the greatest virtue both because it makes us perfect in God's sight and because by it uniquely God is revered and honored to the utmost, as Sirach says: *For great is the might of the Lord: he is glorified by the humble* alone. Only the humble revere God, for the rest seek to glorify themselves, not God. Thus, if all our righteousness and the sum total of the Christian religion consist in honoring God, then it is obvious that total righteousness lies in humility and the greatest virtue in total righteousness. To Dioscorus, seeking to know the summit of gospel perfection, Saint Augustine replied in a way similar to a certain philosopher when asked what should be taught in rhetoric. When asked the first time, he replied: "eloquence;" the second time, again he replied: "eloquence," and the same the third time. Saint Augustine answered likewise: "If you were to ask me what is the summit of gospel perfection, I would answer: humility. Should you ask me a second and

a. Augustine, *De Trinitate,* VIII, c. 8, n. 12, *Corpus Christianorum, Series Latina* (Collected Works of Christian Writers, Latin Series) (hereafter CCSL) 50, 287; *The Trinity,* translated with introduction and notes by Edmund Hill, edited by John Rotelle (Brooklyn: New City Press, 1991), 253.

b. *Glossa ordinaria* in Mt 3:15, in *Bibl. sac. cure glossa Lirani* v, f. 15r.

third time, I would still answer: humility."[a] When one of the holy fathers was asked "What is human perfection?" he replied: "Humility."[b] And the Lord himself, when asked by the disciples to increase in them the grace of faith, answered: *"When you have done all that is commanded you, say 'We are unworthy servants, we have only done what was our duty.'"*

    The fourth fruit of humility is that it leads to eternal glory, its last and perfect fruit. Job says of this: *He who has been humbled shall be in glory: and he who shall bow down his eyes, he shall be saved.* That is to say, through humility every evil is avoided and all good is obtained. How right it is when the text says *he shall be in glory,* for by fair recompense the more humble one is here, the higher and more sublime will be one's place in glory. The more lowly and humble a person is on earth, the closer is he to Christ who sits *in the lowest place.* And the closer one is to Christ in this world, the closer must one be to him in heaven. It is manifest that Christ is raised above all others, and it is therefore entirely proper that his servant be honored among all others, for where Christ is, there shall his servant be also. The more a person cultivates lowliness, the less is he tainted with vainglory. Therefore, as he received no reward whatever in this world, how much greater and more splendid must he appear in that true glory of heaven on which alone his heart is set and to which he is pledged unconditionally!

    We should embrace humility with our whole heart in order to obtain these four fruits. Though outwardly humility seems like a useless, hard old shell, inside it holds a precious kernel. And further, as the farmer sows corn seed in the ground and leaves it there to die while he waits for it to bear fruit, so ought we cheerfully to long to be despised. Saint James writes: *Let the lowly brother boast in his exaltation.*

    Second, let us look at how this noble virtue is acquired. There are four pathways that lead to it. The first is meditation on God. This is a road leading directly to humility for anyone who duly attends to God. We must meditate on God as the author of every good and the one who rewards us according to our deeds. As the author of all good we are obliged to call out to him: *O Lord you have wrought for us all our works,* and so to ascribe every good to him and nothing to ourselves. And that makes us humble. The First Letter of Saint Peter advises us: *Humble yourselves under the mighty hands of God,* and we should keep in mind that it is not by our power or the might of our hands that we have achieved the good that is ours, but *it is the Lord that made us and not we*

Lk 17:10

Jb 22:29

Lk 14:19

Jas 1:9

Is 26:12

1 Pt 5:6

Dt 8:17

Ps 100:3

---

a. Augustine, *Epistola* 118, n. 22, PL 33, 442; *Saint Augustine: Letters,* vol. 2, The Fathers of the Church, vol. 18, translated by Wilfrid Parsons (New York: Fathers of the Church, 1953), 282.

b. Anonymous, *De vitis Patrum,* V, lib. 15, n. 77, PL 73, 966.

ourselves. This rids us of pride which trumpets: *Our hand is triumphant, the Lord has not wrought all this.*

We must also keep before our minds that God will deal with us most justly according to our deeds. God is so strictly just that he remits no punishment. On the contrary, for only one evil act of the will he cast the most noble angelic spirits out of heaven forever. Thus Sirach advises us: *Humble yourselves greatly, for the punishment of the ungodly is fire and worms.*

The second pathway to humility is remembrance of Christ. We should call to mind that Christ was humbled even to the most horrible form of death as the price of our salvation and the pattern of our life. He was the price of our salvation as we read in Isaiah: *We esteemed him stricken, smitten by God, and afflicted.* If Christ humbled himself for our salvation, surely we ought to humble ourselves for his glory. Moreover, he humbled himself as the pattern for our life, as Saint John records: *For I have given you an example, that you also should do as I have done to you.* Therefore, because he is our *Teacher and Lord,* and *a disciple is not above his teacher nor a servant above his Lord,* and we are the servants of Christ, then we ought to be humble and self-effacing. Saint Paul exhorts us to this in Philippians: *Have this mind among yourselves which was in Christ Jesus,* and he continues: *he humbled himself and became obedient unto death, even death on a cross.* How lukewarm is the believer who, seeing his Lord humbled and despised, lifts up his heart and occupies himself with things great and marvelous above him.

The third pathway to humility is just assessment of oneself. A person makes a just estimate of himself when he not only examines his present condition, but also has before his mind the two poles of his life, namely, where he is going and whence he came. Then he reflects on himself in the midst of his afflictions. As we read in the Prophet Micah: *Your humiliation shall be in the midst of you.*

Bear in mind where you came from. You were rescued from the heap of the damned, created out of the dust and slime of the earth, *you were born in utter sin,* you became sinful and now you are in exile from the glory of paradise. Thoughts such as these drive off and keep away the spirit of pride to the extent that one begins to cry out with the three young men in the Book of Daniel: *We are brought low today in all the world because of our sins.*

Consider attentively also the end of your life, that is, where you are going. You are moving toward disintegration and decay. As Genesis tells us: *You are dust, and to dust you shall return;* and as Sirach asks: *How can he who is dust and ashes be proud?* Today you are alive, tomorrow you may be dead; healthy and strong today, sick and weak tomorrow; today a rich man, tomorrow perhaps a beggar; wise today, possibly you will become foolish tomorrow. Who, then, could dare to be proud, surrounded by such adversity? Nobody, except perhaps the person who makes no just assessment of himself, but rivets his attention on present prosperity and says what we read in the Book of Revelation about the proud: *For you say, I am rich in natural gifts; I have prospered in spiritual graces; and I need nothing* of worldly goods. But examine yourself well and you will realize that *you are wretched and pitiable* for lack of natural gifts; *poor and blind* for want of spiritual graces; *and naked* in possessing nothing of this world's goods. For as Job realized: *Naked I came from my mother's womb, and naked shall I return,* and Saint Paul reminds us: *For we brought nothing into the world and we cannot take anything out of the world.*

Rv 3:17

Jb 1:21

1 Tm 6:7

The fourth pathway to humility is respect for one's neighbor. It consists in respecting one's neighbor outwardly, as Saint Peter writes: *Clothe yourselves, all of you, with humility toward one another,* and this especially toward one's superiors. There is also inner respect which is found when a person reckons others better than himself. Each one ought to do this, as Saint Paul advises: *In humility count others better than yourselves.* Undoubtedly, we should all have this inner respect for others, because anyone of our neighbors is blessed with hidden or manifest graces for which we ought to count him better than ourselves. Elijah was reproached for thinking he was the only servant of the Lord left in Israel: *I will leave seven thousand in Israel, all the knees that have not bowed to Baal.* Each one knows his own sins better than the sins of others.

1 Pt 5:5

Phil 2:3

1 Kgs 19:18

Finally, we come to consider the means by which humility is maintained and there are four. Anyone who desires to safeguard humility unfailingly must make his own the means which protect it.

First of all he must maintain a heartfelt sorrow for his sins. We read in the Book of Proverbs: *Grief in a man's heart shall bring him low.* Grief over sins deflates the puffed up spirit, and constant sorrow does not allow one word of praise which would flatter the spirit, to re-echo in the heart. This clearly is what is meant by the words in Job: *No one spoke a word to him, for they saw that his suffering was very great.* Intense sorrow which springs from heartfelt lament turns the attention of the soul wholly toward God, empties the soul of vanity and fills it with humility. As the Psalmist says: *I am afflicted and humbled exceedingly: I roared with the groaning of my heart.*

Prv 12:25

Jb 2:13

Ps 37:9

Secondly, he must observe silence because this protects humility. The Psalmist says: *I was dumb and was humbled and kept silence from good things.* Humility is safeguarded by silence, not about one's sins, but about one's virtues. For a person ought not to parade his virtues,

Ps 38:3

but his vices, as beggars are accustomed to show their afflictions in
Sir 18:21 public. As Sirach advises: *Humble yourself before you are sick and when
you have sinned make known your regret.* We do that by honest and accurate confessions of sins.

Third, he must train himself to hard work and discipline, for these
Est 14:2 protect humility. Scripture tells us that Esther *humbled her body, and
every part that she loved to adorn she covered with her tangled hair.* That is
how one ought constantly to maintain atoning humility in oneself,
Ps 34:13 as the truly penitent Psalmist says: *I humbled myself with fasting.* Consequently, anyone who desires to keep humility intact must persevere in chastising his flesh continually by fasts and vigils, prayers
and penance.

Fourth, he must learn to despise being honored. One achieves this
by striving to be considered worthless, which people generally de-
2 Sm 6:21-22 spise. This is what King David did: *I will make merry before the Lord. I
will make myself yet more contemptible than this and I will be abased in your
eyes.* The same is true of Saint Francis who had himself dragged na-   1C 17, 52; 2C 9
ked like a silly drunkard through a city, and who also took care of lepers.

And so because he left us an outstanding example of humility,
with every right he says to us: Learn from me to be not only meek but
also humble of heart, for I am most meek and humble. Therefore,
Sir 11:12-13 these words from Sirach apply to him: *There is a man who is slow and
needs help,* because of his severe penance; *who lacks strength and
abounds in poverty,* because of the extreme poverty and indigence he
embraced; *but the eyes of the Lord have looked upon him for his good,* by be-
stowing upon him the gifts of grace; *and lifted him out of his low estate
and raised up his head,* by delivering him from the miseries of this life
and leading him to the heights of glory.

May the only begotten Son of God, the Lord Jesus Christ, through
the prayers of Saint Francis lead us to those same heights. Amen.

The Major Legend of Saint Francis

(1260-1263)

Prologue

HERE BEGINS THE PROLOGUE TO THE LIFE OF BLESSED FRANCIS

[1]*The grace of God our Savior has appeared*   Ti 2:11
in these last days   Acts 2:17; Heb 1:2
in his servant Francis
to all who are truly humble and lovers of holy poverty,[a]
who, while venerating in him God's superabundant mercy,
learn by his example
to reject wholeheartedly *ungodliness and worldly passions*,   Ti 2:12
to live in conformity with Christ   Ti 2:13
and to thirst after *blessed hope* with unflagging desire.

In an outpouring of kindness,
the Most High God looked upon him,   Jb 36:22
a little, poor, and contrite man,   Is 66:2
to that He not only *lifted the needy man*   1Kgs 2:8

---

a. With this opening sentence, Bonaventure places Francis within the framework of the history of salvation. Paul's Letter to Titus 2:11, which appears frequently in Bonaventure's sermons, not only underscores the gift of grace, but also articulates the dimensions of the revelation of the Word, cf. IX 52, 114, 129, 141, 187, 270, 480. While reflecting an Augustinian approach to history, Bonaventure's use of Acts 2:17 and Hebrews 1:2 shows the influences of the formulations of Rupert of Deutz (1070-c.1135) and the controversial Joachim of Fiore (c. 1130-1202), cf. Bernard McGinn, *Visions of the End: Apocalyptic Traditions in the Middle Ages* (New York: Columbia University Press, 1979); Joseph Ratzinger, *The Theology of History in Saint Bonaventure*, translated by Zachary Hayes, (Chicago: Franciscan Herald Press, 1971); Gerhart Ladner, *The Idea of Reform: Its Impact on Christian Thought and Action in the Age of the Fathers* (New York, Evanston, and London: Harper and Row, 1967). Thus, Francis appears as a symbolic representation of grace, one that is perceived best by the lowly and the poor.

43

Is 49:6

from the dust of a worldly life;
but also gave him as a light for believers,
a practitioner, a leader, and a herald of Gospel perfection,
that by bearing witness to the light
he might prepare for the Lord a way of light and peace
to the hearts of his faithful.

For this man,
like the morning star in the midst of clouds,
shining with bright flashes of life and teaching,
guided into the light by a resplendent aura
those sitting in darkness and in the shadow of death;
and *like the rainbow among clouds of glory,*
displaying in himself
the sign of the Lord's *covenant,*
he announced to the people
the good news of peace and salvation,
appearing, as well, as *an angel of* true *peace.*
according to a likeness by imitation
of the Precursor designated by God that,
while preparing a path
in the desert of the highest poverty,
he would preach penance
by example as much as by word.

First endowed with gifts of divine grace,
he was then enriched
by the merit of unshakable virtue;
and *filled with the spirit* of prophecy,
he was also assigned an angelic ministry
and was totally aflame with a Seraphic fire
Like a hierarchic man,[a]
lifted up on *a fiery chariot,*
it may be reasonably accepted as true
that he came *in the spirit and power of Elijah,*

Marginal references:
Is 49:6
Jn 1:7
Lk 1:76,79
Sir 50:6
Lk 1:79
Sir 50:8
Gn 9:13
Rom 10:15
Is 33:7
Mk 1:3; Lk 3:4
Lk 24:47
Lk 1:67
2 Kgs 2:11
Lk 1:17
Lk 1:17

---

a. The Latin text reads: *vir hierarchicus* [hierarchic man] a technical term through which Bonaventure refers to the process that restructures the soul according to its place in God's design and to its true image, that is, among other creatures above and below it, and within itself. This approach has its roots in the writings of the Psuedo-Dionysius which had an enormous influence on the writers of the Middle Ages due to the translations of John Scotus Erigena (c. 810-c. 877) and, closer to the time of Bonaventure, Thomas Gallus (+1246). See Bernard McGinn, *The Flowering of Mysticism: Men and Women in the New Mysticism,* Volume III of *The Presence of God: A History of Western Christian Mysticism* (New York: Crossroad, 1998) 93-100. Bonaventure sees this hierarchical dimension of Francis's life, as that of any Christian, as flowing from the presence of grace, that gift "that purges the soul, enlightens and perfects it; gives it life, reforms and stabilizes it; elevates, assimilates, and joins it to God." Cf. *Breviloquium* VI 1 (V 252).

as will appear quite clearly in the course of his life.
　　And so in the true prophecy
　　of that other *friend of the Bridegroom,*　　　　　Jn 3:29
　　John the Apostle and Evangelist,
　　he is considered not without reason
to be like the angel ascending from the rising of the sun
　　bearing the seal of the living God.
　　For *"at the opening of the sixth seal,"*　　　　　Rv 6:12
　　John says in the Apocalypse,
　　　"I saw another Angel　　　　　Rv 7:2
　　ascending from the rising of the sun,
　　having the sign of the living God."[a]

　　²If we consider the height of his extraordinary holiness
we can come to the conclusion, without any doubt,
　　that this messenger of God
　　—worthy of love by Christ,
　　imitation by us,
1C Prol 2　　and admiration by the world—
　　was God's servant, Francis.
　　In this, while living among humans,
　　he was an imitator of angelic purity
and was placed as an example for the perfect followers of Christ.

　　This conviction should be faithfully and devotedly
　　in the forefront of our minds:
　　not only does this advance the mission he held　　　　　Is 22:12
　　of calling to weep and mourn,
　　to shave one's head and wear sackcloth,
　　　and to sign the Tau　　　　　Ez 9:4
　　on the foreheads of those moaning and grieving[b]
　　　with a sign
　　　of a penitential cross,
　　and of a habit conformed to the cross;
　　　even more,
　　it confirms with the irrefutable testimony of truth that
　　the seal of the likeness of the living God,　　　　　Ez 28:12

---

a. The identification of this angel became a controversial point in the apocalyptic traditions of the Middles Ages. It reached its apogee in the Franciscan tradition with Bonaventure's description of Francis. Cf. Bernard McGinn, *Visions; Stanislao da Campagnola, L'Angelo del Sesto Sigillo e l'Alter Christus* (Rome, 1971); Joseph Ratzinger, *The Theology of History in Saint Bonaventure,* translated by Zachary Hayes, (Chicago: Franciscan Herald Press, 1971).

b. 2C 106, FA:ED II 317b.

Ez 28:12
that is, of *Christ crucified,*
was imprinted on his body,
not by natural forces or human skill,
2 Cor 3:3   but by the wondrous power *of the Spirit of the living God.*

³I feel that I am unworthy and unequal to the task of writing the
life of a man so venerable and worthy of imitation.ᵃ I would never
have attempted it if the fervent desire of the brothers had not 1C Prol 2
aroused me, the unanimous urging of the General Chapter had not
induced me,ᵇ and the devotion which I am obliged to have toward
our holy father had not compelled me. For when I was a boy, as I still
vividly remember, I was snatched from the jaws of death by his invo-
cation and merits. So if I remained silent and did not sing his praises,
I fear that I would be rightly accused of the crime of ingratitude. I recognize that God saved my life through him, and I realize that I have
experienced his power in my very person. Although I cannot accomplish this fully, this is my principal reason for undertaking this task:
that I may *gather together* the accounts of his virtues, actions and
Jn 6:12   words—like so many *fragments,* partly forgotten and partly scattered—*that they may not be lost* when those who lived with this servant
of God die.

⁴In order to have a clearer and more certain grasp of the authentic
facts of his life, which I was to transmit to posterity, I visited the sites
of the birth, life, and death of this holy man. I had careful interviews
with his companions who were still alive, especially those who had
intimate knowledge of his holiness and were his outstanding followers. Because of their acknowledged truth and proven virtue, they can 1C Prol 1
be trusted beyond any doubt. In describing what God graciously accomplished through his servant, I decided that I should avoid a cultivated literary style, since the reader's devotion profits more from
simple rather than ornate expression. To avoid confusion I did not al- 1C Prol 2
ways weave the story together in chronological order. Rather, I
strove to maintain a more thematic order, relating to the same theme

---

a. This reference to the Prologue to *The Life of Saint Francis* by Thomas of Celano (hereafter 1C)
   suggests a difference between the two works. Whereas Thomas underscores the veneration,
   admiration, and love due to the newly canonized Francis, Bonaventure adds that he is also "worthy of
   imitation." Bonaventure's portrait is a presentation of how that imitation might be accomplished.
b. The Latin reads *me fratrum fervens incitasset affectus, generalis Capituli concors induxisset instantis*
   [the fervent desire of the brothers had aroused me, the unanimous urging of the General Chapter
   induced me]. The brothers gathered at the General Chapter of Narbonne, 1260, were the force
   behind the composition of this text, undoubtedly motivated by a variety of reasons, not the least of
   which was the need for a liturgical text with a more universal appeal.

events that happened at different times, and to different themes events that happened at the same time, as seemed appropriate.

[5]The life of Francis—in its beginning, progress, and end—is described in the following fifteen chapters:

Chapter One: his manner of life while in the attire of the world.

Chapter Two: his perfect conversion to God and his restoration of three churches.

Chapter Three: the foundation of the Order and the approval of the Rule.

Chapter Four: the progress of the Order under his hand and the confirmation of the Rule.

Chapter Five: the austerity of his life and how creatures provided him comfort.

Chapter Six: his humility and obedience and God's condescension to his slightest wish.

Chapter Seven: his love of poverty and the miraculous fulfillment of his needs.

Chapter Eight: his affectionate piety and how irrational creatures were affectionate toward him.

Chapter Nine: the fervor of his charity and his desire for martyrdom.

Chapter Ten: his zeal for prayer and the power of his prayer.

Chapter Eleven: his understanding of Scripture and his spirit of prophecy.

Chapter Twelve: the efficacy of his preaching and his grace of healing.

Chapter Thirteen: his sacred stigmata.

Chapter Fourteen: his patience and his passing in death.

Chapter Fifteen: his canonization and the solemn transferal of his body.

Finally, there is appended an account of miracles which took place after his happy death.

Here Ends the Prologue

Chapter One

SAINT FRANCIS'S MANNER OF LIFE
IN THE ATTIRE OF THE WORLD[a]

Jb 1:1

[1]*There was a man*
in the city of Assisi,
named Francis

Sir 45:1

whose memory is held in benediction,
because God graciously

Ps 21:4

preceded him with blessings of sweetness,
mercifully snatching him from the dangers of the present life,
and richly filling him with gifts of heavenly grace.

1C 1

Ps 62:9

For **at a young age,** he lived among *foolish children of mortals* and was brought up in foolish ways. After acquiring a little knowledge of reading and writing, he was assigned to work in a lucrative merchant's business. Yet with God's protection, although he indulged himself in pleasures, even among **wanton youths,** he did not give himself over to the drives of the flesh; not even among greedy merchants *did he place his*

Sir 31:8

hope in money or treasures, although he was intent on making a profit.

Jb 31:18

There was to be sure, *growing* with him *from his infancy,* a generous *care* for the poor divinely implanted in the heart of the young Francis.[b] It had so filled his heart with kindness that, even at that time, **he**

Lk 6:30

resolved not to be **a deaf hearer of the Gospel**[c] but *to give to everyone who begged,* especially if he asked out of "**divine love.**"

On one occasion, however, **when** he was caught up in the pressures of business, **contrary to his** usual **manner of acting,** he sent away

1C 3

1C 2

2C 7

1C 17

2C 5

1C 22

2C 5

---

a. The Latin title reads: *De conversatione sancti Francisci in habitu saeculi* [Saint Francis's manner of living in the Attire of the World] referring to the earlier monastic concept of the life embraced by a religious upon entrance into the monastery, this is, after a conversion. In his *Commentary on Ecclesiastes,* Bonaventure describes *conversatio* as the life-style of a person who is unworldly and, therefore, concerned with a virtuous manner of living. In this context, this title reflects the changed understanding of Francis's youth that had been generally accepted at Bonaventure's time, and alludes to and anticipates the description of Francis's "perfect conversion" in the following chapter. Cf. Philibert Schmitz, "Conversatio morum," *Dictionnaire de la Spiritualité Ascetique et Mystique, Doctrine et Histoire* III (Paris: Beauchesne, 1963), 2206.

b. Bonaventure uses *miseratio* [care or pity], the word employed by Jerome in the Vulgate translation of Job, to describe this characteristic of Francis. It has the sense of an act of kindness towards those in need, *miseratio,* and is used five times in this work (I 1; II 2; IV 7; VIII 1–2x). This is also the first of six manifestations of the cross (I 3, 5; II 1; III 3-6; IV 9,10) during Francis's life leading to the seventh, that of LaVerna where he received the stigmata (XIII).

c. Cf. FA:ED I 202c.

empty-handed **a poor man who had begged alms for the love** of God. **Immediately** turning back *to his heart,* he ran after him, and, gently with extravagant alms, he promised God that from that moment, while he had the means, he would not refuse those who begged from him for the love of God. **He observed this** with untiring piety **until his death** and merited an abundant increase of grace and love for God.[a] For afterwards, when he had perfectly *put on Christ,* he would say that even while he was in secular attire, he could scarcely ever **hear** any mention of the divine **love without being deeply moved** in his heart.

At the same time, the sensitivity of his gentleness, together with a refined set of manners, a patience and affability beyond human decorum, and a generosity beyond his means singled him out as a young man of flourishing natural disposition. This seemed to be a prelude to the even greater abundance of God's blessings that would be showered on him in the future. Indeed a certain exceptionally simple man of Assisi, whom, it is believed, God had instructed, whenever he chanced to meet Francis going through the city, used to take off his cloak and *spread the garment* under his feet, claiming that Francis was worthy of reverence, since he was destined to do great things in the near future and would be magnificently honored by the entire body of the faithful.[b]

[2] However, up to this time, Francis **was ignorant** of *God's counsel* for him. For this reason, drawn in several directions to the external by the demand of his father as well as forced down to the inferior by the corruption of his natural origin,[c] he had not yet learned how to contemplate the celestial nor had he become accustomed to savor the divine.

And because *affliction can enlighten* spiritual *awareness,*
the hand of the Lord was upon him,
and *a change of the right hand of the Most High,*

Ps 85:9

2C 196

Gal 3:27

1C 2

Lk 19:36

1C 4

2C 4

Jb 15:8

Is 28:19

1C 2

Ez 1:3

Ps 76:11

---

a. This is Bonaventure's first use of *pietas,* a word that appears forty-two times in LMj. The third book of his *Commentary on the Sentences of Peter Lombard* reveals that, prior to LMj, he had a well-developed theology of *pietas* and perceived that through it God was worshipped and neighbor served. Cf. *III Sent,* Dist. VI, art 1, q. 6. As noted in previous passages of *Francis of Assisi: Early Documents,* the word is not easily translated into English, cf. supra FA:ED I 189c.

b. In one of its liturgical prescriptions, the friars at the Chapter of Narbonne (1260) had changed Julian of Speyer's first antiphon for Matins to *Hic vir in vanitatibus nutritus indecenter/divinis charismatibus preventus est clementer,* cf. FA:ED I 332c. Thus, they accepted the revision of Thomas of Celano's *Remembrance* portraying the young Francis whom Baptism had changed "from a child of wrath to a child of grace" (2C3), FA:ED II 241.

c. Bonaventure is struggling with the effects of original sin, thus his description of Francis as *distractus* [drawn in several directions] and *depressus* [forced down] by nature and by original sin. For a succinct theology of the creation, fall, and restoration of the human, see Bonaventure's "Prologue to the Second Book of Sentences," in *Bonaventure: Mystic of God's Word,* introduced and edited by Timothy Johnson (Hyde Park: New City Press, 1999), 59-64.

afflicting his body with **prolonged illness**   LJS 2
in order to prepare his soul for the anointing of the Holy Spirit.

And **when the strength** of his body **was restored,** dressed as usual   1C 3; LJS 2; 2C 5
in his fine **clothes, he met a knight** who was of noble birth, but **poor**
and badly clothed. Moved by a pious impulse of care for his poverty,[a]
he took off his own garments and clothed the man on the spot. At
one and the same time he fulfilled the two-fold duty of piety by covering over the embarrassment of a noble knight and relieving the
want of a poor human being.

³The following **night,** when he had fallen **asleep,** the divine kind-   1C 5
ness showed him a large and **splendid palace** with **military arms**   2C 6; 1C 5
emblazoned with the insignia of Christ's cross. Thus it vividly indi-   1C 17
cated that the mercy he had exhibited to a poor knight for love of the
supreme King would be repaid with an incomparable reward.[b] When   1C 5
he asked to whom these belonged, the response he received from on
high was **that all these things were for him and his knights.** Therefore, **on waking up in the morning,** since he was not yet disciplined   LJS 3
in penetrating the divine mysteries and did not know how to pass
through the visible appearance[c] to contuit[d] the invisible truth, he

---

a. The Latin reads: *pio affectu* [a pious impulse]. *Affectus* is one of the more difficult words to translate
since Bonaventure's use is very much influenced by that of Bernard of Clairvaux, especially in his
treatise *On Loving God.* Cf. "Affectio, Affectus," *Lexique Saint Bonaventure,* edited by Jacques-Guy
Bougerol, (Paris: Éditions Franciscaines, 1969), 15-16; Bernard of Clairvaux, *On Loving God with
An Analytical Commentary,* by Emero Stiegman (Kalamazoo: Cistercian Publications Inc.,1995),
88-98. The adjective *pius,* closely related to *pietas,* is also difficult to translate in contemporary
English in which it takes on the sense of one "having or showing religious devotion." Thus the
contemporary English translation of *pius* overlooks the richer nuance of *pietas.*

b. At this point Bonaventure introduces the word *misericordia* which appears twelve times in the text (I
3; II 8; III 1; V 4; IX 3; XI 4; XII 11; XXI 5–3x; XXIII 2,3,4. Whereas *miseratio* has the sense of an
act of pity or kindness, *misericordia* has the sense of "heart sensitive to misery," *compassio* the
ability to suffer with another. Bonaventure's sermons suggest that this text reflects his rich theology
of *misericordia.*

c. The Latin text reads: *per visibilum species transire ad contuendam invisibilem veritatem* [to pass
through the visible appearance to contuit the invisible truth]. In this phrase Bonaventure proposes
his understanding of the spiritual journey from the visible to the invisible, a journey articulated in his
Journey of the Soul into God, see *Bonaventure: The Journey of the Soul into God, The Tree of Life, The
Life of St. Francis.* Translated and Introduction by Ewert H. Cousins, Preface by Ignatius Brady (New
York: Paulist Press, 1978).

d. The Latin word, *contuitus,* is used nine times by Bonaventure in LMj, and can be translated as
"concomitant gaze or insight." The most important discussion of the teaching that the divine reason
is "contuited by us" along with created reason in every act of certain knowledge is found in
Questiones Disputatae de Scientia Christi q.4, concl. (V:22b-24b). See also *De reductione artium ad
theologiam* 18 (V:32a), *Sermo Chrisus unus omnium magister* 7-19 (V:569a-572a), and *III Sent.* D.
XXXV, a.1, q.3, conc. (III, 778). For a succinct presentation of the significance of *contuitio* in
Bonaventure's mysticism, see Ewert H. Cousins, "Bonaventure's Mysticism of Language," in
Mysticism and Language, edited by Steven T. Katz (New York, Oxford: Oxford University Press,
1992), 236-253. After a discussion of the journey through the visible to the invisible, Cousins
concludes: "This innate awareness of God can be awakened by the excessive contuition through the
technique of contemplative *reductio,* and it can be brought to ecstatic awareness by divine grace."
Cf. Rossano Zas Friz De Col, "La Contuizione de Simbolo Secondo San Bonaventura," *Collectanea
Franciscana* 69 (1999): 43-78.

assessed the unusual vision to be a judgment of great prosperity in the future. For this reason, still ignorant of the divine plan, he set out to join a generous count in Apulia, hoping in his service to obtain the glory of knighthood, as his vision foreshadowed.

Shortly after he had embarked on his journey and had gone as far as the neighboring city, he heard the Lord speaking to him during the night in a familiar way: "Francis, who can do more for you, a lord or a servant, a rich person or one who is poor?" When Francis replied that a lord and a rich person could do more, he was at once asked: "Why, then, are you abandoning the Lord for a servant and the rich God for a poor mortal?" And Francis replied: *"Lord, what do you want me to do?" And the Lord answered him: "Go back to your own land,* because the vision which you have seen prefigures a spiritual outcome which will be accomplished in you not by a human but by a divine plan."

When morning came, then, he returned in haste to Assisi, free of care and filled with joy, and, already made an exemplar of obedience, he awaited the Lord's will.

⁴From that time on, as he was removing himself from the pressure of public business, he would eagerly beg the divine kindness to show him what he should do. When the flame of heavenly desire intensified in him by the practice of frequent prayer, and already, out of his love for a heavenly home, he *despised* all earthly things *as nothing*; he realized that he had found a *hidden treasure,* and, like a wise merchant, planned to buy *the pearl he had found by selling everything.*

Nevertheless,
how he should do this, he did not yet know;
except that it was suggested to his spirit
that a spiritual merchant must begin with contempt for the world
and a knight of Christ with victory over one's self.

⁵One day, therefore, while he was riding his horse through the plain that lies below the city of Assisi, he met a leper. This unforeseen encounter struck him with not a little horror. Recalling the plan of perfection he had already conceived in his mind, and remembering that he must first conquer himself if he wanted to become *a knight of Christ,* he dismounted from his horse and ran to kiss him. As the leper stretched out his hand as if to receive something, he gave him money with a kiss. Immediately mounting his horse, however, and turning all around, even though the open plain stretched clear in all directions, he could not see the leper

2C 6

LJS 3

1C 6

2C 9

Acts 9:6

Gn 32:9

Jn 21:4

Sg 8:7

Mt 13:44-46

2 Tim 2:3

2 Cor 7:4 **anywhere.** He began, therefore, *filled with wonder and joy,* to sing praises to the Lord, while proposing, because of this, to embark always on the greater.

He then began to seek out **solitary places,** favorable to grieving, 2C 9
Rom 8:26 where, with *unutterable groans,* he concentrated incessantly on meriting to be heard by the Lord after the long perseverance of his prayers.

One of those days, withdrawn in this way, while he was praying and all of his fervor was totally absorbed in God, Christ Jesus appeared to him as fastened to a cross.[a] His *soul melted* at the sight, and 2C 10-11
Sg 5:6 **the memory of** Christ's **passion was so impressed on** the innermost 3C 2
recesses of his **heart. From** that **hour,** whenever **Christ's** crucifixion 2C 11
came to his mind, he could scarcely **contain** his tears and sighs, as he later revealed to his companions when he was approaching the end of his life. Through this the man of God understood as addressed to
Mt 16:24 himself the Gospel text: *If you wish to come after me, deny yourself and take up your cross and follow me.*

[6]From then on he clothed himself with a spirit of poverty, a sense 1C 17; 2C 9
of humility, and an eagerness for intimate piety. For previously not only had association with lepers horrified him greatly, so too did even gazing upon them **from a distance.** But, now because of Christ LJS 12
crucified, who according to the text of the prophet appeared despised 1C 17
Is 53:3 *as a leper,* he, in order to **despise himself** completely, showed deeds of
humility and humanity to lepers with a gentle piety. He visited their 2C 9
houses frequently, generously distributed alms to them, and with a great drive of compassion **kissed their hands** and their mouths.[b]

To **poor** beggars he even wished to give not only his possessions but his very self, sometimes taking off his clothes, at others altering them, at yet others, when he had nothing else at hand, ripping them in pieces to give to them.

To poor priests he also provided help, reverently and piously, especially **in the appointments** of the altar, and, in this way, he both became a participant in the divine worship and provided assistance for the need of its celebrants.

With religious devotion he visited at this time the shrine **of the Apostle Peter.** When he saw a large number **of the poor** before the entrance **of the church,** led partly by the gentleness of his piety,

---

a. This is the first of many ecstatic experiences described in Bonaventure's portrait, cf. I 5; II 1; III 6; VIII 10; IX 2; X 1-4; XI 13; XII 1. It is clear that, for Bonaventure, Francis was a model of the Christian caught in ecstasy.

b. Bonaventure now introduces the word *compassio* [compassion] that appears five times (I 6; VIII 1,5,6; XIV 4) suggesting more than *miseratio* [an act of kindness] or *misericordia* [a heart sensitive to suffering]. Compassion *(com-passio)* has the sense of suffering with another.

1C 16

encouraged partly **by the love of poverty,** he gave his own clothes to one of the neediest among them. **Dressed** in his rags, he spent that day in the midst **of the poor** with an unaccustomed joy of spirit, in order to spurn worldly glory and to arrive, by ascending in stages, at Gospel perfection.

He was more attentively vigilant
to mortifying his flesh
so that he might carry externally in his body
the cross of Christ
which he carried internally in his heart.
The man of God, Francis,
did all these things
while not yet withdrawn from the world
in attire and way of life.

Chapter Two

HIS PERFECT CONVERSION TO GOD
AND HIS REPAIR OF THREE CHURCHES[a]

¹Because the servant of the Most High

had no other teacher in these matters

except Christ,

His kindness visited him once more

in the sweetness of grace.

1C 8

2C 9

For **one day** when Francis *went out to meditate in the fields,* **he walked near the church of San Damiano which was threatening to collapse because of age.** Impelled by the Spirit, **he went inside to pray. Prostrate before** an image **of the Crucified,** he was filled with no little consolation as he prayed. While his tear-filled eyes were gazing at the Lord's cross, he heard with his bodily ears **a voice coming from that cross,** telling him three times: "Francis, go and repair my house which, as you see, is all being destroyed."

Trembling, Francis was stunned at the sound of such an astonishing voice, since he was alone in the church; and as he absorbed the power of the divine words into his heart, he fell into an ecstasy of mind. At last, coming back to himself, **he prepared himself to obey and pulled himself together to carry out the command** of repairing the material church, although the principal intention of the words referred to that which *Christ purchased with his own blood,* as the Holy Spirit taught him and as he himself later disclosed to the brothers.

Then, after fortifying himself with the sign of the cross, he arose, and taking cloth to sell, **he hurried off to a city called Foligno. There, after selling everything he had brought with him, even the horse he was riding, the successful merchant quickly returned with the price he had obtained.** Returning to Assisi, he reverently entered the church he had received the command to repair. **When he found the poor priest there, he showed him** fitting reverence,

Gn 24:63

Acts 20:28

2C 10

1C 8

3C 2

2C 10

2C 11

1C 8

LJS 6

1C 9

LJS 6

LJS 6

---

a. This title also provides insight into Bonaventure's interpretation and must be seen in light of the title of the previous chapter. Whereas the earlier monastic tradition envisioned a *conversio* [conversion] anticipating a *conversatio* [a virtuous manner of living], Bonaventure reverses the order, and does so by adding the adjective *perfecta* [perfect] to it.

Off 11 11

offered him money for the repair of the church and for the use of the poor, and humbly requested that he be allowed to stay with him for a time. The priest agreed to his staying there but, out of fear of his parents, would not accept the money that the true scorner of wealth had thrown on a windowsill, valuing it no more than if it were dust.

1C 10

²When he learned that the servant of God was *spending time* with this priest, his disturbed father ran to the place. But because [Francis] was still a new athlete of Christ, when he heard the threats of his pursuers and learned in advance of their coming, wanting to *leave room for their anger*, he hid himself in a secret pit. There he remained in hiding for some days, imploring the Lord incessantly with flowing tears to *deliver him from the hands of those who were persecuting his soul* and to fulfill the fervent wishes he had inspired. He was then

1 C 11

filled with an excessive joy and began to accuse himself of cowardice. He cast aside his fear, abandoned the pit, and took the road to the city of Assisi.

When the townspeople saw his unkempt face and his changed

1JS 8

mentality, they thought he had gone out of his senses. They threw mud and stones from the streets, and shouted insults at him, as if he

1C 11; 1JS 8

were insane and out of his mind. But the Lord's servant passed through it as if he were deaf to it all, neither broken nor changed by

1C 12; 1JS 8

any wrong. When his father heard the shouting, he ran to him at

1JS 8

once, not to free him but rather to destroy him. With no pity, he dragged him home and badgered him first with words, then with blows and chains. But as a result of this he became more fit and eager to carry out what he had begun, recalling that Gospel passage: *Blessed are they who suffer persecution for justice' sake, for theirs is the kingdom of heaven.*

1C 13

³After a little while, when his father had left the country, his

1JS 8

mother, who did not approve what her husband had done and had no hope of being able to soften her son's inflexible determination, released him from his chains and permitted him to leave.

1C 13; 1JS 8

He gave thanks to the Almighty Lord and went back to the place

1JS 8

he had been before. Returning and not finding him at home, his father reviled his wife with a bitter tongue-lashing and raced to that place shaking so that, if he could not call him back, he might at least drive him from the neighborhood. But strengthened by God, Francis went out on his own to meet his furious father, crying out loudly that binding and beating lead to nothing. In addition, he

Mt 25:5

Rom 12:19

Ps 31:16; 109:31; 142:7

Mt 5:10

declared he would gladly suffer anything for the name of Christ. When the father, therefore, saw that he could not recall him, **he** turned his attention to recovering the money. When he finally found it on the windowsill, his rage was dampened a little, **and his** thirsty greed was somewhat quenched by gulping down the money.

Mt 6:9 (margin note left)

1C 14; LJS 8 (margin)

⁴Thereupon **the father of the flesh** worked on **leading the child of** grace, now stripped of his money, **before the bishop of the city that he** might renounce his family **possessions** into his hands and return everything he had. The true lover of poverty showed **himself eager** to comply and went **before the bishop without delaying or hesitating.** He did not wait for any words nor did he speak any, but immediately took off his clothes and gave them back to his father. Then it was discovered that **the man** of God had **a hair shirt** next to his skin under his fine clothes. Moreover, drunk with remarkable fervor,[a] he even took off **his trousers, and was completely stripped naked before everyone.** He said to his father: "Until now I have called you father here on earth, but now I can say without reservation, *'Our Father who art in heaven,'* since I have placed all my treasure and all my hope in him." **The bishop,** recognizing and admiring such intense **fervor in** the man of God, **immediately stood up** and in tears **drew** him **into his arms,** covering him **with the mantle that** he was wearing. Like **the pious** and good **man** that he was, he bade his servants give him something to cover his body. They brought him a poor, cheap cloak of a farmer who worked for the bishop, which he accepted gratefully and, with his own hand, marked a cross on it with a piece of chalk, thus designating it as the covering of a crucified and half-naked poor man.

1C 13 (margin)

1C 15 (margin)

2C 12 (margin)

1C 15 (margin)

2C 12 (margin)

1C 15 (margin)

LJS 10 (margin)

Thus the servant of the Most High King
was left **naked**
that he might follow
his naked crucified **Lord,** whom he loved.[b]
Thus the cross strengthened him
to entrust his soul
to the wood of salvation
that would save him from the shipwreck of the world.

Wis 14:1-7 (margin)

1C 15 (margin)

---

a. Bonaventure describes spiritual inebriation as the fourth of six steps in the love of God in his *De Triplici Via* II 10: "Inebriation consists in those who love God with such love that they not only find solace burdensome, but even take delight in and seek suffering instead of solace and, out of love of Him whom they love, delight in pain, abuse, and scourging as did the Apostle" (cf. 2 Cor 12:5,10).

b. For a thorough history of spiritual nudity and the uniqueness of Bonaventure's use of the term in this instance, cf. Jean Châtillon, *"Nudum Christum Nudus Sequere:* A Note on the Origins and Meaning of the Theme of Spiritual Nakedness in the Writings of St. Bonaventure." GR 10:3 (1996): 293-340.

^{1C 16}

^{1C 91; 2C 214}

⁵Released now from the chains of all earthly desires,
this scorner of the world left the town
and in a carefree mood
sought the secret of solitude[a]
that alone and in silence
he would hear the mystery of the divine eloquence.

While Francis, the man of God, was making his way through a certain forest, singing with glee praises to the Lord in French, robbers suddenly rushed upon him from an ambush. When they asked who he was, the man of God, filled with confidence, replied in a prophetic voice: "I am the herald of the great King!" But they beat him and threw him into a ditch filled with snow, saying: "Lie there, you stupid herald of God!" After they left, he jumped out of the ditch, and exhilarated with great joy, he began in an even louder voice to make the woods resound with praises to the Creator of all.

^{16; Off 14 IV; LJS 11}

⁶And coming to a certain neighboring monastery,[b] he asked for alms like a beggar and received it like someone unknown and despised. Setting out from there, he moved to Gubbio, where he was recognized and welcomed by an old friend and clothed with a poor little tunic, like one of Christ's little poor.

^{LJS 11}

From there the lover of profound humility
moved to the lepers and lived with them,
serving them all most diligently for God's sake.
He washed their feet,
bandaged sores,
drew pus from wounds
and wiped away filth.
He who was soon to be a physician of the Gospel
even kissed their ulcerous wounds
out of his remarkable devotion.
As a result, he received such power from the Lord
that he had miraculous effectiveness
in healing spiritual and physical illnesses.

^{Lk 10:30-37}

I will cite one case among many, which occurred after the fame of the man of God became more widely known.

---

a. For a thorough study of the role of solitude and the meaning of this phrase "*secretum solitudinis* [the secret of solitude]" cf. Octavian Schmucki, "Place of Solitude: An Essay on the External Circumstances of the Prayer Life of St. Francis of Assisi," GR 2:1 (1988) 77-132.

b. Bonaventure employs the word used by Julian, *coneobium*, to describe Thomas's *claustrum monachorum*.

There was a man in the neighborhood of Spoleto whose mouth and cheek were being eaten away by a certain horrible disease. He could not be helped by any medical treatment and went on a pilgrimage to implore the intercession of the holy apostles. On his way back from visiting their shrines he happened to meet the servant of God. When out of devotion he wanted to kiss his footprints, that humble man, refusing to allow it, kissed the mouth of the one who wished to kiss his feet. In his remarkable piety Francis, the servant of lepers, touched that horrible sore with his holy mouth, and suddenly every sign of the disease vanished and the sick man recovered the health he longed for. I do not know which of these we should admire more: the depth of his humility in such a kind kiss or his extraordinary power in such an amazing miracle.

[7]Grounded now in the humility of Christ, Francis recalled to mind the obedience enjoined upon him **from the cross, to repair the church of San Damiano.** As a truly obedient man, he returned **to Assisi** to obey the divine command at least by begging. Putting aside all **embarrassment** out of love of the poor Crucified, **he begged** from those among whom he was accustomed to have plenty, and he loaded stones upon his frail body that **was weakened by fasting.** With God's help and the devoted assistance of the citizens, he completed repairs on **that church.**

2C 13

2C 14

1C 21

After this work, to prevent his body from becoming sluggish with laziness, he set himself to repair a certain church of Blessed Peter a further distance from town, because of the special devotion which, in his pure and sincere faith, he bore to the prince of the apostles.

[8]When he finally completed this church, he came **to a place** called the Portiuncula **where there stood a church of the most Blessed Virgin Mother of God, built in ancient times but now deserted and no one was taking care of it. When the** man of God saw it so abandoned, **he began to stay** there **regularly** in order to repair it, **moved by the warm devotion** he had toward the Lady of the world. Sensing that angels **often visited** there, according to the name of that church, which from ancient times was called **Saint Mary of the Angels,** he stayed there out of his reverence for the angels and his special love for the mother of Christ.

1C 21

LJS 14

1C 106

2 C 18

1C 19

This place
the holy man **loved more than other places** in the world;
for here he began humbly,
here he progressed virtuously,

1C 18

here he ended happily.
This place
he entrusted to his brothers at his death
as the the most beloved of the Virgin.

1C 20   Before his conversion, a certain brother, dedicated to God, had a vision about this church which is worth telling. He saw countless people who had been *stricken with blindness, on their knees* in a circle around this church, with their faces raised to heaven. All of them, with tearful voices and *uplifted hands, were crying out to God,* begging for mercy and light. Then a great light came down from heaven and, diffusing itself through them, gave each the sight and health they desired.

Gn 19:11; 2 Chr 6:13

Ps 55:17

2C 18   This is the place
where the Order of Lesser Brothers
was begun by Saint Francis
under the prompting of divine revelation.
For at the bidding of divine providence
which guided Christ's servant in everything,
LJS 14   he built up three material churches
before he preached the Gospel
and began the Order not only
to ascend in an orderly progression
from the sensible to the intelligible,
from the lesser to the greater,
but also
to symbolize mystically
in external actions perceived by the senses
what he would do in the future.[a]
For like the three buildings he built up,
so the Church
—where there is victory
for the triple army of those being saved—
was to be renewed in three ways
under his leadership:
1C 37   by the form, rule, and teaching of Christ
which he would provide.
And now we see
that this prophecy has been fulfilled.

---

a. Bonaventure may well be alluding to an interpretation of progress in the spiritual life offered by Richard of Saint Victor, who, in his *Mystical Ark,* described the different stages of the spiritual life in similar terms. Cf. *Richard of Saint Victor: The Twelve Patriarchs, The Mystical Ark, Book Three of The Trinity,* trans. and intro by Grover A. Zinn, preface by Jean Châtillon (New York, Ramsey, Toronto: Paulist Press, 1979), 34-35.

Chapter Three

THE FOUNDING OF THE RELIGION[a]
AND THE APPROVAL OF THE RULE

Mt 25:5

Jn 1:14

IC 21

2C 198

[1]In the church of the Virgin Mother of God,
her servant Francis *lingered*
and, with continuing cries,
insistently begged her
who had conceived and brought to birth
the Word full of grace and truth,[b]
to become his **advocate.**
Through the merits of the Mother of Mercy,
he conceived and brought to birth
the spirit of the Gospel truth.

Mt 10:9

Ex 5:24

IC 22

LJS 22

LJS 15; IC 22

LJS 15

One day while **he was** devoutly **hearing** a Mass of the Apostles, **the Gospel** was read in which Christ sends **out his disciples to preach** and gives them the Gospel form of life, that they *may not keep gold or silver or money in their belts, nor have a wallet for their journey, nor may they have two tunics, nor shoes, nor staff.* Hearing, understanding, and committing this to memory, this friend of apostolic poverty was **then** overwhelmed with an **indescribable** joy. **"This is what** I want," he said, **"this is what I desire with all my heart!"** Immediately, *he took off the shoes from his feet,* put down his staff, denounced his wallet and money, **and, satisfied with one tunic, threw away** *his leather belt* and put on a piece of rope for a belt. He directed all his heart's desire to carry out what he had heard and to conform in every way to the rule of right living given to the apostles.

---

a. The Latin is *religio* which Bonaventure uses in the title of this chapter to contrast it with that of the fourth. While *religio* and *ordo* tended to be synonyms in the twelfth and thirteenth centuries, *religio* had a more generic sense of religious life, while *ordo* designated those who followed the same customs or prescriptions, e.g. different monasteries. Bonaventure uses these words, as do the earlier texts, to show the development of the primitive fraternity, cf. AP 19, FA:ED 43; L3C 37, FA:ED II 90.

b. The use of this passage of John's Gospel reflects Bonaventure's theology of Christ as the Word "full of grace and truth," cf. *III Sent,* Dist. XIII, art 1, q. iii, spoken that we might participate in a life of virtue, I (III, 281), *Breviloquium* IV 5 (V, 246). In his *Itinerarium mentis in Deum* I 7, Bonaventure sees reception of the Word full of grace and truth as the means needed for rectifying sinful human nature (V, 298). Two references to this scriptural passage in Bonaventure's *Commentarius in Evangelium Lucae* (I 47; XI 60) place it in a Marian context, that is, she who is the receptacle as well as the means of bringing into the world the Incarnate Word (VII, 22, 296).

LJS 16

IC 23

²Through divine prompting the man of God began to become a model of evangelical perfection and to invite others to penance. His statements were neither hollow nor worthy of ridicule, but filled with the power of the Holy Spirit, they penetrated the marrow of the heart, so that they moved those hearing them in stunned

IC 24

amazement. In all his preaching, he announced peace by saying: *"May the Lord give you peace."*ᵃ Thus he greeted the people at the begin-

Mt 10:12; Lk 10:5

Test 5

ning of his talk. As he later testified, he had learned this greeting by the Lord revealing it to him.

Thus it happened that,
filled with the spirit of the prophets
and according to a prophetic passage,

Is 52:7

he proclaimed peace,
preached salvation,
and, by counsels of salvation,
brought to true peace
many who had previously lived at odds with Christ
and far from salvation.

LJS 17

³Therefore
as the truth of the man of God's simple teaching and life
became known to many,
some men began to be moved to penance
and, abandoning all things,
joined him in habit and life.

IC 24

The first among these was
Bernard, a venerable man,
who was made a *sharer* in the divine *vocation*

Heb 3:1

and merited to be the firstborn son of the blessed Father,ᵇ
both in priority of time and in the gift of holiness.

2C 15

For this man, as he was planning to reject the world perfectly after his example, once he had ascertained for himself the holiness of Christ's servant, sought his advice on how to carry this out. On

---

a. The significance of this greeting can be seen in the opening paragraph of the Prologue of Bonaventure's *Journey of the Soul into God.* Cf. Bonaventure, *The Journey of the Mind to God,* translated by Philotheus Boehner; edited, with introduction and notes by Stephen F. Brown (Indianapolis/Cambridge: Hackett Publishing Company, 1993), 40, n.5.

b. Bonaventure's identification of Bernard as the *primogenitus* [first born] introduces an important theme of this chapter, one to which Bonaventure alludes in his twice-used phrase "conceived and brought to birth" (III 1). This may possibly be an allusion to the image of Odo of Cheriton, who quotes Francis as declaring "he was the woman whom the Lord had impregnated with his word, and that he had borne these spiritual sons" cf. FA:ED I 590-591. But it is also consistent with Bonaventure's theology of the interiorization and proclamation of the Word.

hearing this, God's servant was filled with the consolation of the Holy Spirit over the conception of his first child. "This requires **counsel** that is from God," he said.

Mt 27:1 *When morning had broken* **they went into the church** of Saint Nicholas, and, after they had prepared with a prayer, Francis, a worshiper of the Trinity, opened **the book of the Gospels** three times   Off 3 IV-VI asking God to confirm Bernard's plan with a threefold testimony. **At**

Mt 19:21 **the first opening of the book** this text appeared: *If you will be perfect,*   1C 92
Lk 9:3 *go, sell all that you have, and give to the poor.* **At the second:** *Take nothing*
Mt 16:24 *on your journey.* **And at the third:** *If anyone wishes to come after me, let him deny himself and take up his cross and follow me.* "This is our life and rule," the holy man said, "and that of all who wish to join our com-
Mt 19:21 pany. Go, then, if you wish to be perfect, and carry out what you have heard."

[4]Not long afterwards five other men were called by the same   1C 25 Spirit, and **the number** of Francis's sons **reached** six. The third among them was the holy father **Giles,** a man indeed filled with God and worthy of his celebrated reputation.[a] Although he was **a simple** and unlearned man, he later became famous for his practice of heroic virtue, as God's servant had prophesied, and was raised to the height of exalted **contemplation.** For through the passage of time, he was continually intent on elevations; [b] and he was so often rapt into God in ecstasy, as I myself have observed as an eyewitness, that he seemed to live among people more like an angel than a human being.

[5]Also at that time **a priest of the town of Assisi, Sylvester,** a man   2C 109 of an upright way of life, was **shown a vision** by the Lord which should not be passed over in silence. Reacting in a purely human way, he had an abhorrence for the bearing and the way of Francis and his brothers. But then he was visited by grace from heaven in order to save him from the danger of rash judgment. **For he saw in a**
Dn 14:22 **dream** the whole town of Assisi encircled by *a huge dragon* which,

---

a. He died near Perugia on April 22, 1262, while Bonaventure was writing the present work. In his *Commentary on Luke's Gospel,* Bonaventure draws attention to the seven degrees of contemplation articulated by Giles. "Although in words that are simple but not scientific, Brother Giles, who was frequently known to be in rapture, distinguished the degrees in this way. There are seven degrees of contemplation. The first is fire; the second, unction; the third, ecstasy; the fourth, contemplation; the fifth, taste; the sixth, rest; and the seventh, glory. Beyond these nothing remains except eternal happiness." Cf. Bonaventure, *Commentarius in Evangelium Lucae* IX 48 (VII, 231-232).

b. The Latin read *sursumactionibus incessanter intentus* a word he frequently uses in the context of the spiritual life as a continuing ascent into God, e.g. *Itinerarium mentis in Deum* I 1, where prayer is seen as the mother and origin of all *sursum-actio* (V 297); *Collationes in Hexaëmeron* XIX 27, XXII 22 (V 24, 440). In general, Bonaventure sees it as the passive elevation of the soul toward ecstatic love. Sylvester is described here and also in LMj VI 9 and LMj XII 2 as a man of "dove-like simplicity" and great prayer.

because of its enormous size, seemed to threaten the entire area with destruction. Then he contuited[a] issuing from Francis's mouth a golden cross whose *top reached the heavens* and whose arms stretched far and wide and seemed to extend to the ends of the world. At the sight of its shining splendor, the foul and hideous dragon was put to flight. When he had seen this vision for the third time and realized that it was a divine revelation, he told it point by point to the man of God and his brothers. Not long afterwards, leaving the world, he clung to the footsteps of Christ with such perseverance that his life in the Order confirmed the authenticity of the vision which he had had in the world.

Gn 28:12

1C 26

[6]On hearing of this vision,
the man of God was not carried away by human glory;
but recognizing God's goodness in his gifts,
he was more strongly inspired to put to flight
our ancient enemy with his cunning
and to preach the glory of the cross of Christ.
One day,
while he was weeping in a solitary place
as he looked back over his past *years in bitterness,*
the joy of the Holy Spirit came over him
and he was assured of the complete forgiveness of all of his sins.
Then he was caught up above himself
and totally engulfed in a wonderful light,
and, with his inmost soul opened wide,[b]
he clearly saw what would transpire for him and his sons
in the future.

Is 38:15

LJS 18

1C 27

After this he returned to the brothers and said: "Be strong, my beloved ones, and *rejoice in the Lord.* Do not be sad because you are so few, nor afraid because of my simplicity or yours. For as the Lord has shown me in truth that He will make us grow into a great multitude and will spread us in countless ways by the grace of his blessing."

Eph 6:10; Phil 3:1, 4:4

---

a. In this instance Bonaventure changes the verb used in 2C 109, *videt* [he sees] to the stronger, more "Bonaventurian" verb, *contuebatur* [he contuited]. *Contuebatur,* cf. LMj I 2, supra, 532 d. By doing so, he underscores the conviction arising in Sylvester from the evidence of the dream that could only be accounted for by divine intervention. This vision of Sylvester becomes important in understanding the significance of the stigmata, cf. LMj XIII 10, infra 156.

b. The Latin reads: *raptus deinde supra se et in quoddam mirandum lumen totus absorptus, dilatato sinu mentis* [Then he was taken above himself and totally engulfed in a wonderful light, with his inmost soul opened wide] is reminiscent of the language of Gregory the Great and later mystics. Cf. Bernard McGinn, *The Growth of Mysticism: Gregory the Great through the 12th Century. The Presence of God: A History of Western Christian Mysticism,* Volume II (New York: Crossroad, 1996).

⁷At the same time, another good man entered the religion,   1C 29
bringing the number of the man of God's blessed offspring to seven.
Then the pious father called all his sons to himself and, as he told
them many things about the kingdom of God, contempt for the
world, the denial of their own wills, and the chastising of their bod-
ies, he revealed his proposal to send them to the four corners of the   LJS 19
world.

> For the poor and sterile simplicity of our holy father
> had already *brought* seven *to birth*
> and now he wished to bring to birth in Christ the Lord
> all the faithful of the world called to cries of penance.

1 Sm 2:5

"Go," the gentle father said to his sons, "while you are announcing peace to the people, *preach repentance for the forgiveness of sins.* Be

Mk 1:4; Lk 3:3

patient in trials, watchful in prayer, strenuous in work, moderate in
speech, reserved in manner, and grateful for favors, for because of all
these things an eternal kingdom is being prepared for you." As
they humbly prostrated themselves on the ground before God's   LJS 19
servant, they accepted the command of obedience with a spirit of
joy. Then he spoke to each one individually: "*Cast your care upon the*

Ps 55:23

Lord, and he will sustain you." He was accustomed to saying this
phrase whenever he sent a brother under obedience.   LJS 19
Knowing he should give himself as an example to others, he too   1C 30
then set out with one companion for one part of the world that he
might first practice rather than preach. The remaining six he sent to
three other parts of the world, thus forming the pattern of a cross.

> After a short time had passed,
> the kind father,   LJS 20
> longing for the presence of his dear children,
> since he could not bring them together as one by himself,
> prayed that this be done
> by the One
> who *gathers the dispersed of Israel.*   Ps 146:2
> So it happened that,
> after a short time,
> without any human summons,
> they all came together according to his desire,
> quite unexpectedly and much to their amazement,
> through the working of divine kindness.
> During those days four upright men joined them,
> increasing their number to twelve.

LJS 20

⁸Seeing that the number of brothers was gradually increasing, Christ's servant wrote for himself and his brothers a form of life in simple words in which, after he had placed the observance of the holy Gospel as its unshakable foundation, he inserted a few other things that seemed necessary for a uniform way of life. As he desired to have what he had written approved by the Supreme Pontiff, he decided to go with his band of simple men before the presence of the Apostolic See, placing his trust solely in God's guidance. As God was looking from *on high* upon their desire, He strengthened the companions' frame of mind, terrified at the thought of their simplicity, by showing the man of God a vision of this sort.

It seemed to him that he was walking along a road beside which stood a tree of great height. When he approached and stood under it, he marveled at its height. Suddenly he was lifted so high by divine power that he touched the top of the tree and easily bent it down to the ground. The man, filled with God, understanding the portent of this vision to refer to the condescension of the Apostolic See, was overjoyed and, after he had comforted his brothers, set out with them on the journey.

⁹When he arrived at the Roman Curia and was brought into the presence of the Supreme Pontiff, he explained his proposal, humbly and urgently imploring him to approve that rule of life. The Vicar of Christ, the Lord Innocent III, a man thoroughly brilliant with wisdom, admiring in the man of God remarkable purity and simplicity of heart, firmness of purpose, and fiery ardor of will, gave his assent to the pious request. Yet he hesitated to do what Christ's little poor man asked because it seemed to some of the cardinals to be something novel and difficult beyond human powers.

Among the cardinals there was a most venerable man, the lord John of St. Paul, Bishop of Sabina, a lover of holiness, and helper of Christ's poor. Inspired by the Holy Spirit, he said to the Supreme Pontiff and his brother cardinals: "If we refuse the request of this poor man as novel or too difficult, when all he asks is to be allowed to lead the Gospel life, we must be on our guard lest we commit an offense against Christ's Gospel. For if anyone says that there is something novel or irrational or impossible to observe in this man's desire to live according to the perfection of the Gospel, he would be guilty of blasphemy against Christ, the author of the Gospel." At this observation, the successor of the Apostle Peter turned to the poor man of Christ and said: "My son, pray to Christ that through you He may show us His will, so that once we know it with more certainty, we may confidently approve your holy desire."[a]

> [10]The servant of Almighty God,   2C 16
> giving himself totally to **prayer**,
> obtained through his devout prayers
> both what he should say outwardly
> and what the pope should hear inwardly.

For when he told **a parable,** as he had accepted it from God, about a rich **king** who **gladly betrothed a poor but lovely woman** who bore him children with **the king's likeness,** and, for this reason **were fed at his table,** he added his own interpretation. **"The sons and heirs of the** eternal **King** should not fear that they will die of hunger. They have been born of a poor mother by the power of the Holy Spirit in the image of Christ the King, and they will be begotten by the spirit of poverty in our **poor little** religion. For if the King of heaven promises his followers an *eternal kingdom,* he will certainly supply them with those things that he gives to *the good* and *the bad* alike."

2 Pt 1:11; Mt 19:28

Mt 5:45

While the Vicar of Christ listened attentively to this **parable** and   2C 17
its interpretation, **he was** quite **amazed and recognized without a doubt that Christ had spoken in this man.** But he also confirmed a vision he had recently received from heaven, that, as the Divine Spirit indicated, would be fulfilled in this man. **He saw in a dream,** as he recounted, **the Lateran basilica almost ready to fall down.** A little poor **man, small and scorned,** was propping it up with his own back bent so that it would not fall. "I'm sure," he said "he is the one who will hold up Christ's Church by what he does and what he teaches." Because of this, **filled with** exceptional devotion, he bowed to the request in everything and **always loved Christ's servant with special love. Then he granted what was asked and promised even more.** He approved the rule, gave them a mandate to   LJS 21

---

a. The following paragraph, except for the first sentence, was added to Bonaventure's text by Jerome of Ascoli, Minister General of the Order, 1274-1279, and later Pope Nicholas IV. He learned of it from Cardinal Riccardo degli Annibaldi, a relative of Innocent III; cf. Arnold of Saurrant, "Chronicle of the Twenty-Four Generals," in AF III, 365: "When he arrived at the Roman Curia and was led into the presence of the Supreme Pontiff, 'he explained his proposal,' asking with humility and persistence that that rule of life be approved. The Vicar of Christ was in the Lateran Palace, walking in a place called the Hall of the Mirror, occupied in deep meditation. Knowing nothing of Christ's servant, he sent him away indignantly. Francis left humbly, and the next night God showed the Supreme Pontiff the following vision. He saw a palm tree sprout between his feet and grow gradually until it became a beautiful tree. As he wondered what this vision might mean, the divine light impressed upon the mind of the Vicar of Christ that this palm tree symbolized the poor man whom he had sent away the previous day. The next morning he commanded his servants to search the city for the poor man. When they found him near the Lateran at Saint Anthony's hospice, he ordered him brought to his presence without delay."

preach penance, and had small tonsures given to all the lay brothers, who were accompanying the servant of God, so that they could freely preach *the word of God.*[a]

Lk 11:28

---

a. The Latin reads *coronas parvulas* [small tonsures], a phrase much different from those of AP 36, FA:ED II 51c *(clericam)* and L3C 51, FA:ED II 98b *(tonsuram).* In this instance, it is the pope who has this imposed upon the lay brothers; the earlier texts state that it was due to the influence of the cardinal, John of Saint Paul, and that it was imposed on all the brothers. Furthermore, this is imposed "so that they could freely preach the word of God." Bonaventure's reference to Lk 11:28, the conclusion to the praise of "the womb that bore you . . . ," may be a fitting thematic conclusion to this chapter in which generative power of the Word and the image of the woman are so central.

Chapter Four

THE PROGRESS OF THE ORDER UNDER HIS HAND
AND THE CONFIRMATION OF THE RULE

[1]Relying on divine grace and papal authority,
with great confidence,
Francis took the road to the Spoleto valley,
that *he might fulfill and teach* Christ's Gospel.
On the way he discussed with his companions
how they might sincerely keep the rule they had accepted,
how they might advance *in* all *holiness* and *justice* before God,
how they should improve themselves
and be an example for others.

The hour was already late as they continued their long discussion. Since they were exhausted from their prolonged activity, the hungry men stopped in a place of solitude. When there seemed to be no way for them to get the food they needed, God's providence immediately came to their aid. For suddenly a man carrying bread in his hand appeared, which he gave to Christ's little poor, and then suddenly disappeared. They had no idea where he came from or where he went.

From this the poor brothers realized
that while in the company of the man of God
they would be given assistance from heaven,
and so they were refreshed more by the gift of divine generosity
than by the food they had received for their bodies.
Moreover,
filled with divine consolation,
they firmly decided
and irrevocably resolved never
to withdraw from the promise to holy poverty,
be it from starvation or from trial.

[2]When they arrived in the Spoleto valley, going back to their holy proposal, they began to discuss whether they should live among

LJS 23
IC 42
IC 40
Lk 11:2
2 Cor 5:15
Ps 79:6
LJS 27; 1C 45
Test 5
1C 80; 1C 62
LJS 41
1C 45
LJS 27

the people or go off to solitary places. But Christ's servant Francis, putting his trust in neither his own efforts nor in theirs, sought the pleasure of the divine will in this matter by the fervor of prayer. Enlightened by a revelation from heaven, he realized that he was sent by the Lord to win for Christ the souls which the devil was trying to snatch away. Therefore he chose to live for everyone rather than for himself alone, drawn by the example of the one who deigned *to die for all.*

³The man of God then gathered with his companions in an abandoned hut near the city of Assisi, where they kept themselves alive according to the pattern of holy poverty in much labor and want, drawing their nourishment more from *the bread of tears* than of delights.

They spent their time there praying incessantly, directing their effort mentally rather than vocally to devoted prayers, because they did not yet have liturgical books from which to chant the canonical hours. In place of these they had the book of Christ's cross which they studied continually day and night, taught by the example and words of their father who spoke to them constantly about the cross of Christ.

When the brothers asked him to teach them to pray, he said: "When you pray, say 'Our Father . . .' and 'We adore you, O Christ, in all your churches throughout the whole world, and we bless you, for by your holy cross you have redeemed the world.' " He also taught them to praise God in all and with all creatures,[a] to honor priests with a special reverence, and to believe with certainty and to confess with simplicity the truth of the faith, as the holy Roman Church holds and teaches. They observed the holy father's teaching in every detail, and prostrated themselves humbly before every church and crucifix which they were able to see from a distance, praying the formula he had taught them.

⁴While the brothers were still staying in the place already mentioned, one Saturday the holy man entered the city of Assisi to preach in the cathedral on Sunday morning, as was his custom. In a hut situated in the garden of the canons, away from his sons in body, the

---

a. This description of the prayer-life of the primitive fraternity and, in particular, Francis's teaching about it, is thoughtfully crafted. As the cross-references indicate, Bonaventure carefully uses the texts of Thomas of Celano, Julian of Speyer, and Francis himself. His addition of *et ex omnibus* [and with all] to Francis's encouragement "to praise God in all creatures" (1C 80, FA:ED I 250) underscores Bonaventure's appreciation for the role of creation in the adoration of God. Cf. infra LMj IX 1. *The Oxford Latin Dictionary* offers twenty-one nuances to the preposition *ex* suggesting that God is praised in and because of, or in accordance with. In light of CtC 3, the preposition is translated "with."

man devoted to God spent the night in his customary way, in the
prayer of God. **About midnight, while some of the brothers were**   1C 47
2 Kgs 2:11-14   **resting and others** were persevering in prayer, behold, *a fiery chariot*
of wonderful **brilliance entering the door of the house moved** *here*
and there **through the little house three times.** On top of it sat a
bright globe that looked like the sun, and it made the night bright
as day. *Those who were awake* were **dumbfounded,** while those
sleeping were disturbed and, at the same time, **terrified;** they
sensed the brightness with their hearts as much as with their bod-
ies, while the conscience of each was laid bare to the others by the   LJS 29
power of that marvelous light.

As they looked into each other's hearts,
they all **understood** together that the **holy father,**
1 Cor 5:3   *while away from them in body,*
was present in spirit
transfigured in such an image
radiant with heavenly **brilliance**
and inflamed with burning ardor
2 Kgs 2:11   in a glowing *chariot of fire,*
as the Lord had shown him to them
Jn 1:47   that they might follow him as *true Israelites.*
Like a second Elijah,
God had made him
2 Kgs 2:12   *a chariot and charioteer* for spiritual men.
Certainly we can believe
Jn 9:32   that *He opened the eyes*
of these simple men at the prayers of Francis
Acts 2:11; Sir 18:5   that they might see *the wonders of God*
just as he had once opened the eyes of a child
2 Kgs 6:17   *to see the mountain full of horses and chariots of fire*
round about Elisha.
When **the holy man** returned **to the brothers,**
he began to probe the secrets of their consciences,   LJS 29
to draw courage for them from this wonderful vision
and to make many predictions about the growth of the Order.
When he disclosed many things   1C 48
that transcended human understanding,
the brothers completely realized
Is 11:2   *the Spirit of the Lord had come to rest* upon him in such fullness
that it was absolutely safe for them
to follow his life and teaching.

⁵After this,
under the guidance of heavenly grace,
the shepherd Francis led

LJS 21   *the little flock* of those **twelve brothers**   Lk 12:32

to St. Mary of the Portiuncula,
that where the Order of Lesser Brothers had had its beginning
by the merits of the mother of God,
it might also begin to grow with her assistance.

1C 36   There, also,

having become a herald of the Gospel,

he went about the cities and towns   Mt 9:35; Lk 9:60

proclaiming the kingdom of God

not in words taught by human wisdom,   1 Cor 2:4, 13

but in the power of the Spirit.
To those who saw him,
he seemed to be a person of another age as,
with his mind and face always intent on heaven,^a
he tried to draw them all on high.

1C 37   As a result,

the vineyard of Christ began

to produce buds with the sweet smell of the Lord   Sir 24:23

and, when it had produced
flowers *of sweetness, of honor, and of respectability,*
to bring forth abundant *fruit.*

⁶For set on fire by the fervor of his preaching, a great number of people bound themselves by new laws of penance according to the rule which they received from the man of God. Christ's servant decided to name this way of life the Order of the Brothers of Penance. As the road of penance is common to all who are striving toward heaven, so this way of life admits **clerics and lay, virgins and married of both sexes.** How meritorious it is before God is clear from the numerous miracles performed by some of its members.

LJS 23

Virgins, too, were drawn
to perpetual celibacy,
among whom was the virgin
especially dear to God,
Clare.

---

a. "Always intent on heaven" is a phrase taken from the fourth antiphon of Lauds in the Office of Saint Martin of Tours, as well as from the *Third Letter,* n. 14, of Sulpicius Severus, (PL 20, p. 182).

As **the first tender sprout,**[a]   2C 109
she gave forth a fragrance
like a lustrous untouched flower
that blossoms in springtime,
and she shone
like a brilliant star.
Now she is glorified in heaven
and fittingly venerated by the Church on earth,
she who was the daughter in Christ
of our holy father Francis, the little poor man,
and the mother of the Poor Ladies.

[7]**Many people** as well, not only **driven** by devotion but also in-   1C 37
flamed by a desire for the perfection of Christ, once they had con-
demned the emptiness of everything worldly, followed the footsteps
of Francis. Their numbers increased daily and quickly reached even
to the ends of the earth.

Ps 18:15

Holy poverty,   1C 39
which was all they had to meet their expenses,
made them prompt for every **obedience,**
robust for work,
and free for travel.
And since they had nothing earthly
they loved nothing and **feared losing nothing.**
They were safe wherever they went,
held back by no fear, **distracted by no cares;**
they lived with untroubled minds,
and, without any anxiety,
looked forward to the morrow
and to finding a lodging for the night.

In different parts of the world   1C 40
many insults were hurled against them
as persons unknown and looked down upon,
but true love of the Gospel of Christ
had made them so **patient,**
that they sought
to be where they would suffer physical persecution

---

a. Curiously, Bonaventure takes Thomas's reference to Bernard of Quintavalle (2C 109, FA:ED II 319)
   and applies it to Clare.

rather than where their holiness was recognized
and where they could glory in worldly favor.

IC 41

Their very poverty
seemed to them overflowing abundance
since, according to the advice of the Wise Man,
a little pleased them
instead of much.

Sir 29:30

When some of the brothers went to the lands of non-believers, a certain Saracen, moved by piety, once offered them money for the food they needed. When they refused to accept it, the man was amazed, seeing that they were without means. Realizing they did not want to possess money because they had become poor out of love of God, he felt so attracted to them that he offered to *minister to all their needs* as long as he had something to give.

1 Kgs 4:7

O ineffable value of poverty,
whose marvelous power moved
the fierce heart of a barbarian
to such sweet pity!
What a horrible and unspeakable crime
that a Christian *should trample upon*
this noble pearl
which a Saracen held in such veneration!

Mt 7:6

[8]At that time a certain religious of the Order of the Crosiers, Morico by name, was suffering from such a grave and prolonged illness in a hospital near Assisi that the doctors had already despaired of his life. In his need, he turned to the man of God, urgently entreating him through a messenger to intercede for him before the Lord. Our blessed father kindly consented and said a prayer for him. Then he took some bread crumbs and mixed them with oil taken from a lamp that burned before the altar of the Virgin. He made a kind of pill out of them and sent it to the sick man through the hands of the brothers, saying: "Take this medicine to our brother Morico. By means of it, Christ's power will not only restore him to full health, but will make him a sturdy warrior and enlist him in our forces permanently." When the sick man took the medicine, prepared under the inspiration of the Holy Spirit, he was cured immediately. God gave him such strength of mind and body that when a little later he entered the holy man's Order, he wore only a single tunic, under which for a long time he wore a hair shirt next to his skin. He was

satisfied with uncooked food such as herbs, vegetables, and fruit; and for many years, never tasted bread or wine, yet remained strong and in good health.

⁹As the merits of the virtues increased in Christ's little poor,
the fragrance of a good reputation spread everywhere
and attracted a great number of people
from different parts of the world
to come and see our holy father.

Among them was **a certain** refined **composer of worldly songs,** 2C 106 **who, because of this, had been crowned by the Emperor and was,** therefore, called **the "King of Verses."** He decided to visit the man of God, who despised the things of the world. When he found him Ez 1:3 preaching in a monastery in the village of San Severino, *the hand of the Lord came upon him.* **He saw** Francis, the preacher of Christ's cross, **marked with two bright shining swords intersecting in the shape of a cross. One of them stretched from his head to his feet, and the other across his chest from one hand to the other. He did not know** Christ's servant by sight, **but once he had been pointed out by such a miracle, he recognized him immediately. Stunned at once by what he saw,** he began to resolve to do better. He was struck in his conscience by the power of his words, as if pierced by a spiritual sword coming from his mouth. He completely despised his worldly **displays** and joined the blessed father by profession. When the holy man saw that he had been completely converted from the restlessness of the world **to the peace** of Christ, he called him **Brother Pacifico.** Afterwards this man advanced in holiness; and, before he went to France as provincial minister—indeed he was the first to hold that office there, he merited **again to see a great Tau on Francis's forehead, which** displayed a variety **of** different **colors** that caused his face to glow with wonderful beauty.

The holy man venerated this symbol with great affection,
often spoke of it with eloquence,
and signed it with his own hand **in the letters he sent,**
as if his whole desire were,
according to the prophetic text,
Ez 9:4   *to mark with a Tau*   LMj Prol 2
the foreheads of those moaning and grieving,
of those truly converted to Jesus Christ.

10With the passing of time when the number of brothers had increased, the watchful shepherd began to summon them to a general chapter at Saint Mary of the Portiuncula to allot to each a portion of obedience *in the land of* their *poverty,* according to *the measuring cord of* divine *distribution.* Although there was a complete lack of all necessities and sometimes the number of the brothers was more than five thousand, nevertheless with the assistance of divine mercy, they had adequate food, enjoyed physical health and overflowed with spiritual joy.

Because he could not be physically present at the provincial chapters, he was present in spirit through his solicitous care for governing, fervor of prayer, and effectiveness of blessing, although, he did sometimes appear visibly by God's wonderful power.

For the outstanding preacher, who is now a glorious confessor of Christ, Anthony, **was preaching to the brothers at the chapter** of Arles on the inscription on the cross: *Jesus of Nazareth, King of the Jews.* **As he glanced at the door** of the chapter, a **brother of** proven virtue, **Monaldo by name,** moved by a divine reminder, **saw with his bodily eyes blessed Francis lifted up in the air with his arms extended as if on a cross, blessing the brothers.** All the brothers felt themselves **filled with a consolation of spirit,** so great and so unusual, that it was certain to them that the Spirit *was bearing witness* **to the** true **presence of the** holy **father** among them. This was later confirmed not only by the evidence of signs, but also by the external testimony of the words of the holy father himself.

> It must be clearly believed that the almighty power of God,
> which allowed the holy bishop Ambrose
> to attend the burial of the glorious Saint Martin
> and to honor that holy prelate with his holy presence,[a]
> also allowed his servant Francis to be present
> at the preaching of his true herald Anthony,
> in order to attest to the truth of his words,
> especially those concerning Christ's cross,
> of which he was both a carrier and a minister.

11When the Order was already widely spread and Francis was considering having the rule which had been approved by Innocent

Marginal references: Gn 41:52; Ps 78:54 — 1C 48 — Jn 19:19 — Jn 1:7

---

a. In the first of his four books describing the miracles of Saint Martin of Tours (+397), Gregory of Tours (+594) writes that Saint Ambrose (+397), while people thought he was dozing at Mass, was present at Martin's funeral that was celebrated at the same time. Cf. Gregory of Tours, *De miraculis sancti Martini Episcopi*, I 5 (PL 71, 918ff).

permanently confirmed by his successor Honorius, he was advised by the following revelation from God.

It seemed to him that he was gathering tiny bread crumbs from the ground, which he had to distribute to a crowd of hungry brothers who stood all around him. He was afraid to give out such little crumbs, fearing that such minute particles might slip between his fingers, when a voice said to him from above: "Francis, make one host out of all the crumbs, and give it to those who want to eat." He did it, whoever did not receive it devoutly, or showed contempt for the gift received, soon appeared obviously covered with leprosy.

2C 209

In the morning the holy man told all this to his companions, regretting that he did not understand *the mystery of the vision.* On the following day, while *he kept vigil in prayer,* he heard this voice coming down from heaven: "Francis, the crumbs of last night are the words of the Gospel; the host is the rule and the leprosy is wickedness."

Dn 2:19
Tb 3:11

Since he therefore wanted **the Rule** that had been taken from a more widespread collection of Gospel passages **to be confirmed,** he went up to a certain mountain led by the Holy Spirit, with two of his companions, to condense it into a shorter form as the vision had dictated. There he fasted, content with only *bread* and *water,* and dictated the rule as the Holy Spirit suggested to him while he was praying.[a] When he came down from the mountain, he gave the rule to his vicar to keep. After a few days had elapsed, the vicar claimed that it had been lost through carelessness. The holy man went off again to the place of solitude and rewrote it *just as before,* as if he were taking *the words* from the mouth of God. And he obtained confirmation for it, as he had desired, from the lord Pope Honorius, in the eighth year of his pontificate.

Dt 9:9

Dt 10:3
Dt 10:4

Fervently exhorting the brothers to observe this rule,
Francis used to say
that nothing of what he had placed there
came from his own efforts
but that he dictated everything
just as it had been revealed by God.
To confirm this with greater certainty by God's own testimony,
when only a few days had passed,

---

a. The allusions to Deuteronomy in this and the following passages suggest that Bonaventure may have been comparing the events surrounding the writing of the Rule to those of Moses' reception of the Ten Commandments. Thus Fonte Colombo may be seen as another Sinai, Francis's fasting on bread and water is similar to that of Moses, as is his vicar, the unnamed Elias, to Aaron who, in Deuteronomy, is also unnamed; and his return to the mountain's top to receive, again, the words of God.

the stigmata of our Lord Jesus were imprinted upon him
by the finger *of the living God,*   Rv 7:2
as the seal of the Supreme Pontiff, Christ,
for the complete confirmation of the rule
and the commendation of its author,
as will be described below,
after our exposition of his virtues.

Chapter Five

THE AUSTERITY OF HIS LIFE
AND HOW CREATURES PROVIDED HIM COMFORT

[1]When the man of God, Francis, saw
that many were being inspired
by his example
to carry the cross of Christ with fervent spirit,
he himself, like a good leader of Christ's army,

Rv 7:9 was encouraged to reach the palm of victory
through the height of heroic virtue.[a]
He directed his attention to this text of the Apostle:

Gal 5:24 *Those who belong to Christ
have crucified their flesh
with its passions and desires.*[b]
To carry in his own body the armor of the cross,
he held in check his sensual appetites with such a rigid discipline
that he scarcely took what was necessary
for the sustenance of nature.

He used to say that it would be difficult **to satisfy the necessity** of   1C 51
the body without giving in to the earthbound inclinations of the

---

a. Pages 81-90 of the Index to Bonaventure's *Commentarius in Quatuor Libros Sententiarum* establish his well-articulated theology of virtue. The *ordo amoris* [the ordering of love], as he calls virtue in the first of the *Disputed Question on Evangelical Perfection*, demands a clear sense of direction since his view of creation sees a "twofold order of things, one within the universe, and another with regard to their end." Cf. *Questiones Disputatae de Perfectione Evangelica*, q. I, concl. (V 123); *Commentarius in Libros Sententiarum* I., dist. XLIV, a.1, q.3, ad 2 (I, 786). While the earlier *legendae* and lives of Saint Francis describe his virtues, especially 2C, they do so in a somewhat unclear fashion. To be true to his own theology of virtue, Bonaventure develops an approach that is well-defined and carefully delineated. Cf. Regis J. Armstrong, "Towards an Unfolding of the Structure of St. Bonaventure's *Legenda Major" The Cord* 39 (1989): 3-17.

b. Curiously *austeritas* [austerity] is seldom used in Bonaventure's writings; aside from the chapter headings, it appears only three times in this work (LMj VI 2; IX 4; XIII 2). Francis is described only twice as *austerus* [austere] in this work (LMj V1, 7). The same may be said of the earlier descriptions of Francis: the word does not appear in any form in Thomas of Celano, and only once in AP 39 (FA:ED II 59) and in L3C 39 (FA:ED II 91). His *Commentary of Luke's Gospel* and his sermons reveal Bonaventure's appreciation for the word. Austerity is seen as (a) the "beginning of human reparation" (IX, 208); (b) the means of freeing us "from the disturbances of sin" (IX, 466); (c) that which enables us to enter the gate of heaven (VII, 350); and (d) that which identifies us with Christ (VII, 16, 228). In commenting on this passage, Gal 5:24, Bonaventure writes: "Austerity is a sign of an interior holiness . . ." (V, 16).

senses.[a] Therefore when he was in good health, he **hardly ever allowed** himself **cooked food; and on the rare occasion when he did so, he either sprinkled it with ashes** or added **water** to make it extremely insipid. **What shall I say about wine, when he would** scarcely **drink** even **enough water** while **he was burning with** a fierce **thirst?** He discovered more effective methods of abstinence and daily improved in their exercise. Although he had already attained the height of perfection, nevertheless always beginning, he was innovative in punishing the lust of his flesh with afflictions.[b]

When he went out among people, he conformed himself to his hosts in the food he ate **because of** the text **of the Gospel.** But when he returned home, he kept strictly his sparse and rigid abstinence. Thus he was austere toward himself but considerate toward his neighbor. Making himself obedient to the Gospel of Christ in everything, he gave an edifying example not only when he abstained but also when he ate.

More often than not, **the naked ground was a bed for his** weary **body; and he would often sleep sitting up, with a piece of wood or a stone** positioned **for his head.** Clothed in a single poor little **tunic,** he served the Lord in *cold and nakedness.*

[2]Once when he was asked how he could protect himself against the bite of the winter's frost with such thin clothing, he answered with a burning spirit: "If we were touched within by the flame of desire for our heavenly home, we would easily endure that exterior cold." In the matter of clothes, he had a horror for softness and loved coarseness, claiming that John the Baptist had been praised by the Lord for this. If he felt the softness of a tunic that had been given to him, he used to sew pieces of cord on the inside because he used to say, according to the word of Truth itself, that we should look for soft clothes not in the huts of the poor but in the palaces of princes. For his own certain experience had taught him that demons were terrified by harshness, but were inspired to tempt one more strongly by what is pleasant and soft.

R IX 13; LR III 14 *(margin)*
Lk 10:7 *(margin)*
1C 52; LJS 31 *(margin)*
LJS 31 *(margin)*
2 Cor 11:27 *(margin)*
Mt 11:8; Lk 7:25 *(margin)*
Mt 11:8 *(margin)*
ER II 14 *(margin)*

---

a. The changes made to Thomas's text are important for obtaining a correct understanding of austerity. Bonaventure changes "it is impossible" (1C 51) to "it is difficult." More importantly, while Thomas adds ". . . without bowing to pleasure," Bonaventure states: "without giving into earthbound inclination of the senses." Thus he directs the readers attention to the larger questions of the significance of the human body in the plan of God, and the role of the senses.

b. Bonaventure uses *libido* [lust] in this passage, a word that appears rarely in these documents. Francis never uses the word, Thomas of Celano once (2C 126), and Bonaventure only three times and only in this chapter (LMj V 1,3,4). Bonaventure's homilies deal with the word sporadically. Following Augustine, he defines it as "the love of those things that someone unwilling can lose," cf. Sermon II on the Purification (IX, 646), and identifies twelve "masks" used by the devil in its promotion, e.g. riches, laziness, luxury, etc, cf. Sermon VI and the XXII Sunday after Pentecost.

One **night,** contrary to his **accustomed** manner, he had allowed a   2C 64
feather pillow to be placed **under his head** because of **an illness** in
his head and **eyes.** The devil got into it, gave him no rest until the
hours **of matins,** and in many ways disturbed him from the fervor **of**
holy **prayer,** until, after he had called a companion, he had him **take
the pillow** with the devil far away out of his cell. But when the
brother went out of the cell **with the pillow, he lost** the strength and
use of his limbs, until **at the voice of the holy** father, **who was aware
of this** in spirit, his former strength of heart and body was fully restored to him.

Is 21:8   ³**Unbending in discipline** *he stood upon his guard,* taking the great-   1C 42
est care to preserve purity of both soul and body.ᵃ Near the beginning
of his conversion, **in wintertime he would** frequently **immerse him-**   LJS 24
self in a ditch filled with icy water in order to perfectly subjugate the
enemy within and preserve the white robe of modesty from the
flames of voluptuousness. He used to say that it should be incomparably more tolerable for a spiritual man to endure great cold in his
flesh rather than to feel even slightly the heat of carnal lust in his
heart.

1 Cor 7:5   ⁴**One night** while *he gave himself to prayer* in a cell at the hermitage   2C 116
1 Sm 3:8   of Sarteano, the ancient enemy *called* him *three times:* "Francis,
Francis, Francis!" When **he replied** to him, he asked **what** he
wanted. And that one continued deceitfully: **"There is no sinner in
the world whom** God **will not forgive if he is converted. But if any-**
Dt 3:39   **one kills himself by hard penance,** *he will find no mercy* for all eternity." **At once by a revelation,** the man of God **recognized the
enemy's treachery, how he was trying to call him back to being
lukewarm.** This was surely shown by what followed. For immedi-
Jb 41:12   ately after this, at the whim of him *whose breath sets coals afire,* **a serious temptation** of the flesh seized him. When that lover of chastity
felt it coming, after **he took off his clothes,** he began **to lash himself
very strenuously with a cord,** saying: "Come on, Brother Ass, that's
the way you should stay under the whip! The tunic has given up on

---

a. This passage of Isaiah 21:8 appears frequently in Bonaventure's writings. In his *Commentary on
Luke's Gospel,* his three references are specifically directed to the struggles of the spiritual life (XII
58; XVII 7; XXI 59), most specifically to the temptations of the contemplative life. A reference in
The Exposition on the Rule of the Friars Minor IV centers on the roles of the Minister and Custodian
which Bonaventure sees in terms of vigilance or keeping guard. *The Treatise on Twenty-Five Points
to Remember* 23 employs the same language as this passage of LMj in speaking of the ancient enemy
that attacks both the inner and outer man. The Latin has *utriusque hominis puritate servanda*
[preserving purity of both persons], a difficult phrase to translate literally. It's soul and body. Cf. VII
326, 427, 539; VIII 419, 517.

religion; it presents a symbol of holiness. It is not lawful for a lustful person to steal it. *If you want to leave, leave!"*

Is 40:4; 1 Sm 30:13

Even more inspired by a wonderful fervor of spirit, once he opened the cell, went out into the garden and, throwing his poor still naked body into the deep snow, began to pack it together by the handful into seven mounds. Showing them to himself, he spoke as if to another person: "Here, the larger one is your wife; those four over there are your two sons and two daughters; the other two are a servant and a maid who are needed to serve them. Hurry, then, and get them some clothes because they are freezing to death! But if the complicated care of them is annoying, then take care to serve one Master!" At that the tempter went away conquered. And the holy man returned to the cell in victory, because while he froze outwardly as penance, he so quenched the fire of lust within, that he hardly felt anything of that sort from that time on.

2C 117

A certain brother, who *was giving himself to prayer* at the time, saw *in the bright moonlight* all these things. When the man of God learned that he had seen this that night, while giving him an account of the temptation, he ordered him to reveal to no living being what he had seen as long as he himself lived.

1 Cor 7:5
Jb 31:36

1C 43

⁵He taught not only that the vices of the flesh must be mortified and its prompting checked, but also that the exterior senses, through which death enters the soul, should be guarded with the greatest care.[a]

2C 112

He solicitously commanded the avoidance of familiarities with women by sight or by conversation, for many are an occasion of ruin; and he maintained that, through these, a weak spirit would be broken and a strong spirit often weakened. He said that avoiding this contagion when conversing with them, except for the most well-tested, was as easy as *walking* in fire *and not burning one's feet.* He himself so *turned aside his eyes, lest they see vanity* of this kind, that, as he once said to a companion, he almost recognized no woman by her face. For he did not think it was safe to drink into one's interior such images of woman's form, which could either rekindle the fire in an already tamed flesh, or stain the brightness of a pure heart. He even used to declare that a conversation with a woman was unnecessary except only for confession or very brief instruction, as their

Prv 6:28
Ps 119:37

2C 114
ER XII 3,4

---

a. *Exteriores sensus* [the exterior senses]: while Bonaventure uses the words of Thomas (1C 43), his theology of the spiritual senses suggests that he perceives much more. The already noted change of Thomas's text in which Bonaventure articulates a different purpose in the practice of austerity, LMj V 1, describes the result of sin as bringing about the "earthbound inclination of the senses." Thus the demand for austerity, i.e., to direct the senses "heavenward" or, in the terminology of this text, "life-giving."

salvation requires and respectability allows. **"What business,"** he asked, **"should** a religious **have with a woman, except when she re-ligiously makes a request for holy penance or for counsel concern-ing a better life?** When one is too secure, one is less wary of the enemy. If the devil can hold onto one hair of a person, he will soon make it grow into a plank."

2C 113

[6]He taught the brothers to flee with all their might from idleness, the cesspool of all evil thoughts;[a] and he demonstrated to them by his own example that they should master their rebellious and lazy flesh by constant discipline and useful work. Therefore he used to call his body **Brother Ass,** for he felt it should be subjected to heavy labor, beaten frequently with whips, and fed with the poorest food.

ER VII 11; LR V 2; Test 21

2C 129

If he saw **someone idle** and vagrant, wanting to eat **the labors** of others, he thought he should be called "**Brother Fly,"** because he did nothing good himself but poisoned the good done by others and so rendered himself useless and obnoxious to all. On account of **this he** once said: "I want my brothers to work and be kept busy, so that, given to idleness, they stray into what is forbidden with heart and tongue."

2C 75

2C 161

He strongly wanted the brothers to observe the silence recom-mended by the Gospel, so that they particularly abstain at all times from *every idle word,* since they would have *to render an account on the day of judgment* But if he found a brother accustomed to shallow talk, **he would reprimand** him bitterly, affirming that a modest silence was the guardian of a pure heart and no small virtue itself, in view of the fact that *death and life* are said to be *in the hands of the tongue,* not so much by reason of taste as by reason of speech.

2C 160

ER XI; RH; Adm X LR III

Mt 12:37

Prv 18:21

[7]Although he energetically urged the brothers to lead an austere life, he was not pleased by an intransigent severity that did not *put on a heart* of piety and **was not seasoned with the salt of discernment.**[b]

Col 3:12

2C 22

---

a. Bonaventure introduces *otium* [idleness] into his discussion of austerity and, in doing so, describes it in words similar to those of his first letter to the entire Order in 1257: "Certain brothers have succumbed to idleness, that cesspool of every vice, where they have been lulled into choosing a monstrous kind of state somewhere between the active life and the contemplative, while cruelly feeding on the blood of living souls." Cf. *Epistolae Officiales* I 2 (VIII, 469), translation is that of Dominic Monti, *Works of Saint Bonaventure V: Writings Concerning the Franciscan Order* introduction and translation by Dominic Monti (St. Bonaventure, NY: The Franciscan Institute, 1994), 59. The theme returns frequently in Bonaventure's writings, especially those to the friars, *Instruction for Novices* IX 1-2; *Constitutions of Narbonne* VI, and the *Defense of the Mendicants* XII 17 (VIII 321, 455, 484, 502).

b. Bonaventure's concept of *discretio* is more in keeping with the contemporary English word, discernment. In his *Commentarius in Ecclesiasten,* C. IX he writes of *discernendum* [distinguishing or discerning] between what is bad and good (VI, 75), a process he maintains in his *Commentarius in Ioannem,* C. XI, coll. Xli, a. 38; coll. Xlii, 7, that is clouded by the sleep of sin (VI, 587, 589). In his *Commentarius in Evangelium Lucae* C. II, v. 45, he describes the time of *discretionis* [discernment] as that of turning to good (VII, 66).

2C 21

One night, when one of the brothers was tormented with hunger because of his excessive fasting, he was unable to get any rest. **The pious shepherd** understood the danger threatening his sheep, called the brother, put some bread before him, and, to take away **his embarrassment, he started eating first** and gently **invited** him to eat. The brother put aside his embarrassment, **took the food,** overjoyed that, through the discerning condescension of his shepherd, he had both avoided harm to his body, and received an edifying example of no small proportion.

When morning came, after the man of God had called the brothers together and recounted what had happened during the night, he added this reminder: **"Brothers, in this incident let charity, not food, be an example for you."** He taught them, moreover, to follow **discernment** as the charioteer of the virtues,[a] not that which the flesh recommends, but that taught by Christ, whose most sacred life expressed for us the exemplar of perfection.

> [8]Encompassed by the weakness of the flesh,
> a human cannot follow
> the spotless crucified Lamb so perfectly
> as to avoid contacting any filth.
> Therefore he taught
> those who strive after the perfect life
> to cleanse themselves daily
> with streams of tears.
> Although he had already attained extraordinary purity
> of heart and body,
> he did not cease to cleanse the eyes of his soul
> with a continuous flood of tears,
> unconcerned about the loss of his bodily sight.[b]
> When he had incurred a very serious eye illness
> from his continuous weeping,
> and a doctor advised him to restrain his tears
> if he wanted to avoid losing his sight,
> the holy man answered:
> "Brother doctor,
> we should not stave off

---

a. The Latin here is *aurigam virtutum* [the charioteer of the virtues]. The phrase comes from Bernard of Clairvaux, *On The Song of Songs*, Sermon 49:5, translated by Kilian Walsh and Irene M. Edmonds (Kalamazoo, MI: Cistercian Publications, 1962), 25.

b. In a passage comparing the tears of Mary Magdalene with those of St. Monica and St. Ambrose, Bonaventure notes: "The blessed Francis wept so much that the doctors told him to stop weeping, otherwise he would be blind. And, because of his tears, he did go blind. Cf. *Sermon 1 on St. Mary Magdalene* ii (IX, 557).

a visitation of heavenly light even a little
because of love of the light
that we have in common with flies.
For the body receives the gift of light
for the sake of the spirit
and not the spirit for the sake of the body."
He preferred to lose his sight
rather than to repress the devotion of his spirit
and hold back the tears
which cleansed his interior vision
so that he could see God.[a]

[9]Once he was advised by doctors, and was strongly urged by the brothers, to undergo the process of cauterization. The man of God agreed humbly because he realized that it would be at the same time salutary and harsh. **The surgeon who had been summoned** then **came and placed an iron instrument in the fire for cauterizing.** But the servant of Christ, **comforting his body, which was struck with panic, spoke to the fire** as a friend: **"My brother Fire, your beauty is the envy of all creatures, the Most High created you strong, beautiful and useful. Be gracious to me in this hour; be courteous! I pray the Great Lord who created you to temper now your heat that I may bear your gentle burning."**

With the prayer finished, he traced **the sign of the cross** over the iron instrument **glowing in the fire, and waited unafraid. The hissing iron was sunk into tender flesh, and the burn is extended straight slowly from the ear to the eyebrow.** How much pain that burning caused, that holy man expressed: "Praise the Most High," he said **to the brothers, "because I tell you truly, I felt neither the heat of the fire nor any pain in my flesh." And turning to the doctor,** he said: **"If my flesh isn't well cooked, then try again!"** The experienced doctor was amazed at the powerful strength of spirit in his weak body, and proclaimed it a divine miracle, saying: "I say to you, brothers, *I have seen wonderful things today.*"

2C 166

Lk 5:26

---

a. This carefully crafted paragraph, a bridge between the more negative section of LMj V 1-7 and the more positive (LMj V 9-12), needs to be understood in light of Bonaventure's theology of the spiritual senses, the "fullest account" of which, according to Karl Rahner's thorough study, "is to be found in the mystical theology of Saint Bonaventure," cf. Karl Rahner, "The Doctrine of the Spiritual Senses in the Middle Ages," *Theological Investigations* XIV 7 (New York: Crossroad-Seabury, 1979) 104-134. Clearly the result of grace, Bonaventure understands this as one of challenges of spiritual growth. Thus the following paragraphs of Bonaventure's portrait of Francis touches on the "spiritualization" of his senses of touch, taste—and smell which is implied, hearing, and sight.

For he had reached such purity
that his **flesh was in** remarkable **harmony**
with his spirit
and his spirit with God.
As a result God ordained
that *creation which serves its Maker*
should be subject in an extraordinary way
to his will and command.

LJS 64

Wis 16:24

3C 17

[10]**For, at another time when** the servant of God **was suffering** from a severe illness at the hermitage of Sant'Urbano, he was feeling the weakness of his nature, **and requested** a drink of wine. He was told that there was no wine that they could give him; so he ordered some water and when it was brought, he blessed it with the sign of the cross. At once what had been brought as pure water became excellent wine; and what the poverty of a deserted place could not provide, the purity of the holy man obtained.

At its taste,
he immediately **recovered with such ease,**
that the newness **of taste**
and the renewal **of health,**
supernaturally renewing the tasted and the taster,
confirmed by a twofold witness,
that he had perfectly stripped away *the old man*
and put on *the new.*

Col 3:9-10

1C 61

[11]Not only did **creation** serve God's servant
at his nod,
but even the Creator's providence condescended everywhere
to his pleasure.

2C 126

For one time when his body was weighed down by many forms of illness, he had a desire to hear some music to arouse the joy of his spirit. But since it seemed inappropriate that this should be done by a human ministry, the deference of angels came to indulge the holy man's pleasure. **One night, as he was keeping vigil and meditating about the Lord, suddenly a lute was playing some wonderful harmony** and *a very sweet melody.* No one was seen, but *the changes in his hearing* suggested that the lute player was moving back and forth from one place to another. With *his spirit turned to God,* there was such delight in that sweet sounding song, that he thought he had exchanged this world for the other.

Sir 40:21; Ez 10:13

Jb 34:14

This did not remain hidden from the brothers who were close to

Lk 1:68; 7:16 him, who, by clear signs, would often see him *visited by the Lord* with such overwhelming and frequent consolation, that he was incapable of keeping them hidden.

[12]At another time when the man of God and a companion were walking on the banks of the Po while on a journey of preaching between Lombardy and the Marches of Treviso, they were overtaken by the darkness of night. The road was exposed to many great dangers because of the darkness, the river and some swamps. His companion said to the holy man: "Pray, father, that we may be saved from these threatening dangers!" Full of confidence, the man of God answered

Lk 3:8 him: *"God is powerful,* if it pleases him in his sweetness, to disperse this darkness and give us the benefit of light." Scarcely had he finished speaking when, behold, such a great light began to shine around them with a heavenly radiance that they could see in clear light not only the road, but also many other things all around, although the night remained dark elsewhere. By the guidance of this light they were led physically and comforted spiritually; singing hymns of praise to God they arrived safely at their lodging, which was a long way off.

Consider that,
at his nod,
that man of admirable purity and great virtue
tempered the heat of fire,
changed the taste of water,
brought comfort with angelic melody
and was led by divine light,
so that, in this way, it might be proved
that the entire fabric of the universe
came to the service
of the sanctified senses of the holy man.[a]

---

a. It is helpful to read the first two chapters of Bonaventure's *Journey of the Soul into God* in order to appreciate his attempts to theologize on the uniqueness of the purification of a human's senses to the extend of returning to the order established by God.

Chapter Six

HIS HUMILITY AND OBEDIENCE AND
THE DIVINE CONDESCENSIONS MADE TO HIM AT HIS NOD

¹Humility,
the guardian and embellishment of all the virtues,
had filled the man of God with abundance.
In his own opinion
he was nothing but a sinner,
though in truth he was a mirror
and the splendor of every kind of holiness.
As he had learned from Christ,
he strove to build himself upon this
like a wise architect laying a foundation.^a
He used to say that it was for this reason
that the Son of God came down
from the height of his Father's bosom
to our lowly estate
so that our Lord and Teacher might teach humility
in both **example** and **word.**

Therefore as Christ's disciple, he strove **to regard himself as worthless** in his own eyes and those of others, recalling what had been said by his supreme Teacher: *What is highly esteemed among mortals is an abomination before God.* He used to make this statement frequently: "What a person is before God, that he is and no more." Therefore, judging that it was foolish to be elated by worldly **favors,** he rejoiced in insults and was saddened by praise. If nothing else, *he* would rather *hear himself blamed* than praised, knowing that the former would lead **him to change his life, while the latter would** push him to a fall. And so **frequently** when people extolled the merits of his holiness, he commanded **one of the brothers to impress** upon his ears words that were, on the contrary, insulting. **When the**

2C 140

2C 26

I Cor 3:10; Heb 6:1

1C 53

1C 4

Lk 16:15

Adm XIX 2

2C 140

Ps 31:14

1C 53

LJS 33

---

a. Bonaventure's theology of humility is clearly stated in his *Disputed Questions on Evangelical Perfection*, Question I, in which he proposes it as "the foundation of all virtue," cf. *Quaestiones Disputatae de Evangelica Perfectione* (V, 117-124). Throughout those writings directed to the friars he continually returns to the theme and repeatedly describes it as virtue's "guardian" and "beauty" or "embellishment," whose primary model is Christ.

brother, though unwilling, called him a boor and a mercenary, un-skilled and useless, he would reply, exhilarated in mind and face: "May the Lord bless you, my beloved son, for it is you who are really telling the very truth and what the son of Peter Bernardone needs to hear."

[2]In order to make himself looked down upon by others,   1C 54
he did not spare himself the shame of bringing up his own faults
in his preaching before all the people.

Once it happened, because he was ill, he somewhat relaxed the   1C 52
rigor of his abstinence in order to recover his health. When his physi-cal strength returned, the authentic scorner of himself was inspired to insult his own flesh. "It is not right," he said, "that people should believe I am abstaining while, in fact, I eat meat secretly." He got up, inflamed with the spirit of true humility, and after he had called the people together in the piazza of the city of Assisi, he solemnly en-tered the principal church with many of the brothers whom he had brought with him. He commanded that he be dragged before the eyes of all, with a cord tied around his neck and stripped to only his underwear, to the stone where criminals received their punishment. Climbing upon the stone, although he had a fever and was weak and the weather was bitter cold, he preached with much vigor and spirit. He asserted to all his hearers that he should not be honored as a spiri-tual man but rather he should be despised by all as a carnal man and a glutton. Therefore those who had gathered there were amazed at so great a spectacle. They were well aware of his austerity, and so their hearts were struck with compunction; but they professed that his humility was easier to admire than to imitate. Although this inci-
Is 20:3   dent seemed to be more *a portent* like that of a prophetic utterance than an example, nevertheless it was a lesson in true humility in-structing the follower of Christ that he must condemn the fame of   1C 53
transitory praise, suppress the arrogance of bloated bragging, and re-ject the lies of deceptive pretense.

[3]He more often did many things in this way,   LJS 33
Ps 30:12   that outwardly he would become *like a discarded utensil*
while inwardly he would possess the spirit of holiness.

Ps 27:13   He strove to hide *the good things of his Lord* in the secrecy of his   2C 133
heart, not wanting to display for his own glory what could be the cause of ruin. For often, when many were calling him blessed, he would utter words of this sort: "Don't praise me as if I were safe! I

can still have sons and daughters. No one should be praised as long as his end is uncertain." This he would say to those who praised him; but to himself: "Francis, if the Most High had given so much to a thief, he would be more grateful than you!"

2C 134

He would often say to the brothers: "No one should flatter himself for big applause for doing anything a sinner can do. A sinner," he said, "can fast, pray, weep, and mortify his flesh. This one thing he cannot do: be faithful to his Lord. So this is the only reason for boasting: if we return to the Lord the glory that is his, if we serve him faithfully, and credit Him for what he has given us."

2C 151

[4]That this Gospel merchant
would profit in many ways
and *melt down* all the present time into merit,
he chose not only to be under, rather than above
but also to obey, rather than command.

Jer 6:29

Therefore, resigning the office as general, he asked for a guardian whose will he would obey in all things. He maintained that the fruit of holy obedience was so abundant, that, for those who submit their necks to its yoke, no time passes without profit. Therefore he always promised obedience to the brother who customarily was with him when travelling. Once he said to his companions: "Among the many other things that divine piety has bestowed upon me, it has granted me this grace: that I would obey a novice of one hour, if he were given to me as my guardian, as diligently as I would obey the oldest and most discerning brother. A subject," he said, "must not consider in his prelate a human being, but rather Him for love of Whom he is a subject. The more contemptibly he presides, the more pleasing is the humility of the one who obeys."

2C 152

One time, when they asked him who should be judged truly obedient, he suggested as an example the likeness of a dead body. "Take a lifeless corpse," he said, "and place it wherever you want! You will see that it does not resist being moved, nor complain about location, nor protest if left. Sit it on a throne, and it will look down, not up; dress it in purple, and it looks twice as pale. This," he said, "is someone truly obedient, who doesn't argue about why he's being moved; he doesn't care where he's placed, he doesn't pester you to transfer him. When raised to an office, he keeps his usual humility; the more he's honored, the more he considers himself unworthy."[a]

---

a. See 2C 152, FA:ED II 345

⁵He once said to his companion: "I wouldn't consider myself a   2C 145
Lesser Brother unless I had the attitude I will describe to you. Sup-
pose, as a prelate of the brothers, I go to the chapter, preach and
admonish the brothers, and, at the end, they speak against me:
'You are not suitable for us, because you are uneducated, inarticu-
late, unlettered, and simple!' So, in the end, I am thrown out in disgrace, looked down upon by everyone. I tell you, unless I hear
these words with the same expression on my face, with the same
joy, and with the same resolution for holiness, I am in no sense a
Lesser Brother!" And he added: "In a prelacy there is a fall, in
praise a precipice, in the humility of a subject profit for the soul.
Why, then, do we pay more attention to dangers than to profits,
while we have time for profit?"

For this reason,   1C 38
Francis,
the pattern of humility,
wanted his brothers **to be called Lesser**   ER I 6-7; LRI II 1
and the prelates of his Order to be called ministers,
that he might use the words of the Gospel
he had promised to observe,
and that his followers
might learn from this very name
that they had come to the school
of the humble Christ
to learn humility.
The teacher of humility,
Jesus Christ,
to instruct his disciples in true humility,
said:
"Whoever wishes to become great among you,   ER V 11-12
let him be your servant;
and whoever wishes to be first among you
will be your slave."

Mt 25:45

Mt 20:26-2

When the Lord of Ostia, the chief protector and promoter of the   2C 148
Order of Lesser Brothers—who afterwards, as the holy man **had**   LJS 65
foretold, was elevated to the honor of the supreme pontificate, and
was called Gregory IX—asked him whether he would allow his
brothers to be promoted to ecclesiastical offices, he responded: **"My**
Lord, my brothers are called 'lesser' precisely so they will not pre-
sume *to become 'greater.'* If you want them to bear *fruit in the Church of*

Mt 20:26; Jn 15:2, 8;
Phil 3:6

God, keep them and preserve them in the status in which *they were*   1 Cor 7:20
called, and do not permit them to rise to ecclesiastical prelacies."

⁶And because he preferred humility to honor
both in himself and in all his subjects,
God, the lover of the humble,
judged him worthy of higher honors
as a heavenly vision revealed to one brother,
a man of outstanding virtue and devotion.

2C 122
2C 123
    For when he was in the company of the man of God and was pray-
ing fervently with him in a deserted church, he passed into ecstasy,
and saw *among the many thrones in heaven* one more noble than the   Rv 4:1-2
rest, adorned with precious stones and glittering with great glory.
He wondered within himself at the splendor of the lofty **throne,** and   Est 15:9
thought quietly about whose it might be. *Then he heard a voice saying*   Dn 4:16; Acts 9:4
to him: "This throne belonged to one of *those who fell,* and now it is   Is 14:9-15; Rv 12:7
reserved for the humble Francis." Finally, when the brother *came*   Acts 12:11
back to himself from the flight of prayer, he followed the blessed man
as he proceeded to act in his usual manner.

2C 123
    As they went along the road, talking to one another about God,
that brother, not unmindful of his vision, skillfully asked him what
he thought of himself. The humble servant of Christ said to him: "I
see myself as the greatest of sinners." When the brother said, to the
contrary, that he could neither say nor feel this with a good conscience, [Francis] continued: "If Christ had pursued so great a crim-
inal with such mercy, I surely think he would be much more
grateful to God than I." At hearing such remarkable humility, the
brother was convinced of the truth of the vision, knowing from the   Mt 23:12; Lk 1:52
sacred testimony of the Gospel that the truly humble will be exalted
to the height of glory from which the proud have been cast out.

2C 202
    ⁷Another time, when he was praying in a deserted church at
Monte Casale in the province of Massa, he realized through the
spirit that sacred relics had been left there. When he sadly reflected
that they had been robbed of the honor due them for a long time, he
ordered the brothers to bring them with reverence to the place. But
when, for an urgent reason he had gone away, his sons, forgetting
the father's order, disregarded the merit of obedience. One day
when they wanted to celebrate the sacred mysteries, after they had
removed the cover from the altar, they discovered—not without
great wonder—some very beautiful and very fragrant bones. They

were gazing upon the relics which had been brought there not by human hands, but by the power of God.

A little later, when he had returned, the man devoted to God dili- gently began to inquire if his orders about the relics had been car- ried out. The brothers humbly confessed their fault of neglecting obedience, and won pardon together with a penance. And the holy man said: *"Blessed be the Lord my God* who himself carried out what you were supposed to do."

Ps 18:47

Consider carefully
the care of divine providence for our dust,
and ponder
the excellent virtue of the humble Francis
in the eyes of God!
Whose commands a human did not heed,
whose wishes God obeyed.[a]

[8] One time when he came to Imola, he went to the bishop of the city and humbly asked, according to his pleasure, to be able to call the people together to preach to them. The bishop replied harshly to him: "Brother, I preach to my people and that is enough!" The gen- uine humble man bowed his head and *went outside,* but less than an hour later *he came back in.* At this, since the bishop was annoyed, he asked him what he was looking for a second time. He responded with a humility of heart as well as of voice: "My lord, if a father throws his son out by one door, he should come back by another." The bishop, overcome by humility, embraced him with a smile, saying: "From now on, you and all your brothers have my general permission to preach in my diocese, because your holy humility has earned it."

Mt 26:75, 58

2C 147

[9] It happened once that he came to Arezzo at a time when the whole city was shaken by a civil war that threatened its destruc- tion. Given hospitality in the outskirts, he saw demons over the city leaping for joy and arousing the troubled citizens to mutual slaugh- ter. In order to put to flight those seditious spiritual powers, he sent Brother Sylvester, a man of dove-like simplicity, before him as a herald, saying: "Go in front of the city gate and, on behalf of Al- mighty God, command the devils to leave at once!" The genuine

2C 108

---

a. In his commentary on the healing of the centurian's son, Bonaventure comments on the power of humility in prompting God to bow to human needs and desires. Thus this sentence provides a transition from the pursuit of humility as a self-emptying to a means of drawing the Almighty to human needs. *Commentary on Luke's Gospel* VII 18 (VII, 170).

obedient man hurried to carry out his father's orders and, caught up in *praise before the face* of the Lord, he began to cry out boldly in front of the city gate: "On behalf of Almighty God and by the command of his servant Francis, get away from here, all you demons." At once the city returned to peace and all the citizens reformed their civil law with great tranquility.

Ps 94:2

> Once the raging pride of the demons,
> which had surrounded the city like a siege,
> had been driven out,
> as the wisdom of a poor man entered in,
> that is, the humility of Francis,
> it brought back peace and saved the city.
> For by his lofty virtue of humble obedience,
> he had gained such powerful control
> over those rebellious and obstinate spirits
> that he could repress their ferocious brashness
> and drive back their savage violence.

> ¹⁰The proud demons flee from the lofty virtues of the humble,
> unless occasionally the divine goodness allows them
> *to be buffeted* to protect their humility,
> as the Apostle Paul writes about himself,
> and as Francis learned through experience.

2C 119

2 Cor 12:7

On one occasion he was invited by Lord Leo, the Cardinal of Santa Croce, to stay with him for a little while in the City, and he humbly accepted out of respect and affection. The first night, when he wanted to rest after his prayer, demons came upon the soldier of Christ, attacking him fiercely. After they beat him long and hard, they finally *left him half-dead.* When they left, the companion he had called came. The man of God told him what had happened, adding: "Brother, I believe that the devils can do nothing, unless God's providence allows it. Therefore, they have now attacked me fiercely in this way, because my staying at the court of the great doesn't offer good example. My brothers, who stay in poor places, hearing that I am staying with cardinals, might suspect perhaps that I am involved in worldly affairs, puffed up by honors and *living in luxury.* And so, I think that one who is set up as an example is better off avoiding courts and living humbly among the humble in humble places, that he might bring about *a strengthening of those who suffer* want, by putting up with the same things." In the morning, then, they went to the cardinal, offered a humble excuse, and said good-bye.

Lk 10:30

Lk 7:25

Prv 28:27

¹¹The holy man abhorred
pride, the source of all evil,
and disobedience, its worst offspring,
but he welcomed the humility of repentance
with no less intensity.

It happened once that **a brother, who** had done something   2C 154
against the law **of obedience,** was brought to him to be punished according to justice. Seeing that the brother showed clear signs of being truly sorry, the man of God was drawn to be easy on him out of
love of humility. However, so this easy forgiveness might not be an
incentive for others to fail in their duty, **he ordered that the brother's
hood be taken off and thrown** into the midst of a fire, so that all
could see what and how harsh a punishment the offense of disobedience deserved. When **the hood** had been within the fire for a while,
he ordered that **it be pulled out of the flames** and returned to the
humbly repentant brother. What a marvel! The hood was pulled out
of the middle of the flames, showing no trace of a burn. This was
done so that, with this one miracle, God might so commend both the
holy man's virtue and the humility of repentance.

Therefore,
worthy of being followed
is the humility of Francis
that obtained such marvelous honor even on earth
that, at his mere nod,
it inclined God to his wish,
changed the attitude of a human being,
repulsed the obstinacy of demons at his command,
and restrained the greed of flames.
In truth,
as it exalts its possessors,
this is what
wins honor from all,
while it exhibits reverence to all.

Chapter Seven

HIS LOVE OF POVERTY
AND THE MIRACULOUS FULFILLMENT OF NEEDS

[1]Among the gifts of charisms[a]

which Francis obtained from the generous Giver,

he merited,

as a special privilege,

to grow in the riches of simplicity

LR VI 6; 2C 55   through his love **of the highest poverty.**

The holy man,

realizing that she was a close friend of the Son of God,

yet was nowadays an outcast throughout almost **the whole world,**

was eager to espouse her *in an everlasting love.*   Jer 31:3

For her sake,

he not only *left his father and mother,*   Gn 2:24; Mk 10:7

but also scattered

everything he could have.

No one coveted gold as he coveted poverty;

no one was as careful of guarding a treasure

as he was of this pearl of the Gospel.   Mt 13:45-46

In this especially would his sight be offended:

if he saw in the brothers

anything which did not accord completely with poverty.

Truly, from the beginning of his religious life until his death,

his wealth was

a tunic, a cord, and underwear,

1C 76   with these he was content.

2C 200   He frequently brought to mind with tears

the poverty of Jesus Christ and his mother,

claiming that she was the queen of the virtues

because she shone so remarkably

---

a. The Latin reads *inter cetera charismatum dona* [among the gifts of charisms]. *Charismata* is a word that does not frequently appear in Bonaventure's writings. Beyond its use here and in the conclusion to Francis's miracles (LMj M X 8), it appears in the *Commentary of Luke's Gospel* I 114 (VII, 370) and the *Commentary on John's Gospel* XVII, Collation LXII 2 (VI, 611). The Lucan Commentary refers to Is 26:8, "Your name and remembrance are the desire of the soul . . ." as Bonaventure suggests that remembrance leads us to charisms that must be sought.

1 Tm 6:15; Rv 19:16
in the *King of Kings*
and in the Queen, his mother.

For when the brothers were seeking at a gathering about which of the virtues makes one a greater friend of Christ, he replied, as if opening the secret of his heart: "You know, brothers, that poverty is the special way to salvation, as the stimulus of humility and the root of perfection, whose fruit is many, but hidden. For this is the

Mt 13:44
hidden treasure of the Gospel *field;* to buy it, everything must be sold, and, in comparison, everything that cannot be sold must be spurned."

[2]"Whoever desires to attain this height," he said, "must renounce in some way not only worldly wisdom but also the expertise of

Ps 70:15-16
knowledge, that, having renounced even this possession, he *might enter into the mighty works of the Lord* and offer himself naked to the arms of the Crucified. For in vain does one perfectly renounce the world, who keeps the money bag of his own opinions in the hidden recesses of his heart."[a]

2C 194
2C 140

Often when he spoke to the brothers about poverty, he would insist on the saying of the Gospel: *The foxes have their holes and the*

Mt 8:20; Lk 9:58
birds of the air have nests, but the Son of Man *has nowhere to lay his head.* Because of this, he taught the brothers to build, like the poor, poor

1 Pt 2:11
little houses, which they should inhabit not as their own but, like *pilgrims and strangers,* as belonging to others. For he would say that the laws of pilgrims was to be sheltered under someone else's roof, to thirst for their homeland, and to travel in peace.[b] Sometimes he ordered the brothers to tear down houses they had built, or to move out of them, if he noticed in them something contrary to gospel poverty because it was appropriated or sumptuous.

2C 56
LR VI 2
2C 59
2C 55

This, he used to say, was the foundation of his Order,
on which primary substratum the structure of religion rests,
so that it is strengthened by its strength,
and weakened by the weakness of its base.

[3]In the same way he would teach,
as he learned from a revelation,
that entering the sacred religion should begin

2C 80

---

a. Whereas Thomas places the curious statement, "the moneybag of his own opinion," in a more general context, Bonaventure inserts it into this description of the poverty demanded of a scholar.
b. Cf AC 23, FA:ED II 136a.

from that Gospel passage:

If you wish to be perfect,
go, sell all that you have,
and give to the poor.

Therefore,
only those who had given up everything and kept nothing
would he admit to the Order,
both because of the words of the holy Gospel
and because they should not cause scandal
by keeping a money bag.

Thus when someone asked to be received into the Order in the Marches of Ancona, the true patriarch of the poor replied: "If you want to join Christ's poor, distribute what you have to the poor of the world." When he heard this, the man went off and, led by love of the flesh, left his goods to his relatives, and nothing to the poor. When the holy man heard him tell of this, he reproached him harshly: "Go on your way, Brother Fly, for you have not yet *left your home and your family.* You gave what you had to your relatives, and cheated the poor; you are not worthy of the holy poor. You began with the flesh; you laid down a crumbling foundation for a spiritual building." The *carnal man* returned to his own and demanded back his goods; refusing to give them to the poor, he soon left his proposal of virtue.

[4]Another time, in the place of **Saint Mary of the Portiuncula,** the destitution was so great, that it was not possible to provide for the brothers coming as guests according to their needs. His vicar went to the man of God, pointing out the indigence of the brothers and asking permission to save some of the goods of those entering as novices to which the brothers could have recourse *in due season.* Not ignorant of heavenly guidance, the man of God said to him: "**Far be it** from us, **dearest brother,** to treat without piety what is in the *Rule* for the sake of anyone. I prefer that you strip **the altar of the** glorious **Virgin, when** necessity requires it, than to use something or even a little that is contrary to the vow of poverty and the observance of the Gospel. For the Blessed Virgin will be **happier to have her altar** stripped and the counsel **of the holy Gospel kept** perfectly, **than to have her altar decorated** and **her Son's** counsel, as promised, neglected."

[5]One time as the man of God was traveling with a companion through Apulia near **Bari,** he found a large bag lying on the road;

2; LR II 5; Test 16

ER II 4; LR II 5

R VII 7; Adm IV 3

2C 81

2C 78

2C 67

2C 68

Mt 19:21

Jn 12:6; 13:29

Gn 12:1

Sir 34:24-25

1 Cor 2:14

Ps 145:15

the kind they call a *fonda*,[a] apparently bursting with coins. His companion alerted the poor man of Christ and urged him to pick the purse up from the ground and distribute the money to the poor. The man of God refused, declaring there was a trick of the devil in this purse they had found, and that the brother was recommending something sinful rather than meritorious, that is, to take what belonged to another and give it away. They left the place and hurried to finish *the journey* they had *begun*. But the brother was not yet at peace, deluded by empty piety, bothering the man of God as if he had no concern to relieve the destitution of the poor. The gentle man agreed to return to the place, not to carry out the brother's wish, but to uncover the devil's trickery. So he returned to the *fonda* with the brother and a young man who was on the road, and after they had prayed, he ordered his companion to pick it up. The trembling brother was dumbfounded, sensing beforehand a diabolical omen. Nevertheless, because of the command of holy obedience, as he was casting out hesitation from his heart, he stretched out his hand toward the bag. Behold, a large snake slid out of the bag and, suddenly disappearing along with it, showed the brother the diabolical deceit. After the enemy's trickery and cunning were grasped, the holy man said to his companion: "To God's servants, brother, money is nothing but a devil and a poisonous snake."

[6]After this something marvelous happened to the holy man while he was going to the city of Siena for some urgent reason. Three poor women, who were exactly alike in height, age, and appearance, met him on the great plain between Campiglia and San Quirico and offered him a small gift of a new greeting. "Welcome, Lady Poverty!" they said. When he heard this, the true lover of poverty was filled with unspeakable joy, for he had in himself nothing that he would so gladly have people hail as what these women had chosen.

Once they had abruptly disappeared,
considering
the remarkable novelty
of the likeness among them,
of the greeting,
of the meeting
and of the disappearance,
the brothers accompanying him weighed,

Jgs 19:14

2C 93

---

a. The Latin term *fonda* literally means a sling and might be translated as *money belt*.

not without reason,
what the mystery meant about the holy man.
Clearly,
it would seem that through those three poor women
so alike in appearance,
offering such an unusual greeting,
and disappearing so quickly,
the beauty of Gospel perfection,
consisting in poverty, chastity, and obedience
was fittingly revealed
to be shining perfectly in the man of God
in an equal way.
Nonetheless,
he had chosen to glory above all
in the privilege of poverty
which he was accustomed to call
his mother, his bride, and his lady.
In this
he desired to surpass others
because he had learned from her
to regard himself inferior to all.

2C 83   Therefore if he saw someone dressed **poorer than himself, immediately** criticizing himself, he set out to be similar, as if contending
2C 84   with **a rival for poverty and afraid to be overcome. It happened one
day that he met a poor man on the road. When he saw the man's
nakedness,** his heart **deeply moved, he said to his companion** in a
sad voice: **"This man's need brings great shame on us, for we have
chosen poverty for its** great **riches; and see, it shines more clearly in
him."**

       [7]For love of holy poverty,
the servant of almighty God
used the alms he had begged from door to door more gladly
than those offered spontaneously.[a]
2C 72   For if **he were invited** by distinguished persons
and honored by a more lavish dinner,

---

a. At this juncture, Bonaventure shifts his considerations of Francis's poverty (1-6) to the acceptance of
begging (7-10). In doing so, he follows the approach he had taken in his *Disputed Questions on
Evangelical Perfection,* Question II, which is divided into three articles: (i) poverty as renunciation;
(ii) poverty as begging; (iii) poverty and manual labor. Cf. V, 124-165. In this shift, Bonaventure is
laying the groundwork for the last section of this chapter devoted to God's miraculous fulfillment of
the brothers' needs (11-13).

he would first seek some pieces of bread at the neighboring houses
and then, enriched by poverty, sit down at table.

And once he did this, **when he** was invited by the Lord Bishop of   2C 73
Ostia, who held Christ's poor man in special affection. After **the**
bishop complained that he had disparaged his honor as would be expected when a dinner guest goes out for alms, God's servant replied:
"My lord, I showed you great **honor while I have honored a greater**
Ps 68:17   **Lord.** *For the Lord is pleased* by poverty and especially when one
freely chooses to go begging for Christ. This is the royal dignity
2 Cor 8:9   which **the Lord** Jesus assumed when he *became poor* for us that he
Mt 5:3   might enrich us by *his want* and *would* make us truly *poor in spirit, as*   LR VI 4; 2C 72
heirs and kings of *the kingdom of heaven.* I do not wish to relinquish
this royal dignity for a fief of false riches granted for only an hour."

8Sometimes, **as he encouraged** the brothers to beg for alms, he   2C 71
1 Jn 2:18   **would use words** such as these: "Go, for *in this last hour* the Lesser
Brothers have been given to the world so that the elect may carry
out for them what will be commended by the Judge as they hear
Mt 25:40   those most sweet words: *As long as you have done it for one of my lesser*
brothers, you did it for me." Then he would say that it was a delight **to**
beg with the title of Lesser Brothers, which the Teacher of Gospel
truth had so clearly expressed by his own mouth in rewarding the
just. When there was an opportunity, he used to go begging even on
the principal feasts, saying that, in the holy poor, the prophecy is ful-
Ps 77:25   filled: *Man will eat the bread of angels.*

He used to say
that bread is clearly angelic,
which holy poverty gathers from door-to-door,
which is sought out of God's love
and is given out of His love
by the blessed prompting of angels.

9Once, on a holy **Easter Sunday,** while he was staying **at a hermit-**   2C 61
age that was so far from any houses that he could not conveniently
go begging, he begged **alms** from the brothers, like **a pilgrim and**
Lk 24:13   **beggar,** mindful of him who *that day* appeared in the guise *of a pilgrim*
to his disciples travelling on the road to Emmaus.

When he had humbly received it,
he taught them with sacred eloquence
to continually celebrate the Lord's Passover,

in poverty of spirit
that is,
his passing *from this world to the Father,*   Jn 13:1
passing through the desert of the world
like *pilgrims and strangers*   1 Pt 2:11
and, like true Hebrews.[a]
And because,
when begging alms,
he was motivated
not by greed for profit but by liberty of spirit,
God, *the Father of the poor,*   Jb 29:16
seemed to have a special care for him.

LR VI 2

2C 77

[10]Once when the Lord's servant was gravely **ill at Nocera,** he was brought back **to Assisi by formally appointed representatives** sent for that purpose out of devotion by the people of Assisi. As they carried Christ's servant back, **they came to a poor little village called Satriano where, since their hunger and the hour called for food, they went out, and finding nothing for sale, returned** empty-handed. The holy man told them: **"You didn't find** anything, **because you trust more in those flies of yours than in God."** For he **used to call coins "flies."** **"But go back,"** he said, **"to the houses which you have visited and, offering the love of God** as a reward, **humbly** ask for an alms. Do not consider this shameful or cheap out of false esteem, **for after sin everything is bestowed as alms, for that great Almsgiver, out of his** abundant **piety, gives to both the worthy and the unworthy."**

The knights overcame their embarrassment, readily **begged for alms, and bought more with the love of God than with money.** Since their hearts were struck with compunction by the divine nod, the poor villagers generously gave not only what was theirs, but also themselves. And so it happened that Francis's wealthy poverty supplied the need which money could not alleviate.

2C 44

[11]**At the time when** he was lying ill **in a hermitage** near Rieti, a **doctor** visited him often to care for him. Since the poor man of Christ was unable to pay him adequately for his services, the most generous

---

a. This is clearly a reference to Francis's role in preparing "in the desert a way of the highest poverty," cf. LMj Prol 1. It further accentuates the biblical and eschatological dimensions of a poverty closely linked to the Paschal or *transitus* that permeates Bonaventure's thought. Cf. Jacques-Guy Bougerol, "Transitus," in *Lexique Saint Bonaventure* (Paris: Éditions Franciscaines, 1969), 127-128; Werner Hülsbusch, "Die Theologie des *Transitus* dei Bonaventura," in *S. Bonaventura 1274-1974*, Vol. IV (Grottaferrata, Rome: Collegio S. Bonaventura, 1974), 533-565; André Ménard, "Spiritualité du *Transitus*," in *S. Bonaventura 1274-1974*, Vol. IV (Grottaferrata, Rome: Collegio S. Bonaventura, 1974), 607-635.

God made up for the poor man and repaid the doctor for his devoted care with the following favor, so that he would not go without payment in the present life. The doctor's new house, which he had just spent all his money building, was threatened with collapse because of a wide crack in the wall, which reached *from the top to the bottom,* a collapse which seemed unavoidable by human means. Fully trusting in the merits of the holy man and out of the devotion of his great faith, he asked his companions to give him something which the man of God had touched with his hands. After many requests he obtained a small amount of his hair which he placed one evening in the crack in the wall. When he rose in the morning, he found that the crack had been so firmly closed that he could not pull out the hairs he had placed there nor could he *find* any *trace* of the crack. And so it happened that because he had dutifully ministered to the body of God's servant in its state of collapse, he avoided the danger of the collapse of his house.

Mt 27:51

Wis 5:10

¹²**Another** time as the man of God **wanted** to go to a hermitage to **spend more time in contemplation, because he was weak,** he rode on **a donkey belonging to a certain poor man. As it was summertime,** that man **climbed up a mountain following** Christ's servant. **Worn out from the long and grueling journey, and weakened further by a burning thirst,** he began to **cry out urgently after the saint:** "Look, **I'll die** of thirst if I don't get a drink **immediately!"** Without delay the man of God **leaped down from the donkey, knelt on the ground, raised his hands to heaven and prayed unceasingly until he understood that he had been heard.** After he had finished his prayer, **he told** the man: "**Hurry over there** to the rock **and you will find living water which at this very hour Christ has mercifully** *brought forth water from the rock* **for you to drink.**"

3C 15

Ps 78:16; Dt 32:13

How amazingly kind God is,
so easily bowing to his servants!
A thirsty man drank *water from the rock*
by the power of another's prayer
and took a drink from *the most solid rock.*
There was no stream of water there before,
nor could any be found since,
even after a careful search.

Ps 78:16; Ex 17:1-7

Dt 32:13

¹³**How Christ multiplied** food at sea
through the merits of his poor man will be noted below.
Here let it suffice to mention

1C 55

that with only a small amount of food
that he had been given as alms,
LJS 34   he **saved** sailors for **a number of days**
from starvation and the danger of death.
From this one could clearly see
that just as the **servant** of Almighty God was
like Moses in drawing *water from the rock,*   Ps 78:16; Ex 17:1-7
like Elisha in the multiplication **of provisions.**   2 Kgs 41

Therefore, let every lack of confidence be far from Christ's poor!
For if the poverty of Francis was so abundantly sufficient
that, by a marvelous power,
it supplied
the destitution of those who came to his aid,
providing food, drink, and housing
when money, skill, and natural means were lacking,
how much more will it merit
those things that are given to all
in the usual plan of divine providence.
If a dry rock gave drink abundantly
to a poor man who was thirsty
at the word of another poor man,
nothing at all
will refuse its service
to those who have left all
for the Creator of all.

Chapter Eight

THE DRIVE OF PIETY
AND
HOW IRRATIONAL CREATURES
SEEMED MOVED TOWARD HIM

1 Tm 4:8

[1]True *piety,*[a]
which according to the Apostle
gives power to all things,
had so filled Francis's heart
and penetrated its depths
that it seemed to have claimed the man of God
completely into its dominion.
This is what,
through devotion, lifted him up into God;
through compassion, transformed him into Christ;
through self-emptying,[b] turned him to his neighbor;
through universal reconciliation with each thing,
refashioned him to the state of innocence.[c]

Through this virtue
he was moved with piety to all things,
especially to souls redeemed by the precious blood of Jesus Christ.
When he saw them being stained by the filth of sin,
he grieved with such tender care

---

a. To place this chapter into a proper historical context, it would be helpful to read André Méhat, Aimé Solignac, Irénée Noye, "Piété," *Dictionnaire de Spiritualité Ascetique et Mystique, Doctrine et Histoire XII* (Paris: Beauchesne, 1986), 1694-1743.

b. The Latin is *condescensionem* [condescension], a word that has negative overtones in contemporary English. In this sense, it implies the stooping of one who is actually exalted in power, rank and dignity, i.e., Christ, so as to accommodate himself to others. Cf. *Webster's Dictionary of Synonyms,* first edition (Springfield, MA: G.& C. Merriam Co., Publishers, 1951), 791.

c. In his *Third Book of Commentary on the Sentences of Peter Lombard,* Bonaventure quotes Augustine's *The City of God* X, c.1, n.3: "The word 'piety' (*eusebeia* in Greek) is generally understood as referring particularly to the worship of God. But this word also is used to describe a dutiful attitude towards parents; while in popular speech it is constantly used in connection with acts of compassion . . . From this application comes the application of the epithet *pius* to God himself." Augustine, *The City of God,* translation by Henry Betterson, introduction by John O'Meara (London, New York, Victoria, Ontario, Auckland: Penguin Books, 1972), 373. Cf. *III Sent.* D. 35, au., q.6, concl. (III, 785b). In this passage, however, Bonaventure extends the meaning of piety to embrace reconciliation with all creation, thus introducing the Franciscan dimension of the word and extending its meaning.

that he seemed like a mother
who was daily bringing them to birth in Christ.
And this was the principal reason for revering
ministers of God's word:
they raise up *seed for their deceased brother*,[a]
Christ, crucified particularly for sinners,
and, with pious concern for their conversion,
they guide them with concerned piety.

2C 172

Dt 25:5

He maintained that a service of this kind of care was more acceptable to *the Father of mercies* than every sacrifice, especially if it were
undertaken with the eagerness of perfect charity. Thus it should be
done more by example than by word, more by tear-filled prayer than
by long-winded sermons.

2 Cor 1:3

2C 164

[2]In the same way **he said that a preacher must be wept over,** as
over someone without real piety, who in preaching seeks not the salvation of souls, but his own **praise,** or who destroys with the deprav-
ity of his life what he builds up with the truth of teaching. He said
that **a simple** tongue-tied **brother** must be preferred who challenges
others to good by his good example. And so **he would explain that
passage** *So that the barren has borne many* in this sense: "The barren
one," he said, "is the **poor little brother who does not have the duty
of producing children in the Church. At the judgment he will** *give
birth to many children,* **for then the Judge will credit to his glory
those he is converting now to Christ by his secret prayers.** *She who
has many children will languish,* **because** the vain and long-winded
preacher, **who rejoices over many** now **as if they were born through
his power, will discover then that he has nothing of his own in
them."**

1 Sm 2:5

1 Sm 2:5

2C 155

[3]*Therefore,*
he yearned with heartfelt piety
and burned with ardent zeal
for the salvation of souls.
He would say
that he *was filled with the sweetest fragrance*
and as if anointed with *precious ointment*
whenever he heard
of many people being converted **to** the way of truth

Ex 29:18

Jn 12:3

---

a. An allusion to the Levirate law through which, in order to perpetuate a family name, a widow who has
no son is taken to wife by her brother-in-law.

by the fragrant reputation of holy brothers in faraway lands.
He rejoiced in spirit upon hearing of such brothers,
and would heap blessings on those brothers
worthy of full acceptance
who, by word or deed, led sinners to the love of Christ.

So also, those who violated sacred religion by evil deeds incurred the very heavy penalty of his curse. "By you," he said, "most holy Lord, and by the whole court of Heaven, and by me, your little one, may they be cursed who break up and destroy by their bad example what you earlier built up and do not cease to build up through holy brothers of the Order!"

He was often so deeply saddened by scandal given to the weak, that he felt he would be overcome unless he had been bolstered by the consolation of the divine mercy.

One time when he was disturbed by some bad examples, he anxiously prayed to the merciful Father for his sons, and brought back a response of this sort from the Lord: "Why are you so upset, poor little man? Have I set you up as a shepherd over my religion so that you can forget that I am its main protector? I have entrusted this to you, a simple man, so that the things that I work in you would be attributed not to human industry, but to divine grace. *I have called, I will preserve, and I will pasture,* and I will raise up others to make up for the fall of some. So that, even if they have not been born, I will have them born! No matter how severely this poor little religion is shaken, it will always remain safe by my gift."

⁴He hated the vice of detraction like a snakebite, as a foe to the source of piety and grace. He firmly held it to be the most atrocious plague and abominable to the most pious God, because the detractor feeds on the blood of the souls which he kills with *the sword of his tongue.*

One time, when he heard one brother blackening the reputation of another, he turned to his vicar and said: "Get up! Get up! Search thoroughly; and if you find the accused brother innocent, make the accuser known publicly by a severe punishment." More than once he decided that a brother should be stripped of his habit if he had stripped his brother of the glory of his reputation, and that he could not raise his eyes up to God until he first did his best to give back what he had stolen. "To the degree that the impiety of detractors is greater than that of thieves," he would say, "so much more does the law of Christ, fulfilled in the observance of piety, oblige us to desire the well-being of souls rather than of bodies."

---

1 Tm 1:15

2 Pt 2:8 — 2C 156

2C 157

2C 158

Is 48:15; Rev 10:3

Ps 56:4

2C 182

Lk 18:13

⁵Emptying himself
through a wonderful tenderness of compassion
for anyone with a bodily affliction,
in the sweetness of his pious heart,
he turned back to Christ
any need, any lack he might notice in anyone.
He certainly had an inborn kindness^a
doubled by the piety of Christ **poured out on him.**
Therefore his soul melted for the poor and the infirm;
to those to whom he could not extend a hand
he extended his affection.

Once it happened that one of the brothers responded more gruffly
to **a poor man begging alms** at an inconvenient time. **When the pi-**
ous lover of the poor heard this, he ordered the brother to strip na-
ked, prostrate **himself at that poor man's feet, confess his fault, and**
beg for his prayers and forgiveness. When he had done this with humility, the father added gently: "Brother, as long as **you see a poor**
person, a mirror of the Lord and his poor Mother is placed before
you. Likewise in the sick, look closely for the infirmities which He
accepted."

In all the poor
that most Christian poor man also saw before him
a portrait of Christ;
he not only gave freely to those he met
the necessities of life, if these had even been given to him,
but he also resolved they should be returned,
as if they truly belonged to them.

It happened once that **a poor man** met him on his return **from**
Siena, when, because of an illness, he was wearing a short mantle
over his habit. When his kind eye observed the man's misery, he said
to his companion: "We must give back to this poor man his mantle,
for it is his! For we accepted it on loan until we should happen
upon someone poorer than we are." But his companion, seeing the
need of his pious father, objected to this stubbornly, lest by providing for someone else, he neglect himself. But he said: "The great
Almsgiver will accuse me of theft if I do not give what I have to
someone in greater need."

Margin references: 2C 83 · 1C 76 · 2C 8 · 2C 85 · Sg 5:6 · Mt 8:17; Is 53:4 · 2C 87 · 2C 77

---

a. LMn I 1, infra 202.

Therefore of all that was given him to relieve the needs of his body,
he was accustomed to ask the permission of the donors
so that he could give it away
should he meet someone in greater need.
He spared nothing at all,
neither mantles nor tunics,
neither books nor even appointments of the altar:
all these he gave to the poor, when he could,
to fulfill his obligation of piety.
Frequently,
whenever he met **poor people burdened with heavy loads,**   1C 76
he would carry their burdens on his own weak **shoulders.**

[6]**From a reflection** on the primary source of all things,   1C 80
filled **with** even more abundant **piety,**
he would call **creatures,**   1C 81
no matter how small,
by the name of "brother" or "sister,"
because he knew they shared with him the same beginning.
However,   1C 77
he embraced more affectionately and sweetly
those which display
the pious **meekness of Christ in a natural likeness**
and portray him in the symbols **of Scripture.**
He often paid to ransom **lambs** that were being led to their death,   1C 79
remembering that most gentle Lamb
Is 53:7   who willed *to be led to slaughter* to pay the ransom of sinners.[a]

One night when the servant of God was a guest at the monastery   2C 111
of San Verecondo in the diocese of Gubbio, a little sheep gave birth
to a baby lamb. There was a very cruel sow there, which did not
spare the life of the innocent, but killed it with her ravenous bite.
When the pious father heard this, he was moved to remarkable
compassion and, remembering the Lamb without stain, lamented
for the dead baby lamb, saying in front of everyone: "Alas, brother
lamb, innocent animal, always displaying Christ to people! Cursed
be the pitiless one who killed you, and neither man nor beast shall
eat of her!" It is amazing to tell! Immediately the vicious sow began
to get sick and, after paying the bodily punishment for three days,
finally suffered an avenging death. She was thrown into the mon-

---

a. The reference to *agnus* [lamb] is obviously to the images of the New Testament: Jn 1:29, 36; Acts
8:32; 1 Pt 1:19; Rv 5:8, 12, 13; 6:1, 16; 7:9, 10, 14, 17; 12:11; 13:8; 14:1, 4, 10, etc.

astery's ditch and, laying there for a long time, dried up like a board, and did not become food for any hungry creature.

Therefore,
let human impiety pay attention
to how great a punishment might at last be inflicted on it,
if such animal cruelty is punished with so horrible a death.
Let also the devotion of the faithful weigh
how the piety in God's servant
was of such marvelous power and of such abundant sweetness
that even the nature of animals acknowledged it
in their own way.

3C 31

⁷When he **was on a journey** near the city **of Siena, he passed a** large **flock of sheep grazing** in a pasture. **He greeted them kindly, as** usual. **After they left the pasture, they all ran to him, lifted their heads,** fixed their eyes on him. They gave him such **a loud bleating** that the shepherds and the brothers were amazed to see the lambs and even the rams frisking about him in such an extraordinary way.

Another time at Saint Mary of the Portiuncula the man of God was offered a sheep, which he gratefully accepted in his love of that innocence and simplicity which the sheep by its nature reflects. The pious man admonished the little sheep to praise God attentively and to avoid giving any offense to the brothers. The sheep carefully observed his instructions, as if it recognized the piety of the man of God. For when it heard the brothers chanting in choir, it would enter the church, genuflect without instructions from anyone, and bleat before the altar of the Virgin, the mother of the Lamb, as if it wished to greet her. Besides, when the most sacred body of Christ was elevated during the Solemnity of the Mass, it would bow down on its knees as if this reverent animal were reproaching the irreverence of those who were not devout and inviting the devout to reverence of the Sacrament.

Once in Rome he had with him a little lamb out of reverence for the most gentle Lamb of God. At his departure he left it in the care of the noble matron, the Lady Jacoba of Settesoli.[a] Now the lamb went with the lady to church, standing reverently by her side as her inseparable companion, as if it had been trained in spiritual matters by the saint. If the lady was late in rising in the morning, the lamb rose and nudged her with its horns and woke her with its bleating, urging her with its nods and gestures to hurry to the church. On account of this,

---

a. Cf. AC 8, FA:ED II 122b.

the lamb, which was Francis's disciple and had now become a master of devotion, was held by the lady as an object of wonder and love.

[8]Another **time at Greccio a small live hare was given** to the man of God, **which he put down on the ground free to run away where it pleased. At the call of the kind father, it leapt quickly into his lap.** He fondled it with the pious affection of his heart and seemed to pity it like a mother. **After warning it with gentle** talk not to let itself be caught again, **he let it go free. But as often as he placed it on the ground** to run away, it always came back to the father's **bosom,** as if it perceived with some hidden sense of its heart the piety he had for it. **Finally, at the** father's **command, the brothers** carried it away **to a** safer place of solitude.   *3C 29*   *1C 60*

In the same way, **on the island in the Lake of Perugia, a little rab-bit** was caught and offered to the man of God. Although it fled from everyone else, it entrusted itself to his hands and his heart as if to natural security.   *3C 30*

When he was hurrying **across the Lake of Rieti to the hermitage of Greccio,** out of devotion a **fisherman offered him a little wa-ter-bird. He received it** gladly **and, with open hands, invited it** to go away, but **it did not want to go. He remained in prayer for a long time with his eyes lifted to heaven. Returning to himself as if after** no more than an hour **stay in another place,** he gently ordered the **little bird** to go away to praise the Lord. **And so the bird, having re-ceived permission with a blessing, flew away expressing its joy in the movements of its body.**   *3C 23*

On the same lake in a similar way **he was offered a large fish that was still alive.** Calling it **by name in his** usual **brotherly way, he put it back in the water next to the boat. The fish kept playing in the water in front** of the man of God; and as if it were attracted by his love, it would in no way leave the boat until it received from him his permission with a blessing.   *3C 24*

[9]Another time when he was walking with a brother through the marshes of Venice, he came upon a large flock of birds singing among the reeds. When he saw them, he said to his companion: "Our Sister Birds are praising their Creator; so we should go in among them and chant the Lord's praises and the canonical hours." When they had entered among them, the birds **did not move from the place;** and on account of the noise the birds were making, they could not hear each other saying the hours. The saint turned to the birds and said: "Sister Birds, stop singing until we have done our duty of   *3C 20*

praising God!" At once they were silent and remained in silence as long as it took the brothers to say the hours at length and to finish their praises. Then the holy man of God gave them permission to sing again. When the man of God gave them permission, they immediately resumed singing in their usual way.

3C 27   **Near the cell of the man of God** at Saint Mary of the Portiuncula, **there was a cricket living and singing on a fig tree.** With its song, it frequently aroused the Lord's servant **to the** divine praises, for he had also learned to marvel at the Creator's magnificence even in insignificant creatures. One day, after he called it, **it flew upon his hand** as if taught from heaven. He said to it: **"Sing, my Sister Cricket, and with your joyful song praise the Lord Creator!"** Obeying without delay, it began to chirp; nor did it stop **until** at the father's command **it flew back to its** own **place. There it remained for eight days,** coming each day, singing and returning at his **command.** Finally **the man of God said to his companions:** "Let us give permission to our sister cricket now, for **while making us so happy with her singing,** she has aroused us to the praises of God over the space of eight days." **As soon as it received permission, the cricket went away and never appeared there again,** as if it did not dare to disobey his command in the slightest way.

3C 26   [10]**When he was sick at Siena, a nobleman sent him a live pheas-**
//2C 170   ant he had recently caught. The moment it saw and heard the holy man, it was drawn to him with such affection that it would in no way allow itself to be separated from him. For many times **it was put down** outside the **brothers' place in the vineyard** so that it could go away if it wanted. But every time it ran right back to the father as if it had always been reared by him. Then it was given to a man who used to visit God's servant out **of devotion** but it absolutely refused to eat, as if it were upset at being out of the sight of the devoted father. It was finally brought back to God's servant, and as soon as it saw him, showed signs of joy and **ate** heartily.

When he went to the hermitage of La Verna to observe a forty-day fast in honor of the Archangel Michael, birds of different kinds flew around his cell, with melodious singing and joyful movements, as if rejoicing at his arrival. They seemed to be inviting and enticing the devoted father to stay. When he saw this, he said to his companion: "I see, brother, that it is God's will that we stay here for some time, for our sisters the birds seem so delighted at our presence."

3C 25   **When** he extended his stay there, **a falcon nesting there bound itself to him in a great covenant of friendship with him.** For at the hour of the night when the holy man usually rose for the divine office, it anticipated him with its noise and song. This pleased God's servant very much because such great concern for him shook out of him all sluggish laziness. But when Christ's servant was more than usually burdened with illness, the falcon would spare him and would not announce such early vigils. As if instructed by God, at about dawn it would ring the bell of its voice with a light touch.

> In the joy of the different kinds of birds
> and in the song of the falcon,
> there certainly seems to have been a divine premonition
> of when this praiser and worshiper of God
> would be lifted up on the wings of contemplation
> and then
> would be exalted with a seraphic vision.

[11]Once while he was staying in the hermitage at Greccio, the people of that place had been stricken by multiple disasters. A pack of raging wolves devoured not only animals, but even people. And every year hailstorms destroyed their wheat field and vineyards. When the herald of the holy Gospel preached to those afflicted in this way, he said to them: "To the praise and honor of Almighty God, I assure you that all the disasters will cease, and the Lord looking down upon you, will multiply your earthly goods. If you believe me, show mercy to yourselves. Once you have made a sincere confession, *bring forth fruits worthy of repentance.* I tell you again, if you are ungrateful for these gifts, and *return to your vomit,* the disasters will return, punishment will double, and even greater *wrath will rage* against you."

2C 35

Mt 3:8

Prv 26:11; 2 Pt 2:22

Jos 22:18

From that hour, therefore, once the people did penance at his exhortation, the disasters ceased, the dangers vanished, and neither the wolves nor the hailstorms caused *any more harm.* And even more remarkable, whenever the hail, falling on neighboring fields, reached the boundaries of Greccio, either it would stop or move off in a different direction.

2C 36

Dn 3:50

> The hail kept the pact of God's servant
> as did the wolves;
> nor did they try to rage anymore contrary to the law of piety
> against people converted to piety,
> as long as, according to their agreement,
> the people did not act impiously
> against God's most pious laws.

Therefore, we should respond piously
to the piety of the blessed man,
which had such remarkable gentleness and power
that it subdued ferocious beasts,
tamed the wild,
trained the tame,
and bent to his obedience
the beasts that had rebelled against fallen humankind.
Truly this is the virtue
that binds all creatures together,
and *gives power to all things*   1 Tm 4:8
having the promise of the life,
that now is and
is yet to come.

Chapter Nine

THE ARDOR OF CHARITY
AND THE DESIRE FOR MARTYRDOM

[1]**Who would be competent to describe** the burning charity
with which Francis, *the friend of the Bridegroom,* was aflame?
Like a thoroughly burning coal,
he seemed totally absorbed in the flame of divine love.
For as soon as he heard "the love of the Lord,"
he was excited, moved, and on fire
as if these words from the outside
were a pick strumming the strings of his heart on the inside.
He used to say that it was a noble extravagance
to offer such a treasure for alms
and that those who considered it less valuable than money
were complete fools,
because the priceless price of divine love alone
was sufficient to purchase the kingdom of heaven,
and
the love of him who loved us greatly
is greatly to be loved!

Aroused by everything to divine love,
he *rejoiced* in all *the works of the Lord's hands*
and through their delightful display
he rose into their life-giving reason and cause.
In beautiful things he contuited Beauty itself[a]
and through the footprints impressed in things
he followed his Beloved everywhere,
out of them all making for himself *a ladder*
through which he could climb up to lay hold of him
who is utterly desirable.[b]
With an intensity of unheard devotion

Margin references:
Jn 3:29

1C 80

2C 196

2C 165

Ps 91:4

Jb 23:11; Sg 5:17

Gn 28:12-13

Sg 5:16

---

a. Once again the Latin is *contuebatur,* cf. supra 50 d.

b. The Latin here is *consurgebat* [he rose], *contuebatur* [he contuited], and *conscenderet* [he would climb up], all words which Bonaventure adds to the text of Thomas of Celano who writes *intuetur* [gazes upon] *cognoscit* [discerns] and *perveniatur* [reaches].

he savored
in each and every creature
—as in so many rivulets—
that fontal Goodness,
and discerned
an almost celestial choir
in the chords of power and activity
given to them by God,
and, like the prophet David,
he sweetly encouraged them to praise the Lord.[a]

Ps 148

[2]Jesus Christ crucified
always *rested like a bundle of myrrh in the bosom* of his soul,[b]
into Whom
he longed to be totally transformed
through an enkindling of ecstatic love.
And as a sign of his special devotion to him,
he found leisure[c]
from the feast of the Epiphany through forty successive days
—that period when Christ was hidden in the desert—
resting in a place of solitude,
shut up in a cell,
with as little food and drink as possible,
fasting, praying, and praising God without interruption.[d]
He was borne aloft into Christ
with such burning intensity,
but *the Beloved* repaid him with such intimate love
that it seemed to that servant of God
that he was aware
of the presence of that Savior before his eyes,
like a yoke,
as he once intimately revealed to his companions.

Sg 1:12

Mt 4:1-11;
Mk 1:12-13; Lk 4:1-13

Sg 1:12

---

a. Bonaventure seems to be alluding here to Francis's *Canticle of the Creatures*, cf. FA:ED I 113-114.

b. The reference to myrrh from the Song of Songs is reminiscent of Bernard of Clairvaux's *Forty-second Sermon on the Song of Songs* 11 in which he writes that under the name of myrrh, the beloved includes "all the bitter trials she is willing to undergo through love of her beloved." Cf. Bernard of Clairvaux, *On the Song of Songs* II, translated by Kilian Walsh, introduction by Jean Leclercq (Kalamazoo, London and Oxford: Cistercian Publications, 1976, 1976), 219.

c. The Latin is *vacabat* [he found leisure], a word difficult to translate but one rich in the contemplative tradition, where it has the sense of vacationing or taking a holiday in God. A thorough study of the word can be found in Jean Leclercq, *Otia Monastica: Études sur Le Vocabulaire de La Contemplation au Moyen Âge* (Rome: "Orbis Catholicus," Herder, 1963), 42-49.

d. The Rules (ER III 11; LR III 6) suggest this extra Lent as a commendable, but optional, practice. It is reckoned from the Epiphany because Christ was taken by the Spirit to the desert immediately after his baptism, which is commemorated on that feast. Cf. 2C 59, FA:ED II 286.

Toward the sacrament of the Lord's Body   2C 201
he burned with fervor to his very marrow,
marveling with unbounded wonder
at that loving condescension and condescending love.
He received Communion frequently
and so devoutly
that he made others devout,
1 Pt 1:19   for at the sweet taste of *the spotless Lamb*
he was often rapt in ecstasy as if drunk in the Spirit.[a]

[3]He embraced the mother of the Lord Jesus   2C 198
with an inexpressible love
since she made the Lord of Majesty a brother to us
1 Pt 2:10   and, through her,
we *have obtained mercy.*

In her, after Christ, he put all his trust **and made her the advocate**
of him and his brothers and, in her honor, he used to fast with great
devotion from the Feast of the Apostles Peter and Paul to the Feast of
the Assumption.[b]

He was joined in a bond of inseparable love   2C 197
to the angels
who burn with a marvelous fire
to pass over into God
and to inflame the souls of the elect.

Out of devotion to them he used to spend **the forty days after the**
Feast of the Assumption of the glorious Virgin **in fasting** and continual prayer. Because of the ardent zeal he had for the salvation of
all, he was more devoted with a special love **to blessed Michael** the
Archangel **in view of his duty of presenting souls to God.**

Ez 28:14, 16   From remembering all the saints like *fiery stones,*
he was re-enkindled into a godlike fire,
embracing with the greatest devotion
all the apostles,
especially Peter and Paul,
because of the burning love they had toward Christ.
Out of reverence and love for them

---

a. Cf. LMj II 4, supra 57 a.
b. From June 20 to August 15.

he dedicated to the Lord a special fast of forty days.
The poor man of Christ
had nothing other than *two small coins*,   Mk 12:42
namely his body and his soul,
which he could give away in generous charity.
But for the love of Christ
he offered them so continuously
that he seemed to be constantly immolating
his body through the rigor of fasting,
and his spirit through the ardor of his desire,
without, sacrificing a *holocaust* in the courtyard,   Ex 30:1, 27-28
and within, burning *incense* in the temple.[a]

[4]The exceptional devotion of his charity
so bore him aloft into the divine
that his loving kindness was enlarged
and extended to those who shared with him nature and grace.
2C 172   Since the piety of his heart **had made him**
a brother to other creatures,
no wonder *the charity of Christ*   2 Cor 5:14
made him
even more a brother to those who are marked
in the image of their Creator
and *redeemed with the blood* of their Author!   Rv 5:9

For he would not consider himself a friend of Christ, unless he
cared for the souls whom He had redeemed. He used to say that
nothing should be preferred **to the salvation of souls,** demonstrat-
ing this forcefully **with the fact that** *the Only-begotten Son of God* saw   Jn 3:18
fit to hang on the cross for the sake of souls.

From this arose
his effort in prayer,
his travel in preaching,
and his excess in giving example.

2C 173   Therefore, **whenever somebody criticized him for the excessive**
austerity of his life, he would reply that he was given as an exam-

---

a. The vocabulary in this passage is reminiscent of *The Soul's Journey into God* in which Bonaventure
continually returns to the images of the courtyard and the temple to describe the soul's journey into
the Holy of Holies. Cf. *Bonaventure: The Soul's Journey into God, The Tree of Life, The Life of Saint
Francis*, translation and introduction by Ewert H. Cousins (New York, Ramsey, Toronto: Paulist
Press, 1978), 53-116.

ple. For although his innocent flesh, which was already submitting freely to the spirit, had no need of the whip because of any offense, he still renewed its punishment and burdens because of example, *staying on the hard paths only* for the sake of others. For he used to say: *"If I speak in the tongues of men and angels*, but without charity and do not show examples of the virtues to my neighbors, it is little use to others, nothing to myself."

Ps 17:4
1 Cor 13:1-3

> [5]In the **fervent** fire of his charity
> he strove to emulate
> the glorious triumph of the holy martyrs
> in whom
> the flame of love could not be extinguished,
> nor courage weakened.
> Set on fire, therefore,
> by that perfect charity *which drives out fear,*
> **he desired** to offer to the Lord
> *his own life* as *a living sacrifice* in the flames of martyrdom
> so that he might repay Christ, who died for us,
> and inspire others to **divine love.**

1C 55

1 Jn 4:18

Rom 12:1

In the sixth year of his conversion, burning with the desire for martyrdom,[a] he decided to take a ship to the region of Syria in order to preach the Christian faith and penance to the Saracens and other non-believers. When he had boarded a ship to go there, he was driven by contrary winds to land on the shores of Slavonia.[b] He spent a little while there and could not find a ship that would cross the sea at that time. Feeling that he had been cheated of his desire, he begged some sailors going to Ancona to take him with them for the love of God. When they stubbornly refused because he could not pay them, the man of God, completely trusting the Lord's goodness, secretly boarded the ship with his companion. A man arrived, sent by God for his poor man, as it is believed, who brought with him the food needed. He called over a person from the ship, a God-fearing man, and spoke to him in this way: "Keep all these things faithfully for the poor brothers hiding on your ship and distribute them in a friendly fashion in their time of need." And it so

LR XII 1

LJS 34

Jb 1:1; Tb 11:4

---

a. The theology of the desire for martyrdom is succinctly expressed in Bonaventure's *De Triplici Via* II 8: ". . . we are crucified for the world when we choose to die for everyone that they might please God as well. We do not reach this perfect love of neighbor unless we first reach that perfect love of God because we love our neighbor who would not be lovable were it not for God." (VIII 9-10) In his *Apologia Pauperum* IV 1, he maintains that the desire for martyrdom is the perfection of love (VIII, 252).

b. Cf. FA:ED I 229 b.

happened that, when the crew was unable to land anywhere **for many days** because of the force of the winds, **they used up all** their food. **Only** the alms given from above to the poor Francis **remained.** Since **this** was only a very small amount, **by God's power** it was multiplied so much that while they were **delayed at sea for many days** by the relentless storm, **it fully supplied their needs until they reached the port of Ancona.** When **the sailors realized that they had escaped** many threats **of death through God's servant,** as those who had experienced the horrifying **dangers of the sea** and *had seen the* wonderful *works of the Lord in the deep,* **they gave thanks to almighty God, who is always revealed through his** friends and **servants as awesome and lovable.**

⁶When **he left the sea,** he began **to walk the earth** and to sow in it **the seed** of salvation, reaping **fruitful** harvests. But, because the fruit **of martyrdom** had attracted his heart to such an extent, he desired a precious death for the sake of Christ more intensely than all the merits of the virtues. So he took the road **to Morocco to preach the Gospel of Christ to the Miramamolin** and his people,^a hoping to attain in this way the palm of martyrdom he so strongly desired. **He was so carried away with desire** that, although he was physically weak, **he would race ahead** of his companion on the journey and hurry to carry out his purpose, flying along, as if **intoxicated in spirit. But af**ter he had gone as far as **Spain,** by the divine design, which had other things in store for him, he was overtaken by a very grave illness which hindered him **from achieving** what he desired.

> Realizing, then,
> that his physical life was still necessary
> for the children he had begotten,
> the man of God,
> while he considered death as *gain* for himself,
> returned *to feed the sheep* entrusted to his care.

> ⁷But with the ardor of his charity
> urging his spirit on toward martyrdom,
> he tried yet a third time to set out to the non-believers,
> hoping to shed his blood
> for the spread of the faith in the Trinity.

Margin references: LJS 34; Ps 107:24; 1C 56; LJS 35; 1C 56; LJS 35; Phil 1:21; Jn 21:17

---

a. Cf. FA:ED I 230 b.

In the thirteenth year of his conversion, he journeyed to the re-   1C 57
gions of Syria, constantly exposing himself to many dangers in order
to reach the presence of the Sultan of Babylon.[a] For at that time there
was a fierce war between the Christians and the Saracens,[b] with
their camps situated in close quarters opposite each other in the field,
so that there was no way of passing from one to the other without
danger of death. A cruel edict had been issued by the Sultan that
whoever would bring back the head of a Christian would receive as a
reward a gold piece.[c] But Francis, the intrepid knight of Christ, hoping to be able to achieve his purpose, decided to make the journey,
not terrified by the fear of death, but rather drawn by desire for it. Af-

1 Sm 30:6
ter praying, *strengthened by the Lord,* he confidently chanted that pro-
Ps 23:4
phetic verse: *"Even if I should walk in the midst of the shadow of death, I
shall not fear evil because you are with me."*

[8]Taking a companion with him, a brother named Illuminato, a
virtuous and enlightened man, after he had begun his journey, he
came upon two lambs. Overjoyed to see them, the holy man said to
Sir 11:22
his companion: *"Trust in the Lord,* brother, for the Gospel text is being
Mt 10:16
fulfilled in us: *Behold, I am sending you forth like sheep in the midst of
wolves."* When they proceeded farther, the Saracen sentries fell upon
them like wolves swiftly overtaking sheep, savagely seizing the servants of God, and cruelly and contemptuously dragging them away,
treating them with insults, beating them with whips, and putting   1C 57
them in chains.

Finally, after they had been maltreated in many ways and were
exhausted, by divine providence they were led to the Sultan, just as
the man of God wished. When that ruler inquired by whom, why,
and how they had been sent and how they got there, Christ's servant,
Francis, answered with an intrepid heart that he had been sent not
by man but by the Most High God in order to point out to him and his
people the way of salvation and to announce the Gospel of truth.

He preached to the Sultan
the Triune God and the one Savior of all, Jesus Christ,
with such great firmness,

---

a. *Syria* was often used as a general name for the Levant. The *soldan of Babylon* was actually the ruler of
Egypt *(Babylon* was the name given to modern Cairo) whose power extended over the Holy Land
except for the small enclaves still held by the Crusaders.

b. The fifth Crusade, which for tactical reasons attacked Egypt rather than Palestine. The Crusaders
were at this time besiging Damietta, on the delta of the Nile. Cf. FA:ED I 231c.

c. In the original *Byzantinum arueum.* The gold *byzant* or *bezant* was a current coin all over
Christendom and Islam.

> such **strength of soul,**
> and such fervor of spirit
> that the words of the Gospel appeared
> to be truly fulfilled in him:
> *I will give you utterance and wisdom*
> *which all your adversaries will not be able to resist or answer back.*

Lk 21:15

For the Sultan, perceiving in the man of God a fervor of spirit and a courage that had to be admired, willingly listened to him and invited him to stay longer with him. Inspired from heaven, Christ's servant said: "If you wish to be converted to Christ along with your people, I will most gladly stay with you for love of him. But if you hesitate to abandon the law of Mohammed for the faith of Christ, then command that an enormous fire be lit and I will walk into the fire along with your priests so that you will recognize which faith deserves to be held as the holier and more certain." "I do not believe," the Sultan replied, "that any of my priests would be willing to expose himself to the fire to defend his faith or to undergo any kind of torment." For he had seen immediately one of his priests, a man full of authority and years, slipping away from his view when he heard Francis's words.

"If you wish to promise me that if I come out of the fire unharmed," the saint said to the Sultan, "you and your people will come over to the worship of Christ, then I will enter the fire alone. And if I shall be burned, you must attribute it to my sins. But if God's power protects me, you will acknowledge *Christ the power and wisdom of God* as *the true God* and the *Savior* of all." The Sultan replied that he did not dare to accept this choice because he feared a revolt among his people. Nevertheless **he offered** him **many precious gifts,** which the man of God, greedy not for worldly possessions but the salvation of souls, spurned as if they were dirt. Seeing that the holy man so completely **despised** worldly possessions, the Sultan **was overflowing with admiration,** and developed an even greater respect for him. Although he refused, or perhaps did not dare, to come over to the Christian faith, he nevertheless devoutly asked Christ's servant to accept the gifts and give them to the Christian poor or to churches for his salvation. But, because he was accustomed to flee the burden of money and did not see a root of true piety in the Sultan's soul, Francis would in no way accept them.

1 Cor 1:24; Jn 17:3, 4:42

57; LJS 36; 1C 57

> [9]When he saw that he was making no progress
> in converting these people
> and that he could not *achieve his purpose,*

2 Tm 3:10

namely martyrdom,
he went back to the lands of the faithful,
as he was advised by a divine revelation.
Thus by the kindness of God
and the merits of the virtue of the holy man,
it came about,
mercifully and remarkably,
that the friend of Christ
sought with all his strength to die for him
and yet could not achieve it.
Thus he was not deprived
of the merit of his desired martyrdom
and was spared to be honored in the future
with a **unique** privilege.   1C 57
Thus it came about
that the divine fire
burned still more perfectly in his heart,
so that later it was distilled clearly in his flesh.

O truly blessed man,
whose flesh,
although not cut down by a tyrant's steel,
was yet not deprived

Rv 5:12   of bearing a likeness of *the Lamb that was slain!*
O, truly and fully blessed man, I say,
whose life
"the persecutor's sword did not take away,
and who yet did not lose the palm of martyrdom"![a]

---

a. *Breviarium Romanum,* antiphon at second Vespers for the feast of Saint Martin of Tours.

Chapter Ten

ZEAL FOR PRAYER
AND THE POWER OF PRAYER

2C 94 [1]Francis,
the servant of Christ,
aware that while *in the body he was away from the Lord,*   2 Cor 5:6, 8
became totally unaware of earthly desires
through love of Christ,
and **strove** to keep **his spirit present** to God
by praying without ceasing   1 Thes 5:17
lest he be without the consolation of the Beloved.
Prayer was a comfort for the contemplative,
even now **a citizen with the angels** in **the heavenly mansions,**
as *he sought* with burning desire *the Beloved*   Sg 3:1-2
2C 94 from whom only the wall of the flesh separated him.
Distrusting his own effort and trusting divine piety,
prayer was a fortress to this worker;
for in everything he did,
he cast his care completely *upon the Lord*   Ps 55:23
through his perseverance.
He firmly claimed
that the grace of prayer
must be desired above all else
by a religious,
believing that without it no one could prosper in God's service.
He used whatever means he could
to arouse his brothers
to be zealous in prayer.[a]
1C 71 For whether **walking or sitting,**
inside or outside,
working or resting,
he was so **focused on prayer**
2C 94 that he seemed to have dedicated to it

---

a. Cf. LMj IV 3, supra 69.

not only whatever was in his heart and body,
but also his effort and time.

[2]He usually neglected no visitation of the Spirit.   2C 95
Whenever it was offered, he would follow it;
and for as long as the Lord granted,
he enjoyed the sweetness offered.
When he was occupied with travel
and felt the breathing of the divine Spirit,
while his companions went on ahead,
he would stop in his tracks,
as he turned a new inspiration into something fruitful.
2 Cor. 6:1   He did not receive grace in vain.
Many times he was suspended   2C 98
in such an excess of contemplation,
that he was carried away above himself and,
experiencing what is beyond human understanding,
he was unaware of what went on about him.

For instance, one time when he was traveling through Borgo
San Sepolcro, a heavily populated town, and was riding on a donkey because of physical weakness, crowds rushed to meet him out of
devotion. He was touched by them, pulled and shoved by them, yet
he seemed not to feel any of this, and as if he were a lifeless corpse,
did not notice what was going on around him. Long after he had
passed the town and left the crowds, he came to a dwelling of lepers,
and the contemplator of heaven, as if returning from somewhere
else, anxiously asked when they would be reaching Borgo.

His mind was so fixed on heavenly splendors
that he was not aware
of the differences of place, time, and people that he passed.
That this happened to him often was confirmed
by the repeated experience of his companions.

[3]And because he had learned in prayer
that the presence of the Holy Spirit for which he longed
was offered more intimately to those who invoke him,
the more It found them
far from the noise of worldly affairs.

Therefore seeking out solitary places, he used to go to deserted   1C 71
and abandoned churches to pray at night. There he often endured   1C 72

horrible struggles with devils who **would assault** him physically, trying to distract him from his commitment to prayer. But armed with heavenly weapons, the more vehemently he was attacked by the enemy, the more courageous he became in practicing virtue and the more fervent in prayer, saying confidently to Christ: *"Under the shadow of your wings, protect me from the face of the wicked who have attacked me."* To the devils he said: **"Do whatever** you want to me, you malicious and deceitful spirits! For you cannot do anything unless the heavenly hand relaxes its hold on you. And I am ready to endure with delight whatever He decrees." The demons retreated **confused,** not tolerating such firmness of mind.

⁴The man of God
remaining more alone and at peace
would fill the forest with groans,
water the places with tears,
strike his breast with his hand,
and, as if finding a more secret hiding place,
would converse with his Lord.
There he replied to the Judge,
there he entreated the Father,
there he conversed with the Friend.
There too the brothers who were devoutly observing him
heard him on several occasions groan with loud cries,
imploring the divine clemency for sinners,
and weeping over the Lord's **passion**
as if it were before him.
There he was seen praying at night,
with his hands outstretched in the form of a cross,
his whole body lifted up from the ground
and surrounded by a sort of shining cloud,
so that the extraordinary illumination around his body
was a witness to the wonderful light that shone within his soul.
There too,
as is proven by certain evidence,
the *unknown and hidden secrets of* divine *wisdom*
were opened up to him,
although he never spoke of them outside
except when *the love of Christ urged* him
and the good of his neighbor demanded.
For he used to say:
"It happens that one loses something priceless

Ps 17:8-9

2C 122

2C 95

2C 11

Ps 51:6

2 Cor 5:14

2C 99

for the sake of a small reward,
and easily provokes the giver not to give again."

When he returned from his private prayers, in which he was *changed almost into a different man,* he tried his best to resemble the others, lest what he might show outwardly, the breeze of favor would *deprive* him *of a reward* inwardly. When he was suddenly overcome in public by *a visitation of the Lord,* he would always place something between himself and bystanders, so that he would not cheapen the sight of the Bridegroom's intimate touch. When he prayed with the brothers, he completely avoided coughs, groans, hard breathing, or external movement, either because he loved to keep secrecy or because he had withdrawn into his interior and was totally carried into God.

Often he would say to those close to him: "When a servant of God is praying and is visited by the divine, he must say: 'Lord, you have sent this consolation from heaven to me, an unworthy sinner, and I entrust it to your keeping, because I feel I am a thief of your treasure.' When he returns from his prayer, he should appear as a poor man and a sinner, as if he had not obtained any new grace."

⁵Once when the man of God was praying in the place of the Portiuncula, the bishop of Assisi happened to come to him, as he often did. As soon as he entered the place, he went more abruptly than he should have to the cell where Christ's servant was praying, knocked on the door, and was about to barge in, when he stuck his head inside and saw the saint praying. Suddenly *struck with trembling,* his limbs froze, and he lost his voice. By the divine will, he was quickly pushed outside by force and dragged backwards a long way. Stunned, the bishop hurried to the brothers, and, when God had restored his speech, at the first word he confessed his fault as best he could.

One time the abbot of the monastery of San Giustino in the diocese of Perugia happened to meet Christ's servant. When he saw him, the devout abbot quickly dismounted from his horse to show reverence to the man of God and to converse with him a bit about the salvation of his soul. Finally, after a pleasant conversation, the abbot, as he left, humbly asked him to pray for him. The dear man of God replied: "I will willingly pray." When the abbot had ridden away a short distance, the faithful Francis said to his companion: "Wait a little, brother, because I want to pay the debt I promised." As he prayed, suddenly the abbot *felt in spirit* unusual warmth and

Margin references:
1 Sm 10:6
Sir 2:8
Lk 1:68
2 Chr 24:9
Jb 21:6
Rom 8:5

2C 94
2C 99
2C 100
2C 101

sweetness like nothing he felt before, and rapt in ecstasy, he totally fainted away into God. This lasted for a short time, and then he returned to his senses and realized the power of Saint Francis's prayer. From that time on, he always burned with ever greater love for the Order, and told many about this miraculous event.

2C 96

⁶The holy man was accustomed to fulfill the canonical hours with no less reverence than devotion. Although he was suffering from diseases of the eyes, stomach, spleen, and liver, he nevertheless did not want to lean against a wall or partition while he was chanting the psalms. He always fulfilled the hours standing up straight and without a hood, without letting his eyes wander about and without dropping the syllables.

If he were on a journey, he would stop at the right time and never omitted this reverent and holy practice because it was raining. For he would say: "If the body calmly eats its food, which along with itself will be food for worms, should not the soul receive the food of life in great peace and tranquillity?"

2C 97

He also thought that he had committed a serious offense if, while he was at prayer, he was distracted by empty imaginings. When such a thing would happen, he did not fail to confess it and immediately make amends. He had made such a habit of this carefulness, that he was rarely bothered by this kind of "flies."

One Lent he had been making one small cup to occupy any spare time so that it would not in any way be wasted. When he was saying terce, it came to his mind and distracted him a little. Moved by fervor of spirit, he burned the cup in the fire, saying: "I will sacrifice it to the Lord, whose sacrifice it had interrupted!"

He used to say the psalms with such attention of mind and spirit, as if he had God present. When the Lord's name occurred in the psalms, he seemed to lick his lips because of its sweetness.

1C 82; 1C 45

He wanted to honor with special reverence the Lord's name not only when thought but also when spoken and written. He once persuaded the brothers to gather all pieces of paper wherever they were found and to place them in a clean place so that if that sacred name happened to be written there, it would not be trodden underfoot.[a] When he pronounced or heard the name Jesus, he was filled with an inner joy and seemed completely changed exteriorly as if some honey-sweet flavor had transformed his taste or some harmonious sound had transformed his hearing.

---

a. FA:ED I 252a.

[7]It happened, **three years prior to his death,** that he decided to   1C 84
celebrate **at the town of Greccio the memory of the birth of the
Child Jesus** with the greatest possible solemnity, in order to arouse
devotion. So that this would not be considered a type of novelty, he
petitioned for and obtained permission from the Supreme Pontiff.

He had **a manger** prepared,   1C 85
hay carried in and an ox and an ass led to the spot.
The brethren are summoned,
the people arrive,
the forest amplifies with their cries,
and that venerable **night** is rendered
brilliant and solemn
by a multitude of bright lights
and **by resonant** and harmonious hymns of praise.   1C 86
The man **of God stands before the manger,**   1C 85
filled **with piety,**
bathed in tears, **and overcome with joy.**
A solemn Mass is celebrated over the manger,
with Francis, a levite of Christ, chanting the holy **Gospel.**
Then he preaches to the people standing around him   1C 86
about the birth of the poor King,
whom, **whenever he means to call him,**
he called in his tender love,   LJS 54
the Babe from Bethlehem.
A certain virtuous and truthful knight,
Sir **John** of Greccio,   1C 84
who had abandoned worldly military activity out of love of Christ
and had become an intimate friend of the man of God,
claimed that **he saw** a beautiful **little child** asleep in that **manger**   1C 86
whom the blessed father Francis embraced in both of his arms
and **seemed to wake it from sleep.**
Not only does the holiness of the witness
make credible
the vision of the devout knight,
but also the truth it expresses
proves its validity
and the subsequent miracles confirm it.
For Francis's example,
when considered by the world,
is capable of arousing
the hearts of those who are sluggish in the faith of Christ.
The hay from the crib   1C 87

LJS 55

was kept by the people
and miraculously cured sick **animals**
and drove away **different** kinds of pestilence.
Thus God glorified his servant in every way
and demonstrated the efficacy of his holy prayer
by the evident signs of wonderful miracles.

Chapter Eleven

THE UNDERSTANDING OF SCRIPTURE
AND
THE SPIRIT OF PROPHECY

¹Unflagging zeal for prayer
with a continual exercise of virtue
had led the man of God to such serenity of mind that,
although he had no expertise in Sacred Scripture through learning,   2C 102
his intellect, nevertheless
enlightened by the splendor of eternal light,
Jb 28:11   *probed the depths* of Scripture
with remarkable incisiveness.^a
For his genius, pure and unstained,
Col 1:26   penetrated *hidden mysteries,*
and where the knowledge of teachers stands outside,
the passion of the lover entered.
Whenever he read the Sacred Books,
and something struck his mind
he imprinted it tenaciously on his memory,
because^b he did not grasp in vain
what his attentive mind heard,
for he would mull over it
with affection and constant devotion.

Once, when the brothers asked him whether he was pleased that the learned men, who, by that time, had been received into the Order, were devoting themselves to the study of Sacred Scripture, he replied:^c "I am indeed pleased, as long as, after the example of Christ, of whom we read that he prayed more than he read, they do

---

a. For an in-depth consideration of Bonaventure's appreciation for this aspect of Francis's spiritual life, see his Prologue to the *Breviloquium.* See *Bonaventure: Mystic of God's Word,* introduced and edited by Timothy Johnson (Hyde Park: New City Press, 1999), 31-46.

b. Cf. 2C 102, FA:ED II 314a.

c. The following section is a collage of similar passages from 2C 102, 163, 189, 194, 195, FA:ED II 315, 352, 367-68, 371-72.

not neglect zeal for prayer;[a] and, as long as they study, not to know what they should say, but to practice what they have heard and, once they have put it into practice, propose it to others. I want my brothers," he said, "to be Gospel disciples and so progress in knowledge of the truth that they increase in pure simplicity without separating the simplicity of the dove from the wisdom of the serpent which our eminent Teacher joined together in a statement from his own blessed lips."[b]

Mt 10:16

2C 103   ²**At Siena**, a religious, **who was a Doctor of Sacred Theology**, once **asked him** about certain questions that were difficult to understand. He brought to light the secrets of divine wisdom with such clarity in teaching, that the learned man was absolutely dumbfounded. With admiration he responded: "Truly **the theology** of this holy father, borne aloft, as it were, on the wings **of purity and contemplation, is** *a soaring eagle;* while our learning *crawls on its belly on the ground.*"

Jb 9:26; Gn 3:14

2C 102

For although he was *unskilled in word,*
nevertheless, full of knowledge,
he often untangled the ambiguities of questions
and brought the hidden into light.
Nor is it inconsistent!
If the holy man had received from God
an understanding of the Scriptures,
it is because,
through his imitation of Christ
he carried in his activity the perfect truth described in them and,
through a full anointing of the Holy Spirit,
held their Teacher in his heart.

2 Cor 11:6
Jb 28:11
1 Jn 2:20

---

a. A thorough presentation of Bonaventure's theology of a prayer based on Scripture can be found in Timothy Johnson, *Iste Pauper Clamavit: Saint Bonaventure's Theology of Prayer* (Frankfurt am Main, Bern, New York, Paris: Peter Lang, 1990). See also Charles Carpenture, *Theology as the Road to Holiness in St. Bonaventure*, Theological Inquiries (New York/Mahwah: Paulist Press, 1999), 13-38.

b. An appropriate commentary on this passage can be found in Bonaventure's *Letter in Response to an Unknown Master*, 10: ". . . [T]hat you might appreciate how much the study of Holy Scripture delighted him, let me tell you what I myself heard from a brother who is still living. Once a New Testament came into Francis's hands, and since so many brothers could not all use it at once, he pulled the leaves apart and distributed the pages among them. Thus each one could study and not be a hindrance to the others. Moreover, the clerics he received into the Order he held in greatest reverence, and at his death he ordered the brothers to venerate the teachers of Sacred Scripture as those from whom they receive the words of life." *Writings Concerning The Franciscan Order*, Works of Saint Bonaventure V, introduction and translation by Dominic Monti, (St. Bonaventure, NY: Franciscan Institute Publications, 1994), 51.

Rv 19:10
[3]*The spirit of prophecy,* too, so shone forth in him   2C 27
that he foresaw the future,

1 Cor 14:25
contuited **the secrets of the heart,**
knew of **events from afar** as if they were present,
and miraculously appeared present to those who were absent.[a]

For at the time **when the Christian army was besieging**   2C 30
Damietta,[b] the man of God was there, armed not with weapons, but
Prv 21:31
with faith. **When Christ's servant heard** that the Christians *were pre-paring for war on the day of the battle,* he sighed **deeply and said to his
companion:** "If a clash of battle is attempted, **the Lord has shown**
Jb 16:7
me that it will not go well for the Christians. But if I say this, they
will take me for a fool; if I keep silent, my conscience won't leave
me alone. What do you think I should do?" His companion replied:
1 Cor 4:3
"Brother, don't give *the least* thought *to how people judge you.* This
won't be the first time people took you for a fool. Unburden your
Acts 5:29
conscience, and *fear God rather than men."*

When he heard this, the herald of Christ leapt to his feet, and
rushed to the Christians crying out warnings to save them, forbid-
Tb 3:4
ding war, and threatening disaster. But they took the truth *as a joke.*
Ex 4:21; Jn 12:40
They hardened their *hearts* and refused to turn back. The whole
Christian army charged, attacked, and retreated fleeing from the
battle carrying not triumph but shame. The number of Christians
was diminished by such a great massacre, that about six thousand
were either dead or captured.

From this
it was abundantly clear
that the wisdom of the poor man was not to be scorned;
Sir 37:18
since *sometimes the soul of a just man will declare truths
more clearly than seven sentinels
searching the horizon from a height.*

[4]At another **time, after his return from overseas, he went to**   2C 31; 3C 41
Celano to preach; and a certain knight invited him very insistently,
with humble devotion, to dine with him. So he came to the knight's
home and the whole **family delighted at the arrival of the poor**

---

a. In this accentuation of the perfect truth contained in Scripture, Bonaventure is laying the foundation
for his consideration of Francis's gift of prophecy. "The Prophet does not give assent to what is
foretold, because of itself," he teaches, "but because of the Truth enlightening and teaching him." *III
Sent,* D. 23, art. 1, q. 2, concl. (III, 514). Furthermore he maintains that "It belongs to a prophet to
recognize the truth." Cf. *Commentary on the Gospel of John* I, coll. 7:3 (VI, 544).
b. Cf. FA:ED I 231b.

guests. Before they took any food, the man offered prayers and praise to God as was his custom, **standing with his eyes raised to heaven.** When he finished his prayer, **he called** his kind **host** aside and confidentially told him: "**Look, brother host, overcome by your prayers, I have entered your home to eat.** Now **heed my warnings quickly because you shall not eat here but elsewhere.** *Confess your sins* right now, contrite with the sorrow of true repentance; and leave nothing in you unconfessed that you do not reveal in a true confession. The Lord will reward you today for receiving His poor with such devotion." The man agreed to the saint's words without delay; and telling all of his sins in confession to his companion, *he put his house in order* and did everything in his power to prepare for death. **Then they went to the table; and while the others began to eat,** suddenly their host **breathed forth his spirit,** carried away by sudden death according to the words of the man of God.

1 Jn 7:44

Is 38:1

> In recompense for the kindness of his hospitality,
> it happened according to the word of Truth that
> *because he had received a prophet,*
> *he received a prophet's reward.*
> Through the prophetic warning of the holy man,
> that devout knight prepared himself for a sudden death
> so that, protected by the armor of repentance,
> he escaped perpetual damnation
> and entered into *the eternal dwellings.*

Mt 10:41

Lk 16:9

2C 41

⁵At the time, while the holy man lay sick in Rieti, a canon named Gedeone, a lustful and worldly man, was seized by a grave illness and was bedridden. When he had himself carried to him, he, together with those present, tearfully begged to be marked by him with that sign of the cross. "How can I sign you with the cross," he asked, "when you once lived according to the desires of the flesh, with no fear of *the judgments of God?* Because of the devout requests of those pleading for you, however, I will sign you with the sign of the cross in the name of the Lord. But you must know you will suffer worse things, if, once set free, you return to *your vomit.* Because of the sin of ingratitude *things worse than the first* are always inflicted. When he made the sign of the cross over him, immediately the man who was lying crippled got up restored to health, and bursting with praise of God cried: "I am free!" Many people there heard the bones of his hips cracking as when someone snaps dry twigs with his hands. But after a short time, the canon, *forgetting God,* turned his body back to its unchaste ways.

Sir 17:24

Prv 26:11
Mt 12:45

Jgs 3:7

One evening he dined at the house of a canon, and slept there that night. Suddenly the roof of the house collapsed on all of them. Others who were there escaped with their lives, only that wretch was trapped and killed.

Therefore,
by a just judgment of God,
the last state of that man became worse than the first
because of his vice of ingratitude
and his contempt for God.
Since gratitude must be shown for forgiveness received,
an offense **repeated doubles displeasure**.

Mt 12:45

[6]Another time, **a noble woman**, devoted to God, came **to the saint** to explain her trouble to him and ask for help. **She had a very cruel husband** whom she endured as **an antagonist** to her **service of Christ**. So she begged the saint **to pray for** him so that God in his goodness would soften his **heart**. When he heard this, **he said** to her: "Go in peace, and without any doubt be assured that you will soon have consolation from your husband." **And he added: "You may tell him for God and for me, that now is the time** of clemency, **and later it will be the time of justice."**

After receiving his blessing, the lady returned home, found her husband and relayed the message. *The Holy Spirit came upon* him and he was changed from the old to the new man, prompting him to reply very meekly: "My lady, *let us serve the Lord* and *save our souls."* At the suggestion of his holy wife, they lived a celibate life for many years. On the same day, they both **departed** to the Lord.

2C 38

Acts 10:44

Jos 22:27; Gn 19:19

The power of the prophetic spirit in the man of God
was certainly extraordinary,
which restored vigor to dried up limbs
and impressed piety on hardened hearts.[a]
The transparency of his spirit
was no less wondrous;
for he could foresee future events

---

a. "Piety," Bonaventure teaches, "is contrary to hardness of heart." Cf. *III Sent*, D. 35, au., q. 6, concl., ad 1, 2, 3, 4 (III, 786b). The same teaching can be found in a more poetic manner: "O human heart, you are harder than any hardness of rocks, if at the recollection of such great expiation you are not struck with terror, nor moved with compassion, nor shattered with compunction, nor softened with piety." Cf. *The Tree of Life* 29, in *Bonaventure: The Soul's Journey Into God, The Tree of Life, The Life of Saint Francis*, introduction and translation by Ewert H. Cousins (New York, Ramsey, Toronto: Paulist Press, 1978), 154.

and even probe obscurity of conscience,
as if another Elisha rivaling *the two-fold spirit* of Elijah.   2 Kgs 2:9

[7]On one occasion he told a friend at Siena what would happen to him at the end of his life. Now when the learned man mentioned above, who consulted him at one time about the Scriptures, heard of this, he asked the holy father in doubt whether he had really said what the man had claimed. He not only confirmed that he had said this but, besides, foretold to this learned man, who was so eager to know another's future, the circumstances of his own end. To impress this with greater certainty on his heart, he miraculously revealed to him a certain secret scruple of conscience that the man had and which he had never disclosed to any living person; and he relieved him of it by his sound advice. The truth of all this was confirmed by the fact that this religious eventually died just as Christ's servant had foretold.

2C 31   [8]When the holy man was returning from overseas, with brother Leonard of Assisi as his companion, he happened to climb on a donkey for a while, because he was weak and tired. But his companion walked behind, and was also quite tired. *Thinking in human*   Rom 6:19
terms, he *began to say to himself*: "His parents and mine did not so-   Lk 7:39
cialize as equals,[a] and here he is riding while I am on foot leading his donkey." *As he was thinking this,* the holy man immediately got   Mt 1:20
off the donkey. "No, brother," he said. "It is not right that I should ride while you go on foot, for in the world you were more noble and influential than I." The brother was *completely astonished*, and *over-*   Est 7:6; Nm 12:14
come with embarrassment: he knew he had been caught. He fell   Est 8:3
down at his feet and, *bathed* in tears, he exposed his naked thought   Lk 7:38, 44
and begged forgiveness.

1C 49   [9]A certain brother, devoted to God and to Christ's servant, frequently turned over in his heart the idea: whomever the holy man embraced with intimate affection would be worthy of divine favor. Whomever he excluded, on the other hand, he would not regard among God's chosen ones. He was obsessed by the repeated pressure of this thought and intensely longed for the intimacy of the man of God, but never revealed the secret of his heart to anyone. The de-
1C 50   voted father called him and spoke gently to him in this way: "Let no thought disturb you, my son, because, holding you dearest among those very dear to me, I gladly lavish upon you my intimacy and

---

a. Cf. 2C 31, p. 281 a.

love." The brother was amazed at this and became even more devoted. Not only did he grow in his love of the holy man, but, through
the grace of the Holy Spirit, he was also filled with still greater gifts.

While he was secluded in a cell on Mount La Verna, one of his companions was yearning with great desire to have something of the Lord's words commented on and written with his own hand. He believed that by this means he would be set free from—or at least could bear more easily—a serious temptation which oppressed him, not in the flesh but in the spirit. Though growing weary with such a desire, he was in a state of inner anxiety because, overcome with embarrassment, he did not dare to disclose it to the venerable father. But what man did not tell him, *the Spirit revealed.* He ordered that brother to bring him paper and ink. And he wrote down with his own hand the *Praises of the Lord* according to the brother's desire, and, at the end, a blessing for him, saying: *"Take* this paper *for yourself* and keep it carefully until your dying day." The brother took the gift he so much desired and his temptation disappeared immediately. The letter was preserved and, since later it worked wonders, it became a witness to the virtues of Francis.

[10]There was a brother who, to all appearances, led a life of extraordinary holiness, but who stood out for his singular ways. *He spent all his time in prayer* and kept such strict silence that he used to make his confession by gestures instead of words. It happened that the holy father came to that place to see and hear the brother, and to have a word with the other brothers about him. While everyone was commending and praising him highly, the man of God replied: "Brothers, stop! Do not sing me the praises of his devilish allusions. *You should know the truth.* This is a diabolical temptation and a fraudulent deception." The brothers took this very hard, judging that it was impossible that contrivances of fraud could paint themselves over with so many signs of perfection. But a few days later, after he left religion, the brilliance of the interior insight with which the man of God perceived the secrets of his heart became abundantly clear.

> Foretelling with unchanging truth
> the ruin of many who seemed to stand firm,
> but also the conversion to Christ of many who were perverse,
> he seemed to have approached
> the mirror of eternal light
> for contemplation,

Margin references:
2C 49
1 Cor 2:10
PrsG; BlL
Gn 28:2
1 Cor 7:5
2C 28
Mt 22:16
1C 48

in whose marvelous brilliance
the gaze of his mind perceived
the physically absent as if they were present.

[2C 34] [Dt 5:5] [11]Once while his vicar was holding a chapter, he was praying in his cell, as *the go-between and mediator* between the brothers and God. One of them, hiding behind the mantle of some excuse, would not submit himself to the discipline of obedience. Seeing this in spirit, the holy man called one of the brothers and said to him: "Brother, I saw the devil perched on the back of that disobedient brother holding him tightly by the neck. With a rider like that on him, he spit out the bit of obedience, and gave free rein to his own will. But when I prayed to God for the brother, the devil retreated suddenly confused. Go, therefore, and tell the brother to submit his neck to the yoke of holy obedience without delay!" Warned by means of a messenger, the brother immediately was converted to God and, with humility, cast himself at the feet of the vicar.

[2C 45] [Lk 2:45] [12]Another time it happened that two brothers came from far away to the hermitage of Greccio to see the man of God and to receive his blessing which they had desired for a long time. When they arrived, *they did not find him,* because he had already left the common area for a cell; so they went away saddened.

And behold,
as they were leaving,
although he could not have known anything
of their arrival or departure through any human means,
he came out of his cell contrary to his custom,
called after them
and blessed them in Christ's name with the sign of the cross,
just as they had desired.

[2C 39] [Acts 21:4] [Lk 15:13; Rom 14:13; Mt 5:22] [13]Once two brothers were traveling from the Terra di Lavoro, and the older one had seriously scandalized the younger one. When they reached the father, he asked the younger how his companion had behaved toward him during the trip. The brother replied: "Well enough." "Be careful, brother," he added, "don't lie under the pretext of humility. I know, I know. But wait a bit and you'll see." The brother was quite amazed that he knew *through the Spirit* such far away events. *Just a few days later,* the one who *had scandalized his brother,* having turned against religion in contempt, left. He did not ask the father's forgiveness nor accept the discipline

of correction that was due. In that single fall, two things shone forth
clearly: the equity of the divine judgment and the penetrating power
of the spirit of prophecy.

¹⁴How he appeared as present to the absent,
through divine power,
is evidently clear from the above,
if it is recalled to mind how he appeared to the brothers,
although absent,
transfigured in a fiery chariot,   LMj IV 4
and how he presented himself at the Chapter of Arles   LMj IV 10
in the image of a cross.
It should be believed that this was done by divine providence
so that from his miraculous appearance in bodily presence
it might clearly shine forth
how present and open his spirit was
Wis 7:24, 27   to the light of *eternal wisdom,*
which is mobile beyond all motion.
Reaching everywhere because of its purity,
spreading through the nations
into holy souls,
it makes them prophets and friends of God.

For the exalted Teacher
is accustomed to opening his mysteries
Prv 3:32; Mt 11:25   *to the simple* and the *little ones*
as first appeared in David, the best of the prophets,
and then in Peter, the prince of the apostles,
and finally in Francis, the little poor man of Christ.
Acts 4:13   For when these simple men were unskilled in letters,
Jn 16:23; Acts 13:9   they were made illustrious by the teaching of the Holy Spirit.
One was a shepherd
Jn 21:15; 1 Pt 5:2   that he would *pasture the Synagogue,*
1 Sm 16:11-12; 2 Sm 5:2   *the flock* God had led out of Egypt;
the other was a fisherman
Mt 13:47-48   that he would *fill the net* of the Church
with many kinds of believers;
Mt 13:44-46   the last was *a merchant*

that he would *purchase the pearl* of the Gospel life,
selling and giving away *all he had*
for the sake of Christ.[a]

---

a. This passage echoes an autobiographical comment in Bonaventure's *Letter in Response to an Unknown Master*, 13: "I confess before God that what made me love Saint Francis's way of life so much was that it is exactly like the origin and the perfection of the Church itself, which began first with simple fishermen and afterwards developed to include the most illustrious and learned doctors. You will find the same thing in the Order of Saint Francis; in this way God reveals that it did not come about through human calculations but through Christ." "A Letter in Response to an Unknown Master," in *Works of Saint Bonaventure: Writings Concerning the Franciscan Order*, introduction and translation by Dominic Monti (St. Bonaventure, NY: Franciscan Institute Publications, 1994), 54.

Chapter Twelve

THE EFFECTIVENESS OF PREACHING
AND THE GRACE OF HEALINGS

¹The truly faithful servant and minister of Christ,
Francis,
in order to do everything faithfully and perfectly,
directed his efforts chiefly
to the exercise of those virtues which,
by the prodding of the sacred Spirit,
he knew pleased his God more.

In this matter it happened that he fell into a great struggle over a doubt which, after he returned from many days of prayer, he proposed for resolution to the brothers who were close to him.

"What do you think, brothers, what do you judge better? That I should spend my time in prayer, or that I should travel about preaching? I am a poor little man, simple and *unskilled in speech;* I have received a greater grace of prayer than of speaking. Also in prayer there seems to be a profit and an accumulation of graces, but in preaching a distribution of gifts already received from heaven.

"In prayer there is a purification of interior affections and a uniting to the one, true and supreme good with an invigorating of virtue; in preaching, there is a dust on our spiritual feet, distraction over many things and relaxation of discipline.

"Finally, in prayer we address God, listen to Him, and, as if living an angelic life, we associate with the angels. In preaching, it is necessary to practice great self-emptying for people and, by living humanly among them, to think, see, speak, and hear human things.

"But there is one thing to the contrary that seems to outweigh all these considerations before God, that is, the only begotten Son of God, who is the highest wisdom, came down from *the bosom of the Father* for the salvation of souls in order to instruct the world by His example and to speak the *word* of salvation to people, whom He would redeem by the price of His sacred blood, *cleanse with* its *washing* and sustain with its draught, holding back for Himself absolutely nothing that He could freely give for our salvation. And because we should do

2 Cor 11:6

ER XXIII 9

Lk 10:11

1 Cor 1:24, 30; Jn 1:18

Eph 5:26

140

everything according to *the pattern* shown to us in Him as *on the heights of the mountain,* it seems more pleasing to God that I interrupt my quiet and go out to labor."

When he had mulled over these words for many days with his brothers, he could not perceive with certainty which of these he should choose as more acceptable to Christ. Although he understood extraordinary things through the spirit of prophecy, this question he could not resolve with clarity on his own.

But God's providence had a better plan, that the merit of preaching would be shown by a sign from heaven, thus preserving the humility of Christ's servant.

²He was not ashamed to ask advice in small matters from those under him, true Lesser Brother that he was, though he had learned great things from the supreme Teacher. He was accustomed to search with special eagerness **in what manner, and in what way** he could serve **God more perfectly** according to His good pleasure.

As long as he lived,
this was his highest philosophy,
this his highest desire:
to ask
from the wise and the simple,
the perfect and the imperfect,
the young and the old,
how he could more effectively arrive
at the summit of perfection.

Choosing, therefore, two of the brothers, he sent them to Brother Sylvester, who **had seen the cross** coming out from his **mouth,** and, at that time, spent his time in continuous prayer on the mountain above Assisi. He was to ask God to resolve his doubt over this matter, and to send him the answer in God's name. He also asked the holy virgin Clare to consult with the purest and simplest of the virgins living under her rule, and to pray herself with the other sisters in order to seek *the Lord's will* in this matter. Through a miraculous revelation of the Spirit, the venerable priest and the virgin dedicated to God came to the same conclusion: that it was the divine good will that the herald of Christ should preach.

When the two brothers returned and told him God's will as they had received it, he rose at once, *girded himself* and without the slightest delay took to the roads. He went with such fervor to carry out the

Ex 25:40

1C 35

1C 91

LMj III 5

Lk 12:47

Jn 21:7

2 Kgs 3:15 divine command, just as he ran along so swiftly as if *the hand of God were upon him,* giving him new strength from heaven.

[3C 20] [LJS 37] [3C 20] [1C 58] [3C 20] [1C 58] [3C 20]

³When he was approaching Bevagna, he came **upon a place** where a large flock of birds of various kinds had gathered. When the holy one of God saw them, he swifty ran to the spot and greeted them as though they had human reason. They all became alert and turned toward him, and those perched in the trees bent their heads as he approached them and in an uncommon way **directed** their attention to him. He approached them and **intently encouraged them** all to hear the word of God, saying: "**My brother birds, you should greatly praise your Creator, who clothed you with feathers, gave you wings for flight,** confided to you purity of the air, and governs **you without your least care."** While he was saying this and similar things to them, the birds fluttered about in a wonderful way. They began to stretch their necks, spread their wings, open their beaks, and look at him. He passed through their **midst** with amazing fervor of spirit, touching them with his tunic. Yet none of them left the place until the man of God **made the sign of the cross and gave them a blessing and permission to leave;** then **they all flew** away together. His **companions** waiting **along the way** contuited all these things.ᵃ **Upon returning** to them, the pure and **simple man began to** accuse himself of negligence because he had not previously preached to the birds.

⁴From there he went **preaching** through the neighboring districts and came to **a village called Alviano.** When **the people were gathered, he called for silence, but he could** scarcely **be heard above the shrieking made by the swallows that were nesting there.** In the hearing of all the people, the man of God addressed them and said: "**My sister swallows, it is now time for me to speak, because you have already said enough. Hear the word of God and stay quiet until the word of the Lord is completed."** As if they had been able to understand **him,** they suddenly became **silent,** and did not leave that place until the whole sermon was over. All who saw this were *filled with amazement* and *gave glory to God.* News of this miracle spread around everywhere, enkindling reverence for the saint and devotion for the faith.

Acts 3:10; Mt 9:8

[3C 21] [1C 59] [3C 21]

---

a. In this instance, Bonaventure uses only three words of 1C 58, *socii* [companions] and *in via* [along the way]. It is significant that once again he uses the verb *contuere* to underscore the conviction arising in those companions from the evidence supplied by the effect Francis had on those birds, effects whose presence can only be accounted for by divine intervention.

3C 22

⁵In the city of **Parma, a scholar,** an excellent young man, was diligently studying with his companions when **he was so annoyed by the bothersome chattering of a swallow. He began to say** to his companions: "**This swallow is one of those** that kept bothering the man of God **Francis when he was preaching** one time, **until he imposed silence on them."** And **turning to the swallow, he said confidently:** "**In the name** of God's servant **Francis, I command you** to come **to me and to be silent at once."** When it heard the name of Francis, it immediately became silent, as if it really had been trained by the teaching of the man of God, and entrusted itself **to his hands** as if to safe keeping. **The surprised scholar** immediately **gave it back its freedom** and **heard its chattering** no more.

⁶Another time when God's servant was preaching on the seashore at Gaeta, out of devotion, crowds rushed upon him in order to touch him. Horrified at people's acclaim, the servant of Christ jumped alone into a small boat that was drawn up on the shore. The boat began to move, as if it had both intellect and motion of itself, and, without the help of any oars, glided away from the shore, to the wonderment of all who witnessed it. When it had gone out some distance into the deep water, it stood motionless among the waves, as long as the holy man preached to the attentive crowd on the shore. When, after hearing the sermon, seeing the miracle, and receiving his blessing, the crowd went away and would no longer trouble him, the boat returned to land on its own.

Who, then, would be
so obstinate and lacking in piety
as to look down upon the preaching of Francis?
By his remarkable power,
not only creatures lacking reason learned obedience,
but even inanimate objects served him
when he preached, as if they had life.

⁷*The Spirit of the Lord,*   Is 61:1; Lk 4:18
who had *anointed and sent* him,
and also *Christ,*   1 Cor 1:24
the power and the wisdom of God,
were with their servant Francis *wherever he went*   Ru 1:16
so that he might abound with words of sound teaching
and shine with miracles of great power.

1C 23

**For his word was like a blazing fire,
reaching the deepest parts of the heart,**

and filling the souls of all with wonder,
since it made no pretense
at the elegance of human composition,
but exuded the breath of divine revelation.

Once when he was to preach **before the pope and cardinals at the**   1C 73
suggestion of the lord of Ostia, he memorized a sermon which he
had carefully composed. When he stood in their midst to offer his edifying words, he went completely blank and was unable to say anything at all. This he admitted to them in true humility and directed
himself to invoke the grace of the Holy Spirit. Suddenly he began to
overflow with such effective eloquence and to move the minds of
those high-ranking men to compunction with such force and power
Acts 6:10   that it was clearly evident it was not he, but *the Spirit* of the Lord who
was speaking.

[8]**Because he first convinced himself by action and then con-**   1C 36
**vinced others by word, he did not fear rebuke, but spoke the truth
boldly. He did not encourage, but struck at the life of sin with a
sharp blow, nor did he smooth over, but struck at the faults of sinners with harsh reproaches. He spoke with the same constancy of**   LJS 58
mind to the great and the small, **and would speak with the same** joy
of spirit **to the few as to the many.**

People of all ages and both sexes hurried   1C 36
to see and hear this **new** man
given to the world by heaven.
Moving about through various regions,
he preached the Gospel ardently,
Mk 16:20   *as the Lord worked with* him
and confirmed his preaching with the signs that followed.[a]
For in the power of His name
Francis, the herald of truth,
Lk 11:15; 9:2   *cast out devils and healed the sick,*
and, what is greater,
he softened the obstinate minds of sinners
and moved them to penance,
restoring at the same time health to their bodies and hearts,

---

a. In his commentary on the missionary mandate, Lk 9:2, Bonaventure clearly reiterates that with the
authority to preach the Lord also conferred the power of healing, cf. *Commentary on Luke's Gospel* IX
3 (VII, 217). The following paragraphs 9-11 touch on some of the miracles performed by Francis
while he lived.

as his miracles prove,
a few of which we will cite below as examples.

LJS 48; 1C 65   ⁹In the city of Toscanella he was warmly taken in as a guest by a
3C 175, 176   knight whose only son had been crippled since birth. At the father's
insistent entreaties, he lifted the child up with his hand and cured
him instantly, so that all the limbs of his body *at once got back their*   Acts 3:7
LJS 48   *strength* in view of all. The boy became healthy and strong and immediately rose, *walking and leaping, and praising God.*   Acts 3:8

LJS 48; 3C 176   In the city of Narni, at the request of the bishop, he made the
sign of the cross from head to foot over a paralytic who had lost the
use of all his limbs, and restored him to perfect health.

3C 174   In the diocese of Rieti a boy was so swollen for four years that he
could not in any way see his own legs. When the boy was presented
to Francis by his tearful mother, he was cured the moment the holy
man touched him with his sacred hands.

3C 178   At the town of Orte a boy was so twisted that his head was bent
to his feet and some of his bones were broken. When Francis made
the sign of the cross over him at the tearful entreaty of his parents,
he was cured on the spot and stretched out immediately.

3C 177   ¹⁰There was a woman in the town of Gubbio whose both hands
were so withered and crippled that she could do nothing with them.
When he made the sign of the cross over them in the name of the
Lord, she was so perfectly cured that she immediately went home
LJS 48; 3C 177   and prepared with her own hands food for him and for the poor, like
Peter's mother-in-law.   Mt 8:14-15

3C 124   In the village of Bevagna he marked the eyes of a blind girl with
his saliva three times in the name of the Trinity and restored the
sight she longed for.

1C 67   A woman of the city of Narni, afflicted with blindness, received
the sign of the cross from him and recovered the sight she longed
for.

At Bologna a boy had one eye covered over with an opaque film so
that he could see nothing at all with it nor could he be helped by any
treatment. After God's servant had made the sign of the cross from
his head to his feet, he recovered his sight so completely that, having
later entered the Order of Lesser Brothers, he claimed that he could
see far more clearly with the eye that had been previously ill than
with the eye that had always been well.

1C 69   In the village of San Gemini, God's servant received hospitality
from a devoted man whose wife was troubled by a demon. After
LJS 50   praying, he commanded the devil to leave by virtue of obedience,

and by God's power drove him out so suddenly that it became evident that the obstinacy of demons cannot resist the power of holy obedience.

In **Città di Castello**, an evil spirit, which had taken possession of a certain woman, departed **furious** when commanded under **obedience** by the holy man, and left the woman who had been **possessed** free in body and mind.   1C 70

[11]**A brother** was suffering from such **a terrible affliction** that many were convinced it was more a case of possession **by a demon** than a natural sickness. **For he was often completely cast down and rolled about foaming at the mouth, with his limbs now contracted, now stretched out, now bent, now twisted, now rigid and hard. Sometimes, when he was stretched out and rigid, with his feet level with his head, he would be lifted into the air and then would fall down** horribly. Christ's servant was **full of pity** for him in such a miserable and incurable illness, and he sent him a morsel of the bread he was eating. When he tasted the bread, the sick man received such strength **that** he never **suffered** from that **illness** again.   3C 195 / LJS 49 / 3C 195 / 1C 68

In the district **of Arezzo, a woman had been in labor for several days** and was already near death; there was no cure left for her in her **desperate** state except from God. Christ's servant **was passing through** that region, riding **on horseback because of physical illness.** It happened that when the animal was being returned to its owner, it was led **through the village where the woman was suffering.** When **the men of the place saw the horse on which the holy** man had been mounted, they took off the reins and placed them **on the woman.** As soon as the reins touched her, **all danger** miraculously **passed, and the woman gave birth safely.**   1C 63 / LJS 51; 3C 108 / 1C 63; 3C 108

A man from Città della Pieve, who was religious and God-fearing, had in his possession a cord which our holy father **had used as a belt.** Since many **men and women in** that town **suffered from various diseases, he went to the houses of the sick and gave the sufferers water to drink which had been touched by the cord.** In this way many were cured.   1C 64; LJS 52

Sick persons who **ate** bread touched by the man of God were quickly restored to health by divine power.   1C 63; 3C 19

[12]Since the herald of Christ
in his preaching
brilliantly shone with these and many other marvelous miracles,
people paid attention to what he said
as if *an angel of the Lord were speaking.*   Jgs 2:4

For excelling in him were:
a privilege of virtues,
a *spirit of prophecy,*   Rv 19:10
a proficiency for miracles,
a sign given by heaven to preach,
an obedience of creatures lacking reason,
a powerful change of hearts at the sound of his words,
an erudition by the Holy Spirit beyond human teaching,
an authority to preach
granted by the Supreme Pontiff guided by a revelation,
moreover,
a Rule confirmed by that same Vicar of Christ
in which the manner of preaching is described, and,
as a seal, the marks of the Supreme King imprinted on his body.
These are like ten witnesses
affirming to the whole world without any doubt
that Francis, the herald of Christ,
celebrated in mission,
authentic in teaching,
admirable in holiness,
because of all this
truly preached the Gospel of Christ
as a messenger of God.

Chapter Thirteen

THE SACRED STIGMATA

1C 91

¹It was a custom for the angelic man Francis
never to rest from the good,

Gn 28:12

rather, like the heavenly spirits *on Jacob's ladder,*ᵃ
he either *ascended* into God
or *descended* to his neighbor.
For he had so prudently learned
to divide the time given to him for merit,
that he spent some of it working for his neighbor's benefit
and dedicated the rest
to the tranquil excesses of contemplation.
Therefore,
when he emptied himself
according to the demand of times and places
to gain the salvation of another,
leaving the restlessness of the crowds,
he would seek the secrets of solitude and a place of quiet,
where freeing himself more freely for the Lord,
he would shake off the dust that might have clung to him
from the time spent with the crowds.

Therefore,

1C 94

two years before he returned his spirit to heaven,

LJS 61

after a variety of many labors,
he was led by divine providence
to *a high* place *apart* called Mount La Verna.ᵇ

Mt 17:1

---

a. The image of Jacob's ladder, Gn 28:12, appears frequently in Bonaventure's writings. It refers to the stages of prayer (*Regula Novitiorum* II 8), understanding Scripture (*Breviloquium*, Prol 3), progressing in virtue (*Breviloquium* V 6), ascending into God from the sensible to the mystical (*Itinerarium* I 9), a life of contemplation (*Collationes in Hexaëmeron* XXII 24). Above all, it refers to Christ (*Christus Unus Omnium* 14) and, in light of Francis's life, to Francis himself (Itin VII 3): "He [Saint Francis] is set forth as an example of perfect contemplation, just as previously he had been of action, like a second Jacob-Israel. And thus, through him, more by example than by word, God would invite all truly spiritual men to this passing over and this transport of soul."

b. In order to appreciate the depth of this image of Mount La Verna as a "high place apart," it is helpful to read Bonaventure's commentary on the Transfiguration in his *Commentary on Luke's Gospel* IX 46-60 (VII, 23-235). The mountain is seen as the summit of an excellent life, as ideal for prayer and contemplation, for divine apparitions, instructions, and for resting in God.

When according to his usual custom
he had begun to fast there for forty days
in honor of Saint Michael the Archangel,
he experienced more abundantly than usual
an overflow of the sweetness of heavenly contemplation,
was on fire with an ever intense flame of heavenly desires,[a]
and began to be aware more fully of the gifts of heavenly entries.
He was carried into the heights,
not as a curious *searcher of the supreme majesty*   Prv 25:27
crushed by its glory,
but as a *faithful and prudent servant,*   Mt 24:45
exploring God's good pleasure,
to which, with the greatest ardor, he desires
to conform himself in every way.

1C 92

1C 93

1C 92; 1C 93

[2]Through a divine sign from heaven he had learned that in opening the book of the Gospel, Christ would reveal to him what God considered most acceptable in him and from him. After completing his **prayer** with much devotion, he took **the book of the sacred Gospels from the altar** and had his companion, a holy man dedicated to God, **open** it three times in the name of the Holy Trinity. All three times, when **the book was opened, the Lord's passion** always met his eyes. **The man filled with God understood that,** just as he had imitated Christ in the actions of his life, so he should be conformed to him in the affliction and sorrow of his passion, before *he would pass out of this*   Jn 13:1 *world.*

And although his body was already weakened
by the great austerity of his past life
and his continual carrying of the Lord's cross,
he was in no way terrified,
but was inspired even more vigorously
to endure martyrdom.
The unconquerable enkindling of love in him
for the good Jesus
had grown into *lamps and flames of fire,*   Sg 8:6-7
that *many waters could not quench so* powerful a *love.*

---

a. This passage is reminiscent of the Prologue to Bonaventure's *Soul's Journey into God*. "No one is in any way disposed for divine contemplations that lead to spiritual transports unless like Daniel, he is also a man of desire." Worthy of note is the footnote explaining this text. Cf. *The Journey of the Mind to God*, translated by Philotheus Boehner, edited, with introduction and notes by Stephen F. Brown (Indianapolis/Cambridge: Hackett Publishing Company, 1993), 2, 42-43, note 16.

Eph 2:4

> ³With the seraphic ardor of desires,
> therefore,
> he was being borne aloft into God;
> and by compassionate sweetness
> he was being transformed into Him
> Who chose to be crucified out of
> *the excess of His love.*

On a certain morning about the feast of the Exaltation of the Cross, while Francis was praying on the mountainside, **he saw a Seraph having six wings,** fiery as well as brilliant, descend from the grandeur of heaven. And when in swift flight, it had arrived at a spot in the air near the man of God, there appeared between the wings the likeness of a man **crucified,** with **his hands and feet extended** in the form of a cross and **fastened to a cross. Two of the wings were raised above his head, two were extended for flight, and two covered his whole body. Seeing this, he was overwhelmed and his heart was flooded with a mixture of joy and sorrow. He rejoiced at the gracious way** Christ looked upon him under the appearance of **the Seraph, but the fact that He was fastened to a cross** *pierced his soul with a sword* of compassionate sorrow.

1C 94

3C 4

Lk 2:35

> He marveled exceedingly
> at the sight of so unfathomable a vision,
> knowing that the weakness of Christ's passion
> was in no way compatible
> with the immortality of the seraphic spirit.
> Eventually he understood from this,
> through the Lord revealing it,
> that Divine Providence had shown him a vision of this sort so that
> the friend of Christ might learn in advance
> that he was to be totally transformed
> into the likeness of Christ crucified,[a]
> not by the martyrdom of his flesh,
> but by the enkindling of his soul.[b]
> As the vision was disappearing,
> it left in his heart a marvelous fire

1C 94

---

a. For the theology behind this statement, see supra 33 a.

b. Bonaventure uses the term *incendium mentis*, literally *the conflagration of his soul*. The term *incendium* appears in the alternate title of Bonaventure's treatise on the three stages of the spiritual life: *De triplici via seu Incendium amoris, On the Triple Way* or *The Fire of Love*. On Francis's desire for martyrdom, cf. LMj IX, 5-9.

and imprinted in his flesh a likeness of signs
no less marvelous.

3C 4   For immediately the marks of nails began to appear in his hands and feet just as he had seen a little before in the figure of the man crucified. His hands and feet seemed to be pierced through the center by nails, with the heads of the nails appearing on the inner side of the hands and the upper side of the feet and their points on the opposite sides. The heads of the nails in his hands and his feet were round and black; their points were oblong and bent as if driven back with a hammer, and they emerged from the flesh and stuck out beyond it. Also his right side, as if pierced with a lance, was marked with a red wound from which his sacred blood often flowed, moistening his tunic and underwear.

2C 135   [4]As **Christ's servant** realized that he could not conceal from his **intimate companions the stigmata** that had been so visibly imprinted on his flesh, he feared to make public the Lord's *sacrament* [a]   Tb 12:7 and was thrown into an agony of doubt whether to tell what he had seen or to be silent about it. He called some of the brothers and, speaking in general terms, presented his doubt to them and sought their advice. One of the brothers, Illuminato, by name and by grace,[b] understanding that Francis had seen something marvelous that made him seem completely dazed, said to the holy man: "Brother, you should realize that at times divine sacraments are revealed to you not for yourself alone but also for others. You have every reason to fear that if you hide what you have received for the profit of many, you will be blamed for *burying* that *talent*." Although the holy man   Mt 25:25 used to say on other occasions: *"My secret is for myself,"* he was moved   Is 24:16 by Illuminato's words. Then, with much fear, he recounted the vision in detail, adding that the one who had appeared to him had told him some things which he would never disclose to any person as long as he lived. We should believe, then, that those utterances of that sacred Seraph marvelously appearing to him on the cross were so *secret* that *people are not permitted to speak of them.*   2 Cor 12:4

---

a. Cf. 2C 9, FA:ED II 248 a. While Bonaventure's use of the *sacramentum* [sacrament] parallels that of Thomas, he uses the word more frequently in reference to the stigmata.

b. Earlier, LMj IX 8, Bonaventure referred to Illuminato as *viro utique luminis et virtutis* [without doubt a man of light and virtue]. In this instance, LMj XIII, he writes of him as *gratia Illuminatus et nomine* [Illuminatus—enlightened—by grace and by name], obviously underscoring his unique qualities and role in the key events of Francis's life. Thomas of Celano, 3C 123, describes the miracle through which he overcame blindness and his entrance into the Order, to which Bonaventure adds by highlighting his growth in holiness, cf. LMj Mir VII 6.

⁵After **true love of Christ**   2C 135

2 Cor 3:18   *transformed* **the lover** *into His image,*

when the forty days were over that he spent in solitude

as he had desired,

and the feast of St. Michael the Archangel

had also arrived,

the angelic man Francis

Ex 19:1   *came down from the mountain,*

bearing with him

the likeness of the Crucified,

Dt 4:13   depicted not on *tablets of stone* or on panels of wood

carved by hand,

but engraved on parts of his flesh

Dt 9:10; Jn 11:27   *by the finger of the living God.*

Tb 12:7   And because *it is good to keep hidden*

the sacrament of the King,

the man aware of the royal secret

would then hide from men those sacred signs.

Since it is for God to reveal what He does for his own great glory,

the Lord himself,

who had secretly imprinted those marks,

openly revealed some miracles through them

so that the hidden and marvelous power of the stigmata

would display a brilliance of signs.

⁶**In the province of Rieti a very serious plague broke out and so**   3C 18
cruelly took the lives of cattle and sheep that no remedy could be
found. **A certain Godfearing man** was told **in a vision at night to
hurry to the hermitage of the brothers and get the water in which**
God's servant Francis, **who was staying there at that time, had
washed his hands and feet, and to sprinkle it** on all the animals. **He
got up in the morning, came to the place,** secretly got the water from
the companions of the holy man, and **sprinkled** it on the sheep and
cattle. Marvelous to say, the moment that water touched the animals, which were weak and lying on the ground, they immediately
recovered their former vigor, stood up and, as if they had had nothing
wrong with them, hurried off to pasture. Thus through the miraculous power of that water, which had touched his sacred wounds, the
plague ceased and deadly disease fled from the flocks.

⁷About the time the holy man stayed on Mount La Verna,

clouds would form over the mountain,

and violent hailstorms would devastate the crops.

> But after that blessed apparition
> the hail stopped,
> to the amazement of the inhabitants,
> so that the unusually serene face of the sky proclaimed
> the excellence of that heavenly vision
> and the power of the stigmata imprinted there.

In wintertime because of his physical weakness and the rough roads, he was once riding on a donkey belonging to a poor man. It happened that he spent the night at the base of an overhanging cliff to try to avoid the inconveniences of a snowfall and the darkness of night that prevented him from reaching his place of lodging. When, however, the saint heard his helper tossing and turning, grumbling and groaning, since, as he had only thin clothing, the biting cold would not let him sleep; burning with the fire of divine love, he stretched out his hand and touched him. A marvelous thing happened! At the touch of his sacred hand, which bore the burning *coal of the Seraph,* the cold fled altogether and the man felt great heat within and without, as if he had been hit by a fiery blast from the vent of a furnace. Comforted in mind and body, he slept until morning more soundly among the rocks and snow than he ever had in his own bed, as he later used to say.

Is 6:6-7

> Thus it is obvious to certain witnesses
> that those sacred marks were imprinted
> by the power of Him Who,
> through a seraphic activity,
> purifies, illumines, and inflames.[a]
> Outwardly,
> by purifying from pestilence,
> with a marvelous effect,
> they brought health, serene skies,
> and warmth to bodies.
> As after his death
> this was demonstrated
> by even more evident miracles
> as we will later record in the proper place.

---

a. A reference to the three hierarchical acts presented by the Pseudo-Dionysius, *The Celestial Hierarchy* III 2. Cf. supra, 526 a; also, *Pseudo-Dionysius: The Complete Works*, trans by Colm Luibheid and Rene Roques, foreword, preface, and notes by Rene Roques, introductions by Jaroslav Pelikan, Jean Leclercq, and Karlfried Froehlich (New York, Mahwah: Paulist Press, 1987), 154-155.

Mt 13:44   [8]Although **he tried** his best **to hide** the *treasure found in the field,* he   2C 135
                could not prevent at least some from seeing **the stigmata in his**   2C 136
                hands and feet, although he always kept **his hands** covered and
                from that time on always wore shoes.

                A number of the brothers saw them **while he was still alive.** Al-   3C 5
                though they were men of outstanding holiness and so completely
                trustworthy, nevertheless to remove all doubt they confirmed under
                oath, touching the most sacred Gospels, that this was so and that
                they had seen it.

                Also some of the cardinals saw them because of their close friend-
                ship with the holy man; and they inserted praises of the sacred stig-
                mata in the hymns, antiphons, and sequences which they composed
Jn 5:33   in his honor, and thus by their words and writings *gave testimony to the*
                truth.[a]

                Even the Supreme Pontiff Lord Alexander,[b] in a sermon preached
                to the people at which many of the brothers and I myself were pres-
                ent, affirmed that he had seen the sacred stigmata with his own eyes
                while the saint was still alive.

                More **than fifty brothers** with the virgin Clare, who was most de-   3C 5
                voted to God, and her sisters, as well as **innumerable laymen,** saw
                them after his death. Many of them kissed the stigmata out of devo-
                tion and **touched** them **with their own hands** to strengthen their
                testimony, as we will describe in the proper place.

                But the wound in his side he so **cautiously** concealed that as long   2C 138
                as he was alive no one could see it except by stealth. One brother   1C 95
                who used to zealously take care of him induced him with a pious care
                to take off **his tunic to shake it out. Watching closely, he saw the**   2C 136; 2C 138
                wound, and he even quickly touched it with three of his fingers de-
                termining the size of the wound by both sight and **touch.** The brother   1C 95
                who was his vicar at that time also managed to see it by similar care.
                A brother who was **a companion** of his, a man of marvelous simplic-   2C 138
                ity, when he was one day **rubbing his shoulders that were weak**   1 C 95
                from illness, put his hand under his hood and accidentally touched
                the sacred **wound, causing him great pain.** As a result, from that
                time on, he always wore underclothes made so that they would reach

---

a. Gregory IX (Cardinal Hugolino) composed the hymn *Proles de caelo,* the response *De paupertatis*
   borreo, the antiphons *Sancte Francisce propere* and *Plange turba paupercula,* and the sequence
   Caput draconis ultimum; Cardinal Thomas of Capua, the hymns *Deus morum* and *In caelesti collegio,*
   the response *Carnis spicam,* the antiphon *Salve sancte Pater,* and the sequence *Laeteabundus*
   Francisco; Cardinal Rainerio Capoci of Viterbo, the hymn *Plaude turba;* Cardinal Stefano di Casa
   Nova, the antiphon *Caelorum candor splenduit.* Most of these were incorporated into the rhymed
   office composed by Julian of Speyer.
b. Alexander IV, pope 1254-1261, who made the same affirmation in his bulls: *Benigna operatio*
   (October 19, 1255) and *Quia longum esset* (June 28, 1259).

up to his armpits to cover the wound on his side. Also the brothers who washed these or shook out his tunic from time to time, since they found these **stained with blood,** were convinced without any doubt from this evident sign of the existence of the sacred wound, **which, after his death,** they along with many others contemplated **and venerated** *with unveiled face.*

3C 5

3C 5

2 Cor 3:18

⁹Come now,
most vigorous knight of Christ,
bear the arms of your invincible Leader!
Visibly shielded with these,
you will overcome all adversaries.
Carry the standard of the Most High King,
by Whose gaze
all combatants of the divine army
are aroused to courage.
Carry the seal of Christ, the Supreme Pontiff,
by which your words and deeds
will be rightly accepted by all
as authentic and *beyond reproach.*

Ti 2:8

For now,
because of *the stigmata of the Lord Jesus*
which you *carry in* your *body,*
no one must *trouble you;*
rather every servant of Christ
must show you with all intensity greater devotion.

Gal 6:17

Now
through these most certain signs,
corroborated
not by the sufficient testimony *of two or three witnesses,*
but by the superabundant testimony of a whole multitude,
God's *testimony* about you and through you
has been made overwhelmingly credible,
removing completely from unbelievers
the veil of excuse,
while they confirm believers in faith,
raise them aloft with confident hope
and set them ablaze with the fire of charity.

Dt 19:15

Ps 92:5

¹⁰Now
the first *vision you saw* is truly *fulfilled,*

Dn 9:24; 4:6

that is, that you should be   1C 5
a future leader in the militia of Christ
and bear heavenly arms
emblazoned with the sign of the cross.

Now   3C 2
the vision that you saw **at the outset of** your **conversion**
must undoubtedly be believed as true,
that is, of the Crucified

Lk 2:35   *piercing* your soul *with a sword* of compassionate sorrow,
but also the sound of the voice **from the cross,**

Nm 7:89   as if proceeding *from* the throne of the lofty Christ
and the secret *mercy seat,*
as you confirmed with your own sacred utterance.

Now   3C 3
in the unfolding of your conversion,
the cross Brother Sylvester saw
marvelously coming from your mouth;
and the swords the holy **Pacifico saw**
piercing your body in the form of a cross;
and the figure of you **lifted up in the air** in the form of a cross
the angelic **man Monaldo** saw
while Saint **Anthony was preaching**
about the inscription on the cross:
these must be truly believed and affirmed
not as an imaginary vision,
but as a celestial revelation.

Now,
finally, near the end,
you were shown at the same time
the sublime similitude of the Seraph
and the humble likeness of the Crucified,
inwardly inflaming you and outwardly signing you

Rv 7:2   as *the other Angel ascending from the rising of the sun*
that *you might have* in you *the sign of the living God:*
this both gives strength of faith to the previous ones

Jn 5:33-34   and *receives* from them *the testimony of truth.*

Behold,
you have arrived
with seven apparitions of the cross of Christ

wondrously apparent and visible in you or about you
following an order of time,
like six steps leading to the seventh
where you finally found rest.[a]
For
the cross of Christ,
both offered to and taken on by you
at the beginning of your conversion
and carried continuously from that moment
throughout the course of your most proven life
and giving example to others,
shows with such clarity of certitude
that you have finally reached
the summit of Gospel perfection
that no truly devout person
can reject this proof of Christian wisdom
ploughed into the dust of your flesh.
No truly believing person can attack it,
no truly humble person can belittle it,
since it is truly divinely expressed
and *worthy of complete acceptance.*

1 Tm 1:15; 4:9

---

a. Note the similarity between the seven stages of *The Soul's Journey into God*, prol., 3; I, 1-7; VII, 1.

Chapter Fourteen

HIS PATIENCE
AND
PASSING IN DEATH[a]

Gal 2:19

[1]*Now fixed with Christ to the cross,*
in both body and spirit,
Francis
not only burned with a seraphic love into God
but also *thirsted* with Christ crucified
for the multitude of those to be saved.

Since he could not walk because of the nails protruding from his feet, he had his half-dead body carried *through the towns and villages* to arouse others to *carry the cross* of Christ. He used to say to the brothers: "Let us begin, brothers, to serve the Lord our God, for up to now we have done little." *He burned with a great desire* to return to the humility he practiced at the beginning; to nurse the lepers as he did at the outset and to treat like a slave once more his body that was already in a state of collapse from his work.

With the Christ as leader,
he resolved "to do great deeds,"
and although his limbs were weakening,
he hoped
for victory over the enemy in a new struggle
with a brave and burning spirit.
For there is no room for apathy and laziness
where the goad of love
always urges to greater things.
There was in him such harmony of flesh with spirit,
such readiness of obedience,
that, when he strove to attain all holiness,

Margin references: Gal 2:19 · Jn 19:28 · Lk 8:1 · Lk 9:23 · Nm 11:4; Mt 2:10 · 1C 98 · LJS 64 · 1C 103 · 2C 209 · 1C 97

---

a. The Latin word here is *transitu* [passing]. It appears on many levels of Bonaventure's thought: that of creation which has a passage through time; that of the People of God and, most especially, of Jesus, i.e., the biblical connotations; and that of every Christian called to journey or pass over into God. Cf. André Ménard, "Spirituaté du *Transitus*," in *S. Bonaventura 1274-1974*, vol. IV (Grottaferrata, Rome: Collegio S. Bonaventura, 1974), 607-635.

not only **did the flesh not resist,**
it even tried **to run ahead.**

²In order that his merits might increase,
for these are brought to perfection *in patience,*   Jas 1:4
the man of God **started** to suffer from various **illnesses,**
so seriously that scarcely **the rest of his body**
remained without intense **pain and suffering.**
Through varied, long-lasting, and continual illness
he was brought to the point
where his *flesh was* already *all consumed,*   Jb 19:20
as if **only** skin *clung to his bones.*   Lam 4:8
But when he was tortured by harsh bodily suffering,
he called his tribulations not by the name of "pains"
but of "Sisters."

Once **when** he was suffering **more intensely than usual,** a certain
brother in his simplicity told him: "Brother, *pray to the Lord* that he   Sir 38:9
treat you more mildly, for he seems to *have laid* his *hand* on you more
heavily than he should." At these words, the holy man wailed and   Ps 31:4; 2 Cor 1:8
cried out: "If I did not know your simplicity and sincerity, then I
would from now on shrink from your company because you dared to
judge God's judgments upon me as reprehensible." Even though he
was completely worn out by his prolonged and serious illness, he
threw himself on the ground, bruising his weakened bones in the
hard fall. Kissing the ground, he said: "*I thank you, Lord God,* for all   Lk 18:11
these sufferings of mine; and I ask you, my Lord, if it pleases you, to
increase them a hundredfold. Because it will be most acceptable to
me, *that you do not spare me, afflicting me with suffering,* since the fulfill-   Jb 6:10
ment of your will is an overflowing consolation for me."

So it seemed to the brothers, therefore,
that they were almost seeing another Job,
for whom, as the weariness of his flesh was increasing,
so too was the vigor of his soul.
He knew **long in advance the time of his death,**
and as the day of his passing **grew near,**
he told the brothers that
laying aside the tent of his body was at hand,   2 Pt 1:14
as it had been revealed to him by Christ.

³For two years after the imprinting of the sacred stigmata
that is, in the twentieth **year of his conversion,**

Left margin references:
1C 105
1C 107
2C 212
2C 213
1C 108
1C 109

under the many blows of agonizing illness,
he was squared like a stone to be fitted
into the construction of the heavenly Jerusalem,
and like **a work of malleable metal**
he was brought to perfection
under the hammering blows of many tribulations.

2C 214

He asked to be taken to Saint Mary of the Portiuncula
so that **he might yield up** *the spirit of life*
where he had received *the spirit of grace.*

LJS 69

1C 106

Gn 6:17

Heb 10:29

When he had been brought there, **he showed by the example of**
Truth that he had nothing in common with the world. In that grave
illness that ended all suffering, he threw himself in fervor of spirit
totally **naked on the naked ground so that in that final hour, when**
the enemy could still rage, he might wrestle naked with the naked.[a] Lying like this *on the ground* stripped of his sackcloth garment,
he lifted up his face to heaven in his accustomed way, **and wholly intent**
upon that glory, he covered with his left hand the wound in his
right side, so that no one would see it. And he said to his brothers: "I
have done what is mine; may *Christ teach you* **yours."**

2C 214

Jb 20:4

Jb 11:15

1 Kgs 19:20; Eph 4:21

[4]Pierced with the spear **of compassion,** the companions of the
saint **wept streams of tears.** One of them, whom the man of God
used to call his **guardian, knowing** his **wish through divine inspira-**
tion, quickly got up. He took the tunic **with a cord and underwear,**
and offered them to the little poor man of Christ, **saying: "I am lend-**
ing these to you as to a poor man, and you are to accept them **with**
the command of holy obedience." At this **the holy** man rejoiced and
was delighted in the gladness of his heart, because he saw that he had
kept faith until the end with Lady Poverty. *Raising his hands to*
heaven, he magnified his Christ, that now set free from all things, he
was going to him free. For he had done all of this out of zeal for poverty, not wanting to have even a habit unless it were borrowed
from another.

2C 215

Sg 3:11

2 Chr 6:13

2C 216

2C 215

In all things
he wished without hesitation
to be conformed to Christ crucified,
who hung on the cross poor, suffering, and naked.

---

a. Cf. FA:ED I 194 a.

Naked he lingered before the bishop
at the beginning of his conversion;
and, for this reason,
at the end of his life,
he wanted to leave this world naked.

2C 217

And so he charged **the brothers** assisting him,
under the obedience of love,
that **when they saw** he was dead,
they should allow **him to lie naked on the ground**
for as long as it takes to walk a leisurely mile.

O truly the most Christian of men,
who strove by perfect imitation to be conformed
while living to Christ living,
dying to Christ dying,
and dead to Christ dead,
and deserved to be adorned
with an expressed likeness!

2C 216

[5]When the hour of his passing was approaching, **he had all the brothers** staying in the place **called to him and, comforting them** about his death with *words of consolation,* he exhorted them to divine love with fatherly affection. He spoke at length about preserving poverty and patience and the faith of the holy Roman Church, placing the holy Gospel ahead of other observances. As all the brothers

Zec 1:13

1C 108

sat around him, *he stretched his hand over* them, crossing his arms in the form of a cross, for he always loved this sign. And **he blessed all**

Gn 48:14

1C 109

the brothers, both present and absent, in the name and power of the Crucified. Then he added: **"Good bye, all my sons,** *in the fear of the*

Tb 2:14

Lord! Remain in Him always! **Because a** *trial* and *tribulation* is coming in the future, happy are they who will persevere in those things they have begun. I am hurrying to God, to whose grace I entrust all

Sir 27:6

2C 217

of you." When he finished this gentle admonition, the man most beloved of God ordered **the Book of the Gospels brought to him and** asked that the Gospel according to John be read to him from the place that begins: *Before the feast of Passover.* He, as best he could,

Jn 13:1

broke out in this psalm: *With my voice I cried to the Lord; With my voice I*

Ps 142:2

beseeched the Lord; and he finished it to the end. *The just,* he said, *will*

Ps 142

await me until you have rewarded me.

[6]At last,

2C 117

when all of the mysteries were fulfilled in him

and that most holy soul was released from the flesh   1C 110
and absorbed into the abyss of the divine light,
Acts 7:60   the blessed man *fell asleep in the Lord.*
One of his brothers and followers saw that blessed soul
under the appearance of a radiant star
Rv 14:14   carried up on *a shining cloud*
to be borne aloft straight to heaven over many waters,
as if shining with the brightness of sublime sanctity,
and filled with the abundance of heavenly wisdom and grace,
by which the holy man merited to enter
the place of light and peace
where he rests with Christ forever.

At that time the minister of the brothers in Terra di Lavoro was   2C 218
Brother Augustine, a man both holy and upright, who was in his
last hour and had already for some time lost his speech. In the
Acts 23:4; Lk 9:39   hearing of those *who were standing about: he suddenly cried out:* "Wait
for me, father, wait! Look, I'm coming with you!" The amazed
brothers asked him to whom he was speaking so boldly. And he
replied: "Don't you see our father Francis going to heaven?" And
immediately his holy soul, leaving the flesh, followed the most holy
father.

At that time the bishop of Assisi had been at the shrine of Saint   2C 220
Michael on Monte Gargano because of a pilgrimage. Blessed Fran-
Jn 16:28   cis appeared to him on the night of his passing and said: "Behold, *I
Gn 24:54   am leaving the world and am going to* heaven." When he *rose in the
morning,* the bishop told his companions what he had seen, and returning to Assisi, he carefully inquired and found out with certainty
that the blessed father had departed this world at the very hour when
he appeared to him in this vision.

Larks are birds,   3C 32
friends of the light dreading the shadows of dusk.
At the hour of the holy man's passing,
when it was already twilight of the falling night,
they gathered in a great flock over the roof of the house
and, circling around for a long time with unusual joy,
Jn 1:7   *they offered testimony,*
giving delight as well as confirmation,
of the glory of the saint,
who so often had invited them to divine praise.

Chapter Fifteen

HIS CANONIZATION
AND
THE TRANSFERAL OF HIS BODY

¹Francis,

1C 95

the servant and friend of the Most High,
the founder and leader of the Order of the Lesser Brothers,
the practitioner of poverty, the model of penance,
the herald of truth,

2C 26

the mirror of holiness,

2C 161

and **the exemplar** of all Gospel **perfection,**
foreordained by grace from heaven,
in an ordered progression
from the lowest level arrived at the very heights.

The Lord made incomparably more brilliant in death
this marvelous man,
whom He had made marvelously bright in life:
rich in poverty, exalted in humility,
vigorous in mortification,
prudent in simplicity,
distinguished in the integrity of his life.
For after this blessed man left the world,
that sacred spirit,
entering a *home of eternity,*   Eccl 12:5
and made glorious by a full draught from *the fountain of life,*   Ps 36:9
left certain signs *of future glory* imprinted on his body;   Rom 8:18
so that,
his most holy flesh,
which *crucified along with its vices,*   Gal 5:24
had already passed into a new creature,   2 Cor 5:17
bore the likeness of Christ's passion
by a singular privilege
and would offer by the newness of a miracle

C 112, 114; 3C 5

a glimpse of the resurrection.

3C 5

²In his blessed hands and feet could be seen **the nails** that had
been marvelously fashioned by divine power out of his flesh, and

163

thus embedded in the flesh. From whatever point **they were pressed, simultaneously, as if by a continuous and tough tendon, they pulsed at the opposite end.** Also **the wound** in his side could be clearly seen, which was not inflicted on his body nor produced by human means; it was like the wound in the Savior's side, which brought forth in our Redeemer the mystery of the redemption and regeneration of the human race. **The nails were as black as iron;** the wound **in his side was red,** and because it was drawn into a kind of circle by the contraction of the flesh looked like a most beautiful rose. The rest of his **skin, which before** was inclined to be **black** both naturally and from his illness, **now shone white in its beauty, prefiguring** the beauty of that glorious second stole.[a]

³**His limbs** were so supple and **soft** to the touch that they seemed **to have regained the tenderness of childhood** and to be adorned with clear signs **of innocence. The nails** appeared black **in his shining skin,** and the wound in his side was red *like a rose* in springtime so that it is no wonder the onlookers were amazed and overjoyed at the sight of such varied and miraculous beauty.

His sons were weeping at the loss of so lovable **a father** but were filled with **no little** joy while **they kissed the seal marks** of the supreme King in him. **The newness of the miracle turned their grief into joy** and transported **into amazement** their attempts at comprehending it. So unique and so remarkable was the sight to all who observed it that it confirmed their faith and incited their love. It was a matter of amazement to those who heard of it and aroused their desire to see it.

⁴When the people heard of the passing of our blessed father and news of the miracle had spread, they hurried to the place to see with their own eyes so that they could dispel all doubt and add joy to their love. A great number of the citizens of Assisi **were admitted** to contemplate those **sacred marks** with their own eyes and **to kiss** them with their lips. One of them, a knight who was educated and prudent, Jerome by name, a distinguished and famous man, had doubts about these sacred signs and *was unbelieving* like Thomas. Fervently and boldly, in the presence of the brothers and the citizens, he did not hesitate to move the nails and *to touch with his hands* the saint's hands, feet, and side. While he was examining with his hands these authentic signs of Christ's wounds, he completely healed the wound

---

a. That is, the glory of the body in heaven. Bonaventure, *Breviloquium* VII, 7 and *The Tree of Life*, 44. (The double stole refers to the two rewards of paradise: the beatific vision and the glorification of the body.)

of doubt in his own heart and the hearts of others. As a result, later along with others, he became a firm witness to this truth that he had come to know with such certainty; and he swore to it on the Gospel.[a]

IC 116

⁵His brothers and sons, who had been called to their father's passing, **with** *the whole multitude of people,* **spent that night in which** the blessed confessor of Christ departed, in the divine praises. They did this in such a way that **it seemed to be a vigil of angels,** not a wake for the dead. *When day was breaking, the crowds that had assembled took branches from the trees* and carried **his sacred body to the city** of Assisi, with a blaze of **many candles and hymns** and songs. As they passed **the church of San Damiano, where** the noble virgin Clare, now glorious in heaven, was then living enclosed **with the virgins,** they stopped for awhile so that those holy nuns could see and **kiss** his sacred body, adorned with its heavenly **pearls. Finally reaching the city with** great rejoicing, with all reverence they placed the precious treasure they were carrying in the church of Saint George.

Ez 27:33

Jn 21:4; Jn 12:13; Mt 21:8

IC 117; IC 118

LJS 72

There **as a boy he learned his letters,**
there he later preached for the first time,
and there, finally, he received his first place of rest.

LJS 73

⁶The venerable father left the shipwreck of this world in the one thousandth, two hundredth, twenty-sixth year of the Incarnation of the Lord, on the fourth day of the nones of October, a Saturday evening, **and was buried on Sunday.**

IC 88

Immediately,
the holy man **began**
to reflect the light radiating from the face of God
and **to glitter with many** great **miracles.**
Thus the sublimity of his holiness
which, while he was still in the flesh,
had been familiar to the world as a guide for conduct
through examples of perfect justice,
was approved from heaven
while he is now *reigning with Christ*

Rv 20:4

---

a. Bonaventure quotes a phrase from Gregory the Great in his interpretation of the doubt of knight Jerome: "he completely healed the wound of doubt in his own heart and in the hearts of others." In his Twenty-Ninth Homily on the Gospels, Gregory comments on the slowness of the disciples to believe and comments, in particular, on Thomas "who remained so long in doubt." "While doubting," Gregory comments, "he touched the scars of the wounds, and cut out of our hearts the wounds of doubt." Cf. Gregory the Great, *Forty Gospel Homilies,* trans. Dom David Hurst (Kalamazoo, MI: Cistercian Publications, 1990), 226.

as a confirmation of faith
through miracles performed by the divine power.

In different **parts** of the world,   1C 120
his glorious **miracles**
and the abundant benefits obtained through him,   1C 121
inflamed many to devotion to Christ
and incited them to reverence for his saint.
The wonderful things
which God was working
through his servant Francis
—acclaimed by word of mouth
and testified to by facts—
came to the ears
of the Supreme Pontiff, Gregory IX.

[7]That **shepherd of the Church** was fully convinced of Francis's re-   1C 121
markable holiness: not only from hearing of **the miracles** after his
death, but also from his own experience **during his life.** *Having seen*   1C 124
with his own eyes and *touched with his own hands,* he had no doubt that
Francis was **glorified in heaven by the Lord.** In order to act in confor-   1C 126
mity with Christ, whose vicar he was, after prayerful consideration
he decided to glorify him on earth by proclaiming him worthy of all
veneration. In order to certify to the whole world the glorification of
this most holy man, he had the known miracles recorded and attested to by appropriate witness. These he submitted to the examina-
tion of those cardinals who seemed less favorable to his cause. This
material was examined carefully and approved by all. He decreed,   1C 126
with the unanimous **advice** and assent **of** his **brothers and of all the**   LJS 74
prelates who were then in the curia, that he should be canonized. He
came **personally** to the city of Assisi **in the one thousandth, two**   1C 126; LJS 74
hundredth, twenty-eighth year of the Incarnation of the Lord, on
the seventeenth day of the calends of August, a Sunday, and en-
rolled the blessed father **in the catalog of the saints, in a great and**
solemn ceremony that would be too long to describe.

1 Jn 1:1 (margin)

[8]In the year of one thousand, two hundred and thirty, **when the**   LJS 75
brothers had assembled **to celebrate a general chapter** at Assisi, his
body, dedicated to God, **was translated on the eighth of the calends**   LJS 76
of June to the basilica constructed in his honor.

While that sacred treasure was being carried,
marked with the seal of the Most High King,
He whose likeness he bore
deigned to perform many miracles,
Sg 1:3   so that through his saving *fragrance*

the faithful in their love
might *be drawn to run after* Christ.
It is truly fitting
that *the blessed bones* of one who,   Sir 46:14
through the grace of contemplation,
was pleasing to God, beloved by Him in life,
and borne by Him into paradise
like Enoch,   Gn 5:24
and of one who,
through the zeal of love,
was snatched up into heaven in a fiery chariot   2 Kgs 2:11
like Elijah,
that these blessed bones,
already blossoming among those *heavenly flowers*   Sir 50:8
of the garden of an eternal spring,
should flower again   Sir 46:14
with a wonderful permeating fragrance
from their place of rest.

LJS 76   ⁹**Just as** that blessed man
had shone in his life with **marvelous** signs of virtue,
so from the day of his passing until the present,
in different parts of the world,
he shines with outstanding examples of **miracles**
through the divine power that glorifies him.
Remedies for all sicknesses, necessities, and dangers
are conferred
through his merits
on the blind and the deaf,
the mute and the crippled,
the paralytic and the dropsical,
the possessed and the leper,
the shipwrecked and the captive.
But also many dead are miraculously brought back to life
through him.
Thus the magnificence
of the power of the Most High   Lk 1:35
doing wonders for his saint   Ps 4:3
shines forth to the faithful.
To Him be honor and glory   Rom 16:27
for endless *ages of ages.*

Amen.

HERE ENDS THE LIFE OF BLESSED FRANCIS.

HERE BEGIN SOME OF THE MIRACLES
SHOWN AFTER HIS DEATH

Chapter I
IN THE FIRST PLACE
THE POWER OF THE SACRED STIGMATA

¹To the honor of almighty God
and the glory of our Blessed Father Francis,
as I begin to write down
some of the approved miracles
worked by our Blessed Father
after his glorification in heaven,
it seems to me that I ought to begin by that one
which manifests most clearly the power of Jesus' cross
and by which its glory is newly shown forth.
For *the new man,* Francis,
became famous for a new and stupendous miracle.
By a singular privilege, not granted in previous ages,
he appeared marked,
adorned with the sacred stigmata,
and *conformed in this body of death*
to the body of the Crucified.
Whatever human speech can say about this will be less than the
praise it deserves.
Indeed, all the striving of the *man of God,*
whether in public or in private,
revolved around the cross of the Lord.
So that the mark of the cross
stamped on his heart at the beginning of his conversion
might mark his body externally
he enclosed himself in the cross itself
when he put on the habit of a penitent,
bearing the image of the cross.
Just as, internally, his mind *had put on* the crucified Lord,
so, externally, his body also put on the arms of the cross;
and, in the sign by which God had vanquished the
powers of the air
his army would battle for the Lord.^a

Eph 4:24

3C 2

Phil 3:10, 21; Rom 7:24

1 Sm 9:6

1C 90

Gal 3:27

---

a. The term *arma crucis* could mean both "the armor of the Cross" and "the insignia of the Cross," as in
the coat of arms on a shield. Both senses fit the context, and both were probably intended by
Bonaventure.

From the very first moment
in which he began to do battle for the Crucified,
the mysteries of the cross began to shine forth in him
in manifold and diverse ways,
as will be clear to anyone who considers the events of his life.
For by the sevenfold apparitions of the Lord's cross
which he experienced,
he became an image of the Crucified in his thoughts,
in his feelings and in his actions,
being transformed by his ecstatic love of Christ.
The mercy of the Supreme King toward those who love Him,
something beyond anything humans can imagine,
stamped the banner of His cross upon his body,
**that one who so wonderfully excelled in love of the cross
should also wonderfully become a wonder in honor of the cross.**

3C 3

²The unassailable certainty of this stunning miracle is supported
not only by the witness
—which is in every way *worthy of our trust*—   Ps 92:5
of those who *saw these wounds, and touched them,*   Lk 24:39
but also by the wondrous apparitions and miracles
which have shone forth after his death
to drive away **every cloud** from our **minds.**

1C 101

Indeed, before he had inscribed this standard-bearer of the cross in the catalog of the saints, the Lord Pope Gregory the Ninth, of happy memory (about whom this holy man had prophetically foretold that he would be raised up to the apostolic dignity) carried a certain scruple of doubt in his heart about whether he had really received a wound in his side. But one night—as that blessed pontiff himself used to tell with tears in his eyes—blessed Francis *appeared to*   Mt 1:20; 2:13,19
him in a dream with a certain show of sternness in his face. Reproving him for his inner uncertainty, blessed Francis raised up his right arm, uncovered the wound on his side, and asked him for a vial in which to gather the spurting blood that flowed from it. In the dream the Supreme Pontiff brought him the vial requested, and it seemed to be filled to the brim with the blood which flowed abundantly out of the side. From that day he began to feel such devotion towards this sacred miracle, and to burn with such a zeal for it, that he would not allow anyone to obscure these signs with arrogant presumption without striking him with a severe rebuke.[a]

---

a. Three declarations of Gregory IX, promulgated in 1237, praise the Stigmata of Francis, and defend their genuineness against those who attacked it. The texts of these declarations are in BFr I, 211-214.

[3]A certain brother, Lesser by Order, preacher by office, and a man of outstanding virtue and reputation, was firmly convinced of the holy stigmata. But, as he tried to examine the reason for this miracle by the light of human understanding, he began to be irritated by a scruple of doubt. As he struggled for many days over these questionings, which grew stronger as he turned them over in his mind, one night, as he slept, Saint Francis appeared to him with muddy feet, humbly stern, and patiently irritated. And he spoke, "Why all these conflicting struggles in you? Why these filthy doubts? *See my hands* and my feet!" He saw the pierced hands, but he did not see the stigmata on the muddy feet. "Remove the mud from my feet," he said, "and examine *the place of the nails.*" As the brother devoutly took hold of the feet, it seemed to him the mud washed away, and *he touched with* his *hands the places of the nails*. Then suddenly, as the brother awoke, he was flooded with tears, and he cleansed himself of his earlier muddy feelings both with the flow of his tears and by public confession.

[4]In the city of Rome a certain matron of upright life and noble family chose Saint Francis for her advocate, and kept his image *in the secluded chamber*, where she prayed to the Father in secret. One day as she gave herself to prayer, she noticed that the Saint's image did not show the sacred marks of the stigmata. She was very sad and surprised. No wonder they were not in the painting: the painter left them out! For several days she wondered anxiously about the reason for this lack, when suddenly, one day those wonderful signs appeared in the picture, just as they are usually painted in other images of the Saint. The woman, shaken, quickly called her daughter, who was devoted to God, inquiring whether the image before then had been without the stigmata. The daughter affirmed and swore that before it had been without the stigmata, but now truly appeared with the stigmata. But, since the human mind sometimes stumbles over itself, and calls the truth into doubt, harmful doubts again entered the woman's heart: perhaps the image had those marks from the beginning. So the *power of God* added a second, so that the first would not be denied. Suddenly the marks disappeared, and the image remained denuded of those privileged signs. Thus the second sign became proof of the first.

Jn 20:27

Jn 20:25

1 Jn 1:1

Jdt 8:5

Mt 6:6

Acts 8:10

3C 10

3C 8

3C 9

3C 11   ⁵In the city of Llerda^a in Catalonia a certain man called Juan, who was devoted to blessed Francis, happened to pass by one evening on the road where there was concealed a deadly ambush—not for him, actually, for he harbored no hostilities, but for another man who looked like him and who often was in his company. One of the men who lay in ambush leaped out of hiding and, taking him for his enemy, stabbed him with deadly blows, wounding him repeatedly, so there was no hope of his recovery. Indeed, the first blow he struck practically lopped off the man's arm and shoulder, and another thrust just below the man's nipple left such a gaping wound that his breath came out through the opening strongly enough to put out the flames of six candles at once.

3C 12   The physicians pronounced his healing to be impossible, for gangrene had begun to set in his wounds, giving out such an unbearable stench that even his own wife could not bear it. So, since he was beyond all human aid, he turned with all possible devotion to beg the protection of the blessed Father Francis, on whom (as well as on the blessed Virgin) he had called with great trust even in the middle of the ambush. And behold, as the poor man lay all alone on his bed, unable to sleep and moaning Francis' name over and over, it seemed to him that someone dressed in the habit of a Lesser Brother came in through the window and approached him. This person *called him by name* and said: "Since you have placed your trust in me, behold, the Lord will deliver you." When the wounded man asked him who he was, he answered that he was Francis. And as soon as he said this, he approached the man's wounds, undid the bandages, and seemed to anoint all the wounds with an ointment. No sooner did he feel the gentle touch of those sacred hands, which had the capacity to heal by the power of the Savior's stigmata, than the gangrene was driven out, the flesh was restored and the wounds were closed, so that he was once again in perfect health. After doing this, the blessed Father disappeared. The man, feeling himself healed, burst out exultantly into shouts of praise to God and Saint Francis, and cried out for his wife. She hurried in at a run, and, as she saw the man standing up whom she had expected to bury the next day, she was utterly

Is 40:26

---

a. A cathedral city and capital of the province of the same name; also known by the Castilian name of Lérida. There are significant differences between this miracle account and that in 3C 11-13. It is possible that two similar events may be involved. While both miracles take place in Spain, in 3C the event occurs "in the kingdom of Castile;" here it takes place in Catalonia. The nature and location of the victim's deadly wounds in both accounts are carefully described, but differ completely, as do the circumstances of his cure. However, if the accounts describe two different events, a certain amount of contamination must have affected the narratives early on, since the words of the cured man in 3C fit better with Bonaventure's narrative here. Cf. also AF III, 191-3 for another allusion to this miracle, and where the man is further identified as "Ioannes de Castris."

terrified and stunned, so that by her screams she gathered the whole neighborhood.

The people of the household hurried in, and tried to force him back into bed, thinking he was in delirium, while he fought them off, insisting that he was cured, and showing them that this was so. At this they were stupefied, **struck with such amazement that they all seemed out of their minds. They thought what they were seeing a fantastic vision,** since they saw the man who just a while ago had been mangled with frightful wounds, and practically withered away, now standing before them in the pink of health and in high spirits. **But the one who was healed said, "Do not be afraid! Do not believe that what you see is false, because Saint Francis has just left this place and has cured me completely of every wound by the touch of those sacred hands."** As the news of this miracle spread, the whole town hastened there. Seeing the power of blessed Francis's stigmata by means of such an obvious miracle, they were at the same time filled with wonder and with joy, and extolled **Christ's standard bearer** with loud cries of praise.

3C 13

3C 149

It was fitting indeed that the blessed Father,
now already dead in the flesh, and living with Christ,
should give health to a mortally wounded man
by the wonderful manifestation of his presence
and the gentle touch of his sacred hands,
since *he bore upon his body the brand marks*
of the One who,
by His merciful death and wondrous resurrection,
had healed the human race
—which had been wounded and *left half alive*—
healing us by the power of His wounds.

Gal 6:17

Lk 10:30

⁶**In Potenza, a city of Apulia, there was a cleric named Ruggero,** an honorable man and a canon of its major church. He was weakened by illness, and one day he entered a church to pray. In the church there was a painted image of blessed Francis, showing the glorious stigmata. He began to doubt that exalted miracle, thinking it was an altogether unprecedented and impossible thing. As, inwardly, his wounded mind **thought useless things, he instantly** felt himself **struck** painfully **in the palm of his left hand** under his glove **as he heard the noise** of a shot, like that **of an arrow from a bow. Instantly, as he was injured by the wound and stunned by the noise, he took off the glove from his hand,** to verify by sight what he sensed through touch and hearing. **Though there had previously**

3C 6

2 Mc 14:45

been no mark in his palm, he now saw a wound in mid-hand, like that from the shot of an arrow. So much heat was coming from it that he thought he would pass out because of it. What a wonder! There was no mark on the glove, so the pain of the hidden wound inflicted on him corresponded to the hidden wound of his heart. [7]He cried out and roared, afflicted with severe pain for two days, and unveiled his unbelieving heart to all. He declared that he believed that the sacred stigmata were truly in Saint Francis, and swore to affirm that all shadow of doubt was gone. He humbly prayed *the holy one of God* to come to his aid through his sacred stigmata, and he seasoned his many prayers with an abundance of tears. Amazing! His unbelief discarded, bodily healing followed the healing of the spirit: all the pain calmed, the fever cooled, and no sign of the wound remained. Everything worked in such a way that the hidden illness of the spirit was by God's mercy healed by means of a manifest cautery of the flesh and, as the spirit was healed, the flesh was at the same time also cured. He became a man humble before God, devoted to the saint, and subject in lasting friendship to the brothers of the Order. The miraculous nature of this incident was attested by a signed oath, fully corroborated by a document bearing the seal of the bishop, by which the news of it has come to us.

Concerning the sacred stigmata
let there be no room for ambiguity;
let *no one's eye* be clouded
because God *is good*;
as if the granting of such a gift
were incompatible with the outpouring of everlasting goodness!
If only *the many members* were joined
in that same seraphic love *to Christ their head!*
If only they were to be found worthy of such *armor* in a similar battle,
and be raised to the same glory in the Kingdom!
No one of sane mind would not attribute this to the glory of Christ.[a]

Mk 1:24

Mt 20:15

1 Cor 12:12

Eph 1:22

Eph 6:11

Rv 1:9

Mk 5:15

Chapter II
THE DEAD RAISED TO LIFE

3C 40

Jos 23:14

[1]There was a woman in Monte Marano near Benevento who clung to Saint Francis with special devotion, and she went *the way*

---

a. The meaning of this obscure passage seems to be: there is no need to be shocked that God should allow a human being to bear the wounds of Christ, since the members of the Body are one with Christ their Head, and will share in His glory.

of all flesh. The clergy came at night with their psalters to sing the wake and vigils. Suddenly, in the sight of all, the woman sat up in bed and called to one of them, a priest who was her godfather, "I want to confess, Father, hear my sin! I have indeed died, and was destined for a harsh prison because I had never confessed the sin I will reveal to you. But Saint Francis prayed for me as I served him with a devout spirit while I was alive. I have now been permitted to return to my body so that after confessing my sin I might merit eternal life. So now, as all of you watch, after I reveal that to you I will hurry off to my promised rest." She then shakily confessed to the shaken priest, and after receiving absolution, composed her-self peacefully on the bed and happily *fell asleep in the Lord.*

Acts 7:60

²In the village of Pomarico, in the mountains of Apulia, a mother and father had an only daughter, tender of age and tenderly loved. When she became seriously ill and close to death, her parents considered themselves dead with her, as they did not expect any future offspring. Relatives and friends gathered for a very sad fu-neral. The unhappy mother lay grief stricken, and the depth of her sorrow kept her from noticing what was going on. In the mean-time, Saint Francis with one companion kindly appeared to visit the desolate woman, whom he knew was devoted to him, and spoke these pious words, "*Do not weep,* for the quenched light of your lamp, which you mourn, will be restored to you through my in-tercession!" The woman jumped up immediately, and told every-one what Saint Francis had told her, and would not allow the body of the deceased to be removed, but with great faith, invoking the name of Saint Francis, took hold of her dead daughter, and lifted her up safe and sound, to the wonder of all the bystanders.

3C 46

Lk 7:13

³The brothers of Nocera [Umbra] asked a man named Peter for a certain cart that they needed for a short time. He foolishly replied by hurling insults at them in place of what they asked, and for the alms requested in honor of Saint Francis he spat out blasphemy at his name. The man immediately regretted his foolishness, as the fear of God came upon him, a fear that the vengeance of the Lord would follow, and it did come soon after. His firstborn son soon took sick and after a short time gave up his spirit. The unhappy fa-ther rolled about on the ground and called out to Saint Francis again and again, shouting tearfully, "*It is I who have sinned*; I spoke evil; you should have punished me personally. Give me back, dear saint, the one you took from this wicked blasphemer, for now I have repented. I surrender myself to you; I promise you lasting ser-vice, and will always offer to Christ a devout *sacrifice of praise* in honor

3C 43

2 Sm 24:17

Ps 50:14

of your name." **Amazing! At these words the boy arose, called for a halt to the wailing, and said that as he was dying, he was led** forth from his body, led along **by blessed Francis, and led back** by him.

3C 42

[4]**The barely seven-year-old son of a notary of the city of Rome wanted in his childish way to follow his mother who was going to the church of San Marco.** Forced by his mother to stay at home, he threw himself from the window of the building and, shaking with a last tremor, he immediately breathed his last. **The mother had not gone far, and the sound of someone falling made her suspect the fall of her treasure. She quickly** turned back and discovered her son taken from her by that miserable fall. **She turned avenging hands on herself; and with her cries of anguish moved the neighbors to tears.** A certain **brother named Rao, of the Order of Lesser Brothers, was on his way to preach there. He approached the boy and, full of faith, spoke to the father. "Do you believe that Francis, the saint of God, is able to raise your son** *from the dead* **because of the love he al-** Acts 17:31 ways had for Christ, who was crucified to give life back to all?" The father replied that he firmly believed it and faithfully confessed that he would forever be the servant of the saint, if only he could receive such a great favor through his merits. **That brother knelt with his companion in prayer** and urged the others present there **to pray. With that the boy began to yawn a little, to open his eyes, lift his arms and sit up. In the sight of all, the boy, unharmed, immediately began walking, restored to life** and health through the amazing power of the Saint.

3C 44

[5]**In the city of Capua a lad was playing carelessly with his friends on the bank of the river Volturno. From the bank of the river he fell into the deep. The** *force of the river* **quickly swallowed him up** Ps 46:5 **and buried him, dead, beneath the sand. The children who had been playing near the river with him shouted, and a large crowd** gathered there. **All the people were humbly and devoutly invoking the merits of blessed Francis,** that he might look upon the faith of the boy's parents, who had a great devotion to him, and save their child from the danger of death. **Some distance away a swimmer heard their cries and approached them.** After some searching, and having **invoked** the help of blessed Francis, he found the place where mud had covered over the boy's cadaver like a tomb. He dug and dragged him out, and was saddened to find him dead. Even though the crowd saw that the youth was dead, they still wept and cried out, "Saint Francis, give the father back his child!" The same phrase was also said by the Jews who had come, moved by natural piety: "Saint Francis, give the father back his child!" The boy got

up immediately, unharmed, as all marveled and rejoiced, and begged to be led to the church of blessed Francis, so that he could give thanks to him devoutly, because he knew it was thanks to his power that he had been wondrously revived.

[6]In the city of Sessa, in the neighborhood called "Le Colonne," a house suddenly fell, trapping a youth and instantly killing him. Men and women heard the crash of the house and came running from all around. Raising beams and stones here and there, they succeeded in restoring the dead son to his poor mother. She sobbed bitterly, and cried out in a pain-filled voice, "Saint Francis, Saint Francis, give me back my son!" She was not alone: all there implored the help of the blessed father. But since there was no sign of speech or feeling, they placed the cadaver on a bed, waiting to bury him the following day. The mother however, having faith in the Lord through the merits of His saint, made a vow to cover the altar of blessed Francis with a new altar cloth, if he would bring her son back to life. About the hour of midnight the young man began to yawn; warmth returned to his limbs; and he got up alive and well and burst into shouts of praise, and urged the clergy and all the people gathered there to give praise and thanks to God and to blessed Francis with joyful hearts.

3C 45

[7]In Sicily, a young man named Gerlandino, from Ragusa, went out with his parents to the vineyard at harvest time. He crawled into a wine vat beneath the press to fill some skins. The wooden supports shifted, and the huge stones instantly struck his skull a lethal blow. The father quickly hurried over to his son, but he could not help him; he left him under the weight where it had fallen. Other vineyard workers rushed to the scene when they heard the loud wail and cry. Filled with great sorrow for the boy's father, they pulled the young man from the ruin already dead. But the father fell at the feet of Jesus, and humbly prayed that he give him back his only son through the merits of Saint Francis, whose solemnity was coming soon. He groaned his prayers, he promised works of piety, and promised to visit the holy man's body with his son, if he were raised from the dead. What a wonderful thing! Suddenly the boy whose body had been completely crushed stood up rejoicing in front of everyone, restored to life and perfect health. He told them to stop crying, and declared that he had been brought back to life through the help of Saint Francis.

3C 47

[8]He raised up another dead person in Germany: the Lord Pope Gregory recounted this event in his apostolic letter on the occasion of the translation of the Saint. Through it he informed and gladdened

3C 48

all the brothers who had gathered for the translation and the chapter. I did not write the account of this miracle because I did not know of it, believing that papal testimony is a proof that surpasses any other assertion.[a]

Chapter III
THOSE HE DELIVERED FROM THE DANGER OF DEATH

3C 49

[1]In the vicinity of the City **a nobleman named Rodolfo and his wife**, who was devoted to God, **had given hospitality to Lesser Brothers** as much out of hospitality as out of love and **reverence** for blessed **Francis**. That same **night the** castle **guard was sleeping at the very top of the tower. He lay upon a pile of wood on the top edge of the wall.** Its fastening came loose, **and he fell onto the roof of the palace, and** then **to the ground. The loud crash** of his fall **awoke the whole family and,** learning of the guard's fall, the lord and lady of the castle, together with the brothers, **ran outside**. But the one who had fallen from that height was so **deeply asleep that he did not wake, either at his double fall nor at the loud noise** of the family running to him and shouting. Finally he was awakened **by the hands** of those pushing and pulling him, and began to complain about being **deprived of pleasant rest,** declaring that **he had been sleeping sweetly in the arms of blessed Francis. When he learned** from the others about his fall, and he saw himself on the ground, not up above where he was lying, he was amazed that he had not felt what had happened. **He** then **promised** before everyone there to do penance out of reverence for God and blessed **Francis**.

3C 50

[2]**In the town of Pofi, located in Campagna, a priest named Tommaso went with many others to repair a mill belonging to his church. He carelessly walked along the edge of the channel, where there was a deep gorge** filled with **rapidly flowing** water, and suddenly fell and was thrust against the wooden blades whose force turned the mill. There he remained, pinned against the wood, unable to move at all. Because he was lying face down, the flow of water flooded his mouth. **But with his heart he called plaintively on Saint Francis,** since he could not do so with his voice. He remained there a long time, and his companions despaired of his life. With a struggle they turned the mill in reverse, and they saw the trembling priest thrown into the water's current. Suddenly there ap-

---

a. Oddly enough, Bonaventure's text here copies verbatim Thomas of Celano's personal excuse for not writing an account of this miracle.

peared a Lesser Brother in a shining tunic bound with a cord. With great gentleness he drew him by the arm out of the water, and said, "I am Francis, the one you called." The man was stunned to be freed in this way and wanted to kiss his footprints. He ran here and there, anxiously questioning his companions, "Where is he? Where did the saint go? Which way did he go?" But they were terrified: they *fell prostrate to the ground*, extolling the glorious deeds of the great God and the powerful merits of His humble servant.

Nm 14:5

³Some young people from the town of Celano went out together to cut grass in some fields where an old well lay hidden, its opening covered with plant growth, holding water with a depth of almost four paces. While the children ran about, each going a different direction, one accidentally fell into the well. As the deep pit was swallowing his body, his soul's spirit rose up to call on the aid of blessed Francis, calling out with faith and confidence even as he was falling, "Saint Francis, help me!" The others *turned around this way and that*, and when they noticed that the other *boy was missing* they went in search of him, shouting and crying. When they discovered that he had fallen into the well, they ran crying back to the town, explained what had happened and begged for help. They returned with a large crowd of people, and a man was lowered by a rope into the well. He found the boy floating on the surface of the water totally unharmed. When the boy was lifted out of the well, the boy said to all the bystanders, "When I suddenly fell, I called for Saint Francis's protection, and he instantly arrived while I was still falling. He reached out his hand and gently held me and did not leave until, along with you, he pulled me from the well."

1 Kgs 18:45

Gn 37:30

3C 51

⁴While the Lord Bishop of Ostia, who later became the Supreme Pontiff Alexander,[a] was preaching in the Church of Saint Francis at Assisi in the presence of the Roman curia, a large and heavy stone carelessly left above the raised stone pulpit was pushed out by the strong pressure, and fell onto a woman's head. Since the bystanders assumed that she was definitely dead, with her head completely crushed, they covered her with the mantle she was wearing, intending to take the pitiful corpse out of the church when the sermon ended. She, however, commended herself with faith to Saint Francis, before whose altar she lay. And behold, when the sermon was finished, the woman rose up in the sight of everyone, unharmed, not

---

a. This miracle is not found in any of the texts of Thomas of Celano. Rinaldo dei Conti de Segni, a nephew of Gregory IX, was made Cardinal Bishop of Ostia in 1234, and elected pope as Alexander IV in 1254. As a young cleric he was privileged to see the wounds of Francis while the saint still lived, as he affirmed in a public sermon in the presence of Bonaventure (LMj XIII 8) and in the bulls *Benigna operatio* (October, 1255) and *Quia longum esset* (June, 1259).

showing the least trace of a wound. And, what is even more amazing, she had for many years and up to that very hour suffered from almost uninterrupted headaches, but now was completely freed from them, as she herself later attested.[a]

3C 54

[5]Some devout men gathered in the brothers's place at Corneto for the casting of a bell. An eight-year-old boy named Bartolomeo carried to the brothers a gift for those who were working. All of a sudden a *great wind came up and shook the house;* with great force it blew down the large, heavy door of the entrance onto the boy. It was feared that such a great weight pressing upon him had crushed him to death. He was so completely buried under its weight that nothing of him could be seen from the outside. Everyone present ran to him, calling on the strong right hand of blessed Francis. The father of the boy, however, could not move, his limbs frozen *from grief.* Vowing out loud, he offered his son to Saint Francis. Finally, the deadly weight was lifted off the boy, and there he was! The one they thought was dead appeared cheerful, like someone waking from sleep, with no sign of injury on him at all. When he reached the age of fourteen he became a Lesser Brother and later became a learned man and a famous preacher.

Jb 1:19

Is 65:14

3C 57

[6]Some men of Lentini cut a huge stone from a mountain. It was to be set over the altar of the church of blessed Francis which was soon to be consecrated. A good forty men strained to load that stone on a cart, but after several attempts the stone fell on one man and covered him like a tomb. In their mental confusion they did not know what to do: most of the men left in despair. But ten who remained plaintively invoked Saint Francis not to allow this man who was in his service to die so horribly. With renewed courage, those men then so easily lifted the stone that no one doubted that the power of Francis was involved. The man stood up, unharmed in all his limbs. What is more he recovered his clear eyesight, which earlier had been dimmed: further proof to all that the merits of blessed Francis have great power in desperate cases.

3C 58

[7]A similar incident took place at Sanseverino in the Marches of Ancona. While a very large stone, brought from Constantinople, was being transported to the basilica of blessed Francis by the efforts of many, it suddenly tipped over on top of one of those pulling it. It appeared he was not just dead, but totally crushed too, but

---

a. There is no other extant written source for this incident. Bonaventure would not have been present, since he was in Paris as a student or young professor during the whole period in which Alexander was Cardinal of Ostia, but he may have heard it from one of the friars or members of the Curia who witnessed it.

blessed **Francis** helped him, lifting the stone, and he jumped out without any injury, healthy, and unharmed.

[8]Bartolomeo, a citizen of Gaeta, was very hard at work on the construction of the church of blessed Francis. A beam, in an unsteady position, crashed down, and he was severely crushed, pinned down by the neck. Sensing that his death was imminent, and being a faithful and pious man, he asked one of the brothers for Viaticum. The brother was not able to bring it that quickly, and thinking he would die at any moment, quoted to him the words of blessed Augustine, "Believe, and you have eaten."[a] That night blessed Francis appeared to him with eleven brothers; he carried a little lamb between his breasts. He approached the bed, *called him by name,* and said, "Do not fear, Bartolomeo, because the enemy *will not prevail against you.* He wanted to keep you from my service. Here is the lamb you asked for: you have received it because of your good desire. What is more, by His power you will also obtain health in body and spirit." Then drawing his hand across the wounds, he told him to return to the work he had begun. The man got up very early the next morning, and the workers who had left him half-dead were shocked and amazed when he appeared, unharmed and happy, inspiring their spirits to love and respect for blessed Francis as much by his example as by the miracle of the Saint.

[9]A man named Niccolò from the town of Ceprano one day *fell into the hands* of cruel enemies. With beastly cruelty they struck him with blow upon blow, and did not stop their cruelty until they thought him dead or soon to die. When the first blows fell on him, Niccolò called out in a loud voice, "Help me, Saint Francis! Save me, Saint Francis!" Many heard his voice from far away even though they could not help him. When he had been carried home drenched with his own blood, he confidently affirmed that *he would not see death* as a result of those wounds, and that he did not feel any pain, because Saint Francis had come to his aid and begged the Lord that he be allowed *to do penance.* So, cleansed of blood and contrary to any human hope, he was rescued.

[10]The son of a nobleman of Castel San Gimigniano suffered from a severe illness; all hope was abandoned and he seemed near the end. A stream of blood trickled from his eyes, like the flow of blood from the severed vein of an arm. Other signs of death's approach appeared in the rest of his body, so he was considered as good as dead. Because of the weakness of his breathing and strength,

Marginal references: Gn 4:17 — Jer 1:19 — Jgs 15:18 — Lk 2:26 — Mk 6:12; 3C 59 — 3C 56 — 3C 61

---

a. Cf. Augustine, *In Joh. Evang.* 25:12, (PL 35, 1602).

lack of feeling or movement, he seemed already completely gone. His friends and family, as is usual, gathered for mourning and all that remained was the burial. His father, having faith in the Lord, rushed off to the church of blessed Francis, which had been built in that same town. With a cord hanging around his neck he humbly *threw himself on the ground*. He *made a vow* and *prayed repeatedly*. With sighs and groans, he gained Saint Francis as his patron with Christ. As the father returned quickly to his son and found him restored to health, his *mourning turned into joy*.

Jdt 10:23; 1 Sm 1:11; Jb 40:27

Lam 5:15

[11]*The Lord worked* similar things by the merits of the saint for a girl in the town of Tamarit in Catalonia, and for another **girl of Ancona**. Both of them were **at their last breath** because of grave illness, but **blessed Francis**, whom their parents had faithfully invoked, restored them to perfect health at once.

3C 52

Prv 16:4

[12]A cleric from Vicalvi named Matteo *drank* some *deadly poison*. He was so afflicted that he could not speak at all; he awaited only his end. Even a priest who encouraged him to confess could not pry a single word from him. But he humbly prayed to Christ *in his heart*, to deliver him from the jaws of death through the merits of blessed Francis. Soon after, strengthened by the Lord, he spoke out the name of blessed Francis with faithful devotion, and with witnesses present, he vomited up the poison, and gave thanks to his deliverer.

3C 187

Mk 16:18

Ps 14:1

Chapter IV
THOSE DELIVERED FROM SHIPWRECK

3C 81

[1]Some sailors were placed in grave danger at sea when a fierce storm came up while they were ten miles out from the port of Barletta. Anxious for their lives, they let down the anchors. But the *stormy wind* swelled the sea more violently, breaking the ropes and releasing the anchors. They were tossed about the sea on an unsteady and uncertain course. Finally at God's pleasure the sea was calmed, and they prepared with all their strength to recover their anchors, whose ropes were floating on the surface. As they were unable to achieve this by their own efforts they invoked the help of many saints and were worn down by their exertion, but could not recover even one after a whole day. There was one sailor named Perfetto, though he was anything but perfect in his behavior, who scoffed and said to his companions, "Look, you have invoked the aid of all the saints, and as you see not one of them has helped.

Ps 11:6

Let's call that Francis. He's a new saint; let him somehow **dive into the sea and get our anchors back.**" The others agreed, seriously, not scoffing, with Perfetto's suggestion. Rebuking his scoffing words, by common agreement **they made a vow** with the saint. At that very moment the anchors were suddenly floating on the water with no support, as if the nature of iron had been changed into the lightness of wood.

²**A pilgrim, feeble in body,** from the symptoms of an acute fever he had recently suffered, was traveling from regions overseas[a] on board a ship. This man also had a special feeling of devotion for blessed Francis, and had chosen him as his advocate before the heavenly King. As he was not completely free of his illness, he was tormented by a burning thirst. As the water had run out, he began to shout loudly, "Go confidently, pour me a cup! Blessed Francis has filled my flask with water!" What a wonder! The flask that had been left *void and empty* they now found filled with water. Some days later a storm came up and the boat was being *swamped by the waves* and shaken by strong winds so that they feared they would be shipwrecked. That same sick man suddenly began to shout around the ship, "Get up, everyone, come to meet blessed Francis. He is here to save us!" And with a loud voice and tears he *bowed down to worship.* As soon as he had seen the saint the sick man recovered his full health; and, on *the sea, calm* ensued.

³**Brother Giacomo of Rieti** was crossing a river in a little boat with some other brothers. At the shore, his companions disembarked first, and he prepared to get out last. But that little craft accidentally overturned, and while the pilot swam, the brother was plunged *into the depths.* The brothers on shore with tender cries called on blessed Francis and with tearful sobs begged that he save his son. The drowning brother too, in the belly of a great whirlpool, could not call with his mouth, but called out from his heart as well as he could, imploring the aid of his pious father. See! With the help of his blessed father's presence he walked across the depths as if on dry land. He caught hold of the overturned little boat and reached the shore with it. More wonderful still, his clothes were not wet: not a drop of water clung to his tunic.

⁴**A brother named Bonaventure** was crossing a lake with two men when a side of the boat split, and, with the force of the water rushing in, he sank into the depths along with his companions and the boat. From the *pit of misery* they called on the merciful father

Gn 1:2
Mt 8:24

Jn 9:38

Mt 8:26

3C 82

Mt 18:6

3C 83

3C 86

Ps 40:3

---

a. That is, from a pilgrimage to the Holy Land. Cf. 3C 82, FA:ED II 434 a.

Francis with great faith. **Shortly the water-filled boat** floated up to the surface and, **with the saint** guiding it, safely **reached the shore with them in it.**

Similarly a **brother from Ascoli was saved by the merits of Saint Francis when he fell into a river.**

3C 84 Also **some men** and women who were in similar danger **on the Lake of Rieti** safely escaped a dangerous shipwreck in the midst of *many waters* by calling on the name of **Saint Francis.**   Ps 32:6

3C 85 ⁵**Some sailors from Ancona were caught in a violent storm and knew they were in danger of sinking. In desperation for their lives, they humbly invoked Saint Francis. A great light appeared on the ship,**[a] **and with the light a heaven-sent calm,** as if the holy man, through his admirable power, could *command the winds and the sea.*   Mt 8:26

> I do not believe it possible to tell one by one
> all the **outstanding miracles**
> by which this holy Father has been and is still **glorified**
> on the sea,
> or how often he has brought help
> to those in desperate straits there.
> But it is not surprising
> that authority over the waters has been granted to him
> now reigning in heaven,
> when, even while he was in this mortal life,
> all earthly creatures served him marvelously,
> restored to their original condition.[b]

Chapter V
THOSE SET FREE FROM CHAINS AND IMPRISONMENT

3C 88 ¹**In Romania**[c] **it happened that a Greek servant of a certain lord was falsely accused of theft. His lord ordered him to be shut in a narrow prison and heavily chained. The lady of the household,** however, *had pity on the servant,* for she had no doubt that he was in-   Mt 18:27
nocent of the crime of which he stood accused, and with **devout prayers** entreated her husband **to free him. But her husband remained firm and rejected her request. The lady turned humbly to**

---

a. 3C 85 has "on the sea" (*in mari*).
b. That is, to the harmony of creation before human sin. Cf. 1C 61, FA:ED I 235-36; 2C 166, FA:ED II 254-55;
c. The "Empire of Romania," (1204-1261) established in parts of Greece (Macedonia, Thrace, and coastal regions) taken by Latin crusaders, whose subjects referred to themselves as "Romans" (*Romaioi*).

Saint Francis and, by a vow, commended the innocent man to his compassion. Quickly the helper of the afflicted was present, and mercifully *visited the imprisoned* man. He loosened the chains, broke open the jail, took the innocent man by the hand, and led him out. "I am the one to whom your mistress devoutly commended you," he said. The man shook with fear as he wandered at the edge of a precipice, looking for a way to descend from the very high cliff. Suddenly he found himself on level ground through the power of his deliverer. He went back to his lady and told her his miraculous story, all in order. He inspired his devout lady to the even greater love for Christ and reverence for his servant Francis.

[2]In Massa San Pietro[a] a poor fellow owed a certain knight a sum of money. Since he had no means of paying the debt, the knight had him confined as a debtor. He humbly asked for mercy and, interjecting prayers, requested a deferral for love of Saint Francis. The knight haughtily scorned his prayers; he stupidly mocked the love of the saint as something stupid. He obstinately replied, "I will lock you up in such a place and *put you in* such a *prison* that neither Francis nor anyone else will be able to help you." And he attempted to do what he said. He found a dark prison and threw the chained man into it. A short time later Saint Francis arrived and broke open the prison; he shattered the man's leg-irons and led him to his own home unharmed.

> Thus the strength of Francis plundered the proud knight
> and *delivered from evil*
> the captive who had made himself his subject,
> and turned the knight's impudence into meekness
> by an amazing miracle.

[3]Alberto of Arezzo was being held tightly in chains for debts unjustly charged to him. He humbly placed his innocence before Saint Francis. He greatly loved the Order of the Lesser Brothers and venerated Francis with special affection among all the saints. His creditor had made the blasphemous statement that neither God nor Francis would be *able to deliver him from his hands*. On the vigil of the feast of Saint Francis, the bound man had eaten nothing, but out of love for the saint had given his meal to someone in need. As night fell, Saint Francis appeared to him during his vigil.[b] At the

Mt 25:36,42

3C 89

Gn 41:10

Mt 6:13; 2 Tm 4:18

3C 91

Dn 3:17

---

a. Also known as Massa Trabaria.

b. Fasting and keeping night-vigil were common observances on the eve of great feasts; Franciscan tertiaries fasted on the eve of Saint Francis as late as the mid-twentieth century.

saint's entry, the *chains fell from his hands* and his feet. The doors *opened by themselves* and the boards on the roof fell down; the man got away free and returned to his home. From then on he kept his vow to fast on the vigil of Saint Francis and, as a sign of his increasing devotion, each year to add an extra ounce to the candle he usually offered annually.

[3C 93] [4]When the Lord Pope Gregory IX was occupying the See of blessed Peter there arose an inevitable persecution of heretics. A certain Pietro from Alife was among those accused of heresy, and he was arrested in Rome. By order of the same Pontiff he was handed over to the bishop of Tivoli for safekeeping. The bishop took him, under threat of losing episcopal office, and so that he would not escape, bound him in leg irons and had him confined in a dark jail cell, providing him food *by weight* and drink *by measure*. But that man, with much weeping and praying, began to call on blessed Francis to take pity on him, as he had heard that the vigil of his solemnity was near. And since in purity of faith he had renounced every error of perverse heresy, and clung wholeheartedly to Christ's most faithful servant Francis, he merited to be heard by God through the intercession of blessed Francis's merits. So, on the night before his feast, around dusk, blessed Francis mercifully came down into the prison, called him by name, and ordered him to stand up. The man asked *in great fear* who was calling him, and heard that it was blessed Francis. He saw the chains on his feet break and fall suddenly to the ground by the powerful presence of the holy man; he saw the timbers of the cell opened with their nails sprung outward: there was a clear path for his escape. But once free, he was so astounded that he did not know enough to flee. Instead, he let out a cry and frightened all the guards. When the bishop was told that the man had been freed from his chains, once he understood what had happened, that pontiff devoutly went to the prison, and openly *acknowledging the power of God*, he there *worshiped the Lord*. The chains were sent to the Lord Pope and the Cardinals: on *seeing what had happened*, with much wonder *they blessed God*.

[3C 94] [5]Guidalotto of San Gimignano was falsely accused of poisoning a man, and further of intending to kill the man's son and the whole family with the same deadly means. He was arrested by the local podestà, who had him heavily chained and confined in a tower. But since he knew that he was innocent, he placed his trust in the Lord, and committed the defense of his cause to the patronage of blessed Francis. The podestà thought about what punishment he

Margin references:
Acts 12:7
Acts 12:10
Ez 4:16
1 Chr 10:4
Mk 5:30; Gn 24:26
Lk 23:47; Dn 13:60

could inflict on him, and through torture to make him confess his crime. He was to be lead to punishment in the morning, but that night he was visited by the presence of Saint Francis. He was surrounded by an immense bright light, and he remained in its light until morning, *filled with joy* and great confidence, sure of being rescued. In the morning the executioners arrived, took him out of the cell, and suspended him from a revolving rack, weighing him down with weights of iron. Several times he was let down and raised up again, so that with one torment after another he would be forced more quickly to confess his crime. But the man's face seemed joyful in an innocent way, showing no sign of sorrow in his pain. Then a rather large fire was lit beneath the man, but not a hair of his head was harmed even though his head hung toward the ground. Finally, burning oil was poured over him, but by the power of the patron to whom he had entrusted his defense, he overcame all these things. Therefore he was set free, and went away unharmed.

Ps 126:20

Chapter VI
ON THOSE WHO WERE DELIVERED FROM THE DANGERS OF CHILDBIRTH

[1]A certain countess of Slavonia, illustrious in nobility and a friend of goodness, had an ardent devotion to Saint Francis and a sincere affection for the brothers. She suffered severe pains at the time of childbirth; she was so afflicted with pain that it appeared that the expected birth of the child would mean the demise of the mother. She seemed incapable of bringing the child into life unless she departed from life; and, by this effort, not to give birth but to perish. But the fame of blessed Francis, his *glory and might*, sustained her heart. Her faith aroused, her devotion kindled, she turned to the effective helper, the trusted friend, the comforter of those devoted to him, the refuge of the afflicted. "Saint Francis," she said, *"all my bones* cry out to your mercy, and I vow in spirit what I cannot say aloud." O the speed of mercy! The end of her speaking was the end of her suffering, and the end of her labor was the beginning of giving birth. Just as soon as the pains ceased, she safely gave birth to a child. Nor did she forget her vow or run away from her promise. She had a beautiful church built and, once it was built, donated it to the brothers in honor of the saint.

3C 95

Rv 19:1

Ps 35:10

[2]A certain woman named Beatrice from the region of Rome was close to giving birth. For four days she had been carrying a dead fetus in her womb. She was much distressed and beset by deadly

3C 96

pain. The dead fetus was causing the mother's death, and the abortive offspring, still not brought to light, was an obvious threat to the mother. The help of doctors proved fruitless; every human remedy *labored in vain.* Thus did the ancient curse fall heavily upon the unfortunate woman. Her *womb became a grave,* and she certainly *awaited the grave* soon. Finally, by means of messengers, she entrusted herself with great devotion to the Lesser Brothers. She humbly asked in great faith some relic of Saint Francis. By divine consent a piece of a cord was found, one that the saint had once worn. As soon as the cord was placed on the suffering woman, all her pain was relieved with ease. The dead fetus, cause of death, was released and the woman was restored to her former health.

³Giuliana, wife of a nobleman of Calvi, passed a number of years in mourning over the death of her children: she constantly mourned those unhappy events. All the children she had carried with pain, after a short time, and with even greater anguish, she had carried to the grave. So when she was four months *with child,* because of her earlier experiences, she was more concerned for the death of the offspring she had conceived than about its birth. She faithfully prayed to the blessed father Francis for the life of her unborn fetus. Then one night as she slept, a woman *appeared* to her *in a dream.* The woman carried a beautiful infant in her hands and joyfully offered him to her. But she was reluctant to accept something that she feared she would soon lose. So that woman added, "Take this child confidently; the one that Holy Francis sends to you, out of compassion for your grief, *shall surely live* and enjoy good health." The woman immediately awoke and understood from the heaven-sent vision that the help of Saint Francis was with her, and from that moment was filled with more abundant joy. She increased her prayers and offered vows for having a child, according to the promise. The time for delivery arrived and the woman *gave birth* to a son. He thrived in the vigor of youthful age and, as he had received the kindling of life through the merits of blessed Francis, he offered his parents a stimulus for more devoted affection for Christ and His saint.

The blessed father did something similar to this in the city of Tivoli. A woman had borne several daughters. She was worn out by the desire for male offspring, and groaned prayers and vows before saint Francis. The woman then conceived through his merits, and the one she had implored allowed her to bear twin boys, even though he had been asked for only one.

3C 97
3C 99

Ps 127:1

Jer 20:17

Jb 3:21,22

Mt 1:23

Mt 1:20

Ez 18:9,19

Lk 1:57

3C 98

[4]A woman was near to childbirth in Viterbo, but considered nearer to death. She had severe abdominal pains and suffered the misfortunes that befall women. As her natural strength was collapsing, and all the efforts of medicine failed, the woman called upon the name of blessed Francis. She was immediately healed and gave birth in good health. But when she got what she wanted, she forgot the favor she received, not returning it to the honor of the saint, and she *stretched out her hand* to *servile work* on his birthday.[a] Suddenly she was unable to draw back the right arm she had extended to work; it remained rigid and withered. When she tried to pull it back with the other arm, it too withered with a similar punishment. *Struck with fear* of God the woman reaffirmed the vow, and through the merits of the merciful and humble saint to whom she vowed herself again, deserved to regain the use of her limbs, which she had lost because of ingratitude and contempt.

Prv 31:20; Lv 23:7

Acts 10:4

3C 106

[5]A woman from the region of Arezzo bore the pains of labor through seven days, and was turning black. As people had despaired of her, she made a vow to blessed Francis and began calling on his aid as she was dying. But when she had made her vow, she quickly fell asleep, and *saw in a dream* blessed Francis. He spoke sweetly to her and inquired whether she recognized his face, and if she could recite that antiphon of the glorious Virgin, the *"Salve, Regina misericordiae"* in honor of the same glorious Virgin. When she answered that she recognized both, the saint said, "Start the holy antiphon, and before you finish you will safely give birth." At this cry, the woman woke up and anxiously began "Salve regina *misericordiae.*" When she reached the words *"illos misericordes oculos,"* and *"fructum,"* commemorating the fruit of the virgin's womb, she was immediately freed from all her labor pains, and gave birth to a lovely child, giving thanks to the *"Regina misericordiae,"* who through the merits of blessed Francis was kind enough to have mercy on her.

Gn 28:12

Chapter VII
THE BLIND WHO RECEIVED SIGHT

3C 116

[1]A brother named Roberto of the convent of the Lesser Brothers in Naples had been blind for many years. Excess flesh grew in his eyes and impeded the movement and use of his eyelids. Many brothers from other places had gathered there on their way to different parts of the world. Blessed father Francis, that mirror and

---

a. The *dies natalis* of a saint is the anniversary of death, "birth" into eternal life: in this case, October 4.

exemplar of holy obedience, in order to encourage them on their journey with a new miracle, cured the aforesaid brother in their presence in this way. One night the aforesaid Brother Roberto lay deathly ill and his soul had already been commended, when suddenly the blessed father appeared to him along with three brothers, perfect in holiness, Saint Anthony, Brother Agostino, and Brother Giacomo of Assisi. Just as these three had followed him perfectly in their lives, so they readily accompanied him after death. Saint Francis took a knife and cut away the excess flesh, restored his sight and snatched him from the jaws of death, saying, "Roberto, my son, the favor I have done for you is a sign to the brothers on their way to distant countries that I go before them and *guide their steps.* May they go forth joyfully and fulfill the charge of obedience with enthusiasm!"

Ps 40:3

3C 118

[2]A blind woman of Thebes in Romania, spent the vigil of Saint Francis fasting on bread and water, and was led by her husband at early dawn of the feast to the church of the Lesser Brothers. During the celebration of the Mass, at the elevation of the Body of Christ, she opened her eyes, saw clearly, and devoutly adored. In the very act of adoration she broke into a loud cry, "Thanks be to God and to his saint," she cried, "I see the Body of Christ!" All those present broke *into cries of gladness.* After the Mass the woman *returned to her home* with joy of spirit and the sight of her eyes. The woman rejoiced, indeed, not only because she had recovered the sight of bodily light, but also because, by the merits of blessed **Francis**, helped by the power of faith, the first thing that she saw was that **wonderful** sacrament which is the true and living **light** of souls.

Ps 47:2; Lk 1:56

3C 119

[3]A fourteen-year-old boy from the village of Pofi in Campania suffered a sudden attack and completely lost use of his left eye. The acuteness of the blow thrust the eye out of its socket so that it hung over the cheeks for eight days, by a loose muscle an inch long, and had nearly dried up. Cutting it off seemed the only choice when medical remedies proved hopeless. Then the boy's father turned his *whole mind* to the help of blessed Francis. The tireless helper of the afflicted did not fail the prayers of his petitioner. He marvelously returned the dried eye to its socket and former vigor with the rays of light so longed for.

Mk 12:30

3C 120

[4]In the same province, at Castro, a beam of great weight fell from a high place and crushed the skull of a priest, blinding his left eye. Flat on the ground, he began to cry out mournfully to Saint Francis, "Help me, holy father, so that I can go to your feast as I promised your brothers!" It was the vigil of the saint's feast. He quickly got

up fully recovered and broke into shouts of praise and joy. And all the bystanders who were mourning his accident were amazed and jubilant. He went to the feast and there told everyone how he had experienced the power and mercy.

⁵A man from Monte Gargano was working in his vineyard and while he was cutting wood with a blade struck his own eye and sliced it in half, so that almost half of it was hanging out. Since the danger was desperate and he despaired that human help could save him, he promised that he would fast on the feast of Saint Francis if the saint would help him. Right then the saint of God replaced the man's eye to its proper place, closed the wound and restored his earlier sight in such a way that there remained no trace of the wound.

⁶The son of a nobleman was born blind and obtained the sight he longed for through the merits of Saint Francis. He was called Illuminato,ᵃ named for the event. When he was old enough he joined the Order of blessed Francis, not ungrateful for the gift he received, and made such progress in the light of grace and virtue that he showed himself *a son of the true light* and fulfilled a holy beginning with an even holier ending.

⁷In Zancato, a village near Anagni, a knight named Gerardo had entirely lost his sight. Now it happened that two Lesser Brothers arriving from abroad sought out his home for hospitality. The whole household received them devoutly out of reverence for Saint Francis and treated them with every kindness. Giving thanks to God and their host, they went on to the brothers' place nearby. One night blessed Francis *appeared* to one of the brothers *in a dream* saying, *"Get up*, hurry with your companion to the home of your host. He received Christ and me through you. I want to repay the gift of his piety. He has become blind, which he deserves for the offenses he has not tried to wash away by confession." When the father had gone, the brother got up and hurried with his companion to carry out the command quickly. Arriving at the home of their host, the one related what he had seen *all in order*. The man was quite astonished as he confirmed the truth of all that was said. He broke out in tears, and freely made his confession. He promised amendment and, as soon as the inner man was thus renewed, he immediately regained his outer eyesight. The news of this miracle not only

Marginal references:
- 3C 122
- Jn 9:1
- 3C 123
- Jn 1:9; Eph 5:8
- 3C 117
- Mt 2:13
- Est 15:9

---

a. "Enlightened," cf. LMj XIII 4, supra 151 b.

encouraged many to reverence for the saint, but also to humble confession of their sins and to the gift of hospitality.[a]

Chapter VIII
THOSE FREED FROM VARIOUS ILLNESSES

3C 125

[1]In Città della Pieve there was a young man, a beggar who was deaf and mute *from birth*. His tongue was so short and thin that, to those who many times examined it, it seemed to be completely cut out. A man named Marco received him as a guest for God's sake. The youth, sensing the good will shown him, stayed on with him. One evening that man was dining with his spouse while the boy stood by. He said to his wife, "I would consider it the greatest miracle if blessed Francis were to give back to this boy his hearing and speech. I vow to God," he added, "that if Saint Francis in his goodness will do this, for the love of him I will support this boy as long as he lives." A marvelous promise indeed! Suddenly the boy's tongue grew, and he spoke, saying, "Glory to God and Saint Francis, who granted me speech and hearing!"

Jn 9:1

Ps 132:2

Gn 8:15

3C 109

[2]Brother Giacomo of Iseo, when he was a tender youth in his parental home, suffered a serious rupture of his body. Inspired by the heavenly Spirit, though he was young and ill he devoutly entered the Order of Saint Francis without revealing to anyone the infirmity that troubled him. It happened that when the body of blessed Francis was transferred to the place where the precious treasure of his sacred bones is now kept, this same brother was in the joyful celebrations of the translation in order to show due honor to the most

---

a. This account was inserted in the text by order of the general minister, Jerome of Ascoli, later Pope Nicholas IV. "In Assisi a man falsely accused of theft was blinded through the severity of secular justice; the knight Ottone, by means of the public executioners, put into effect the sentence of the judge Ottaviano, that the eyes of the accused should be torn out. His eyes were therefore dug out of their sockets and his optic nerves cut with a knife, and thus disfigured he was led to the altar of Saint Francis. There he implored the Saint's clemency and proclaimed his innocence of the crime of which he had been accused. And by the Saint's merits within three days he received new eyes—smaller than the ones of which he had been deprived, but no less clear in their capacity to see. This amazing miracle was attested under oath by the aforementioned knight Ottone before Lord Giacomo, abbot of San Clemente, on the authority of Lord Giacomo, bishop of Tivoli, who held an inquest on this miracle. A further witness to the miracle was Brother Guglielmo of Rome, who was obliged to tell the truth as he knew it by Brother Jerome, minister general of the Order of Lesser Brothers, under obedience and under pain of excommunication. Being thus compelled, he affirmed this in the presence of many provincial ministers of the same Order, and of other brothers of great merit. While he was still a layman, he had seen the man when he still had his eyes, and later had seen him as his eyes were being torn out — indeed, he himself out of curiosity had pushed around the eyes of the blinded man with a stick as they lay on the ground — and later on had seen the same man seeing very clearly with the new eyes he had received by divine power." Jerome also wrote a letter to the friars of Assisi about this miracle. See *The Chronicle of the Twenty-four General Ministers*, in AF III, 358, note 1.

holy body of the father who was already glorified.[a] **Approaching the tomb in which the** sacred bones were placed, out of devotion of spirit he embraced the holy grave. **His inner parts suddenly and wonderfully returned to their proper place and he felt himself healed. He laid aside his truss and was from then on totally free of his pain.**

Through the mercy of God and the merits of Saint Francis, the following, as well as many others, were miraculously healed from similar infirmities: **Brother Bartolo of Gubbio**; Brother Angelo of Todi; Niccolò, a priest of Ceccano; Giovanni of Sora; a man from Pisa; and another from the town of Cisterna; Pietro from Sicily; and a man from the town of Spello near Assisi.   3C 110-115

³A woman in the Marittima had lost her mind for five years and was unable to see or hear. She tore her clothes with her teeth and had no fear of the dangers of fire or water. And lately she suffered terribly from falling sickness she had contracted. But one night, as divine mercy prepared to show her mercy, she was brilliantly illuminated by the brightness of a healing light. She saw blessed Francis *seated on a* high *throne,* and prostrate before him she humbly asked for her health. As he still had not granted her request, she made a vow, promising for love of God and the saint never to refuse alms, as long as she had them, to anyone who asked. The saint immediately recognized the same pact he had once made with the Lord,[b] and signing her with the sign of the cross he restored her to full health.   3C 152

Is 6:1

A truthful source reports that the Saint of God Francis mercifully delivered from similar afflictions a girl from Norcia and the son of a nobleman, among others.   3C 153-154

⁴Pietro of Foligno went one time to visit the shrine of blessed Michael, but he was not making the pilgrimage very reverently. He drank from a fountain and was filled with demons. From then on he was possessed for three years, he was physically run down, vile in speech, and dreadful in expression. But as he had some lucid moments, he humbly called on the power of the blessed man, which he heard was effective in driving away the powers of the air. On reaching the tomb of the pious father, as soon as he touched it, he was marvelously delivered from the demons that cruelly tormented him.   3C 150

In a similar way the mercy of Francis came to the aid of a woman of Narni who was possessed by a devil, and of many others, but the   3C 151

---

a. May 25, 1230; see above, LMj XV 8.
b. Cf. 1C 17, FA:ED I 195; 2C5, FA:ED II 244.

details of their sufferings and the different ways in which they were cured would be too long to tell one-by-one.[a]

3C 147

[5]A man, named Buonuomo, from the city of Fano, a leper and paralytic, was brought by his parents to the church of blessed Francis, and there he recovered his health completely from both illnesses.

3C 146

A young man named Atto from San Severino was covered with leprosy. Having made a vow, and brought to the tomb of the saint, he was cleansed of his leprosy through the saint's merits.

This saint, furthermore, had an outstanding power for curing this disease because, out of love for humility and piety, he had humbly dedicated himself to the service of lepers.

3C 148

[6]A noblewoman named Rogata, from the diocese of Sora, had been troubled by *hemorrhages* for twenty-three years, and had suffered as many kinds of pain as there were doctors. The illness was so great that it often appeared that the woman would soon breathe her last, and whenever the flow of blood was stopped, her whole body swelled up. But one day she heard a boy singing in Roman dialect a song about the miracles that God had performed through blessed Francis. Sadness overwhelmed her, and as she broke into tears her faith moved her *to say within herself:*"O blessed father Francis, so many miracles radiate from you: if you would see fit to free me of my illness it would add to your glory, because you have not yet done such a great miracle." What happened? After saying this she felt herself freed through the merits of blessed Francis.

Mt 9:20

Lk 11:38

Also, her son Mario, who had a withered arm, after he made a vow, was cured by Saint Francis.

Christ's blessed standard bearer also healed a woman from Sicily who was worn out by suffering a flow of blood for seven years.

3C 149

3C 181

[7]In the city of Rome there was a woman named Prassede known for her religiosity. From her tender infancy she had, for love of her eternal Spouse, withdrawn for nearly forty years to a narrow cell. She earned the favor of a special friendship with blessed Francis. One day in the course of her tasks, she went up to the attic of her cell and, under some imaginary impulse, fell, breaking her foot and leg, and her shoulder was totally separated from its place. The kindly father appeared to her, clothed in white, *in glorious garments,* and began speaking to her in sweet words, "Get up, *beloved daughter, get up and do not fear! He took her hand, lifted her up,* and disappeared. Turning here and there in the cell, she still thought she was *seeing a vision.* When, at her cries, a lamp was brought, feeling

Is 52:1

Ru 3:10; Lk 6:8; 1:30

Mk 9:27

---

a. Several more accounts of these miracles are in 3C 155-156, FA:ED II 455-56.

Acts 12:9
completely healed through the servant of God Francis, **she re-counted** *in order all* **that had happened.**

Est 15:9

Chapter IX
THE PUNISHMENT OF THOSE WHO WOULD NOT KEEP HIS FEAST
OR HONOR HIM AS A SAINT

[1]In the village of Le Simon, which is in the region of Poitiers, there was a priest called Renaud who had a great devotion to Saint Francis, and who taught his parishioners to keep his feast day as a holy day. But one among the people, who did not realize the Saint's power, held his priest's command in contempt.[a] *He went out* into his field to chop some wood, but as he prepared himself to start the work, he three times *heard a voice that said:* "Today is a holy day; it's a sin to work!" But since neither the priest's command nor the words of a voice from heaven were enough to curb the serf's audacity, without delay the power of God added a miracle and a scourge to vindicate his Saint's honor. The man already had his forked stick[b] in one hand, and was raising up an iron tool with the other one, when the divine power stuck his hands to both tools so that he was not able to open his fingers and let go of either.

Lk 22:62

Acts 9:4

He was utterly amazed at this, and had no idea what to do, so he hastened to the church, where many people gathered from all around to see the miracle. There he went before the altar, pierced to the heart by repentance, and at the suggestion of one of the priests—for many priests had been invited and had come to the cele-bration—he humbly consecrated himself to Saint Francis, and *made three vows* to him, because of the three times that he had heard the warning voice. First, that he would always keep his feast day, then that on that feast he would always come to this church in which he now was present, and finally that he would personally go on pilgrim-age to the Saint's tomb.[c] (During this, the great crowd which had gathered was imploring the Saint's mercy with great devotion.) Wonderful to tell, as he made his first vow, one of his fingers was set free; as he vowed the second one, another finger became unstuck; and as he vowed the third one, the third finger was freed, as well as

1 Sm 1:11

---

a. The Middle Ages saw a great proliferation of holy days, to the point that the precept to abstain from servile work became a real burden, since in an economy based on fruits rather than wages, a day without work necessarily meant a day without earnings. Hence new holy days were often resisted by the laity.

b. Presumably used to hold a high branch steady while it was being cut down with a long-handled ax.

c. "Personally," because it was not uncommon for persons who had vowed pilgrimages to do so vicariously by paying the expenses of another person, who would go as a proxy.

the whole hand, and also the other one. And so the man was brought back to his original freedom of movement and put down the tools by himself, while everyone *praised God* and the miraculous power of his Saint, which could so wonderfully strike and also heal. The actual tools were hung as a memorial before the altar that was raised there in honor of Saint Francis, and hang there to this day.[a]

Many other miracles,
worked there and in nearby places,
show that this Saint is outstanding in heaven
and that his feast should be kept on earth
with great veneration.

[Lk 2:13]

[3C 100]
[Prv 31:19]

²Also in the city of Le Mans a woman *put her hand* to the distaff, *her fingers plied the spindle*. Then **her hands stiffened with pain and her fingers** began **to burn. The pain** taught her, and she recognized the power of the saint, and with a contrite heart **hurried to the brothers. As the** devout **sons begged** for the mercy **of the holy Father she was immediately healed, and** no wound **remained on her hands**, except for just **a trace of the burn** as a reminder of the event.

[3C 101-103]

Likewise **a woman in Campania**, another **in the town of Olite** and a third one in the **town of Piglio** disdained to celebrate the blessed Father's **feast** and were at first punished for their wrongdoing. But once they had repented they were miraculously delivered by the merits of **Saint Francis.**

[3C 129]

³**A knight from Borgo in the province of Massa shamelessly dismissed the works and miraculous signs of blessed Francis. He taunted the pilgrims on their way to observe the saint's feast, and he publicly babbled foolishness against the brothers.** One time, however, as he was mocking the glory of the Saint of God, **he added** to his other **sins a detestable blasphemy. "If it's true that this Francis is a saint,"** he said, **"let my body fall by the sword today, and if he's not a saint, I'll be unharmed!"** *The anger of God rose* to inflict a fitting punishment, and *his prayer was turned to sin*. After a short time, the blasphemer **insulted his nephew, and the latter drew his sword and bloodied it with his uncle's bowels. The accursed man died the same day and became a slave of hell and a** *son of darkness*. Thus others might learn not to attack Francis's wonderful works with **words** of blasphemy, but honor them with devout praises.

[Ps 78:21,31]
[Ps 109:7]

[1 Thes 5:5]

---

a. This miracle does not appear in any previous source; Bonaventure may have heard about it during his stay at Paris, or during his visitation of the French friaries as General Minister.

3C 128

Wis 11:16

[4]A judge named Alessandro, who led away as many as he could from devotion to blessed Francis, was deprived of speech by divine judgment, and for six years was mute. *Tormented by the very things through which he sinned,* great repentance overcame him, and he was sorry that he had ridiculed the saint's miracles. So the merciful saint's anger did not last, and he restored his favor by repairing the man's speech, since he was repentant and humbly invoked him. From then on the judge dedicated his blasphemous tongue to praise of the saint, accepting both discipline and devotion instead of suffering.

Chapter X
SOME OTHER MIRACLES OF DIFFERENT KINDS

3C 16

[1]In the town of Gagliano in the diocese of Valva a woman named Maria subjected herself devoutly to the service of Christ Jesus and Saint Francis. One day during the summer she went out to acquire with her own hands the food she needed. The heat was unbearable and she began to faint from thirst, having nothing to drink, since she was alone on a mountain that was totally deprived of water. Lying nearly lifeless on the ground, she began intently to call upon her patron, Saint Francis, with pious spiritual feeling. As the woman persevered in humble and deeply-felt prayer, in her exhaustion from work, thirst, and heat, she drifted off to sleep. And there was Saint Francis, who *called her by name.* "Get up," he said, "and drink the water that is provided by divine gift for you and for many!" On hearing the sound the woman, strengthened, got up from her sleep. She grabbed a fern next to her and plucked it from the earth. Digging around it with a twig, she found living water and what first seemed a *little* drop *grew into a spring* through divine power. The woman drank, and when she had had enough, she washed her eyes, which earlier had been clouded by a long illness, and from that moment she felt them flooded with new light. The woman ran home and told everyone about the great miracle, to the glory of Saint Francis. At the *news* of the miracle many came running from every direction, and learned by their own experience the marvelous power of this water. For on contact with it, after confession, many were freed of the affliction of their illnesses. That clear spring still flows, and a chapel in honor of blessed Francis has been built there.

Is 40:26

Est 10:6

Mt 9:26

3C 189

[2]In the Spanish town of San Facondo against all hope he marvelously restored leaves, blossoms, and fruit to a man's dried up cherry tree.

3C 190

He freed the people of an area near Villesilos by his miraculous help from an infestation of worms that were destroying the nearby vineyards.

3C 191 He also completely cleansed **the grain barn of a priest near Palencia, which** annually used to be **full of grain worms,** after the priest faithfully commended himself to his care.

3C 192 He also preserved **unharmed from a plague of locusts the land of a lord of Pietramala in the kingdom of Apulia who humbly put** himself under his care while that pestilence devoured *all its surroundings.* Jer 21:14

3C 183 ³A man named Martino led his oxen far from home to find pasture. The leg of one ox was accidentally broken so badly that Martin could think of no remedy for it. He was concerned about getting the hide, but since he had no knife for skinning it he returned home and left the ox in the care of Saint Francis, and faithfully entrusted it to the custody of the faithful saint **lest wolves devour it before his** return. Early next morning he returned to the ox with his skinning knife, but found the ox grazing peacefully, unharmed. He could not distinguish its broken leg from the other. He thanked *the good shepherd* who *took* such loving *care* of him, and procured the remedy. Jn 10:11 Lk 10:34

This humble Saint
knows how to help *all those who call* on him, Ps 85:5; 144:18
nor does he consider it beneath his dignity
to help men in their needs,
small though they may be.

3C 184 To **a man of Amiterno**
he restored **a stolen donkey;**

3C 185 for a woman **of Antrodoco**
he repaired a new **dish**
which had been accidentally **shattered;**
and he re-joined **the plowshare**

3C 186 of a **man of Monte dell'Olmo** in the Marches
when it had **broken** in pieces.

3C 182 ⁴In the diocese of Sabino there was an eighty-year-old woman whose daughter died, leaving behind her nursing baby. The poor old woman was full of poverty but empty of milk, and there was no other woman who would give **a drop of milk to the thirsty** little child as necessity demanded. **The poor old woman did not know where** to turn at all. As the baby **grew weaker, one night,** deprived of any human help, she turned her whole mind to the blessed father Francis begging for help with an outpouring of tears. The lover of the age of innocence was immediately there. "Woman," he said, "I am Francis whom you called with so many tears. Put your breasts in the baby's mouth, for the Lord will give you milk in abundance." The old woman did what she was told, and straightaway her eighty-year-old breasts filled with milk. The marvelous gift of the

saint became known to all, and many came, both men and women
hurrying to see. Their tongues could not call into doubt what their
eyes had seen, and they encouraged all to praise God in the wondrous
power and loving piety of His saint.[a]

⁵At Scoppito a man and wife had but one son, but he was the   3C 158
cause of daily lament, a sort of disgrace to their family line. His
forearms were joined to his neck, his knees to his chest, and his
feet joined to his buttocks, he appeared to be a monster, not the
offspring of humans. The wife, overcome with greater sorrow over
this, called to Christ, invoking the help of Saint Francis, to see fit to
lift her from her unhappy and shameful condition. One night,
while she was overcome with sad sleep because of her sad state,
Saint Francis appeared to her and kindly addressed soothing
words to her. He urged her to carry the boy to the place nearby dedi-
Ps 19:8   cated to his name, so that once bathed *in the Lord's name* with water
from the well of that place he would be completely healthy. She
failed to carry out the saint's command, so Saint Francis repeated it a
second time. He appeared to her a third time and, walking ahead as
guide, took the woman together with the boy, to the door of that
place. Some noble matrons were arriving at that place out of devotion, and when the woman carefully explained to them about the vision, they along with her presented the boy to the brothers.
Drawing some water from the well, the noblest among them
washed the infant with her own hands. The boy instantly appeared
healthy, with all his limbs in their proper place. The greatness of
this miracle aroused wonder in them all.[b]

---

a. Cf. Ps 150:1 and 68:36. Where modern translations say "Praise the Lord in His *sanctuary*" and
"God is wonderful in His *sanctuary*," the Vulgate has "in His *saints*."

b. At this point Jerome of Ascoli made another addition to the text: "A young man from Rivarolo
Canavese called Ubertino joined the Order of Friars Minor in Susa. But during the time of his
novitiate he suffered a horrible fright, as a result of which he lost his wits, became paralyzed on his
whole right side, and became so seriously ill that he lost his speech and hearing as well as feeling and
movement. When he had been confined to his bed in such a miserable state for quite a few days, to
the great sorrow of the other brothers, the solemnity of blessed Francis arrived. On the eve of this
solemnity he had a lucid interval, and called upon his merciful Father the best he could, with a barely
intelligible voice, but with a faith-filled heart. "That night at the hour of matins, while all the brothers
were in church intent on singing God's praises, the blessed Father, dressed in the habit of the
brothers, appeared to this novice in the infirmary, and *a great light shone in that room* (Acts 12:7).
Stretching out his hand (Mk 7:33), he gently ran it over the novice's right side, touching it from head
to toes, then *he put his fingers into his ears*, and impressed a certain mark upon his right thigh. 'This,'
he said, 'will be a sign to you that God has fully restored you to health through me, since you entered
the religious life led by my example.' Then he tied a cord around his waist—he was lying in bed
without a cord—and said to him: 'Get up and go into the church, and with your brothers return the
praises due to God!' When he had said this, as the boy tried to touch him with his hands and kiss his
footprints in gratitude, the blessed Father disappeared from his sight. And the young man, having
recovered physical health and the use of reason, along with lively feeling and speech, went into the
church to the great amazement of the brothers and of the laity who were present there, and who had
seen the young man paralyzed and witless. He joined in the divine praises and then narrated the
miracle from beginning to end, thus kindling in many people devotion towards Christ and Saint
Francis."

3C 159   ⁶In the village of Cori of the diocese of Ostia, a man had so totally lost the use of a leg that he could not walk or move at all. He
was thus confined in bitter agony and had lost hope in any human
assistance. One night he began to spell out his complaint to
blessed Francis as if he saw him there present. "Help me, Saint
Francis! Think of all my service and devotion to you. I carried you
on my donkey; I kissed your holy hands and feet. I was always devoted to you, always gracious, and, as you see, I am dying of the
torture of this harsh suffering." Moved by his complaint and recalling his good deeds and devotion gratefully he came immediately
and, with one brother, appeared to the man keeping vigil. He said
that he had come at his call, and that he carried the means of healing. He touched the source of the pain with a small stick bearing
the figure of the "Tau." The abscess healed quickly, as he gave him
perfect health. What is even more amazing, he left the sacred **sign of
the "Tau"** stamped **on the spot** of the healed ulcer as a reminder of
the miracle. **Saint Francis signed his letters with this sign whenever charity or necessity led him to send something in writing.**

⁷But see now how our mind,
wandering about through the diverse miracles
of the glorious Father Francis,
and distracted by the variety of the stories,
comes at last,
by the merits of that glorious standard bearer of the cross,
and not without divine guidance,
to the Tau,
the symbol of salvation.
From this we can understand that,
just as while he was among *the militant* following Christ,   2 Tm 2:4
the Cross was the peak of merit for his salvation
so also, now that he is triumphant with Christ,
the Cross has become the foundation of *testimonies* for his glory.   Ps 93:5

⁸Indeed, in this great and awesome mystery of the cross,
the *charisms* of graces,   1 Cor 12:31
the merits of virtue,
and the *treasures of wisdom and of knowledge*   Col 2:3
are concealed in such profound depths
as to be hidden

Mt 11:25; Lk 10:21   *from the wise and the prudent* of this world.
But it is *revealed* in such fullness *to the little one* of Christ,
that in his whole life
1 Pt 1:21   *he followed* nothing except *the footsteps* of the cross,
he tasted nothing except the sweetness of the cross,
and he preached nothing except the glory of the cross.
In the beginning of his conversion
he could truly say with the Apostle:
Gal 6:14   *Far be it from me to glory*
except in the cross of our Lord Jesus Christ.
In the course of his life
he could more truly add:
Gal 6:16   *Whoever follows this rule,*
peace and mercy be upon them.
In the finishing of his life
he could most truly conclude:
Gal 6:17   *I bear in my body*
the brand marks of the Lord Jesus.
As for us,
our daily wish is to hear him say:
Gal 6:18   *May the grace of our Lord Jesus Christ*
be with your spirit, brothers. Amen.

Gal 6:14   [9]Now, therefore, safely glory in the glory of the cross,
glorious standard-bearer of Christ!
For you began from the cross;
you went forward according to the rule of the cross,
and in the end you finished on the cross.
By the evidence of the cross
you make known to all believers
how great is your glory in the heaven.
Now too you may be safely followed
Ps 114:1   by those who *come forth from Egypt.*
Ps 136:13   With *the sea parted* by the staff of Christ's cross,
Ps 68:8   *they shall cross the desert;*
Dt 27:3   *crossing the Jordan* of mortality,
Acts 7:5   they shall enter *the promised land,*
Ps 142:6   *the land of the living,*
by the wonderful power of the cross.
May we be brought there

by the true Leader and Savior of the people,
Christ Jesus crucified,   Gal 3:1
through the merits of His servant Francis,
to the praise and glory of God,
One and Three,
who lives and reigns forever and ever.   Rv 10:6; 11:15

Amen.

HERE END THE MIRACLES OF SAINT FRANCIS
SHOWN FORTH AFTER HIS PASSING.

The Minor Legend of Saint Francis

(1260-1263)

Chapter I
HIS CONVERSION

First Lesson

Ti 2:11

The grace of God, our Savior, has appeared in these last days in his servant Francis. *The Father of mercy and light*[a] came to his assistance with such an abundance of **blessings of sweetness** that, as it clearly appears in the course of Francis's life, God not only led him out from the darkness of the world into light, but also made him renowned for his merits and the excellence of his virtues. He also showed that he was notably illustrious for the remarkable mysteries of the cross displayed in him. Francis was born **in the city of Assisi** in the regions of **the Spoleto valley.** First *called John* by his *mother,* and then **Francis** by his father, he held on to the name his father gave him, but did not abandon the meaning of the name given by his mother. **At a young age he lived in vain pursuits among the idle sons of men, and after acquiring a little knowledge of reading and writing he was assigned to work in a lucrative merchant's business; yet with God's protection, neither did he give himself over to the drives of the flesh among wanton youths,** nor did he *put his hope in money or in treasures* among **greedy merchants.**

LMj prol 1

LMj I 1

Lk 1:60

IC 1

2C 3

LMj I 1

Sir 31:18

---

a. The reference to the Father of light found in Jas 1:17, which is not found at the beginning of LMj, underscores the liturgical aspect of LMn. Jas 1:17 is among the most frequently cited biblical texts in Bonaventure's writings. The imagery of light at the opening of LMn takes on particular significance in the context of liturgical worship. Medieval art and architecture favored an aesthetic-practical appreciation of light in liturgical space and medieval theologians like Bonaventure considered light symbolic of divine grace sought and experienced in prayer.

Second Lesson

LMj I 1

For there was to be sure a generous care for the poor together with kindness and gentleness implanted in the heart of the youthful Francis. Increasing in him from early childhood, it had filled his heart with such kindness that, even at that time, he resolved not to be a deaf hearer of the Gospel, but to give an alms to everyone who begged, especially if he asked out of divine love. From the first flower of his youth he bound himself to the Lord by a firm promise that, **if it were possible, he would never refuse those who begged** from him for the love of God. Since he did not cease to fulfill so noble a promise **until death,** he attained **forevermore abundant increase of grace and love for God.** Even though a small flame of God's fiery love flourished constantly in his heart, as a young man involved with worldly concerns, **he was ignorant** of the **mystery of the divine eloquence.** *When the hand of the Lord was upon him,* he was chastened exteriorly by a long and severe illness and enlightened interiorly **by the anointing of the Holy Spirit.**

1C 89

LMj I 1

Mj II 1; LMj II 5

LMj II 1

Ez 1:3

Third Lesson

LMj I 2

After Francis's **strength of body was** somehow **restored** and his mental attitude changed for the better, he had an unexpected meeting **with a knight who was of noble birth** but **poor** in possessions. He was reminded of Christ, the poor and noble king. He was moved toward this man with such **piety** that he removed the fine garments which he **had just acquired** for himself and **immediately dressed** the soldier, leaving **himself** without clothes. **The following night, when he had fallen asleep,** a worthy revelation **showed him a large and splendid palace with military arms emblazoned with the insignia of the cross.** He was promised with earnest certitude that **all these things were for him and his soldiers,** if he constantly bore the standard of the **cross of Christ. From that time as he was removing** himself from the pressure of public business, he began to seek out solitary places favorable for grieving, where, with unutterable groans, he concentrated incessantly on meriting to be heard by the Lord after the long perseverance of his prayers during which he begged the Lord that the way to perfection be shown to him.

LMj I 3

LMj I 4

Fourth Lesson

LMj I 5

One of those days, withdrawn in this way, while he was praying, Christ Jesus, appeared to him as fastened to a cross and repeated for him so efficaciously **this Gospel text:** *if you wish to come*

Mt 16:24

after me, deny yourself, and take up your cross, and follow me.[a] Inwardly, this both kindled his heart with the fire of love and filled it with the painfulness of compassion. **His soul melted at the sight, and the memory of Christ was so impressed on the innermost recesses of his heart,** that with the eyes of his mind he continually, as it were, discerned interiorly the wounds of his **crucified** Lord and **could scarcely contain his tears and sighs.** When now for the love of Christ Jesus *he despised all the goods of his house* by considering them *as nothing*, he felt that he had found the *hidden treasure* and the brilliant *pearl* of great price. Moved by the desire to possess it, he arranged to leave all his possessions, and by a divine method of commerce, he exchanged the business of the world for the business of the Gospel.

Sg 8:7

Mt 13:44, 45

Fifth Lesson

Gn 24:63

One day when *he went out to meditate in the fields*, he walked near the church of San Damiano, which was threatening to collapse because of age. Impelled by the Spirit, he went inside to pray. Prostrate before an image of the Crucified, he was filled with no little consolation as he prayed. When his tear-filled eyes were gazing at the Lord's cross he heard in a marvelous way **with his bodily ears a voice coming from that cross, telling him three times: "Francis, go, rebuild my house which, as you see, is all being destroyed!"** At the wonderful suggestion of this **astonishing voice** the man of God first was indeed thoroughly terrified, then filled with joy and admiration. **Coming back to himself, he arose** immediately **to carry out the command of repairing the material church; although the principal intention of the voice referred to that Church which Christ** *purchased by* precious exchange with *his own blood*, just as the Holy Spirit taught him, and as he revealed later to his close companions.

Acts 20:28

LMj II 1

Sixth Lesson

Soon afterwards Francis, for the love of Christ, put aside all the things he could and offered **money to the poor priest of that church for the repair of his church and for the use of the poor. He humbly asked the priest that he be allowed to stay there for a short time. The priest agreed to his staying there, but out of fear of Francis's**

LMj II 1

---

a. This encounter with the Crucified Christ, which is not present in Thomas of Celano's account of Francis's life, has a heightened sense of immediacy compared with LMj I 5, where Francis appears to grasp the personal import of Mt 16:24 later. Subsequent reference to vision and memory has a narrative function, as prelude to the San Damiano event, and anticipate the stigmata. Heard in a liturgical context, however, these same terms encourage meditation on the image of the Crucified Christ prominent in early Franciscan churches.

LMj II 2
parents he refused the money. But Francis, now a true scorner of wealth, threw a large number of coins on a windowsill, valuing it no more than if it were dust. Hearing this had enraged his father, and wanting to leave room for his anger, he hid himself for some days in a dark cave where he fasted, prayed and wept. Finally, filled with a spiritual joy and *clothed with power from on high,* he confidently came Lk 24:29 forth from the cave and calmly entered the city. When the young people saw his unkempt face and his changed mentality, they thought that he had gone out of his senses. They considered him a fool. They threw mud from the street and shouted insults at him. But this Lord's servant was neither broken nor changed by any wrong. He passed through it as though he were deaf to it all.

Seventh Lesson

LMj II 2
His father, raging and fuming because of all this, seemed as if he were forgetful of natural pity. He began to torment with blows and chains the son who had been dragged home. By wearing down Francis's body with physical abuse, he hoped to turn his mind to the LMj II 3 attractions of the world. Finally Francis's father learned by experience that this servant of God was most willing to bear any harsh LMj II 4 treatment for Christ and that he could not restrain him. He began to insist vehemently that Francis go with him to the bishop of the city and renounce into the bishop's hands his hereditary right to all his father's possessions. The servant of the Lord was determined to carry this out further, and as soon as he came before the bishop, he did not delay nor hesitate or speak or listen to a word. He took off all his clothes instead and, in the presence of those standing around him, discarded even his undergarments. Drunk in spirit,[a] he was LJS 9 not afraid to stand naked out of love for Him who for us hung naked on the Cross.[b]

Eighth Lesson

LMj II 5
Released now from the chains of all earthly desires, this scorner of the world left the town. While free and in a carefree mood, he was singing praises to the Lord in French in the middle of woods when robbers came upon him. As the herald of the great King he

---

a. Liturgy is conducive to the ecstasy of spiritual intoxication. Francis was often *spiritu ebrius* after receiving the Eucharist, see: LMj IX 2 (VIII, 530b). Spiritual intoxication is also linked with love and mystical union in prayer, as Christ was inebriated out of love for his bride in *The Collations on the Six Days,* coll. 14, n. 19 (V, 396b) and the bride, or soul, is intoxicated as well with Christ in *On the Perfection of Life,* c. 5, n. 9 (VIII, 119b-120a).

b. See LMj II 4, supra, 538 b.

was not afraid nor did he stop singing, inasmuch as a half-naked and penniless wayfarer he, like the apostles, *rejoiced in tribulation.* **Then as a lover of total humility** he gave himself to **the service of lepers,** so that while he was subjecting himself to miserable and outcast people under the yoke of servitude, he could first learn perfect contempt of himself and of the world before he would teach it to others. Surely, since he used to fear lepers more than any other group of people, grace was given to him in more abundance. He **moved to the lepers** and gave himself up to their service with such a humble heart that **he washed their feet, bandaged their sores, drew the puss from wounds, and wiped the filth from them.** In an excess of unheard of fervor, he would fall down to kiss their ulcerous sores, putting his *mouth to the dust,* so that, *filled with reproaches,* he might efficaciously subject the **pride of the flesh to the** *law of the spirit* and, once the enemy within him was subdued, possess peaceful dominion over himself.

2 Cor 7:4

LMj II 6

LMj I 6

Lam 3:29, 30

Ninth Lesson

Thereafter, Francis **was grounded in the humility of Christ** and made rich in his poverty.[a] Even though he possessed absolutely nothing, he, nevertheless, began to turn his careful attention to **rebuilding the church** according to the **command given to him from the cross.** Although his **body was weakened by fasting** and bore the burdens of the stone, he did not shrink from earnestly begging the help of alms even from those among whom he had been accustomed to live as a rich man. **With the devoted assistance** of the faithful, who now began to realize the remarkable virtue this man of God possessed, he restored not only the church of San Damiano, but also the abandoned and ruined churches of the **Prince of the Apostles** and of the glorious Virgin. He **mysteriously foreshadowed, by an exteriorly perceptible work,** what the Lord disposed to do **through him in the future.** For according to the likeness of the threefold buildings he built up under the guidance of the holy man himself, the Church was to be renewed in three ways according to the form, rule, and teaching of Christ. The voice from the Cross, which repeated three times the command concerning the rebuilding of the house of God, stands out as a prophetic sign. **We recognize now that it is fulfilled** in the three Orders established by him.

LMj II 7

LMj II 1; LMj II

---

a. Humility and poverty are integral dimensions of the poverty of spirit which is the summation of the evangelical perfection espoused by the Franciscan community, see: *The Commentary on the Gospel of Luke* VII 41 (VII, 175).

Chapter II
THE INSTITUTION OF THE RELIGION
AND THE EFFICACY OF PREACHING

First Lesson

LJS 15

After the work on the **three churches was finished,** he **[1C 21] stayed** at the church dedicated to the Virgin. By the merits and prayers of her who gave birth to the price of our salvation, he merited

LMj III 1

to find the way of perfection through the **spirit of evangelical truth**

LJS 15

infused into him by God. One day **during the solemnity of the Mass,**

LMj IIII

that part **of the Gospel was read in which the evangelical** norm for living was prescribed **for the disciples who were sent to preach;** namely, *do not keep gold, or silver, or money in your girdles, no wallet for*   Mt 10:9-10

LJS 15

your journey, nor two tunics nor sandals, nor staff. **Hearing** such words, he was soon anointed and adorned by the Spirit of Christ with such power that it transformed him into the described manner of living not only in mind and heart, but also in life and dress. He immediately

LMj III 1

took off his shoes, put down his staff, and discarded **his wallet and its money.** He was **satisfied with one tunic;** he rejected **his leather belt and put on a piece of rope for his belt. He directed all his heart's desire to carry out what he had heard and to conform in every way to the rule of right living given to the apostles.**

Second Lesson

LMj III 2

Inflamed totally by the fiery vigor of the Spirit of Christ, **he began,** as another Elias, **to be a model** of truth. He also began to lead some to **perfect** righteousness and **still others to penance. His statements were neither hollow nor ridiculous; they were, instead, filled with the power of the Holy Spirit, and they penetrated to the marrow of the heart. They moved his listeners with great amazement, and their powerful efficacy softened the minds of the obstinate.** As his holy and sublime purpose became known to many through the truth of his simple teaching and life, some began to be moved to penitence by his example.[a] After they left all things, they joined

---

a. Bonaventure's theology of preaching is evident in Francis who united word and example in a compelling invitation to follow Christ. While the power of the spoken word is not to be overlooked, example is crucial if the import of the message is to be effectively conveyed and received. When the two come together, there is a forceful witness to the Gospel, see: *The Sermon for the Second Sunday after Easter* (1), (IX, 294b).

him in habit and life. That humble man decided that they should be called "Lesser Brothers."

Third Lesson

When at the calling of God the **number of brothers reached six,** their devoted father and shepherd found a **place for solitude** where, **in bitterness** of heart, **he deplored** his life as a youth which he had not lived without sin. He also begged for pardon and grace for himself and for his offspring which *he had begotten in Christ.* **When an excessive joy filled his being, he was assured of complete forgiveness** *to the last penny* of all his debt. **Then caught up above himself and engulfed totally in a vivifying light he saw clearly what the future held for him** and his brothers. He disclosed this later in confidence for the encouragement *of his little flock,* when he foretold the Order would soon expand and grow through the clemency of God. After a very few **days had passed, certain others joined him, and their number increased** to twelve. **This servant** of the Lord **decided, therefore, to approach the presence of the Apostolic See.** Together with that band of simple men, he wished to beg earnestly and humbly that the way of life, shown to him by the Lord and **written down by him in a few words,** be confirmed by the full authority of that same most Holy See.

Fourth Lesson

According to his proposal, he hurried with his companions to come **into the presence of the Supreme Pontiff, Lord Innocent III.** *Christ, the power and wisdom of God,* arrived in his clemency before him. By means of a vision, it was communicated to the **Vicar that he should agree to listen calmly to this poor little suppliant and give him a favorable assent.** For *in a dream* the Roman Pontiff himself *saw* that the Lateran basilica was almost ready to fall down, and a poor little man, small and scorned, was propping it up with his own bent back so that it would not fall. While the wise bishop was contemplating the **purity of the simple mind in this servant of God,** his contempt of the world, his love of poverty, the **constancy** of his perfect **proposal,** his zeal for souls, and the **enkindled fervor of his will,** he said: "Truly, this is he who will hold up Christ's Church by **what he does and what he preaches."** As a result, the pope from that time on held a special **devotion** toward this man. **He bowed to the request in all things, the pope approved the Rule, gave him the mandate to preach penance, granted everything he asked, and promised generously to concede even more in the future.**

Margin references:

1 Cor 4:15

1 Cor 1:24

Lk 12:32

LMj III 4
LMj III 6

LMj III 7
LMj III 8

LJS 21

1 Cor 1:24

Gn 28:12

LMj III 9

LMj III 10

LMj III 9

LMj III 10

Fifth Lesson

Strengthened then by grace from on high and by the authority of the Supreme Pontiff, **Francis with great confidence took the road to the Spoleto valley.** He wanted to **teach** by word and **carry out** by deed the truth of the **evangelical** perfection which he had conceived in his mind and solemnly vowed to profess. When the question was raised with his companions **whether they should live among the people or go off to solitary places,** he sought the pleasure of the divine will by the fervor of prayer.[a] **Enlightened by a revelation from heaven, he realized that he was sent by the Lord to win for Christ souls which the devil was trying to snatch away.** Discerning, therefore, he chose to live for everyone rather than for himself alone, he went to an abandoned hut near Assisi to live with his brothers according to the norm of **holy poverty** in every hardship of religious life and preach the word of God to the people whenever and wherever possible. **Having been made a herald of the Gospel, he went about the cities and towns** *proclaiming the kingdom of God not in* such *words taught by human wisdom, but in the power of the Spirit* with the Lord directing **him** by revelations as he spoke *and confirming the preaching by the signs that followed.*

LMj IV 1
LMj IV 2
LMj IV 3
LMj IV 5

Lk 9:60; 1 Cor 1:13

Sixth Lesson

Mk 16:20

Once, **as was his custom,** he was spending the night **in prayer** apart from his sons. Around midnight, while some of them were resting and others were praying, a fiery chariot of wonderful brilliance came **through the little door** of the brothers' dwelling. **Over this chariot, which moved here and there three times throughout the little house,** there rested a bright ball of light which resembled the sun. **Those who were awake were stunned** at this remarkable, brilliant sight. **Those who were asleep were terrified and dumfounded.** They experienced a brightness with their hearts as much as with their bodies, while the conscience of each was laid bare to the others by the power of that marvelous light. With one accord, they all understood, as they looked into each other's hearts, that it was their holy father Francis **who had been transfigured in such an image.** Shown to them by the Lord as one coming *in the spirit and*

LMj IV 4

---

a. Bonaventure holds that constant prayer proffers divine illumination, see: *The Commentary on the Gospel of Luke,* c. 18, n. 3 (VII, 449a-b). Francis's decision to forgo a strictly contemplative life, which was reinforced for the friars and laity in the depiction of his preaching activities in frescoes and panel paintings, mirrors Bonaventure's theological methodology. Bonaventure maintains the end of theology is found in the moral realm, not in contemplation alone, see: *The Commentary on the First Book of Sentences,* proëm, q. 3, concl. (I, 13b).

power of Elias, and *as Israel's chariot and charioteer*, he had been made
leader for spiritual men. When the holy man rejoined his brothers,
he began to comfort them concerning the vision they had been
shown from heaven, probe the secrets of their consciences, predict
the future, and radiate with miracles. In this manner, he revealed
that the *twofold spirit* of Elias *rested* upon him in such plenitude that
it was absolutely safe for all to follow his life and teaching.

Lk 1:17
2 Kgs 2:12

2 Kgs 2:9, 15

Seventh Lesson

At that time a religious of the Order of the Crosiers, whose name
was Morico, was suffering in a hospital near Assisi from an illness
so serious and so prolonged that it was believed that he was very
close to death. Through a messenger he solicited the man of God,   LMj IV 8
earnestly asking him to be willing to intercede for him with God.
The holy man kindly assented to his request. After first praying, he
took some bread crumbs and mixed them with oil taken from a
lamp that burned before the altar of the Virgin. He made a kind of
pill out of them and sent it to the sick man through the hands of his
brothers, saying: "Take this medicine to our brother Morico. By
means of it Christ's power will not only restore him to full health,
but also will make him a sturdy warrior and enlist him in our forces
permanently." When the sick man took the medicine which had
been prepared under the inspiration of the Holy Spirit, he was
cured immediately. God gave him such strength of mind and body,
that when a little later he entered the holy man's religion, he wore
only a single tunic, under which for a long time he wore a hair shirt
next to his skin. He neither drank wine nor tasted anything that
was cooked.

Eighth Lesson

At that time there was a priest from Assisi, whose name was
Sylvester, who was certainly a man of an upright way of life and
possessed dove-like simplicity. *In a dream he saw* that whole region
encircled by a huge dragon whose loathsome and frightful image, it   LMj III 5
seemed, threatened imminent destruction to different areas of the
world. After this, he contuited a glittering golden cross issuing from
Francis's mouth. The top of the cross *reached the heavens*. Its arms,
stretched wide, seemed to extend to the ends of the world, and the
glittering sight of it put that foul and hideous dragon to flight forever. While this vision was being shown to Sylvester for the third
time, this pious man, who was devoted to God, understood that
Francis was destined by the Lord to take up the standard of the glori-

Gn 28:12
Gn 28:12

ous cross, to shatter the power of the evil dragon, and to enlighten the minds of the faithful with the glorious and splendid truths of both life and teaching. **Not long after he gave an account of all this to the man of God and his brothers, he left the world.** In accord with the example of his blessed father, **he clung to the footsteps of Christ with such perseverance that his life in the Order confirmed the authenticity of the vision which he had in the world.**

Ninth Lesson

When he was still living the secular life, a certain brother whose name was Pacifico, found the servant of God **at San Severino where he was preaching in a monastery.** *The hand of the Lord came upon him,* and he saw Francis marked with two bright shining swords intersecting in the shape of a cross. One of them stretched from his head to his feet, and the other across his chest from one hand to the other. **He did not know the man by sight, but once he had been pointed out by such a miracle, he recognized him immediately. He was** exceedingly amazed, frightened, and goaded by the power of his words. Pierced as it were by a spiritual sword coming from his mouth, he completely despised worldly displays and joined himself to his blessed father by profession. Afterwards, he made progress in every moral aspect of religion. Before he became minister in France, as indeed he was the first to hold the office of minister there, he merited to see a great *Tau* on Francis's *forehead,* which displayed a variety of different colors that caused his face to glow with wonderful beauty. The man of God venerated this symbol with great affection.[a] He often spoke of it with eloquence and used it at the beginning of any action. In those letters which out of charity he sent, he signed it with his own hand. It was as if his whole desire were, according to the prophetic text, *to mark with a Tau the foreheads of those moaning and grieving,* of those truly converted to Jesus Christ.

LMj IV 9

Ez 1:3

Ez 9:4

Ez 9:4

---

a. The symbol of the Tau, together with every other representation of the cross, is a reminder of the most assured path to Christ. Bonaventure preached that those seeking the Lord need only look to the cross, cf. *Sermon on Saint Andrew* (1) (IX, 465b).

Chapter III
THE PREROGATIVES OF THE VIRTUES

First Lesson

As a loyal follower of the crucified Jesus, Francis, that man of God, *crucified his flesh with its passions* and desires from the very beginning of his conversion **with such rigid discipline,** and checked his **sensual** impulses according to such a strict law of moderation, **that he would scarcely take what was necessary to sustain nature. When he was in good health he hardly and rarely allowed cooked food. When he did,** however, **he made the food** bitter by either mixing **ashes** with it or **made it as insipid as possible** by pouring **water** over it. *Withdrawing his flesh from wine in order to turn his mind to the light of wisdom,* he preserved such strict control over drinking that we can clearly understand that **when he was suffering from a burning thirst, he scarcely would dare to drink enough cold water to satisfy himself. He often used the naked ground as his bed for his weary body, a stone or a piece of wood for his head. The clothes** covering him were simple, wrinkled, and rough. **Established experience had taught** him that malignant spirits are put to flight by using things difficult and harsh, but they are more **strongly animated to tempting by things luxurious and delicate.**

Gal 5:24

Eccl 2:3

LMj V 1

LMj V 2

Second Lesson

Unbending in discipline, he kept an exceedingly attentive *watch over himself.* **He took** particular **care** in guarding the priceless treasure *in a vessel of clay,* that is, chastity, which he strove *to possess in* holiness and *honor* through the virtuous **purity of both body and soul.** For this reason, **around the beginning of his conversion during the winter cold, he would plunge himself many times,** strong **and fervid in spirit, into a ditch** filled **with icy water** or snow. **He did this to subjugate the enemy within and to preserve the white robe of modesty from the flames of voluptuousness.** Practices such as these enabled him to use **his bodily senses** in an appealing, modest manner. His mastery over the flesh was now so complete that he seemed *to have made a covenant with his eyes;* he would not only flee far away from carnal sights, but also totally avoid even the curious glance at anything vain.

Is 21:8

2 Cor 4:7; 1 Thes 4:4

Jb 31:1

LMj V 3

Third Lesson

LMj V 8

Truly, **even though he had attained purity of heart and body,** and in some manner was approaching the height of sanctification, **he did not cease to cleanse the eyes of his soul with a continuous flood of tears.** He longed for the sheer brilliance of the heavenly light and disregarded the loss of his bodily eyes. **When he had incurred a very serious eye illness from his continuous weeping, a doctor advised him to restrain his tears if he wanted to avoid losing his sight.** He, however, would not assent to this. **He asserted that he preferred to lose sight than repress the devotion of the spirit and impede the tears which cleansed his interior vision so that he could see God.**[a] He was a man devoted to God, who, drenched in spiritual tears, displayed a serenity in both mind and face. The luster of a pure conscience anointed him with such joy that his *mind was* forever *caught*   2 Cor 5:13; Dt 14:29; Ps 91:5

LMj IX 1   *up* in *God,* and *he rejoiced* at all times *in the works of his hands.*

Fourth Lesson

LMj VI 1

Humility, that guard and embellishment of all virtues, had by right so filled the man of God that, although a manifold privilege of virtues was reflected in him, nevertheless, it sought its special domain in him as though in the least of the lesser ones. **In his own**

LMj VI 6   **opinion,** by which he accounted himself the **greatest of sinners,** he

LMj VI 1   was really nothing more than some dirty *earthen vessel,* **while in truth**   Jer 22:28
he was an elect *vessel of sanctification,* set apart by sanctity and glittering with the adornment of many kinds of virtue and grace. Moreover, **he strove to regard himself as worthless in his own eyes and**

LMj VI 2   **in those of others,** to reveal by public confession his **hidden faults,**

LMj VI 3   and to keep the Giver's gifts hidden **in the secrecy of his heart.** He
did this so that he would in no way **be subject to praise which could**

LMj VI 4   **be an occasion for his downfall.** Certainly, in order that he might *fulfill all justice* regarding perfect humility, he so strove to subject himself not only to superiors but also even to inferiors, that he was **accustomed to promise obedience** even to his companion on a journey, no matter how simple he was. As a result, he did not give orders as a **prelate** with authority. **In his humility, he would** rather **obey** those subject to him as their **minister and servant.**

---

a. Spiritual tears are indicative of conversion and a salient feature of prayer as contemplation, cf. supra, 565 b. Bonaventure's debt to Hugh of Saint Victor's *On the Sacraments* is evident in the reference to the physical eye and inner eye. While the physical eye is capable of sight, the inner or contemplative eye requires cleansing because of the blinding influence of sin, see: *The Collations on the Six Days,* coll. 5, n. 24 (V, 358a). On Francis's tears and medieval spirituality, see: Keith Hanes, "The Death of Saint Francis of Assisi" in *Franciscan Studies* 58 (1976): 43-45.

Fifth Lesson

Jer 31:3
This perfect follower of Christ **was so eager** *in everlasting love* to   LMj VII 1
espouse poverty, the companion of humility, to himself that **he not**
Gn 2:22; Mk 10:7 **only** *left his father and mother* **for her, but also scattered everything**
he could have. No one coveted gold as he coveted poverty; nor was
anyone as careful in guarding of a treasure as he was of the pearl of
the Gospel. Since from the beginning of the Religion until his
death, his wealth was a tunic, a cord, and breeches, it would seem
that **he gloried** in want and rejoiced in need. **If at any time he saw**   LMj VII 7
anyone dressed poorer than himself, he would criticize himself im-
mediately and set out to be similar. It seemed as if he were contending with a rival and feared that he would be conquered by the
spiritual nobility of that man. Since the **pledge of his** eternal **inheri-**   1C 74
tance, he had preferred poverty to everything perishable, **counting**   LMj VII 7
as nothing riches which are granted to us as a fief the false riches
granted for only an hour. He loved poverty more than great wealth,
and he, who had learned from it to regard himself inferior to all,   LMj VII 6
hoped to surpass all in its practice.

Sixth Lesson

Through the love of the most sublime poverty, the man of God   LMj VII 1
prospered and grew rich in holy simplicity. Although he certainly
possessed nothing of his own in this world, he seemed to possess all
good things in the very Author of this world. With the steady gaze of
a dove, that is, the simple application and pure consideration of the
mind, he referred all things to the supreme Artisan and recognized,
loved, and praised their Maker in all things.[a] It came to pass, by a
heavenly gift of kindness, that he possessed all things in God and
God in all things. **In consideration of the primal origin of all things,**   LMj VIII 6
he would call all creatures, however insignificant, **by the names of**
brother and sister since they come forth with him **from the one**
source. He embraced those, however, **more tenderly and passion-**

---

a. Bonaventure's usage of literary and artistic terminology in his theology of God bears consideration in
the context of liturgy. As the book of Creation, the world speaks eloquently of the divine Author.
Learning to read the book of Creation parallels the process of learning how to read the Psalter, as both
activities are synonymous with prayer; see: *The Commentary on the Gospel of Luke*, c. 18, n. 16 (VII,
470b-471a) and *The Rule for Novices*, c. 1 (VIII, 475a-476b). The supreme Artisan's activity in the
world offers insight into the ultimate significance of the religious art. Just as creatures are visual
expressions reflecting the divine Artist's creativity, so, too, is liturgical art a visual reminder of God's
presence in the world, see: *The Commentary on the First Book of Sentences*, d. 3, art. unicus, q. 2,
concl. (I, 72b) and *The Commentary on the Fourth Book of Sentences*, d. 9, art. 1, q. 2, concl. (III,
203b). Bonaventure likens God's presentation of saints to the Church to the actions of a master
painter who offers students models to reproduce in their own paintings. By attempting to depict these
models, they themselves will become masters, see: *The Sermon on the Birth of John the Baptist* (1),
(IX, 539a).

ately, who portray by a natural likeness the gracious gentleness of Christ and exemplify it in the Scriptures. It came to pass by a supernatural influx of power that the nature of brute animals was moved in some gracious manner toward him. Even inanimate things obeyed his command, as if this same holy *man, so simple and upright,* had already returned to the state *of innocence.*

LMj VIII 7-9

Jb 2:3

Seventh Lesson

The source of piety pervaded the servant of the Lord with such fullness and abundance that he seemed to possess a mother's heart for relieving the misery of suffering people. He had an inborn kindness doubled by the piety of Christ poured out on him. His soul melted for the poor and infirm, and to those to whom he could not extend a hand he extended his affection. With tenderness of a pious heart, he referred to Christ anyone he saw in need or deprivation. In all the poor he saw before him a portrait of Christ. He not only freely gave to those he met the necessities of life if these had been given to him, but he also resolved they should be returned as if they truly belonged to them. He spared nothing at all, neither mantles nor tunics, neither books nor even appointments of the altar; all these he gave to the poor when he could to fulfill his obligation of piety, even *to the utter privation of himself.*

LMj VIII 5

2 Cor 12:15

Eighth Lesson

His zeal for fraternal salvation, which emerged from the furnace of love, pierced the inmost parts of this man like a *sharp* and *flaming sword.* Aflame with the ardor of imitation and stricken with the sorrow of compassion, this man seemed to be completely consumed. Whenever he became aware that souls redeemed by the precious blood of Jesus Christ were stained by the filth of sin, he would be pierced by a remarkable sting of sorrow. He grieved with such tender care that he seemed like a mother who was daily bringing them to birth in Christ. For this reason, he struggled to pray, was active in preaching, and outstanding in giving good example. He did not think that he was a friend of Christ unless he cherished the souls which Christ redeemed. Although his innocent flesh subjected itself freely to his spirit, it had no need of the lash due to offenses. Nevertheless, for the sake of example, he kept on subjecting it to pain and burdens, *keeping the difficult ways* because of others, so that he perfectly followed the footsteps of He who *in death handed over his life* for the salvation of others.

LMj VIII 1

Rv 1:16

Ps 16:4

Is 53:12

Ninth Lesson

Given **the fire of his charity** which carried the friend of the Spouse   LMj IX 5
into God, one is able to perceive that he thoroughly desired **to offer to**
the Lord his own life as a *living sacrifice* in the flames of martyrdom.
It was for this reason that he attempted on **three** occasions **to jour-**   LMj IX 7
ney to the territory of the **non-believers.** Twice he was restrained by
the will of God. On the third attempt, after much abuse, **many**   LMj IX 8
chains, floggings, and innumerable hardships, **he was led** with the
help of God into the presence of the **Sultan of Babylon.** *He preached*
Jesus with such an efficacious *demonstration of spirit and of power* that
the **Sultan was overflowing with admiration,** and became docile by
the will of God and granted Francis a kind audience. Recognizing in
him a **fervor of spirit, a constancy** of mind, a **contempt** for this present life, and the efficacy of God's word, the Sultan **conceived** such a
devotion toward **him** that he deemed him worthy of great honor. **He**
offered him precious gifts and earnestly invited him to prolong his
stay with him. This true **despiser** of himself and **of the world**
spurned as dirt all that was offered to him. When he realized that he   LMj IX 9
was **not able to accomplish his purpose** after he had truly done all
that he could to obtain it, he made his way back to **the lands of the**
faithful as he was advised by a revelation. So it was that this friend
of Christ with all his strength sought to die for him and yet could
not achieve it. He did not lack the merit of his desired martyrdom,
and he was spared to be honored in the future with a unique privilege.

Rom 12:1

1 Cor 2:4; Acts 5:12

Chapter IV
THE ZEAL FOR PRAYER AND THE SPIRIT OF PROPHECY

First Lesson

LMj X 1

Since he was made totally insensible to earthly desires through his *love of Christ*, aware that while in the body he was exiled from the Lord, the servant of Christ strove to keep his spirit present to God, *by praying without ceasing*, and thus he would not be without the consolation of his Beloved. For whether walking or sitting, inside or outside, working or resting, he was so focused on prayer that he seemed to have dedicated to it not only whatever was in his heart and body but also his effort and time. Many times he was suspended in such an excess of contemplation that he was carried away above himself and, experiencing what is beyond human understanding, he was unaware of what went on about him.

2 Cor 5:14

1 Thes 5:17

LMj X 2

Second Lesson

That he might receive the infusion of spiritual consolations more quietly, he went at night to pray in solitary places or abandoned churches. Although even there he experienced horrible struggles with demons who, fighting as it were hand to hand with him, tried to distract him from his commitments to prayer.[a] After these demons retreated from the unrelenting power of his prayers, the man of God, remaining alone and at peace, and, as if finding a more secret hiding place, would fill the forest with groans, water the places with tears, strike his breast with his hand. Now he entreated the Father; now he played with the Spouse; now he conversed with the Friend. There he was seen praying at night, with his hands and arms outstretched in the form of a cross, his whole body lifted up from the ground and surrounded by a sort of shining cloud, so that the extraordinary illumination around his body together with its elevation, was a witness to the wonderful light and elevation within his soul.

LMj X 3

1C 72; LMj X 3

LMj X 4

2 C 95; LMj X 4

---

a. Francis demonstrated a predilection for solitary sites such as abandoned churches and wilderness areas where he could seek divine consolation. Nevertheless, these same places often served as sanctuary for demons, giving rise to spiritual combat, a common theme in the monastic tradition and medieval hagiography. The struggle with demons is essential to the development of virtue, see: Thomas Heffernan, *Sacred Biography: Saints and Their Biographers in the Middle Ages* (New York: Oxford University Press, 1988): 152-153.

Third Lesson

By the supernatural power of such **ecstatic experiences, as has**   LMj III 4; LMj X
been proven by certain evidence, the *unknown and hidden secrets of*
divine *wisdom were opened to him unless* his zeal for fraternal welfare
urged him and the impulse of heavenly revelation forced him. **His**   LMj XI 1
unflagging zeal for prayer with his continual exercise of virtues
had led the man of God to such serenity of mind that, although he
had no expertise in Sacred Scripture which comes through study in
human learning, **nevertheless, enlightened by the splendor of eter-**
nal light, he probed the depths of Scripture with a clear, **remarkable**
incisiveness. The manifold *spirit* **of the prophets** also *rested* upon him   LMj XI 3
with a plenitude of various graces. By its wonderful power, the man
of God was **present to others who were absent,** had certain knowledge of those far distant, saw the secrets **of hearts,** and also foretold
future events, as the evidence of many examples prove, some of
which are included below.

Ps 50:8

Is 11:2

Fourth Lesson

At one time the holy man, Anthony, then an **outstanding**   LMj IV 10
preacher but now a **glorious confessor of Christ, was preaching elo-**
quently to the brothers at a provincial chapter at Arles on the title
of the Cross: *Jesus of Nazareth, King of the Jews.* **The man of God,**
Francis, who at that time was busy faraway, appeared **lifted up in**
the air at the door of the chapter. With his hands extended as if on a
cross blessing the friars, he filled their spirits with such manifold
consolation that it was certain to them that this **wonderful appari-**   LMj XI 14
tion had been endowed by the power of heaven. Furthermore, that
this did not lie hidden from the blessed father **is evidently clear from**
how open his spirit was to the light of *eternal wisdom which is mobile*
beyond all motion, reaching everywhere because of its purity, spreading
through the nations into holy souls, it makes them prophets and friends of
God.

Jn 19:19

Wis 7:25, 27

Fifth Lesson

At one time when the friars were entering the **chapter** according   LMj XI 11
to custom at St. Mary of the Portiuncula, **one of them, hiding behind**
the mantle of some excuse, would not submit himself to the disci-
pline. The holy one, who was then **praying in** his **cell** as a **mediator**
between those same **brothers and God,** saw all this in spirit. He had
one of the brothers **called to him and said:** "Brother, I saw the devil
perched on the back of that disobedient brother, holding him

tightly by the neck. Constrained by such a rider and having spurned the reins of obedience, the brother was being impelled to follow the devil's reins. Go, therefore, and tell the brother to submit to the yoke of obedience without delay because he, at whose earnestness in prayer this **demon left in confusion,** suggests that this be done." **The brother, warned by the messenger,** perceived the light of truth and conceived the spirit of compunction. *He fell forward on his face* before the vicar of the holy man, recognized that he was culpable, sought pardon, accepted and bore the discipline, and from then on **humbly** obeyed in all things.

Mt 26:39

Sixth Lesson

LMj XI 9

While he was secluded in a cell on Mount La Verna, one of his companions was yearning with great desire to have something of the Lord's words commented on and written with his own hand. This companion was being plagued by a serious temptation, not of the flesh but of the spirit, and he believed that by this means he would be set free from, or at least could bear more easily, the temptation. Though growing weary with such a temptation, he was in a state of anxiety because he was humble, modest, and simple. He was overcome by embarrassment and did not dare to disclose it to the venerable father. But what man did not tell him, *the Spirit revealed.* He ordered the brother to bring him paper and ink. And, he wrote down with his own hand the *Praises of the Lord* according to the brother's desire. He graciously gave the brother what he had written, **and the entire temptation** vanished immediately. **This little note, preserved for posterity,** brought healing to a great number of people. This made it clear to all how much merit before God this writer had whose writing left such efficacious power in a small leaf of paper.

1 Cor 2:10

Seventh Lesson

LMj XI 6

At another time, a noble woman, devoted to God, went confidently to the **holy** man and **implored** him with all her strength to intercede with the Lord on behalf of her husband, so that his hard heart might be softened by a plentiful infusion of his grace. The husband was **very cruel to her and opposed her service of Christ. After listening** to her, the holy and pious man confirmed her in her good intention with holy words, assured her that **consolation would shortly** be **hers,** and finally ordered her to declare **to her husband on the part of God and of himself that now is the time for clemency; later it will be the time for justice.** The woman put her trust in the words which the servant of the Lord had spoken to her, received his blessing, and in haste returned home. There she met her husband and told him about the conversation she had with that man, and without any doubt, she waited for the hoped for promise to be fulfilled. Without any delay, as soon as [Francis's] words reached his ears, the spirit of grace fell upon him and softened his heart in such a way that from that time on he permitted his devoted wife to serve God freely and offered himself to serve the Lord with her. At the suggestion of the holy wife, they lived a celibate life for many years, and then departed to the Lord on the same day; she in the morning as a *morning*

Ps 140:2

sacrifice, and he in the evening as an *evening sacrifice.*

Eighth Lesson

At the time when the servant of the Lord was lying ill at Rieti, a certain canon named Gedeon, who was deceitful and worldly, was   LMj XI 5
seized with a serious illness. Lying on a stretcher, he was brought to him, and with tears in his eyes, he, together with the bystanders, asked that he bless him with the sign of the cross. [Francis] said to him: "Since you once lived according to the *desires of the flesh* and

Sir 17:4   not in fear of the *judgment of God*, I will sign you with the sign of the
Gal 5:16   cross. This is not for your own sake but because of the devout petitions of those interceding for you. I do this with the provision that I let you know, from this moment on, that certainly you will suffer more serious things if, when you are free, you return to your vomit." After the sign of the cross was made from his head to his feet, the bones of his loins resounded and it sounded to all as though dry wood was being broken by hand. Immediately, he who had been lying there constricted, arose cured, and, bursting forth in praise of God said: "I have been freed." Then a short time elapsed when, forgetful of God, he returned his body to impurity, and on a certain evening dined in the lodging of a canon and slept there that night. The roof of the house collapsed suddenly on all but killed only him, while all the others escaped death. In this one event it was made manifest how strict is God's zeal for justice with ungrateful people, and how true and certain was the *spirit of prophecy*

Rv 19:10   which had filled Francis.

Ninth Lesson

At that time after his return from overseas, he went to Celano to preach. A knight with humble devotion invited him to dinner, and   LMj XI 4
with great insistence, forced him, as it were, to come. Before they took any food, the devout man, who offered according to his cus-

tom, praise and prayers to God, saw in spirit that this man's judgment was imminent. He stood there, lifted up in spirit, *with his eyes raised to heaven*. Finally, when he completed his prayer, he drew his kind host aside, predicted that his death was near, admonished him to confess his sins, and encouraged him to do as much good as he could. The soldier agreed to what the blessed man had said and in confession, he revealed all his sins to his companion, put his house in order, committed himself to the mercy of God, and prepared as much as he could to accept death. While the others were taking refreshment for their bodies, the soldier, who seemed strong and healthy, suddenly breathed forth his spirit according to the word of the man of God. Even though this soldier was carried off by a sudden death, nevertheless, he was so protected by the armor of repentance through the spirit's prophetic warning that he escaped perpetual damnation, and according to the promise of the Gospel, entered into the eternal dwellings.

Jn 17:1

Chapter V
THE OBEDIENCE OF CREATURES
AND THE DIVINE CONDESCENSION

First Lesson

Lk 4:18; 1 Cor 1:24
LMj XII 7

Surely, the *Spirit of the Lord* who *had anointed* him and also *Christ, the power and the wisdom of God,* were with the servant, Francis. It was this grace and power that brought it about that not only did *uncertain and hidden things* become evident to him, but even the elements of this world obeyed him. At one time doctors **advised him, and the brothers strongly urged him, to allow** his eye affliction to **undergo the process of cauterization. The man of God humbly agreed** because this would be not only a remedy for a bodily weakness, but also a means for practicing virtue. Given the sensitivity of the flesh, **he was struck with panic** at the sight of the **still-glowing iron.** The man of God **addressed the fire as a brother,** admonishing it in the name and in the power of its Creator **to temper** its heat that **he might be strong enough to bear its gentle burning. When the** hissing iron was sunk into his tender flesh and the burn was extended from the ear to the eyebrow, the man filled with God, exulted in spirit and **said to the brothers: "Praise the Most High, because I** confess **what is true; neither the heat of the fire** troubled me, nor did **pain in the flesh** afflict me."

Ps 50:8
LMj V 9

Second Lesson

LMj V 10

While the servant of God was suffering from a very serious illness at the hermitage of Saint Urban he felt a natural weakness. He requested a drink of wine but was told that there was no wine to give him. He then ordered some water brought to him, and, with the sign of the Cross, he blessed it. What had been pure water, immediately became excellent wine, and what the poverty of this deserted place could not provide, the purity of the holy man obtained. At the taste of it, he recovered so easily that it became evidently clear that the desired "drink" was given to him by a bountiful Giver not as much to please his sense of **taste** as to be efficacious for his health.

Third Lesson

LMj VII 12   At another time, the man of God wanted to go to a certain hermitage to spend some time in contemplation.[a] He rode on a donkey belonging to a poor man because he was weak. While this man followed the servant of God and climbed into mountainous country on a hot day, he became worn out from the journey over a rather rough and long road. When he became weakened from a burning thirst, he began to cry out urgently and say that unless he had a little something to drink, he would die immediately. The man of God leaped down from the donkey without delay, knelt on the ground, raised his hands to heaven, and did not cease praying until he understood that he had been heard. When he finally finished his prayer, he told the man: "Hurry to the rock over there, and there you will find running water, which Christ in his mercy has produced from a rock for you to drink at this very hour." The thirsty man ran to the place pointed out to him and drank the *water* produced *from the rock* by the power of another's prayer, and he consumed the drink furnished for him by God *from the most solid rock*.

Ps 77:16

Dt 32:13

Fourth Lesson

LMj XII 6   At one time, when the servant of Lord was preaching on the seashore at Gaeta, he wished to escape the adulation of the crowd, which in its devotion was rushing upon him. He jumped alone into a small boat that was drawn upon the shore. The boat, as though it were guided by an internal source of power, moved itself rather far from land without the help of any oars. All who were present saw this and marveled. When it had gone out some distance into the deep water, it stood motionless among the waves as long as, with the crowd waiting on the shore, it pleased the man of God to preach. After listening to the sermon, witnessing the miracle, and receiving the blessing they asked for, the crowd went away. By the influence of no other command but a heavenly one, the boat reached the shore; it subjugated itself without rebellion, as if it were *a creature serving its Maker*, to the perfect worshiper of the Creator and obeyed him without hesitation.

Wis 16:24

---

a. This account of Francis bringing water from the rock through prayer and the sermon to the birds in the sixth lesson are depicted above the main doors inside the Upper Basilica of Saint Francis in Assisi. The juxtaposition of these stories indicates a reliance on LMn, instead of LMj, at this point in the Giotto cycle. The resultant architectronic-artistic diptych serves as an arresting reminder, to those in the choir area as well as those departing the church, of the necessary synthesis of the contemplative-active dimensions of life.

Fifth Lesson

Once while he was staying in the hermitage of Greccio, the peo-   LMj VIII 11
ple of that place were burdened by many disasters. Every year hailstorms destroyed their wheat fields and vineyards while a pack of
raging wolves devoured not only animals but even people. The servant of the all powerful Lord was filled with a benevolent compassion for those sorely afflicted people. He promised and guaranteed
them personally in a public sermon that the entire pestilence would
Mt 3:8   vanish if they would confess their sins and be willing *to bring froth*
fruits worthy of repentance. From the very time that the people began
doing penance at his exhortation the disasters ceased, the dangers
Dn 3:50   vanished, and neither the wolves nor the hail caused *any more trou-*
ble. And even more remarkable, whenever the hail, falling on
neighboring fields, reached the boundaries of these people, either
it would stop or move off in a different direction.

Sixth Lesson

At another time the man of God was journeying around the valley
of Spoleto in order to preach. As he was approaching Bevagna, he   LMj XII 3
came upon a place where a very large flock of birds of various kinds
Jude 14:6   had gathered. Looking at them with affection, the *Spirit of the Lord*
came upon him, and he hurriedly ran to the spot, eagerly greeted
them, and commanded them to be silent, so that they might attentively listen to the word of God. While he recounted many things
about the benefits of God to these creatures, who were gathered together, and about the praises that should be returned to him by
them, they began to flutter about in a wonderful way; they
stretched their necks, spread out their wings, opened their beaks,
and looked attentively at him, as if they were trying to experience
Gn 41:38   the marvelous power of his words. It was only proper that this *man,*
full of God, was led by a humane and tender affection to such irrational creatures. For their part, those birds were drawn to him so remarkably that they listened to him when he was instructing them,
obeyed him when he commanded them, flocked to him without fear
when he bid them welcome, and, without distress, remained with
him.

Seventh Lesson

When he had tried to go overseas to pursue the palm of martyr-   LMj IX 5
dom, he was impeded by storms at sea from accomplishing his purpose. The Director of all things remained with him to such an extent

that His providence snatched him, together with many others, from the **dangers of death** and showed forth his wonderful **works** on his behalf **in the depths** of the sea. When he was proposing to return from Dalmatia to Italy and had **boarded a ship** without any provisions at all, a man **sent from God came,** as Francis stepped aboard, **with necessary food for Christ's little poor man.** Then this man gave the provisions to a God-fearing man whom he called from the ship, that **he might administer them** at the proper **time** to those who had absolutely nothing. **When the crew were unable to land anywhere because of the force of the winds, they used up all their food.** All that remained was a **small** portion **of the alms which was given from above** to the blessed man. Because of his prayers, merits, and the **power** of heaven, **these alms were multiplied so much that for many days, as the storm at sea continued, they fully supplied their needs** until the ship reached the desired **port of Ancona.**

Eighth Lesson

LMj V12 **At another time when the man of God was on a preaching journey with a brother companion between Lombardy and the Marches of Treviso, the darkness of night overtook them on the banks of the Po River. The road was exposed to many great dangers** because of the river, the marshes, and the darkness. His companion insisted that he should implore, in such a necessity, divine assistance. The man of God replied with great confidence: *"God is power-* Lk 3:5 *ful.* If it pleases him, he will make light for us by putting the darkness of night to flight." What followed was marvelous! **He had scarcely finished speaking when, behold, by the power of God such a great light began to shine around them that, while the darkness of night remained in other places, they could see in clear light not only the road but also many other things** on the other side of the river.

Ninth Lesson

The brightness of heavenly splendor went before them amid the dense darkness of the night in a fitting manner indeed. This proved that those who follow the light of life on a straight path are not able to be overwhelmed by the shadow of death. By the remarkable splen- LMj V 12 dor of such a light, **they were led physically and comforted spiritually. Singing hymns of praise to God, they arrived safely at their lodging, which was quite a stretch of road away.** He was a truly outstanding and admirable man, **for whom fire tempers its burning** LMj VII 13 **heat, water changes its taste, a rock provides abundant drink,** inanimate things obey, wild animals become tame, and to whom ir-

rational creatures direct their attention eagerly. In his benevolence
the Lord of all things listens to his prayer, as in his liberality he provides food, **gives guidance** by the brightness **of light, so that every**
creature is subservient **to him as a man** of extraordinary **sanctity,**   <small>LMj V 12</small>
and even the Creator of all condescends to him.[a]

---

a. This nuanced transition from self-emptying to the stigmata, with reference to the theme of light, is not
found in LMj where the account of the stigmata in Chapter XIII is preceded by accounts of preaching
and miracles. The theme of condescension or *condescensio*, which is woven through Bonaventure's
thought, sets the stage for the stigmatization of Francis. Divine condescension, witnessed in the
incarnation of Christ and manifested in stigmata, is rooted in God's love for humanity. Self-emptying
presupposes the radical poverty of created reality which looks to the Creator for redemption.

Chapter VI
THE SACRED STIGMATA

First Lesson

II 1; LMj XIII 1
The truly faithful servant and minister of Christ, Francis, two years before he returned his spirit to heaven, began a forty day fast in honor of the Archangel Michael in a high place apart called Mount La Verna. Steeped more than usual in the sweetness of heavenly contemplation and on fire with an ever intense flame of heavenly desires, he began to be aware more fully of the gifts of

LMj XIII 3
heavenly entries. With the seraphic ardor of desires, therefore, he was being borne aloft into God; and by compassionate sweetness he was being transformed into Him Who was pleased to be crucified out of the excess of His love. While he was praying one morning on the mountainside around the Feast of the Exaltation of the Holy Cross, he saw the likeness of a Seraph, which had six fiery and glittering wings, descending from the grandeur of heaven. He came in swift flight to a spot in the air near to the man of God. The Seraph not only appeared to have wings but also to be crucified. His hands and feet were extended and fastened to a cross, and his wings were arranged on both sides in such a remarkable manner that he raised two above his head, extended two for flying, and with the two others he encompassed and covered his whole body.

Second Lesson

LMj XIII 3
Seeing this, he was overwhelmed. His mind flooded with a mixture of joy and sorrow. He experienced an incomparable joy in the gracious way Christ appeared to him so wonderful and intimate, while the deplorable sight of being fastened to a cross *pierced his soul with the sword* of compassionate sorrow. He understood, as the one whom he saw exteriorly taught him interiorly,[a] that the weakness of suffering was in no way compatible with the immortality of the seraphic spirit; nevertheless, such a vision had been presented to his sight, so that this friend of Christ might learn in advance that he had to be transformed totally, not by a martyrdom of the flesh

Lk 2:35

---

a. Christ is the teacher who speaks to the inner spirit through the exterior senses, cf. Bonaventure, *Christ, The One Teacher of All*, 11-14 (V, 570-571), in *What Manner of Man: Sermons on Christ by St. Bonaventure*, translated with introduction and commentary by Zachary Hayes (Chicago: Franciscan Herald Press, 1974), 30-34.

but by the enkindling of his soul, into the manifest likeness of Christ Jesus crucified. The vision, which disappeared after a secret and intimate conversation, inflamed him interiorly with a seraphic **ardor** and marked **his flesh** exteriorly with a **likeness** conformed **to the Crucified;** it was as if the liquefying power of fire preceded the impression of the seal.

Third Lesson

The marks of nails began to appear immediately in his hands   LMj XIII 3
and feet. The heads of these appeared on the inner side of the hands and the upper side of the feet and their points on the opposite sides. The heads of the nails in his hands and feet were round, and their points, which were hammered and bent back, emerged and stuck out from the flesh. The bent part of the nails on the bottom of his feet were so prominent and extended so far out that they did not allow the sole of his feet to touch the ground. In fact, the finger of a hand could be put easily into the curved loop of the points, as I heard from those who saw them with their own **eyes. His right**   LMj XIII 8, LMj
side also appeared as though it were pierced with a lance. It was covered with a red wound from which his sacred blood often flowed. His tunic and underwear were soaked with such a quantity of blood **that his brother-companions,** when they **washed** these   LMj XIII 8
clothes, **undoubtedly** observed that the servant of the Lord had the impressed **likeness of the Crucified** in his **side** as well as in his hands and feet.

Fourth Lesson

Gn 41:38   The man, *filled with God,* realized that the stigmata which was im-   LMj XIII 4
pressed so splendidly on his flesh, could not be concealed from his intimate companions; nevertheless, he feared making public the
Tb 12:7   Lord's sacrament. He was thrown into an agony of doubt as to whether to tell what he had seen or be silent about it. Forced by the sting of conscience, he finally recounted with great fear the vision in detail to some of the brothers who were closer to him. He added that He who appeared to him told him some things which he would never disclose to any person as long as he lived. After the
2 Cor 3:18   true love of Christ *transformed* the lover into his *image,*[a] the forty

---

a. The transformative power of love is an ubiquitous current in Bonaventure's works and an example of his appropriation of the Pseudo-Dionysian heritage, see: *The Commentary on the First Book of Sentences,* d. 15, dubia 5 (I, 275b) and *The Sermon on the 14th Sunday after Pentecost* (1), (IX, 408a).

days on that mountain of solitude were completed and the feast of St. Michael the Archangel arrived. The angelic man, Francis, *came down from the mountain* bearing the likeness of the Crucified, depicted not on *tablets of stone* or on panels of wood, but engraved on parts of his flesh by the *finger of the living God.*

Mt 17:9

Ez 31:18

Fifth Lesson

LMj XIII 5

This holy and humble man tried afterwards with all diligence to conceal these sacred marks; nevertheless, it pleased the Lord to reveal through them certain marvelous things for his glory. Their hidden power, therefore, could be made manifest by clear signs and irradiate like a bright star amid the dense darkness of a darkened age.

LMj XIII 7

For about the time the holy man stayed on Mount La Verna, for example, dark clouds would form over the mountain and violent hailstorms would devastate the crops. Truly, after that blessed apparition, the normal hail stopped to the amazement and joy of the inhabitants. The very aspect of the sky, tranquil beyond usual, proclaimed the supreme worth of that vision from heaven and the power of the stigmata impressed there.

Sixth Lesson

LMj XIII 6

At that time a very serious plague swept through the province of Rieti and began to afflict the sheep and the cattle to such an extent that almost all of them seemed to languish under an incurable illness. A God-fearing man was admonished by a vision one night to hurry to the brothers' hermitage where the blessed father was then staying and to request from his companions the water he used to wash his hands and feet. He was then to sprinkle this water on the suffering animals and, thereby, put the plague to an end. After the man diligently completed this task, God gave great power to the water which had touched the sacred wounds. Even a little of the water completely drove out the plague from the suffering animals it touched. Once they recovered their former vigor, they ran to their fodder as if they had nothing wrong with them earlier.

Seventh Lesson

LMj M I 5

Finally, from that time on, those hands attained such marvelous power that their saving touch returned both robust health to the sick and living sensation to limbs now dry and paralytic. What is greater, they restored unimpaired life to those who had been mortally wounded. I will anticipate and recall briefly to mind for you two of his many miracles. Once at Lerida, a man, whose name was John and who was devoted to blessed Francis, was so cut and savagely wounded one night that one could hardly believe that he would survive until the next day. Our holy father appeared marvelously to him and with his sacred hands touched those wounds. At the very same hour John was so restored to full health that all the region proclaimed that this wonderful standard bearer of the cross was most worthy of all veneration. Who would not be surprised to look upon a person he knew well, who, at almost the same moment of time, was mangled by the most cruel wounds and then rejoiced in unimpaired health? Who would be able to recall this without giving thanks? Finally, who could ponder in a spirit of faith such a tender, virtuous, and remarkable miracle without experiencing devotion?

Eighth Lesson

At Potenza, a city of Apulia, a cleric named Ruggero was thinking foolish things about the sacred stigmata of our blessed father. He received a blow to his left hand under his glove, as though from an arrow shot from a bow. His glove, however, remained untouched. He was subject to the sting of excruciating pain for three days. Feeling remorseful, he called upon and entreated Francis earnestly to help him by means of those glorious stigmata. He received such perfect health that all the pain disappeared and not a trace of a blow remained. From this it seems perfectly clear that those sacred marks of his were impressed by a power and provided with the strength of Him whose characteristic it is to inflict wounds, to provide remedies, to strike the obstinate, and *to heal the contrite.*

Lk 4:18

LMj M 1 6

Ninth Lesson

This blessed man certainly appeared worthy to be marked with this singular privilege since his whole endeavor, both public and private, centered around the cross of the Lord. What else than his wonderful gentleness, the austerity of his life, his profound humility, his prompt obedience, his extreme poverty, his unimpaired chastity; what else than the bitterness of his compunction, his flow of tears, his heartfelt compassion, his zeal for emulation, his desire for martyrdom, his outstanding charity, and finally the privilege of the many virtues[a] that made him Christ-like: what else stood out in him

LMj M 1 1

---

a. This concise compendium of virtues is a meditation on the remarkable conformity of Francis with Christ as preamble and confirmation of the stigmata. These virtues, which are developed in LMn III, are key to understanding Bonaventure's hagiographical hermeneutic. Literary consideration of the virtues was accompanied by their artistic depictions in liturgical books and churches, see: Adolph Katzenellenborgen, *Allegories of the Virtues and Vices in Medieval Art* (Toronto Press: University of Toronto Press, 1989).

than these similarities to Christ, these preparations for the sacred stigmata? For this reason, the whole course of his life, from the time of his conversion, was adorned with the remarkable mysteries of the cross of Christ. Finally, at the sight of the sublime Seraph and the humble Crucified, he was transformed totally by a fiery, divine power into the likeness of the form which he saw. Those who saw them, touched them, and kissed them testified to this; and after having touched these most sacred wounds, they confirmed them with greater certitude by swearing that they saw them and that they were exactly as reported.

Chapter VII
THE PASSING OF DEATH

First Lesson

Gal 2:19
The man of God was now, *fixed to the cross* in both body and spirit. LMj XIV 1
Just as he **was being born aloft into God** by the fire of seraphic love, LMj XIII 3
he was also being transfixed by a fervid zeal for souls. **He thirsted** LMj XIV 1
with the crucified Lord for the deliverance of all those **to be saved**[a].
Since **he could not walk because of the nails protruding from his**
Lk 8:1
feet, he had his half-dead body carried *through the towns and villages,*
Rv 7:2; Lam 2:3
so that like *another angel ascending from the rising of the sun,*[b] he *might*
Lk 1:79
kindle the hearts of the servants of God with a divine *flame of fire, direct*
Rv 7:3
their *feet into the way of peace,* and *seal* their *foreheads* with the sign *of* the
living *God.* **He burned with a great desire to return to the humility**
he practiced at the beginning, so that he might, just as he did at the
outset, nurse lepers and treat his body once more like a slave that
was already in a state of collapse from his work.

Second Lesson

With Christ as leader, he resolved to do great deeds, and al- LMj XIV 1
though his limbs were weakening, he was strong and fervid in
spirit, and he hoped for a victory over the enemy in a new struggle.
In order that his merits might increase, for these are brought to per- LMj XIV 2
fection **in patience, the little one of Christ started to suffer from** various **illnesses.** The painful agony of **suffering** was diffused
Jb 19:2; Lam 4:8
throughout his limbs, his *flesh was all consumed,* **as if only skin clung**
to his bones. While he was tortured by harsh bodily suffering, he
called those punishing conditions not by the name of "pains" but
rather "sisters." He gave such praise and **thanks to the Lord** in the
joyful bearing of them, that **it seemed to the brothers** taking care of
him that they were looking upon Paul in his joyful and humble glory-
ing, and that they were seeing another Job in the vigor of his imper-
turbable spirit.

---

a. Francis's thirst for the salvation of others is indicative of the fourth and highest degree of love
described by Richard of Saint Victor, see: Jean Châtillon, "Richard of Saint Victor," *Dictionnaire de
Spiritualité Ascétique et Mystique, Doctrine et Histoire* XIII (Paris: Beauchesne, 1937-1995), 646.
The return to evangelization after the stigmata demonstrates the *reductio* of Franciscan mysticism
whereby the ecstatic experience of God in prayer leads back into the world. This is evident in
Francis's decision to return to preaching and ministering to lepers.

b. The literary identification of the stigmatized Francis with the angel of the apocalypse bearing the
seal of Rv 7:2 was mirrored in Franciscan liturgical art, as evidenced in an angel bearing the
stigmata in the Lower Basilica of Saint Francis in Assisi.

Third Lesson

LMj XIV 2

He knew long in advance the time of his death. As this day grew near, he told the brothers that *laying aside the tent* of his body was at hand, as it had been pointed out to him by Christ. Two years after the imprinting of the sacred stigmata and in the twentieth year of his conversion, he asked to be brought to Saint Mary of the Portiuncula. He wished to pay his debt to death and arrive *at the prize* of eternal *recompense* there where he had conceived the spirit of perfection and grace through the Virgin Mother of God. After he was brought to the above mentioned place, he showed by a true example that there was nothing in common between him and the world. In that grave illness that ended all suffering, he placed himself in fervor of spirit totally naked on the naked ground, so that in that final hour, when the enemy could still rage, he might wrestle naked with the naked. Lying thus on the ground and in the dust, this naked athlete covered with his left hand the wound in his right side, lest it be seen. With his serene *face raised* in the customary manner *toward heaven* and his attention directed entirely toward that glory, he began to praise the Most High because, released from all things, he was now free to go to Him.

2 Pt 1:14

Phil 3:14; Col 3:24

Jb 11:15

Fourth Lesson

LMj XIV 5

Finally, when the hour of his passing was approaching, he had all the brothers staying in the place called to him. Consoling them in preparation for his death with comforting words, he exhorted them with fatherly affection to divine love. Then leaving them their rightful inheritance, the possession of poverty and peace, he charged them to strive toward things eternal and fortify themselves against the dangers of this world. He carefully admonished them and persuaded them with all the efficacy of speech he could muster to follow perfectly the footsteps of Jesus crucified. As his sons were sitting around him, the patriarch of the poor, whose *eyes had been dimmed* not *by age* but by tears; the holy man, blind and now near death, crossed his arms and *stretched his hands over* them in the form of the cross, for he always loved this sign. He then blessed all the brothers, both present and absent, in the name and in power of the Crucified.

Mass II
LMj XIV 5

Gn 48:10

Gn 48, 14

Fifth Lesson

LMj XIV 5
2 C 94

After this he ordered the Gospel according to John be read to him from the place that begins: *Before the feast of the Passover*. He wished to hear the *voice of the Beloved* knocking, from whom only the wall of flesh now separated him. Finally, when all the mysteries were fulfilled in him, the blessed man, praying and singing psalms, *fell asleep in the*

Jn 13:1

Sg 5:2

LMj XIV 6

Acts 7:60

Lord. His most holy soul, released from the flesh, was absorbed into the abyss of eternal light. At that very hour one of his brothers and disciples, a man certainly famous for his sanctity, saw that happy soul in the likeness of a brilliant star, borne aloft by a *little cloud over many waters* straight to *heaven.* This soul, glittering with the clear luster of his conscience and glistening with the sure sign of his merits, was being raised on high so effectually by an abundance of graces and divine virtues that nothing would be able to detain it at all from its vision of heavenly light and glory.

Ps 28:31

Sixth Lesson

The minister of the brothers at that time in Terra di Lavoro was Augustine, a man who was certainly dear to God, and in his last hour. For a long time he had been without the power of speech, but now *he called out* to those listening *who were standing about* and said: "Wait for me, father, wait! Look, I am coming with you!" The amazed brothers asked him to whom he was speaking, he asserted that he saw blessed Francis going to heaven. As soon as he said this, he also happily went to his rest. At the same time the Bishop of Assisi had gone to the shrine of Saint Michael at Monte Gargano. Blessed Francis, filled with delight, appeared to him in the hour of his *transitus*, and said that he was leaving the world and passing exultantly into heaven. Arising in the morning, the bishop told his companions what he had seen. Then, after returning to Assisi, he carefully inquired and found out for certain that the blessed father had departed from this life at the very hour when he appeared to him in this vision.

LMj XIV 6

Lk 9:39

Acts 23:4

Seventh Lesson

The immensity of celestial goodness deigned to show, by many outstanding examples of miracles after his death, just how remarkable this man was for outstanding sanctity. Because of his merits and at his intercession, the power of almighty God restored sight to the blind, hearing to the deaf, speech to the mute, walking to the lame, and feeling and movement to the paralyzed; he gave robust health, moreover, to those who were withered, shriveled, or ruptured, and effectively snatched away those who were in prison; he brought the shipwrecked to the safety of port, granted an easy delivery to those in danger during childbirth, and put demons to flight from those possessed. Finally, he restored those hemorrhaging and lepers to wholesome cleanliness, those mortally wounded to a perfectly sound condition, and what is greater than all these, he restored the dead to life.

LMj XV 9

Eighth Lesson

LMj Prol 3

Because of him innumerable benefits from God do not cease to abound in different parts of the world, **as even I myself who wrote** the above have experienced in my own life. When I was just a child and very seriously ill, my mother made a vow on my behalf to the blessed father Francis. I was snatched from the very jaws of death and restored to the vigor of a healthy life. Since I hold this vividly in my memory, I now publicly proclaim it as true, lest keeping silent about such a benefit I would be accused of being ungrateful. Accept, therefore, blessed father, my thanks however meager and unequal to your merits and benefits.[a] As you accept our desires, excuse, too, our faults through prayer, so that you may both rescue those faithfully devoted to you from present evils, and lead them to everlasting blessings.

Ninth Lesson

LMj XII 12

It is fitting, therefore, that these words be concluded with a brief recapitulation of everything that has been written. Whoever has read thoroughly the things above should ponder carefully these final considerations: the conversion of the blessed father Francis which took place in a marvelous way; **efficacy** in the divine word; **privilege** of exalted **virtues**; *spirit of prophecy* together with an **understanding** of the Scriptures; **obedience of creatures lacking reason**; the impression of the sacred stigmata; and his celebrated **passage** from this world to heaven. These seven **testimonies** clearly attest and show **to the whole world** that he, the glorious **herald of Christ,** *having in himself the seal of the living God,* **should be venerated** by reason of his accomplishments, and for the fact that he was **authentic in his teaching and admirable in his holiness.** So let those who *are leaving Egypt* feel secure in following him. With the *sea divided* by the staff of the cross of Christ, *they will traverse the desert* and in crossing the Jordan of mortality, they will enter, by the wonderful power of that cross, *into the promised land of the living.* Through the prayers of our blessed father may they, there, be conducted to that glorious Savior and leader, Christ, to whom with the Father and the Holy Spirit, in perfect Trinity be all praise, *honor, and glory forever. Amen.*

Rv 19:10

Rv 7:2

LMj M X 9

Ex 13:17; Ps 113:1

Acts 7:5

Ps 135:13; 67:8; Dt 27:3

Acts 7:5

Rom 16:27

THE END OF THE MINOR LIFE OF SAINT FRANCIS.

---

a. In addition to justifying his efforts to recount the life of Francis, Bonaventure's boyhood memory of healing becomes an invitation to the friars gathered in liturgical prayer to seek assistance from the Poor Man of Assisi. The intercession of Francis lies at the heart of prayer as *oratio*, see: *The Journey of the Mind into God,* prol. 1 (V, 295a).

The Evening Sermon on Saint Francis
Preached at Paris, October 4, 1262

According to Sophronius Clasen this dates from October 4, 1258, and was the only sermon preached before the *Major Legend*,[a] and according to John F. Quinn it was preached on October 4, 1269.[b] However, on the basis of the content of this sermon, several passages of which correspond almost literally to the *Major Legend*, Ignatius C. Brady established that this sermon was preached at Paris in the evening of October 4, 1262.[c]

Mt 24:30 *Then will appear the sign of the Son of Man in heaven*

Introduction

Eccl 11:6 *In the morning sow your seed and at evening withhold not your hand; for you do not know which will prosper, this or that: and if both together, it shall be the better.*

The wise Ecclesiastes addresses these words to the preacher of God's truth, that he should not rest content with having preached in the morning, but should preach and go on preaching at every hour in 2 Tm 4:2 the evening, as Saint Paul admonishes Timothy: *Preach the word; be urgent in season and out of season, convince, rebuke, and exhort; be unfailing in patience and in teaching.*

Today the cardinal preached to you and I trust that with God's help the seed he sowed will bear fruit in you.[d] If now I also can say something that will bear fruit in you, that will be excellent.

Of course, some may say: "What is the point of so many sermons, when they have become occasions of boredom and ridicule?" But that is not true. A person with a well-disposed heart does not get bored; on the contrary, he listens willingly at any time to words

---

a. Cf. Srm1 Introduction, supra 26.

b. John F. Quinn, "Chronology of St. Bonaventure's Sermons" AFH 67 (1974) 161, 183.

c. Ignatius C. Brady, "The Writings of Saint Bonaventure Regarding the Franciscan Order," *San Bonaventura Maestro di vita francescana e di sapienza cristiana.* Atti del Congresso Internazionale per il VII Centenario di San Bonaventura I (Roma, 1976) 101-102; "Saint Bonaventure's Sermons on Saint Francis," *Franziskanische Studien* 58 (1976), 132-137.

d. A reference to the sermon of Eudes of Châteauroux, Chancellor of the University of Paris from 1238-1244, preached on the morning of October 4, 1262, cf. FA:ED II 811-818.

about his God and Creator. A person with a mind eager to learn will attend lectures at any time of the day in order to grow in knowledge. Nor will he miss hearing a lecturer in the afternoon because he heard a professor in the morning. Rather, he will attend it willingly.

The same applies to a person with a heart well-disposed to hear God's word. He will not miss an evening sermon because he heard one in the morning but will go willingly to the evening sermon. And even if he does not profit by it or sometimes gets little of it, nevertheless, if he was pleased to attend and listened willingly to the sermon about his Creator, there is great merit in that. Among the accepted customs here, it is one of the better ones that the students of this city come eagerly to hear the Word of God.

So, the Word of God is to be preached and sown in the morning and the evening; and just as a natural seed will produce little or nothing unless rain pours down to make it germinate and bear fruit, so the seed of my word will bear little fruit unless the rain of God's blessing comes down upon it. Here at the outset, therefore, let us ask Him who, according to the Psalm, shed rain in abundance and re- *Ps 68:9* stored His heritage, to grant me to say something in His honor, to the praise and commendation of Saint Francis and for the consolation of our souls.

I

We began with the text: *Then will appear the sign of the Son of Man in* *Mt 24:30* *heaven.*

LMj XIII 3; XV 2   Among all the gifts which God bestowed on this humble and poor little man, Saint Francis, there was one special and if I dare to say, unique privilege: that he bore on his body the stigmata of our Lord *Gal 6:17* Jesus Christ, for two years before he died. His side was pierced and blood flowed from it, and on his hands he had wounds in which there were black nails bent over at the back. This is certain, as certain LMj XIII 8   as anything in this world can be. Many saw the stigmata on his body, some of whom are still alive. The Lord himself imprinted this sign on that most humble and poor little man, who in his humility made himself a servant of lepers, as you heard today. In praise of this special or, as I would rather say, unique, privilege, I have quoted the text from Saint Matthew's Gospel.

In its literal sense and according to its historical meaning this text refers to the Lord's sign, that is the cross, which will appear on the Day of Judgment; in its allegorical meaning, it refers to the marks of the cross which will be seen then on Christ's body, put on it at the crucifixion; and in its tropological or moral meaning, it refers to the stigmata of the Lord Jesus which appeared on the body of Saint Francis.

In the literal sense "the heavens" refer to the reality we see above us. Understood in this sense, the sign of the cross will appear in the heavens on Judgment Day as a sign of the Judge's severity, so that *all tribes of the earth will wail on account of him* and as Habakkuk says: *The sun and moon . . . shall speed in the brightness of your glittering spear.* This spear by which David brought down Goliath, namely, the Devil, is the cross of Christ. Saint John Chrysostom remarks that it will appear on Judgment Day more splendid than all the stars.[a]

The sign of the cross appeared in heaven which can be understood allegorically; that is, it appeared on the body of our Lord Jesus Christ on the day of the crucifixion. We read in Isaiah: *In that day the root of Jesse shall stand as an ensign to the peoples,* that is, as a sign of mercy. The cross which Christ carried and on which he suffered is a sign of mercy to all peoples and to every nation, as Isaiah continues: *him shall the nations seek and his tomb shall be glorious.* The Jews who refuse to recognize and accept Christ ought to consider all this carefully and acknowledge its truth. Let them search to see if the tomb of any other man is as glorious.

This sign also appeared in the mystical body of Christ and it will be seen on his members, as Saint Paul says: *Those who belong to Christ Jesus have crucified the flesh with its passions and desires.* Only those who bear his sign belong to Christ's army, that is, the sign of Christ's cross. Therefore, everyone will have to bear this sign. God revealed the sign of the cross, however, in a special way to two members of Christ's mystical body: to Emperor Constantine I and to Saint Francis.

For many generations up to the time of Constantine, kings and emperors had been pagans and there had been war and dissension among the peoples of the earth. It was as though the blessings of Christ's cross had been consigned to oblivion. Then the sign of the cross appeared in the heavens to Constantine when he had to go to war against Maxentius. It appeared as a sign of victory for Constantine was told: τούτῳ which means "in this sign, conquer" or "In this sign you will be victorious."[b] At that moment he acknowledged the Crucified One and made the sign of the cross on his forehead. From then onwards the cross was transformed from being a gibbet for brigands into a sign on the foreheads of emperors. After this Constantine sent his mother, Saint Helen, to Jerusalem to search for the wood of the cross. She found it and sent it to Jerusa-

Rv 1:7

Hb 3:11

1 Sm 17:41-51

Is 11:43

Gal 5:24

---

a. Saint John Chrysostom, *Homilia II de Cruce et Latrone*, n. 4, (PG 49, 414).

b. Eusebius, *De vita Constantini*, Lib. 2, c. 28, (PG 20, 943).

lem. From it all the relics of the wood of the cross which are found throughout the whole world have been taken.

It was the Lord's good pleasure at the time of Constantine that he willed to put an end to wars and tribulations through the sign of victory, that is, the sign of the cross, which appeared to Constantine. As he willed to imprint the sign of victory on Constantine, so he chose to imprint the sign of penance on Saint Francis. In so doing he chose a simple, poor, and humble man to be the model of penance to all who were to come after him. Therefore, the text from Revelation can be understood of him: *I saw another angel ascend from the rising of the sun with the seal of the living God*, and this that he might *put a mark upon the foreheads of the men who sigh and groan.* Rv 7:2 Ez 9:4

There are two elements in the text quoted at the beginning. The first concerns the privilege of a special grace which Saint Francis received by being conformed to Christ, as the text says: *Then will appear the sign of the Son of Man*; the second touches on his surpassing merits, as the text continues: *in heaven*, for the Holy Spirit fills the heavens—that is, heavenly men—with his gifts.

II

You will know that the heavens possess numerous characteristics. Leaving aside many others, I want to concentrate on these: their very presence above us, their vast extent which encompasses everything, and their effects on the earth.

First, then, they stand above us in lofty heights which may be taken as referring to the exalted poverty embraced by holy people, and by Saint Francis in particular; they are adorned with splendor, which may be understood as unblemished purity; and they remain unalterable in their position, which I take as referring to Saint Francis's humble obedience.

Saint Francis was like the heavens in their lofty heights because of his exalted poverty. We read in Isaiah: *Heaven is my throne and the earth my footstool*, and a little later: *To whom shall I look but to him who is poor and little contrite in spirit and trembles at my words.* O Lord God, how do you bring together in the same passage *a poor little man* and *heaven*? Of which heaven are you speaking? In which heaven is the Lord pleased to place his throne? Beyond doubt *in the poor little man* who may be called a *heaven*. I will prove this by the Psalm which says: *The Lord is in his holy temple, the Lord's throne is in heaven*, and then adds: *His eyes behold the poor man.* To the avaricious, poverty is a detestable thing, but not so in the eyes of God. For though in appearance it is most base, in truth it is exalted and most high. Saint Paul writes to the Corinthi-

Is 66:1-2
Ps 10:4
Ps 10:5

2 Cor 8:2
ans: *Their extreme poverty has abounded to the riches of their simplicity.* As the heavens are arranged in spheres of high, higher, and highest heavens, so there is a poverty borne in patience that is good, a poverty that is desired and longed for which is better, and poverty embraced with joy in which a person glories and rejoices, which is best of all. Poverty, therefore, is the reason why a person can be likened to the heavens, because it leads to the kingdom of heaven. Our Lord says:

Mt 5:3
Blessed are the poor in spirit, for theirs is the kingdom of heaven. Poverty excludes those who do not love it, or who malign it, from the kingdom

Mt 19:24
of heaven, as Scripture says: *It is easier for a camel to go through the eye of a needle than for a rich man to enter the kingdom of God,* that is, for a rich man who has set his heart on riches and placed his trust in them. Av-

1 Tm 6:9
arice drags a person down because *those who desire to be rich fall into temptation, into a snare, into many senseless and hurtful desires that plunge men into ruin and destruction.* Take note that avarice casts a person into the depths. Poverty, on the other hand, uplifts a person to the state of heavenly life and, above all, that poverty in which a person glorifies and rejoices.

You will not find anyone who embraced poverty like Saint Francis, nor who gloried in it as he did. He refused to possess anything at all, either personally or in common, nor did he want his brothers to own anything. The cross of Christ is the sign of poverty because on it he was reduced to the utmost poverty, not having had even an old rag with which to cover his nakedness. Saint Francis also chose the highest poverty. It is fitting, therefore, that the sign of the Son of Man, namely, Christ's cross, should be found on Saint Francis. LMj VII 1-3

At this point someone may remark that self-praise is distasteful, and so I ought not to be saying these things in praise of ourselves, of our own Orders and of our holy father Saint Francis. But really one should not remain silent about these things by which the Holy Spirit himself approved and confirmed the life of poverty by the sign of the cross. For at the very time Saint Francis sought approval of his Order from the pope, the stigmata of our Lord were imprinted on his body. This was God's approval, not man's, for men can be deceived. And so not only did a human being issue a bull approving poverty, the Lord himself issued his own bull approving poverty by imprinting the stigmata of his passion on the poor and humble Saint Francis. It is not granted to everybody to observe such poverty or to choose it, but it is given to all to admire it. And it ought to be a source of joy to anyone who cannot be poor like this, that such poverty was embraced by someone.[a] LMj IV 11

---

a. Saint Bonaventure may well be excusing himself here.

We noted also that the heavens are adorned with splendor. Saint Francis can be compared to this aspect of the heavens because of his unblemished purity. We read in the book of Sirach: *The firmament on high is his beauty, the beauty of heaven with its spectacle of glory.*

Sir 43:1

The firmament which is arrayed with beauty may be likened to a soul that is marked by purity, as an impression is made by a seal in wax. It says in Exodus that the elders of Israel *saw the God of Israel; and there was under his feet as it were a pavement of sapphire stone, like the very heaven for clearness.* The latter words may be understood of a soul that has been cleansed of every impurity, of all stain and corruption of sins of the flesh. Such as this were the souls of the Nazarites of whom the Book of Lamentations says: *Her Nazarites were whiter than snow, purer than milk, more ruddy than coral, fairer than sapphire.* These words are said of men who had been consecrated to the Lord and were obliged to observe chastity. The Nazarites are described as *whiter than snow*, which is rightly said of people vowed to chastity because of their bodily purity, *purer than milk*, because of the integrity of their desires and the uprightness of their thoughts; *more ruddy than coral*, because all these virtues blend into a unity; and *fairer than sapphire*, which is to say, fairer than the serene blue heavens, because the sapphire has the same color as the clear sky.

Ex 24:9-10

Lam 4:7

Saint Francis, then, can be compared to the heavens adorned with splendor on account of his utter purity. He made himself a eunuch for the sake of the kingdom of heaven, by chastising, severely punishing, and mortifying his flesh so that it would not bring forth thorns and thistles, that is, the passions of unchaste thoughts and desires. Saint Benedict did likewise. At the beginning of his conversion he was so troubled for a short time by temptation of the flesh "that he almost considered abandoning his solitary retreat. Then suddenly God graciously looked upon him and he flung himself naked upon stinging thorns and burning nettles. In so doing he changed his lust to pain, and from that time on he never again experienced a sensation like that."[a]

Mt 19:12

Gn 3:18

LMj V 3

Saint Francis also in the early days of his conversion suffered temptations of the flesh. As he wrestled with these temptations one winter's night, he threw himself naked into the snow and mastered them thoroughly. From that time he scarcely needed to go to such lengths because of the other penance he endured which were quite

---

a. Gregory the Great, *Dialogues* II 2 (PL 77, 132).

sufficient to conquer such temptations. His desire was to overcome completely both the lust of the flesh and evil thoughts and desires of the heart. This man was totally possessed of bodily purity, or better, heavenly purity. And I would remind you, dear brothers, that purity enhances the other virtues, it adorns and ennobles them all. When we hear it said of someone that he leads an honorable life and is chaste and pure, that means in fact that he has honor and glory in the sight of God. The cross of Christ is the sign of chastity, of bodily mortification, and of lamb-like simplicity and purity. Therefore, how right it is that this sign should have been found on Saint Francis.

I pointed out, finally, that the heavens remain unalterable in their position. They suffer no disturbance and everything they contain is fixed according to an order. Saint Francis can be compared to this characteristic of the heavens on account of his humble obedience. We read that Job was asked: *Do you know the order of the heavens?* And we may ask: "What is the order of the heavens?" We know that the higher sphere draws all the other spheres by its movement. Though these move in their course by their own power, nevertheless they move with the higher sphere which draws them all with itself in such a way that in the heavens there is no toil, disorder, or hardship.

Jb 38:33

There is a similar order in the ranks of heaven where the activity of the highest determines all the rest. And who established that order? Beyond doubt its origin is this: the highest order of angels, the supreme spirits, conforms to the eternal law, and the lower ranks of angels, in their turn, are subject to the higher ranks. If you were to ask an angel of one of the lower ranks: "Why do you obey the higher angels when you, like them, were created directly by God?" he would reply: "Why should it be strange that I obey an angel of a higher rank? He commands nothing of himself, but only what has been entrusted to him by God. And I must needs obey my Creator." According to this pattern there is an established order both in God's Church, where the lower ranks are subject to the higher and should obey them, and in the soul of the just man, where the lower faculties are subject to the higher and should obey them.

Why then does the flesh rebel against the spirit? This was not the case at the beginning, for it is unthinkable that God should have created humanity in such disorder. If humanity had remained in original innocence our lower nature and the desires of the flesh would never have rebelled against reason, and we should not have been ig-

norant of the truths we ought to know. All this was the result of original sin. There lies the reason why our highest spiritual powers are
not obedient to God, why our senses do not submit to reason, and
why our lower faculties are not subject to the higher. But these disor-
ders can be set right by humble obedience. A person lives by the obedience born of humility when he submits to God's law without any
resistance or hesitation, and guides his life by the truth. Anyone who
conducts himself in this way can be compared to the heavens where
the lower spheres are unconditionally obedient to the further and
higher spheres.

LMj II 7-8   Saint Francis possessed true humility and it was his desire that
both he himself and his Order should be named from it. Therefore,
his Order is called simply "the Order of Lesser Brothers." He was, or
LMj IV 9   at all events he reckoned himself, the least of all men. The first provincial minister of the brothers in France was a brother named
Pacifico.ª He was a companion of Saint Francis who was sent by him
LMj VI 6   to establish the Order in France. One day in a dream it seemed to him
that he was taken up into paradise. He saw there a large number of
thrones which were all occupied, and higher than the rest a more august throne which was unoccupied. On inquiring whose throne it
might be, he was told it was reserved for Saint Francis. Sometime
later he asked Saint Francis how he saw himself and what he
thought of himself. He answered: "It seems to me I am the greatest
sinner in the world. Yes, beyond question, that is what I think of myself." Pacifico protested: "How can you say that? Aren't there numerous thieves, fornicators, and murderers in the world?" Saint Francis
replied: "Listen. There is no one in the world who, if God has bestowed on him so many and such great graces as he has on me, would
not be more pleasing to God than I am. That is the reason I consider
myself the worst of sinners. Saint Paul said the same of himself: *I am
the first of sinners.*" He did not mean first in time, for there had been   1 Tm 1:15
many sinners before him, but the first in the sense of foremost. And
Saint Paul was a most humble and lowly man as his name reveals. In
fact, he was a most humble and lowly lesser brother.

A great burden has been placed on us by the name we bear: *Lesser
Brothers*, because it obliges us to account ourselves worse and more
sinful than others. If it causes us displeasure to find a brother of our
own Order who is proud, how much more must it be displeasing to

---

a. Cf. AC, 65, FA:ED II 167-68.

God. All this is abundantly clear from the fact that Christ's cross is
above all the sign of humility. Listen to Saint Paul: *Christ humbled
himself and became obedient unto death, even death on a cross.* Christ's cross
is the sign of the most perfect humility and self-abasement because
on the cross he humbled and abased himself to such an extreme for
our sake. So again, how right it is to find this sign on Saint Francis
who possessed the greatest humility and reckoned himself the lowest and meanest of sinners. He used to implore in prayer: "Why, O
Lord, have you laid this burden on me? Why have you made a simple,
unlettered, despicable creature like me the head of this Order?" And
the Lord would reply: "I have placed you over this Order so that what
I achieve in you may be attributed to my grace and not to man's inge-
nuity."

Second, we admire the heavens because of their vast extent. They
contain all things. Saint Francis can be likened to this feature of the
heavens because of his all-embracing love which went out to everyone. We read in the Book of Sirach: *I alone have compassed the circuit of
heaven.* This can be said of the love that is in God and in us for it also
has compassed the heavens which contain everything. Yet only the
righteous dwell in heaven. Love embraces all that love commands,
but such love is found only in the virtuous. It was through love that
the divine nature was united to flesh and through love that Christ
humbled himself and underwent death. The Book of Sirach tells us:
Look upon the rainbow and praise him who made it. What is this rainbow
except the cross of Christ? Therefore, the sign of Christ's cross had to
be found on this man of heavenly virtue, Saint Francis, whose love
was boundless. He had love without limit for everyone. Love spends
itself for sinners without counting the cost. Saint Francis was not
content with preaching God's word only to the Christian faithful
who listen with glad hearts and accept it willingly. He even went to
the Saracens to proclaim the Gospel in the hope that he might be put
to death for his faith in Christ and so become a martyr.

How is it that we, wretched as we are, have such cold hearts that
we are not prepared to endure anything for our Lord's sake? Our
hearts neither burn nor glow with love. Ardent love is a quality of the
heart and the stronger this love burns in a person's heart, the more
heroic and virtuous are his deeds. Do you desire to imprint Christ
crucified on your heart? Do you long to be transformed into him to
the point where your heart is aflame with love? Just as iron when
heated to the point where it becomes molten can take the imprint of

Phil 2:8

LMj VIII 3

Sir 24:8

Sir 43:12

LMj IX 5-8

any mark or sign, so a heart burning fervently with love of Christ crucified can receive the imprint of the Crucified Lord himself or his cross. Such a loving heart is carried over to the Crucified Lord or transformed into him. That is what happened with Saint Francis.

LMj XIII 1-5

Some people express surprise that when the stigmata of Christ's passion were to be imprinted on Saint Francis, a Seraph was sent to him. Surely none of the Seraphim was crucified! But the Seraphim are the angels whose name comes from "burning flame."[a] Thus, what this detail tells us is that Saint Francis was aflame with love when the Seraph was sent to him. The cross or sign of the cross imprinted on his body symbolized his love of Christ crucified and by the flame of that love he was totally transformed into Christ.

LMj XIII 6

I want to tell you something that happened in the province of Rieti which confirms what I have been saying. There was a fatal epidemic which had attacked the animals of the region so that they could not take food. Suddenly, all the animals were dying and the people did not know what to do to save them. One of the local people went to see a devout man and told him how the animals were dying and asked his advice. The devout man advised him to get some of the water in which Saint Francis had washed his hands and feet, sprinkle it over the animals and they would be cured. He did this and the animals came running for their food. I was told this by someone who saw it happen.

So, because Saint Francis had a love as vast as the heavens, and the cross is the sign of the greatest love in the world, it is to be expected that we should find this sign on him.

Moreover, the heavens contain mysteries. The Latin word for heaven, *caelum*, is derived from the verb *celare* meaning to keep secret or conceal.[b] Saint Francis can be compared to this feature of the heavens because he reached the heights of contemplation. It says in the Psalms: *You stretched out the heavens like a tent and covered its higher rooms with waters.* Waters are indeed limpid, refreshing, and shimmering with light and are a symbol of contemplation. There where the waters meet a man sees the reflection of his own image and the splendor of God's light. Saint Francis reached such

Ps 103:2-3

---

a. Gregory, *Homilia in evangelia* I, 34, nn. 10, 12, (PL 76, 1251, 1254); *Gregory the Great: Forty Gospel Homilies*, Cistercian Studies Series 123, translated by David Hurst (Kalamazoo: Cistercian Publications, 1990), 289, 291.

b. *Isidore, Etymologae*, XIII, c. 4, n. 1, (PL 82, 474).

heights of contemplation that he foretold the future, saw the se- LMj XI 3-14
crets of people's hearts, and appeared to those who were absent,
just like Saint Anthony the Hermit of whom Saint Augustine
speaks in the prologue to his work *On Christian Doctrine.*[a] The cross
of Christ is the sign of wisdom and of the revelation of God's mys-
Rv 5:12, 9, 2 teries. This is clear from the Book of Revelation where we are told
that *the Lamb who was slain opened the scroll sealed with seven seals,*
which means he unveiled by his cross all the mysteries of Holy
Rv 3:17 Scripture. The cross of Christ is the key of David; Christ is the
Holy One *who opens and no one shall shut, who shuts and no one opens.*
Because Saint Francis soared to such heights of contemplation
and wisdom, we should expect yet again to find on him the sign of
Christ's cross.

Mt 10:16   The Gospel tells us: *Be simple as doves.* We should love simplicity
and innocence of heart if we desire God to enlighten us with the brilliant light of wisdom. When the moon is directly opposite the sun, it
is all lit up and appears radiant; when it is in eclipse with the sun neither its light nor radiance can be seen. But in fact the nearer it is to
the sun and the closer it draws to it, the more light it receives. For in
truth it has more light then than it receives when directly opposite
the sun. Similarly, with us: the more a person parades his wisdom
and wants to appear wise, so much the less is he enlightened. But
when a person flees human company, enters into himself and reflects on his union with God, then is he so much the more enlightened. Though someone may appear enlightened, to be truly so it is
utterly necessary to draw close to God in the greatest humility and
simplicity of heart. I will give you an example. Students at the University of Paris went to Praepositivus the Chancellor and asked him:
"What do you believe? Tell us what we ought to believe." So
Praepositivus called in a simple man who was passing in the street
and the question was put to him. With simplicity he replied: "I believe in God the Father Almighty and in his Son and in their Spirit
and likewise that there is one God." "Excellent," answered
Praepositivus, "that is how I want to believe, in simplicity and humility."[b]

---

a. Augustine, *De doctrina christiana*, prol., n. 4; *Teaching Christianity*, translated with introduction
   and notes by Edmund Hill, edited by John Rotelle (Hyde Park: New City Press, 1991), 102.
b. See G. Lacombe, "Prevostin de Cremone," in *Dictionnaire de Theologie Catholique* xm, 1 Part.,
   162-69; J.N. Garvin, "Praepositinus of Cremona," in *New Catholic Encyclopedia* XI (Washington,
   1967), 660. His dates are 1130/5-1210. He was Chancellor of Paris from 1206 to 1209. His name is
   found in various forms: Praepositus, Praepositinus, Praepositivus.

Lastly, the heavens encompass everything, they contain all things, yet they are contained by nothing. Saint Francis can be likened to this aspect of them because he was filled with God's sevenfold grace. We read that God said to Abraham: *Look toward heaven and number the stars, if you are able to number them . . . so shall your descendants be.* There is no star however small whose immensity would not fill the earth and give it light. Though the light and rays of each star coalesce in the atmosphere, they are found to be distinct when we look up at the stars themselves.[a] It is something similar with devout souls whom the Holy Spirit enlightens with divine radiance. These are the posterity of the Holy Spirit and his posterity is as the stars of heaven, for the Holy Spirit brings forth devout souls in an altogether wondrous way. The Book of Job says: *His Spirit has adorned the heavens*—that is, men of heavenly virtue—*and with a midwife's skill his hand brought forth the winding serpent.* The marvel of Holy Scripture is how it brings together ideas which appear disparate but in fact are not. What is this hand of God whereby his works are wrought? As regards the creation of the world the Son can be called the hand of God through whom he made all things; as regards the variety of gifts, the Holy Spirit is God's hand who distributes the diverse gifts of grace *and apportions to each one individually as he wills.* Therefore, the Holy Spirit is the hand of God which bestows the manifold gifts of grace. How many are the graces placed in our hands? They are fourteen. The winding serpent will only be brought out of us if this hand of God, that is, the Holy Spirit, showers down on us his sevenfold grace: the four cardinal virtues and the three theological virtues, so that we can set out on the path of holiness and persevere to the end. The seven gifts of the Holy Spirit are given to us that we may do good works with zeal. Christ's cross is the sign of God's boundless grace because from the cross, that is, from Christ's sufferings, flow all the gifts of grace. So, once again, we should expect to find the sign of the Son of man, the cross of Christ, on Saint Francis who was filled with the gifts of the Holy Spirit.

Finally, I wish to say a word about the four effects the heavens have on the earth. They light up the earth by their luster, moisten it with rain from the clouds, bestow warmth on it from their heat and give it brilliance in flashes of lightning. In a similar way these effects of the heavens may be attributed to Saint Francis. He shed light on his neighbors,

Margin references: Gn 15:5 · Gn 1:11 · Jb 26:13 · Jn 1:1-5 · 1 Cor 12:11

---

a. Cf. *II Sent.*, d. XIII, a. III, q. 2 (II, 327).

less advanced on the way of perfection, by his manifest virtue; refreshed them with ardent love by his devout prayers; and filled them
with wonder by the miracles wrought through his holiness and goodness. The cross of Christ is the sign of God's perfect works and of all his
wonderful deeds. And because Saint Francis may be likened to the
heavens in all that he did, we should expect to find the cross imprinted
on him, so that by this sign he would be raised on high. The Lord regards the lowly and therefore he looked upon this humble and poor lit-
Ps 138:6   tle man, Saint Francis, and imprinted on him the sign of the cross; but
the haughty and proud he knows from afar. As Saint James reminds
Jas 4:6   us: *God opposes the proud, but gives grace to the humble.*

Therefore, let us ask God to grant us so to humble ourselves in this
life like Saint Francis, that by his merits and prayers we may be exalted in the next. May the Lord Jesus Christ who loves and lifts up the
humble, hear our prayer. Amen.

Sermon on Saint Francis
Preached at Paris , October 4, 1266

Three opinions exist regarding the date of this sermon. John F. Quinn maintains that it was delivered as early as October 4, 1254.[a] Sophronius Clasen, on the other hand, maintains that it was delivered after the composition of the *Major Legend*.[b] While sympathetic to an early date, Ignatius C. Brady concurs with Clasen and offers as his proof the text of Revelation 7:2, the angel bearing the seal of the living God. In light of a sermon Bonaventure delivered to the General Chapter of the Friars in 1266,[c] Brady proposes October 4, 1266 as the day on which Bonaventure delivered this sermon.[d]

> *I will take you, O Zerubbabel my servant, the son of Shealthiel, and make*   Hg 2:23
> *you like a seal, for I have chosen you*

This text from the Book of Haggai can be applied to Saint Francis. For as Zerubbabel, whose name means "leader of the exodus," led the people out of Babylon and rebuilt the Temple, so Saint Francis brought many people from the disorder of sin to Christ, and he founded a religious order. The saint is commended in this text on three accounts: for his worthy service which was pleasing to God: *I will take you . . .* for the seal of his outstanding holiness: *and make you like a seal;* and for the privilege of having been chosen by God: *for I have chosen you.*

I

As regards the first, we should take note that his service was pleasing to God because he was humble, for he spurned worldly honors. As the Apostle Paul says: *For though I am free from all, I have made*   1 Cor 9:19

---

a. John F. Quinn, "Chronology of St. Bonaventure's Sermons" AFH 67 (1974) 177.

b. Sophronius Clasen, *Franziskus Engel des Sechsten Siegels. Sein Leben nach den Schriften des heligen Bonaventura* (Werl/West, 1962), 153.

c. Clasen, *Franziskus Engel*, 156, 180, n. 239; Brady "The Writings," 102, n. 52; S. Bihel, "S. Franciscus fuitne angelus sexti sigilii?" *Antonianum* 2 (1927) 66, 73.

d. Ignatius C. Brady, "Saint Bonaventure's Sermons on Saint Francis," *Franziskanische Studien* 58 (1976), 130-131.

myself a slave to all that I might win the more. In this way Saint Francis imitated Christ *who though he was in the form of God emptied himself, taking the form of a servant.* And indeed, the service of God begins with humility. In this connection Saint Gregory says: "The person who acquires other virtues but not humility, is like someone carrying dust against the wind; he becomes all the more blinded by what he is seen to be carrying."[a]

Phil 2:6, 7

Saint Francis was so humble that he also served lepers. Because of his great humility he was taken to the heights of knowing divine mysteries. We read in Isaiah: *Behold my servant shall understand, he shall be exalted, and shall be exceeding high,* and in Saint Matthew's Gospel: *You have hidden these things from the wise and revealed them to babes.*

LMj 16; II 6

Is 52:13

Mt 11:25

Furthermore, he was pleasing to God because of his steadfastness through mortification of the flesh. The Psalm says: *I will lift up the cup of salvation . . . O Lord, for I am your servant.* The cup signifies mortification of the flesh. Saint Paul writes: *Our old self was crucified with him so that the sinful body might be destroyed, and we might no longer be enslaved to sin.* By this kind of mortification we serve God as Saint Paul makes clear: *I am speaking in human terms . . . For just as you once yielded your members to serve impurity and greater and greater iniquity, so now yield your members to serve righteousness for sanctification.*

Ps 115:4, 6

Rom 6:6

Rom 6:19

That is precisely what Saint Francis did. Even in the severest winter he rolled himself in the snow to curb temptations of the flesh. On account of his self-denial he was found worthy to receive divine consolations. Commenting on the text of Saint Luke's Gospel: *let your loins be girt,* Saint Gregory explains: "We gird our loins when we curb the lusts of the flesh by continence."[b] Saint Luke goes on to say that when the Lord finds servants such as these *he will gird himself and make them sit down,* that is, be consoled. All the unchaste will be excluded from this consolation, as the Book of Revelation testifies: *Outside are the dogs and sorcerers and unchaste.*

LMj V 3

Lk 12:35

Lk 12:37

Rv 22:15

Third, Saint Francis was pleasing to God because he was faithful by having renounced all earthly desires. We read in the Book of Numbers: *My servant Moses is the most faithful in all my house.* A faithful servant is one who does not look for human praise, as we learn from the text of Saint Paul: *If I yet pleased men, I should not be the servant of Christ.* On this Saint Bernard writes: "You are indeed a faithful ser-

Nm 12:17

Gal 1:10

---

a. Gregory, *Homilia in evangelia* I, hom. 7, n. 4, (PL 76, 1103); *Gregory the Great: Forty Gospel Homilies,* Cistercian Studies Series 123, translated by David Hurst (Kalamazoo: Cistercian Publications, 1990), 27.

b. Gregory, *Homilia in evangelia* I, hom. 13, n. 1, (PL 76, 1123); *Gregory the Great: Forty Gospel Homilies,* Cistercian Studies Series 123, translated by David Hurst (Kalamazoo: Cistercian Publications, 1990), 151.

vant when nothing of the Lord's abundant glory remains clinging to your hands. That glory comes not from you, it is channeled through you."[a]

More faithful still is the servant who does not seek bodily rest. In Saint Matthew's Gospel the Lord asks: *Who then is the faithful and wise* Mt 24:45 *servant, whom his master has set over his household to give them their food at the proper time?* He continues: *Blessed is that servant whom his master* Mt 24:46 *when he comes will find so doing.* The Lord comes to us at our death and prior to that we must not rest from our labors. Of the Prophet Samuel Scripture says: *And all Israel from Dan to Beersheba knew that Samuel was* 1 Sm 3:20 *a faithful prophet of the Lord,* and again, *money, or anything, even to a shoe,* Sir 46:22 *he had not taken of any man and no man did accuse him.*

LMj VII 1-3 Saint Francis observed all this literally for he fulfilled the gospel law perfectly. He had *neither money in his belt nor sandals on his feet.* In Mk 6:8; Mt 10:9 this way he imitated the Lord Jesus, for as Saint Jerome remarks: "The Lord could not himself possess what he had forbidden to his servants."[b] Because of his fidelity Saint Francis was found worthy to be raised to regal honors as the Gospel says: *Well done, good and faithful* Mt 25:21 *servant; enter into the joy of your master.* The covetous will not be taken into this joy, as Saint Paul tells us: *No immoral or impure man or one* Eph 5:5 *who is covetous, that is, an idolater, has any inheritance in the kingdom of Christ and of God.* Therefore, anyone who proclaims that we should love earthly goods is a blasphemer. Saint Jerome wrote to Bishop Nepotian: "You are the priest of a crucified Lord, one who lived in poverty and on the bread of strangers, and it is a shameful thing for a consul's attendants and bodyguards to keep watch before your door."[c] And we should note well that *a servant is not greater than his* Jn 13:16 *master.*

Lastly, Saint Francis was pleasing to God because he was devoted in carrying out God's commands in a way similar to Job: *Have you con-* Jb 1:8 *sidered my servant Job, that there is none like him on the earth, a blameless and upright man, who fears God and turns away from evil?* Of the service of God Scripture says: *Serve him only and he will deliver you.* Jesus himself 1 Sm 7:3 tells us: *No one can serve two masters,* that is, no one can serve the devil Mt 6:24 and God, except by some such agreement as Nahash the Ammonite wanted to make with the sons of Israel when he proposed: *On this* 1 Sm 11:2

---

a. Bernard of Clairvaux, Sermon 13:3, *On the Song of Songs,* translated by Kilian Walsh, introduction by M. Corneille Halflants (Spencer, MA: Cistercian Publications, 1971), 90.

b. Jerome, *Epistula XXII ad Eustochium,* n. 19, in *Corpus Scriptorum Ecclesiasticorum Latinorum,* Vienna (Collected Works of Latin Church Writers) (hereafter CSEL), 168; *Select Letters of Saint Jerome,* Loeb Classical Library, translated by Frederick Wright (London: Heinemann, 1975), 95.

c. Jerome, *Epistula LII ad Nepotianum Presbyterum,* n. 11, CSEL, 433; *Select Letters of Saint Jerome,* Loeb Classical Library, translated by Frederick Wright (London: Heinemann, 1975), 217.

condition I will make a treaty with you, that I gouge out all your right eyes, and thus put disgrace upon all Israel. The right eye is the one fixed on eternal things, the left on earthly things. The devil wants his servants to lose their longing for eternal things even when they do something good.

In everything he did Saint Francis had his right eye fixed on eternal things, for he was *blameless and upright.* And because he possessed a blameless eye, the *whole body* of his actions was *full of light.* He was found worthy to be raised to the heavenly dwelling place on account of his devoted service of God. We read in Isaiah: *Behold my servant, whom I uphold, my chosen in whom my soul delights; I have put my spirit upon him.* Whoever refuses to carry out God's commands is not fit to enter this heavenly dwelling place, as it is written in Saint Matthew's Gospel: *Cast the worthless servant into the outer darkness.*

Saint Francis, then was a servant pleasing to God because he was humble, steadfast, faithful, and devoted. That is to say, he resisted vainglory, the lusts of the flesh, worldly desires, and the powers of evil.

Mt 6:22

Is 42:1

Mt 25:30

II

We come now to the second part of the text: *and make you like a seal.* Saint Francis is commended here for the seal of his outstanding holiness. The marks of the passion imprinted on his body bear eloquent witness to this.

Hg 2:23

LMj XIII 1-10

First of all it should be noted that he was like a seal that has been refashioned, made new, through lament and sorrow for the sins of his past life. The Book of Job says: *The seal shall be restored as clay and shall stand as a garment.* A fallen angel who once bore the seal of God cannot be restored to his original state, because there can be no repentance for an angel. But for human beings it is quite different. The first half of Job's text says: *The seal shall be restored as clay.* That takes place by the waters of sorrow and the earth of humility. The text continues: *and shall stand as a garment.* A garment does not stand of itself but only when it clothes a body. Saint Francis was like a seal restored like clay through sorrow for his sins, and he stood like a garment of the Holy Spirit.

Jb 38:14

Second, he was like a seal transformed by the fire of love. The Song of Solomon says: *Set me as a seal upon your heart.* Speaking of God's love Hugh of Saint Victor writes: "I feel, O my soul, such is the power of love, that you are being transformed into the likeness of him you love."[a]

Sg 8:6

---

a. Hugh of St. Victor, *De arrha animae,* (PL 176, 954); *Soliloquy on the Earnest Money of the Soul,* translated with introduction by Kevin Herbert (Marquette: Marquette University Press, 1956), 16.

Third, he was like a seal that has been imprinted, through being an example of perfect virtue. For this there is a text in Romans: *He received circumcision as a sign or seal of the righteousness he had by faith.* Saint Paul is referring of course to spiritual not bodily circumcision. Rom 4:11

Lastly, he was like a declaratory seal by his ardent desire for the salvation of others. We read in the Book of Revelation: *Then I saw another angel ascend from the rising of the sun, with the seal of the living God.* This seal is the ardent desire for the salvation of all people. Then there is this text in Ezechiel: *And the Lord said to him: "Go through the city, through Jerusalem, and mark Tau upon the foreheads of the those who sigh and mourn over all the abominations that are committed in it."* So it is that God smote those in the land of Egypt who did not bear this sign. Rv 7:2
Ez 9:4
Ex 12:29

In summary, Saint Francis was like a seal refashioned, transformed, imprinted, and declaratory.

III

In the third part of the text: *for I have chosen you,* Saint Francis is commended for the privilege of having been chosen by God. It should be emphasized at the outset that no other cause of divine election can be assigned except the will of him who has said: *I will be gracious to whom I will be gracious and will show mercy on whom I will show mercy.* However, signs of divine election can be discerned and they are chiefly seven. Ex 33:19

The first is reverence for God's name. Scripture tells us: *The fear of the Lord is the beginning of wisdom, and was created with the faithful in the womb, it walks with chosen women, that is, with souls, and is known with the just and faithful.* A few verses earlier we read: *With him that fears the Lord, it shall go well at the end, and on the day of his death he will be blessed.* And in the same chapter: *For he who is without fear, cannot be justified: for the wrath of his high spirits is his ruin.* The whole of Sacred Scripture is directed toward arousing in us reverence for the Lord, as Ecclesiastes teaches: *Fear God, and keep his commandments; for this is the whole duty of a human being.* Sir 1:16
Sir 1:13
Sir 1:28
Eccl 12:13

The second is love of bodily purity. Saint Paul tells us that *God . . . chose us in him before the foundation of the world, that we should be holy and blameless before him,* and Saint Peter says: *You are a chosen race, a royal priesthood, a holy nation, God's own people.* Eph 1:4
1 Pt 2:9

The third is the graciousness of natural compassion. As the Apostle writes: *Put on then as God's chosen ones, holy and beloved, compassion.* In another text he shows Timothy that this is a sign of divine election: *Godliness is of value in every way, as it holds promise for the present life and also for the life to come.* We read, on the one hand, in the Book of Col 3:12
1 Tm 4:8

Jb 31:18
Sir 3:27
Ex 7:13, 21

Job: *For from my infancy mercy grew up with me: and it came out with me from my mother's womb.* On the other hand, Sirach warns: *A hard heart shall fear evil at the last;* and Saint Bernard advises: "If you want to know what a hard heart is, ask Pharaoh."[a]

Is 48:10
Jas 2:5
Mt 5:3

The fourth is joy in voluntary poverty whether the poverty was chosen or inflicted initially. As Scripture tells us: *I have chosen you in the furnace of poverty,* and in another place: *Has God not chosen the poor in this world, rich in faith, and heirs of the kingdom which God has promised to those who love him;* and again: *Blessed are the poor in spirit, for theirs is the kingdom of heaven.*

1 Cor 1:26-27
2 Sm 6:21-22
Lk 16:15

The fifth is the humility of a devoted heart. As Saint Paul writes to the Corinthians: *For consider your call, brethren; not many of you were wise according to worldly standards, not many were powerful, not many were of noble birth, but God chose what is foolish in the world to shame the wise, God chose what is weak in the world to shame the strong.* This in fact, on the one hand, was a sign of divine election in David who said to Michaël: *It was before the Lord, who chose me above your father . . . and I will make merry before the Lord. I will make myself yet more contemptible than this, and I will be abased in your eyes.* On the other hand, Jesus told the Pharisees: *What is exalted among humans is an abomination in the sight of God.*

Sir 45:4
Prv 6:16, 19

The sixth is the humanity of inherent gentleness. As Sirach says: *He sanctified him in his faith and meekness and chose him out of all flesh.* On the other hand, Proverbs warns: *There are six things which the Lord hates and the seventh his soul detests: a man who sows discord among brothers.*

Wis 4:15
Jn 15:16

The seventh is the help of heavenly grace. As the Book of Wisdom says: *God's grace and mercy are with his elect.* Here God's grace and mercy signify his providence over us. Saint John records the words of Jesus: *You did not choose me, but I chose you and appointed you that you should go and bear fruit and that your fruit should abide.*

Therefore, because these seven signs were plainly found in Saint Francis, they show that he was chosen by God.

---

a. Bernard of Clairvaux, *Five Books on Consideration: Advice to a Pope,* The Works of Bernard of Clairvaux, vol. 13, translated by John Anderson and Elizabeth Kennan (Kalamazoo: Cistercian Publications, 1976), 28.

Sermon on the Feast of the Transferal
of the Body of Saint Francis
Probably preached at Paris, May 25, 1267

Bonaventure preached this sermon on the thirty-seventh anniversary of
the transferal of Saint Francis's body from its temporary resting place in the
church of San Giorgio in Assisi to the newly built basilica in his honor. The
occasion was the Vigil of the Solemnity of the Ascension.[a]

Friend, go up higher   Lk 14:10

Introduction

You who dwell in the gardens, my companions listen for your voice; deign   Sg 8:13
to let me hear it.

This text tells us why the word of God must be preached often.
One reason that should inspire us to preach is love of Christ, and another is love of our neighbor. The words of Holy Scripture provide
spiritual nourishment for our neighbor, just as material food sus-
tains the body.

In the same way that a person listens to news of a friend, and a
sick person pays close heed to the advice of the doctor, so those who
love God listen attentively to his word. By the mouth of the contemplative soul dwelling in the gardens of Holy Scripture, because of the
consolations to be found there, the Lord, the Holy Spirit says: I will
come to listen.

A third reason that ought to inspire us to preach is that the Lord
desires to be honored. He wishes to be praised in our prayers, homilies, and sermons, and he wishes our neighbor to be edified by all
these. As it is written: *Let us praise the Lord and he will be glorified.* We   1 Thes 3:1
learn in lectures to distinguish essential and related purposes. The
essential purpose of our sermons ought to be to praise God and the

---

a. The friars of Quaracchi had published this sermon, cf. S. Bonaventurae, (IX 534-535). A more
complete edition can be found in a manuscript in Munich, Staatsbibliothek, Clm 23372, ff.
119v-24r. It was published by R.E. Lerner, "A Collection of Sermons given in Paris c. 1267,
including a new text by Saint Bonaventure on the Life of Saint Francis," *Speculum* 49 (1974):
466-98. Because of internal evidence, the sermon has not been called into question.

related purpose to edify our neighbor. No man of himself can intend or achieve these purposes, but only with the help of God. So here at the beginning ask the Lord to grant me the grace to be able to say something to his praise, in commendation of Saint Francis, and for our edification. Let each one say an *Our Father* and *a Hail Mary.*

I

I began with the *text: Friend, go up higher.* These are Christ's words inviting to the wedding feast those guests found to be humble whom the Lord exalts and desires to exalt. Immediately before these words, the Lord advises: *When you are invited, go and sit in the lowest place.* Saint Francis, having been invited to Christ's wedding feast, sat in the lowest place. That is to say, he clothed himself in a shabby habit and he founded the Order of Lesser Brothers. He did not qualify the word "Lesser" in any way, but simply and unconditionally called his Order the Order of Lesser Brothers. The Lord said to the humble guest, the one who had taken a lower place, *Friend, go up higher.* Notice the Lord calls the humble his friends, and this text may be taken as addressed to the holy confessor Francis who so humbled himself that he wanted to be a lesser brother and *sit in the lowest place.* To this man who made himself humble and lowly for Christ's sake, the Lord says: *Friend, go up higher,* raising, as it were, *the poor from the dust.*

Ps 113:7

The wisdom of God draws the mind to three noteworthy features in this text, which correspond to its three component parts. First, it indicates the presence of grace by the idea of friendship, and so the text says: *Friend.* Second, it signifies "glory" by the spatial adverb *higher.* And third, it symbolizes "pass over from grace to glory" by the verb *go up.* Therefore, in saying *Friend* it means: because you are endowed with grace *go up higher,* that is, come to heavenly glory.

Grace, then, is rightly symbolized by the first word *Friend.* The word refers to the power of grace and eternal wisdom in devout souls, which has been bestowed on many saints for generation after generation. In these latter times grace was given to this holy man, making him a model of repentance to us all.

Jesus calls Saint Francis his friend for a number of special reasons. First, due to his truly humble spirit in all that was committed to him, he was a faithful friend of the Lord. Second, because of his utter purity of heart in everything he pledged himself to do, he was a congenial friend of the Lord. Third, on account of the serenity of his contemplative soul, he was an intimate friend of the Lord. And fourth, because the marks of Christ's cross were imprinted on his body, he became, as Christ's friend, conformed to his likeness. The word LMj XIII 3

Friend, therefore, is addressed to Saint Francis because he was a faithful, congenial and intimate friend of the Lord, conformed to him by the marks of the stigmata on his body.[a]

First, he was a faithful friend on account of his true humility. We read in Sirach: *There is nothing so precious as a faithful friend.* The Lord greatly loves his faithful friends, and that is because he has few faithful ones; and though many nominal friends, few true ones. Saint Gregory advises: "In God's service we must beware of two things: deceit and negligence."[b] Excessive love of self leads to deceit; minimal love of our neighbor leads to negligence, and reduces the love of God to less than it ought to be. A faithful friend possesses a truly humble heart. He observes all God's commandments and attributes nothing to his own glory that is accomplished by God. Saint Bernard writes: "You are indeed a faithful servant of the Lord when nothing of the Lord's abundant glory, which does not come from you but is channeled through you, remains clinging to your hands."[c]

Many achieve nothing for God, because when they see that something of his glory is being channeled through them, they desire to be praised and honored themselves. And who is there these days who does not seek to steal this glory and have it attributed to himself, even from good works which he has not performed? Many are frauds and deceivers. Dear brothers, Saint Francis made himself subject to everyone and was obedient even to the tiniest commandment of God. If anyone ordered him to do anything he was ready to carry it out and be obedient to all.

Moreover, he sought no glory for himself in this world. On the contrary, he always acknowledged himself the greatest and vilest sinner. We read in the account of his life that he used to ask the Lord in prayer: "Why, O Lord, have you put me, wretched and stupid as I am, in charge of this Order?" And the Lord answered: "Have you not considered that I am above you in governing and caring for the Order? Since I am above you, you can put me in your place in governing and directing the Order." For the Lord's sake he attributed everything to the glory of God. Dear brothers, we should learn to be faithful like this ourselves.

Second, he was a congenial friend in everything he pledged himself to do, due to his utter purity of heart. We read in Proverbs: *He who*

(margin: Sir 6:15)

(margin: LMj V 3)

(margin: Prv 22:11)

---

a. The Latin text is: *amicus conformis in ornamento corporis per Christi corpore ad exemplum conformitatem*, literally translated, a friend conformed in the adornment of body by conformity to the example of Christ's body.

b. Gregory I, *Moralia in Job* IX, c.34, n. 53, CCSL 143, 494.

c. Bonaventure had quoted this passage of Bernard of Clairvaux in his sermon of October 4, 1266, cf. *supra* 732-733.

loves purity of heart and whose speech is gracious will have the king as his friend, and not merely an earthly king, but the everlasting King of glory whose friendship ensures that we will arrive at the eternal kingdom. For the Son of God who is *the reflection of eternal light and untarnished mirror of God's active power,* loves only the pure of heart. As the Book of Wisdom tells us: *Wisdom will never make its way into a crafty soul nor stay in a body enslaved to sin.* Saint Francis cherished innocence and purity and so he won the friendship of the everlasting King. Dear brothers, anyone who desires to preserve innocence and purity of heart has to fulfill two necessary conditions. First, he must do penance by willingly undertaking afflictions; and second, he must have patience in tribulations inflicted by others. These are two refining virtues which purify the soul: the first as by water, the second as by fire. We read in the Psalms: *We went through fire and water and you have brought us out to a place of rest.* Just as it is impossible to clean dirty clothes without washing them, so the soul cannot be purified without passing through the refining fire of penance and patience. Because a friend is *a friend at all times,* he has to be pure of heart. Sirach reflects: *If a man washes after touching a corpse, and then touches it again, what is the good of his washing?*

Saint Francis was purified through penance in fasting, abstinence and afflictions. There is a remarkable similarity between him and Saint Benedict. Once when Saint Benedict was troubled by temptations of the flesh, he flung himself naked upon thorns and stinging nettles to drive the temptations away.[a] Saint Francis also when he was once in the Alps threw himself into thorns and freezing snow to curb temptations of the flesh.

Dear brothers, if from your earliest years, you have subdued the flesh, you will withstand its temptations all the more easily and be free of its lusts. I have an example to tell you about a young man who joined the Order of Lesser Brothers.[b] After he had been in the Order for a short time, he became troubled with temptations of the flesh. He was so aroused by lust that he was convinced he could neither withstand nor control it. He went to his provincial minister who was staying in the friary at that time, and confided to him how tormented he was with lust, and told him that he felt he ought to leave the friary, he was so plagued by the flesh. The provincial spoke many words of comfort to him, but to no avail. Subsequently, another brother told him how Saint Francis had overcome temptations of the flesh,

Wis 7:26

Wis 1:4

Ps 66:12

Prv 17:17

Sir 34:30

LMj V 3-4

---

a. Gregory, *Dialogue* II 2.

b. Bonaventure may well have heard of this incident from one of the brothers. There is no written account of it.

and that once in the Alps he had flung himself stark naked into the snow and upon stinging nettles. So the young man decided that the best thing for him to do was subdue his flesh. So, for many days he fasted and abstained from tasty foods and undertook much discipline and for a long period severely scourged his flesh. The result was that whenever he was roused in one part of his flesh by lust or unchaste desires, some other part became so terrified with the scourges it had received, that his whole body began to tremble, even as soon as a thought about lust and sins of the flesh came into his head. He succeeded in chastising his flesh to the point where it was completely under control, and he became so chaste that he lived on in the Order untroubled and died in it a good and holy man. That is one way of safeguarding purity of heart.

A second refining virtue is patience in tribulations. When we are beset with sorrow and adversity caused by others, patience enables us to bear them willingly and joyfully and in this way to purify the soul. Saint Francis desired to undergo tribulations for Christ's sake

_{LMj IX 5-8} and to suffer in order to do something for him. Indeed, so much did he want to bear trials on behalf of his neighbor that he offered himself to the pagan Sultan, that he might be put to death on account of Christ. He used to say: "The Lord chose to undergo death for our justification and I earnestly desire to be put to death for purity of heart."

Dear brothers, when temptations of the flesh come upon you, be mindful of the sufferings and chastisements of the flesh. When tribulations assail you have patience in mind and strength of soul. Saint Jerome tells of a young man who was tempted by lust and greatly troubled. He advised him: "Chastise your body."[a] Then he told another: "Go to the young man, chastise him, torment him with harsh words and cover him with insults." Then in front of their brethren he made accusations against the young man and said such terrible things to him, that the young man was covered with such confusion that he did not know what to do. First, one accused him; then another. Finally, his superior said to him: "My friend, how do you feel?" He replied: "So many scornful and such awful things have been said to me, that I cannot go on living. How could I take pleasure in fornication?" You see, through the reproaches he suffered, the young man lost the desire to commit fornication. There are some, even a great number of people nowadays, who say they want to be chaste; yet, they take on no purifying penance. Without these, I tell you, we can-

---

a. The complete text may be found in Jerome, *Epistula CXXV ad Rusticum*, (PL 22, 1079-1080); *Select Letters of Saint Jerome*, Loeb Classical Library, trans. by Frederick Wright (London, Cambridge, Boston: Harvard University Press, 1933), 396-438.

not be chaste. Moreover, we ought to practice these purifying penances at all times, unlike so many who choose to do penance only during one period of the year, for example, in Lent. Afterwards, they fall away again. Dear brothers, that is simply not enough. We ought rather to be stamped with these purifying penances as with a seal.

Jn 3:29   Third, Saint Francis was an intimate friend of the Lord because of the serenity of his contemplative soul. *The friend of the bridegroom,* that is, of Christ, *who stands and hears him, rejoices greatly when he hears the*

Ex 2:10   *bridegroom's* voice. We read in the Book of Exodus that Moses, whose name means "drawn out of the water," spoke with the Lord as with a

Ex 33:11   friend: *the Lord used to speak to Moses face to face, as a man speaks to his*

Ex 2:5-7; 15   friend. Moses was rescued from the river, and he had to flee from Pharaoh, that is to say, he was poor. The Lord gave him nothing other than a staff; no riches, just a staff with which to make his way in the desert. Later he came to be on such intimate terms with the Lord that

Ex 3:1   he spoke with him as a friend. Moses was a shepherd and tended flocks. What we read of Moses can be said of Saint Francis: the Lord spoke with him as a friend. As Moses was rescued from the river, so Saint Francis was saved from the dangerous currents of a worldly life. God gave him the staff of the cross to lead the people out of the Egypt of vice into the desert of the Order of Lesser Brothers. He carried in his hand nothing other than the staff of Christ's cross at the beginning of his conversion, during his life, and at its end. The Lord does not make his call through riches and learning, but through the

Ex 5:1; 14:26-29   cross. Exodus tells us that God called Moses to lead his people through the desert into the Promised Land. Likewise, the Lord calls his chosen ones to the cross to lead others into the desert of repentance and at the end of this life into the Promised Land, that is, to the glory of the heavenly kingdom.

Ex 19:3-6; 18-24   Moses received heavenly grace because the Lord invited him to a unique companionship with himself. We read in Exodus that he spoke with God and God spoke with Moses and gave him the Law. The same, I tell you, happened to Saint Francis. He was called by the Lord to a unique grace of friendship. Through his prayers he found LMj III 8 the *Rule* of the Lesser Brothers, and when he lost it he returned to the mountain where he had found it and prayed again. And there once LMj IV 11 more by divine revelation and through the power of his prayers he found the lost rule. Then it was confirmed for him.

After this the stigmata of Christ crucified were imprinted on his LMj XIII 3 body. The Lord revealed himself to Saint Francis in the likeness of a Seraph. God appeared to him in the form of a Seraph. He appeared to him as the Crucified Lord so that he could speak with him as with a friend. Perhaps you might ask: "How could this happen?" But it surely did. Saint Paul was so caught up that he saw God's glory. Yet early in his life he had been a most cruel persecutor of God's Church and he had been present at the stoning of Saint Stephen. I assure you, if we are true and faithful friends of Christ, he will still speak to us.

2 Cor 12:1-4

Acts 7:58

Fourth, as Christ's friend, he was made like him in appearance by having the marks of the crucified body of Christ imprinted visibly on his own. The text from the Book of Maccabees about Alexander and Jonathan can be applied to Saint Francis: *he sent him a purple robe and a golden crown and you are to take our side and keep friendship with us.* Alexander, that is, Christ, dispelling the darkness sent Saint Francis *a purple robe,* namely, the marks of his passion. He imprinted on him the stigmata of his own wounds. Hence Saint Paul's saying applies to him: *I bear on my body the marks of Jesus.*

1 Mc 10:20

Gal 6:17

LMj IV 4

What was the *purple robe?* I tell you that among the wondrous and well-nigh unheard of things we read about Saint Francis, there is one of a transfiguration when he appeared to his brothers in a burning chariot in the garden of the canons where he prayed for a whole night. While the brothers watched, the door opened and the burning chariot came in and went round the whole of the little house and they saw Saint Francis like a horseman in the chariot. He told his brothers that this happened for their consolation. Furthermore, he used to tell his brothers their own thoughts and the temptations they had. Thus, the Lord sent him the *purple robe* when he enlightened his mind.

LMj XIII 3

He also sent him a *crown* on the feast of the Exaltation of the Cross when the golden sign appeared to him and within its wings the likeness of the Crucified Lord. He sent him first a chariot, then a likeness of the Seraph and the marks of the stigmata. So, I tell you, the passion of Jesus Christ was renewed in Saint Francis. He used to say that everyone who loved the Crucified Christ was his brother. He bore the stigmata of our Lord Jesus Christ on his hands, feet, and side. On his hands and feet what looked like nails with the points bent over at the back appeared, and they were made of what seemed like dark, sinewy skin. The points under his feet were bent back in such a way that you could put your middle finger into the ring they made. None of this is ancient history. I have seen and been in the company of some one who saw all this and told it to me.[a]

LMj XIII 8

---

a. Alexander IV saw the stigmata while Saint Francis was still alive.

Dear brothers, God could truly call Saint Francis his friend and so he said to him: *Friend, go up higher.* What we have said so far provides the first reason why he was named God's friend.

II

Second, the text adds: *go up higher.* He addresses Saint Francis in these words as if to say to him on the feast of the Ascension,[a] "*Go up* with my help by calling on me in prayer. *Go up* after me, by following my example in your life. *Go up* to God's presence by contemplating the divine splendor. *Go up* because of me whom you shall see at last in glory."

The Lord says to him: *Go up* with my help, for I am the ladder on which you can ascend. This is signified by the ladder which Jacob saw: *set up on the earth, and the top of it reached to heaven.* What is this ladder other than our Lord Jesus himself, the Son of God who through his humanity is set up on earth and by his divinity transcends the heavens? The flesh of Christ, though transformed, remains in union with our earth, and his divinity unites him to the Father who is in heaven. On that ladder, Genesis tells us, *the angels of God were ascending and descending.* They were descending to the humanity of Christ who came in the flesh for us; and, sighing after divine wisdom, they were ascending to heaven. So the Lord says: *Go up* with my help. How is this achieved? By calling on God the Father through the Lord Jesus Christ. In that way you ought to ascend so that it may be said of you what is said of the devout soul in The Song of Solomon: *Who is this that is going up from the desert, like a column of smoke, breathing of myrrh and frankincense, and every perfume the merchant knows?* The desert signifies penance; myrrh, which is bitter, the hardship of sorrow and tears; frankincense, devotion to God; and the perfumes, the spectrum of the virtues. Saint Francis followed Christ by praying constantly and by shedding tears for his sins. He was always at prayer, and he wept so much that he lost his sight. He told those who asked him why he wept so much, as many rebuked him for it: "I do not consider my own sight more precious than the light the angels see."

Then the Lord says to him: *Go up* after me by following my example perfectly in your life. We read in the Book of Samuel: *Then Jonathan climbed up on his hands and feet and his armor-bearer after him.* Jonathan may be taken here as a figure of Christ who was crucified through his hands and feet, and the armor bearer as Saint Francis, filled with the Holy Spirit, who carried the arms of Christ, namely,

Gn 28:12

Gn 28:12

Sg 3:6

LMj X 1-4

1 Sm 14:13

---

a. The sermon was delivered on the vigil of the Ascension.

the cross, the nails, and the spear. These were the arms of our Redeemer and Saint Francis bore them as second nature to him. He taught us to observe poverty like Christ, and he left this world naked just as Christ did. After he had become famous and was sick with fever, he was told to eat some meat, and he did so. Then on Laetare Sunday he preached on the slave and the free woman,[a] and afterwards stripped himself naked [because he had eaten meat]. Both in his life and preaching he desired to be poor and to be seen to be poor. When he was dying he ordered his brothers to lay him completely naked on the ground with his arms outstretched in the form of a cross, and even to be buried like that. And so, I tell you, he was made utterly Christ-like and configured to him. Stretched out as it were on the cross on high, he went up higher. He was totally obedient to the command: *Go up* after me by following me literally.

Third, the Lord said to him: *Go up* to God's presence by contemplating the divine splendor. Moses was told by the Lord: *Ascend this mountain,* that is, the established mountain which is Christ. For the Lord himself is the established mountain. And standing before the people I will show you *the holy city Jerusalem.*

We read in the Book of Job: *he hides the light in his hands.* It is a characteristic of light that no one can claim it as his own. Light is given only to spiritual men. As you know, as long as matter is devoid of form, it can have no ability to receive spiritual light.[b] In a similar way, when a person is tied to temporal possessions which waste away and are dark and tainted, he cannot perceive the brilliance of divine light. That was the kind of advice Saint Francis gave to his brothers, having in mind the words of the Psalm: *fire has fallen on them,* that is, the fire of avarice and possessiveness, *and they shall not see the sun* of justice. The fire of avarice and possessiveness causes blindness, whereas the fire of poverty gives brightness and solace. As you know yourselves, an eagle untied and set free soars gracefully on high; but when the leaden ball is tied to its foot, it can neither fly nor soar on high, but falls to the ground. Likewise, when the soul of a Christian is shackled by the things of this earth, it cannot rise up to contemplate God. For this reason the Lord tells us: *Do not lay up for yourselves treasures on earth . . . for where your treasure is, there will your heart be also.* I assure you that love of earthly possessions can no more be harmonized with love of heavenly treasures than the earth can be united to the heavens. All this is the teaching of our Lord Jesus Christ. However, I am not con-

Marginal references: LMj VII 1; XV 9 — LMj VI 2 — Gal 4:22 — LMj VII 1-6 — LMj XIV 3-5 — Dt 32:49 — Rv 21:10 — Jb 36:32 — LMj VII 1-2 — Ps 58:9 — Mt 6:19, 21

---

a. Gal 4:22. This text occurred in the epistle for that Sunday.
b. Cf. *In II Sent.*, d. XII, dub. 2, (II, 307).

demning those who have riches, but have not set their hearts on them.

Fourth, the Lord said to him: *Go up* because of me whom you shall contemplate at last and in that you will be glorified. We read in The Song of Solomon: *I will climb the palm tree and lay hold of its branches.* The palm tree has a trunk whose lower part is very narrow. The section nearest the ground is thinner than the higher section of the trunk, which is not the case with any other tree. The palm tree is a figure of Jesus Christ, who in his humanity was made *a little less than the angels,* and was small and weak in this world, and in his divinity is Lord and Creator of the angels and of all things. The fruit of this tree is nothing less than the joys of eternal sweetness and everlasting glory which consists in the vision, possession, and enjoyment of God. The Lord Jesus Christ, the Son of God, led our patron, Saint Francis, to eternal glory. So it is that the Son of God could say to him: *Friend, go up higher* to my presence that with me and in me you may be glorified forever. The miracles that he performed during his life prove that he was and remains the friend of God. There is a text about Mordecai in the Book of Esther that we may apply to Saint Francis: *The man whom the king desires to honor is to be clothed with the king's apparel and set upon the horse which the king has ridden and to have the royal crown upon his head.* During his life he bore the stigmata of our Lord Jesus Christ. At his death he rode upon the king's horse, that is, on the cross of Christ, when a cloud appeared on which he was taken to heaven. We can say of him what Scripture says of Christ: *a cloud took him out of their sight.* Furthermore, the royal crown was put upon his head when he was canonized and taken to heaven to be in the company of the saints. I tell you, they consider themselves blessed who were able to touch his body.

His glory has been made great on earth. The Lord honored shepherds, prophets, and lawgivers. He gave his love to fishermen and made them princes. God loved all these and finally, after them, he set his love on merchants. He greatly loved Saint Francis who was a merchant. He made him a true merchant which Saint Francis became when he found the pearl of heavenly glory. He teaches us also to purchase the pearl.

Let us ask the Lord to give us in this life the grace to buy that pearl so that together with Saint Francis we may obtain the reward of the heavenly kingdom. May he grant us this who lives and reigns forever and ever. Amen.

Sg 7:8

Ps 8:7

Est 6:7-8

Acts 1:9

LMj XV 1-9

1 Kgs 19:19

Mt 13:44-46

The Morning Sermon on Saint Francis
Preached at Paris, October 4, 1267

The reference to the "Sisters of Saint Clare," enables us to date this sermon at a point after October 18, 1263, when Pope Urban IV changed the title of the Order of Saint Damian to that of the Order of Saint Clare.[a] A manuscript found in Troyes dates the sermon at October 4, 1267.

> *Behold my servant whom I uphold,*   Is 42:1
> *my chosen in whom my soul delights;*
> *I have put my spirit upon him, he will bring forth justice to the nations.*

Introduction

Who, do you think, is a faithful and wise servant, whom his master has set   Mt 24:45 *over his household, to give them their food at the proper time?* These words from Saint Matthew's Gospel tell us how difficult it is to find a man fit to preach God's word, for such a man must be faithful and wise.

Who, do you think, is faithful? We read in Proverbs: *Many men are*   Prv 20:6 *called merciful; but who shall find a faithful man?* A faithful man is one who seeks nothing but God's glory in everything that he does. He seeks nothing to his own advantage, no praise, no favor, his only concern is God's glory and the salvation of others. It is indeed difficult to find a faithful man.

Nor is it easy to find a wise man. According to Scripture, a wise man is one who gives *them their food at the proper time;* or as Saint Luke has it, who gives *them their portion of food at the proper time.* It is a great   Lk 12:42 art in preaching to gauge wisely the mental range of the hearers, so as not to speak at too great a length or in words too condensed, nor too far beyond them or in words patronizingly simple. And who can achieve this? If a preacher manages it once, he fails in it often. I must confess, when I think about the standard required in a preacher of

---

a. Clare was canonized in 1255. The change in name was made by Urban IV on Oct. 18, 1263, see Ignatius C. Brady, "St. Bonaventure's Sermons on Saint Francis," *Franziskanische Studien* 58 (1976): 132.

God's word, that I am getting old,[a] and I acknowledged I am hardly fit to do it. However, it is God who speaks in preaching. A preacher believes that sometimes he has preached well and thought out many fine ideas; sometimes he may have said nothing, for we read in Proverbs: *It is a human's part to prepare the soul; it is the Lord's to govern the tongue.*

Prv 16:1

I am afraid that if I preach with too much restraint, God will be angry with me. On the other hand, if I set myself to speak at great length on the glories of Saint Francis, I fear that some may think that in praising him I am really seeking praise for myself. It is difficult for me to speak on this matter. My aim, however, is to describe to you a holy and perfect man so that each of you may strive to imitate him. And in doing this I wish to put before you the example of Saint Francis, adhering all the while to the truth. At the beginning let us pray to the Lord that he will grant me to say and you to hear what is to his praise and glory and for our salvation.

We began with the text from Isaiah: *Behold my servant . . .* The meaning of these words refers primarily to our Lord Jesus Christ. However, what is true of the head may be applied to the members on account of their likeness and closeness to the head. Thus, these words may fittingly be understood of any holy and perfect person. But they highlight in a pre-eminent way the unique and perfect holiness of Saint Francis with regard to its root, its loftiness, and its radiance.

The root of perfect holiness lies in deep humility, its loftiness in well tried virtue, and its radiance in consummate love. Endowed with deep humility we are sustained by God; by well tried virtue we are made pleasing to him; and in consummate love we are taken up to God and brought closer to our neighbor. Consequently, in this text Saint Francis is commended for his deep humility, for which he was sustained by God, as its opening words say: *Behold my servant whom I uphold.* Then he is commended for his well tried virtue which made him pleasing to God, as the text continues: *my chosen, in whom my soul delights.* Third, he is commended for his consummate love whereby he passed over into God and opened his heart to his neighbor, as the text concludes: *I have put my spirit upon him . . .*

---

a. The Latin text has *senex* [old]. The Quaracchi editor questioned the word, (IX, 575). Saint Bonaventure was about fifty when he preached this sermon, 1267. According to his own words this puts him in the fifth age of man, since *"senectus"* suggests the period that runs from fifty to seventy. See *IV Sent.*, d. XL, q.3, dub. III (IX, 854): *"quarta, iuventus usque ad quinquagesimum; quinta, gravitas sive senectus usque ad septuagesimum; sexta, senium sive aetas decrepita usque in finem* [the fourth, youth until the fiftieth year; the fifth, dignity or maturity until the seventieth; the sixth, old age or failing age until the end]."

Who, then is such a perfect saint? Listen well. It is the person endowed with deep humility, well tried virtue, and consummate love. The root of holiness begins in humility, develops through well tried virtue, and is crowned in consummate love. Humility moves God to sustain us, well-tried virtue makes us pleasing to Him, but consummate love brings us to be totally rapt in God and to share what we have with others.

I

First of all, Saint Francis is commended here by the mouth of God for his deep humility: *Behold my servant whom I uphold.* What the Lord says in Haggai may be applied to him: *In that day I will take you, O Zerubbabel my servant, and make you like a seal, for I have chosen you.* This text says: *I will make you like a seal* and that by the signs and marks of the passion impressed on you by the Word of the Almighty. And why does he say this? Because Saint Francis was a servant of God, humble in his reverence for Him, more humble still in caring for his neighbor, and most humble of all in despising himself. I admire the humility of Saint Francis more than all his other virtues.

He was a humble servant of God in the reverence he had toward Him. For this reason what the Lord says in the Book of Job may be applied to Saint Francis: *Have you considered my servant Job, that there is none like him on the earth, a blameless and upright man, who fears God and turns away from evil?*

God calls Job his servant on account of his humility. He was committed to God's service and reckoned a *servant* of outstanding reverence for God because he was blameless in his motives, *upright* in what he chose, *God-fearing* in his feelings, and *turned away* from evil in his actions. In all that he did and suffered he praised God. Moreover, we read of Job that *there were born to him seven sons and three daughters.* The name Job is interpreted "sorrowing," and this truly describes Saint Francis, because his life was filled with sorrow. He was always in tears weeping over his own sins or the sins of others. Looking back to the very early days of the Order, we find that Saint Francis had seven friars and he was the eighth. At the Lord's bidding he sent them out two by two in the four directions of the compass, and in accordance with his desire the Lord brought them back together again.

Saint Francis also had three "daughters." At the outset of his religious life he repaired three churches: one dedicated to Saints Cosmas and Damian, another dedicated to Saint Peter the Apostle and another to the Blessed Virgin Mary. It was in the last mentioned church that the Lord revealed to him the form of life he was to lead. Besides

Hg 2:23

Jb 1:8

Jb 1:2

LMj X 4
LMj III 7

LMj II 7-8

this, he founded three religious Orders: the first, the Order of Friars Minor; the second, the Order of Sisters of Saint Clare. Earlier these had been called the Poor Ladies of Saints Cosmas and Damian, but now, with Saint Clare having been canonized, they are called the Sisters of Saint Clare. The third is called the Order of Penitents, known as the Penitent Brethren. These Orders may be understood as his three "daughters," and they were founded for the purpose of honoring God. We see, then, that Saint Francis revered God and was his humble servant. With the Psalmist he could say: *O Lord I am your servant, I am your servant, the son of your handmaid.* We should follow the example of Saint Francis and serve God with reverence.

Scripture admonishes us that we should *fear him who can destroy both body and soul in hell.* We ought to revere God and submit ourselves to His will. Otherwise, He will reproach us, saying: *If I am a father, where is my honor? And if I am the Lord, where is my fear?* And likewise those words from Job: *I called my servant, and he gave me no answer.* The Lord calls us through interior inspirations, through preaching, through chastisements, blessings, and the good example of holy people. Yet we remain unmoved despite what is written in Saint Luke's Gospel: *That servant, who knew his master's will but did not make ready or act according to his will, shall receive a severe beating.* Let us recall once more that Saint Francis was a humble servant of God through the reverence he bore Him.

Second, this servant of God was humbler still in caring for his neighbor. As Saint Paul writes to the Corinthians: *For though I am free from all men, I have made myself a slave to all.* Our holy Father Francis became all things to all men and the servant of everybody. He wanted even to be the servant of the most despised. And once, walking along the road, he promised obedience to one of his brothers. When he was still in the world he had a great loathing for lepers. But after his conversion he devoted himself to taking care of them. He washed their feet, bandaged their ulcers and sores, cleaned away the pus and rotten blood, and kissed their feet. He cared for his neighbor to this extent in order to make himself contemptible and to implore God's grace. Saint Paul tells the Galatians: *For you were called to freedom, brethren; only do not use your freedom as an opportunity for the flesh, but through love be servants of one another.* Such should our freedom be.

Someone might object that while it is true we must serve our neighbor, we are not obliged to serve lepers. But God himself did not disdain this kind of service. He bent down to wash the dirty feet of his disciples, and then said to them: *You call me Teacher and Lord; and you are right, for so I am. If I then, your Lord and Teacher, have washed your feet, you also ought to wash one another's feet. For I have given you an example,*

Ps 116:16

Mt 10:28

Mal 1:6

Jb 19:16

Lk 12:47

1 Cor 9:19

Gal 5:13

Jn 13:13-16

LMj IV 6

LMj VI 4
Test 1-3
LMj II 6

that you also should do as I have done to you. Truly, truly, I say to you, a servant is not greater than his master; nor is he who is sent greater than he who sent him. Commenting on this passage Saint Augustine remarks: "Let us with humility do to one another what in humility was done by the Most High. Great is this commendation of humility. And in fact the brethren do this to one another even literally when they receive one another as guests. And among the brethren where this custom of washing the feet is not practiced, they do in their hearts what they do not do with their hands. But it is much better that it should be done with the hands, for what Christ did, the Christian ought not to disdain to do. When the body stoops down to the feet of a brother, then in the heart itself the affection of humility is either enkindled or, if it is already there, confirmed."[a]

Pope Gregory the Ninth, who was a man full of wisdom, because of his great friendship with Saint Francis, followed his example closely. He kept a leper in his room and, dressed in the habit of a friar, looked after him. One day the leper said to him: "Has the Supreme Pontiff no one but an old man like you, to look after me?" The Pope was exhausted.[b] We do good in serving our neighbor. This is why Saint Paul tells us: *I pommel my body and subdue it,* and the Book of Lamentations says: *It is good for a man that he has borne the yoke from his youth.*

We have seen, then, that Saint Francis was humble through his reverence for God, and humbler still in taking care of his neighbor. Coming now to the third point, we find him humblest of all despising himself, and he did so in order to follow him of whom it is written: *He emptied himself, taking the form of a servant.* Christ was conceived in the form of a servant and, therefore, He could say of Himself: *I am small and despised. I am a worm and no man; scorned by men, and despised by the people.* The Lord revealed His glory in heaven, and for coveting it, Lucifer and the angels who copied him came to perdition. Together with himself, Lucifer brought down humanity, created in God's image. Christ did not reveal His humility in heaven, but desiring to show us the root of wisdom, He humbled Himself. Anyone who desires to possess the wisdom of Christ must begin at the root of holiness, just as Saint Francis did. When he first changed his way of life the townsfolk pelted him with mud from the streets and threw stones at him, he went naked in front of the bishop and all the people announcing

Margin notes: 1 Cor 9:27 · Lam 3:27 · Phil 2:7 · Ps 119:141; 22:6 · Gn 1:27-3:24 · LMj II 2 · LMj II 4

---

a. Augustine, *In Iohannis Evangelium tractatus* CXXIV, tr. 58, CCSL 36, 399-400; *St. Augustine: Tractates on the Gospel of John* 55-111, The Fathers of the Church, vol. 90 (Washington: The Catholic University of America Press, 1994), 21-22.

b. It seems clear enough from this passage that the leper did not know that it was the pope who was serving him.

that he had given up all his worldly goods. Later, after he had become LMj VI 2
a man of outstanding holiness, he had himself dragged naked
through mud. He could not bear to hear himself praised. From all
this we see that he reached the summit of perfect holiness and humility. Saint Bernard writes: "The truly humble man wants to be
considered despicable rather than to be proclaimed a humble man;"[a]
and Saint Gregory writes: "As the proud glory in their superiority, so
the humble rejoice in being despised."[b] Where does humility have its
source? Most surely in the depths of the heart.

Brother Pacifico, who first introduced the Order of Lesser LMj IV 9
Brothers into France, was a man of great holiness. One day while LMj VI 6
praying in a church with Saint Francis, he fell asleep. In his sleep he
saw heaven opened and there in heaven a glorious throne. When he
asked whose throne it might be, he was told it was the throne which
Lucifer had lost because of his pride, and it was now reserved for
Saint Francis because of his humility. When he woke up he asked
Saint Francis: "What do you think of yourself?" Saint Francis answered: "I think I am the greatest sinner in the world." Pacifico re-
joined: "But there are murderers and robbers and all kinds of wicked
people." "Even the greatest sinner in the world," replied Saint Francis, "would be holier than I am if he had received so many graces."

We should take careful note of this remarkable fact. Of everything
that can cause us to wonder, it is among the greatest wonders that of
all the figures in the Old and New Testaments, God has exalted only
those who were humiliated and despised.

In the Old Testament the Lord firmly exalted three men. Saul was
not among them because he was not steadfast in virtue. These three
were Joseph, Moses, and David. What do we read of Joseph? The
Ps 105:17, 18 Psalmist says: *He sent a man before them: Joseph who was sold for a slave.*
The text goes on to say that he was imprisoned and bound with fet-
ters; and he served his fellow prisoners. Then afterwards Pharaoh
Ps 105:21 *made him lord of his house.*

Ex 3:1 Moses was adopted as son by Pharaoh's daughter. The Lord did
not promise him exaltation in the land of Egypt, but when Pharaoh's
anger blazed against him and he had become a shepherd in the
desert, then the Lord appeared to him and revealed to him his judgments.

And what is said about David, what do we read of him? He himself
Ps 78:70-71 tells us: *And he chose his servant David, and took him from the sheepfolds;*

---

a. Bernard of Clairvaux, Sermon 16:10, *On the Song of Songs*, translated by Kilian Walsh, introduction
by M. Corneille Halflants (Spencer, MA: Cistercian Publications, 1971), 121.

b. Gregory, *Dialogue* I 5.

from tending the ewes that had young he brought him to be shepherd of Jacob, his people, and Israel his inheritance. We find also in the New Testament that [all Christ's disciples] humbled themselves, and Christ greatly cherishes the humble.

If someone owned a precious gem which the more worthless it was considered, the more precious it became, how willingly he would show it to those who disparage it. Strength of spirit increases through reproaches; what folly it is, therefore, to seek praise. The Saints wanted to be despised by others in order to be pleasing to God. As Saint Gregory says: "If holy people who achieve so much, reckon themselves as practically worthless, what is to be said of those puffed up with pride, yet devoid of virtue?"[a] Saint Anselm tells us that there are six degrees of humility, and he who succeeds in arriving at the sixth, possesses the fulness of grace.[b] The first degree of humility is to account oneself despicable; the second is to speak of oneself as despicable; the third, to convince others that one is despicable; the fourth, to want to be judged despicable; the fifth, to want to be spoken of as despicable; and the sixth, to want to be treated as despicable. At this point one is close to God and is his humble servant. Saint Francis himself says: "What a man is before God, that he is and no more." A man is worth no more than God reckons him. It is extraordinary that we want to find favor with other people whose approval does nothing for us, and we care little to be pleasing to him whose favor is the summit of holiness. So it is that Saint Francis is commended in this text for his deep humility.

For his humility Saint Francis was sustained by a threefold mercy of God. We read in the Psalms: *Uphold your servant for good: let not the proud calumniate me. Deal with your servant according to your mercy.* This humble servant who revered God, took care of his neighbor and despised himself, and was found worthy to be sustained by God's mercy. Because he despised himself he was sustained by God's forgiving mercy; then because he took care of his neighbor, he was sustained by God's protecting mercy; and third, because he so revered God, he was sustained by God's liberating and uplifting mercy.

First, Saint Francis despised himself and for that he was sustained by God's forgiving mercy. Mary says in the Magnificat: *He has put down the mighty from their thrones and exalted the humble. He has helped his servant Israel, in remembrance of his mercy.* Israel, also named Jacob, struggled with the angel and was crippled. But he was sus-

<small>adm XX; LMj VI 1</small>

<small>Ps 119: 122, 124</small>

<small>Lk 1:52, 53</small>

<small>Gn 32:24-25</small>

---

a. Gregory I, *Homiliarum in evangelia* I, hom. 7, n. 4, (PL 76, 1103); *Gregory the Great: Forty Gospel Homilies*, Cistercian Studies Series 123, translated by David Hurst (Kalamazoo: Cistercian Publications, 1990), 27.

b. Pseudo-Anselmus, *De Similitudo*, c. 100-109, (PL 159, 665-68); cf also *Epistola* 75, (PL 159, 112).

Gn 32:25
tained by God's mercy because from his stock the Son of God was to be born, through whom all sins were to be forgiven. It was first of all necessary for the sinew of his thigh to shrink, which may be interpreted as "to mortify the flesh." In the Book of Daniel the three

Dn 3:38-39
young men prayed: *And at this time there is no prince . . . no place to make an offering before you or to find mercy. Yet with a contrite heart and a humble spirit may we be accepted* by the Lord. If you desire to be sustained by God's forgiving mercy, you must first struggle with the angel in

Ps 50:17
prayer in order to curb evil desires, and then you can offer the sacrifice of a contrite heart. Here on earth the soul is set on fire by evil desires and objects enticing the senses, as if it were burning in a fiery furnace. But if the angel comes down into the furnace and penetrates our spirit with God's grace, then we will humble ourselves and begin to mortify the flesh and so be pleasing to God. As the Book of Daniel

Dn 3:50
records, the angel will make *the midst of the furnace like the blowing of wind bringing dew,* and so the young will not feel the flame of sensual desires, and should they feel them, they will do them no harm.

Saint Francis did not cease from weeping for his sins from the mo- LMj III 6
ment of his conversion to the time the Lord appeared to him and as-

Lk 7:47; Mt 5:26
sured him that his *many sins were forgiven him down to the last farthing.* I would like to have this assurance more than anything else in the

Lk 7:36-50
world. It was given also to Mary Magdalene. And so, because Saint Francis despised himself, he was sustained by God's forgiving mercy.

Second, because he took care of his neighbor he was sustained by

Is 41:9-10
God's protecting mercy. We read in Isaiah: *You are my servant. I have chosen you and not cast you away. . . . I have strengthened you and helped*

Lk 9:62
you and the right hand of my Just One has upheld you. Saint Francis did not turn back; after putting his hand to the plough, he did not look back. He was chosen and not cast away. He avoided not only mortal

Is 41:10
sin, but also venial sin, as far as this is humanly possible. *The right hand of my Just One has upheld you,* says Isaiah. Who is this Just One?

1 Jn 2:1
Saint John gives us the answer: *We have an advocate in heaven with the Father, Jesus Christ the just. The right hand of my Just One* is the right hand of Almighty God who kept him safe from all his enemies. When demons attacked him and thrashed him bodily, he always had re-

Ps 63:7-8
course to God's help. He was able to make his own the words of the Psalm: *In the shadow of your wings I sing for joy. My soul clings to you; your right hand upholds me.* Anyone who seeks protection must place himself under God's right hand.

Third, Saint Francis revered God and for this he was sustained by

Ps 72:24
God's liberating mercy. As the Psalm says: *You have held me by the right hand; and by your will you have guided me and with your glory you have*

received me. Moreover, we read in the Book of Proverbs: *Humiliation* Prv 29:23
follows the proud: and glory shall uphold the humble of spirit. So it is that
the Lord himself says: *For those who honor me I will honor . . . For great is* 1 Sm 2:30; Sir 3:20
the power of God alone and he is honored by the humble.

Only those who honor God will be honored and glorified by him.
Since only the humble honor God, only the humble will be glorified.
Therefore, if you desire to be sustained by this threefold mercy, be a
humble servant by despising yourself, taking care of your neighbor,
and revering God. This is the first stage of the Christian philosophy of
his life. When Dioscorus asked Saint Augustine what the Christian
philosophy of his life chiefly consists of, Saint Augustine replied: "If
you were to ask me what is the most important factor in rhetoric, I
would answer: eloquence. If you were to ask me a second or third
time or even a hundred times, I would still reply: eloquence. This is
how I would answer your question. If you ask me what is the essence
of the Christian philosophy of life, I answer: humility. And were you
to ask me a second or a third time, or even a hundred times, I would
still reply: humility."[a] The Gospel also teaches this and there is not a
page nor a line in Holy Scripture which does not proclaim humility. If
we are proud, we fall from true wisdom, as Saint Paul remarks:
Claiming to be wise they become fools. True wisdom was that of the Rom 1:22
Prophets and Apostles.

From these reflections Saint Francis's deep humility will now be
apparent to everyone.

II

We pass now to say something about the well tried virtue of this
man. Let us recall the words: my chosen, in whom my soul delights.
The word "election" signifies eminence, which raises the person
higher than others. Saint Francis was chosen not merely to be taken
from among sinners, but also to be raised high among the virtuous.
Hence a text from Sirach about wisdom can be applied to him: *In the* Sir 24:4
multitude of the elect she shall have praise, and among the blessed she shall be
blessed. There are three reasons why Saint Francis is to be accounted
as chosen by God and of well tried virtue: his perfect observance of
the Law and Gospel, his indomitable zeal for the Christian faith, and
his exceedingly fervent love of the Crucified Savior.

First of all, Saint Francis was chosen because of his perfect observance of the Law and Gospel. We read in Isaiah: *Behold, I have refined* Is 48:10

---

a. Augustine, *Epistola 118*, n. 22, (PL 33, 442); *Saint Augustine: Letters*, vol. 2, The Fathers of the
Church, vol. 18, translated by Wilfrid Parsons (New York: Fathers of the Church, 1953), 282.

you, but not like silver; I have chosen you in the furnace of poverty. Poverty is a furnace which consumes some and refines others. It consumes those whose poverty is coupled with impatience and covetousness for worldly goods. As the Book of Sirach says: *Poverty is evil in the opinion of the ungodly.* On the other hand, voluntary poverty which carries with it imitation of Christ and conformity to him, is a furnace which purifies God's chosen ones. The three young men mentioned in the Book of Daniel were in a furnace of this kind. Commenting on this Chrysostom says: "And as one like the Son of God appeared in the midst of the fiery furnace with the three young men, so in a similar way the Son of God appears in the world among the poor." The Lord Jesus says: *Whoever of you does not renounce all that he has cannot be my disciple.* Having spoken earlier about the need to hate one's very life in order to be his disciple, he adds: *Whoever does not bear his own cross and come after me, cannot be my disciple.* That poverty which is inseparable from bearing one's own cross, is like a refining furnace, and is an integral part of gospel discipleship. Life according to the Gospel consists in self-denial, purity, simplicity, and every form of kindness. Self-denial eradicates greed; purity, lust; simplicity, inquisitiveness; humility, pride; and kindness drives away anger. By keeping these virtues, a person is a follower of the naked Christ in the furnace of poverty. If I choose to be greedy, unchaste, or proud, this is not to be in the furnace which refines, but in that which destroys.

Saint Francis was like pure gold, refined in the furnace of poverty. How wretched are those who go into this furnace and then jump out again. They are not worthy to be purified. Dear brothers, it is a noble thing to enter this furnace, for as we said earlier: *The angel made the midst of the furnace like the blowing of a wind bringing dew.*

A brother who stayed with Saint Francis at Montepulciano near Siena, related how one day they could find only some stale bread to eat.[a] They went to the entrance of a church where they ate the bread and drank water. When they had finished eating they went into the church where Saint Francis was filled with great joy. He stood there for a whole hour and this tired the other friar. Afterwards, he asked Saint Francis what he had experienced. He told him that he had never felt such sweetness from the time of his conversion. How pleasing to God is poverty combined with self-denial, purity, simplicity, humility, and kindness. Afterwards, he went to Saint Peter's in Rome so that the Apostle might be his surety that he never deflected from his promise to observe poverty. Anyone who seeks earthly com-

Sir 13:24

Lk 14:33

Lk 14:27

Dn 3:50

---

a. Unknown until this point, the incident was afterwards transcribed in the *Actus Beati Francisci et Sociorum eius.* Ed. Paul Sabatier in *Collection d'Etudes et de Documents* IV (Paris, 1902).

fort, forfeits heavenly consolation, as when God *rained down upon the sons of Israel manna to eat, a food having in it all that is delicious and the sweetness of every taste, not sensing its sweetness, they pined after the melons and garlic.* Furthermore, God made streams come out of the rock for the Jews. Therefore, to everyone in the furnace of poverty observing self-denial, purity, simplicity, humility, and kindness, God will give his grace and make them like pure gold.

Second, Saint Francis was chosen by God because of his indomitable zeal for the Christian faith. Of Saint Paul it is written: *He is a chosen instrument of mine to carry my name before the Gentiles and kings and the sons of Israel.* The Apostle Paul was endowed with this zeal because he was consumed with desire to spread faith in Christ among the Jews, then the Greeks, and afterwards among the Romans. Saint Francis wanted to be poor for Christ's sake, and because of his zeal for the faith he became God's chosen instrument. He journeyed into many countries to spread the Christian faith. On three occasions, he attempted to go overseas but was prevented by shipwreck. He travelled to Miramamolin in Spain and then to Morocco, where later our friars were martyred.[a] On a third occasion, he went to the Sultan of Egypt and proclaimed the Christian faith to him, longing to be torn to pieces for the faith. The Sultan said to him: "Let us bring in our wise men so that we can debate our faith and yours." Saint Francis replied: "Our faith is beyond human reason and reason anyway is of no use except to a believer. Besides, I cannot argue from Holy Scripture because your wise men do not believe the Scriptures. Instead, make a fire of wood, and I will go into it together with your wise men. Whichever of us is burnt, his faith is false." On hearing this the Sultan's wise men withdrew. The Sultan began to smile and said: "I don't think I will find anybody to go into the fire with you." "Then," answered Saint Francis, "I will go into the fire alone, and if I am burnt, account it to my sins; if I am not, then embrace the Christian faith." The Sultan replied: "I could not dare do that, for fear my people would stone me. But I believe that your faith is good and true." And from that moment the Christian faith was imprinted on his heart.

Third, Saint Francis was chosen by God on account of his exceedingly fervent love of Christ crucified. He could make his own the words of The Song of Solomon: *My beloved is all radiant and ruddy, chosen out of thousands.* Christ himself was *radiant* in the incarnation because of his sinlessness and *ruddy* in his passion. Saint Francis had

---

a. AF III, 579-96; La *scimitarra del Miramolino: Relazione dei primi martiri francescani del Marrocco (1220)*, translated by A. Ghinato (Roma, 1962).

the greatest devotion to the incarnation and the cross of Christ. On account of his love of the cross, his skin became a dark reddish color, he was interiorly crucified and transformed into Christ. Because of his love of the Virgin's Son he was transformed, even while still alive, into the Crucified, by the Seraph with six wings that appeared to him. He was pierced with huge, strong nails, the points of which were bent over under the soles of his feet, and there was a wound in his side. In the words of the Song of Solomon he could say: *You have wounded my heart.* He was dark-skinned, which was accentuated because of his austerities. Yet at his death his flesh became radiant white and ruddy. He asked the brothers to let him lie naked on the ground, when he was dead, for the length of time it takes to walk a mile. With Saint Paul he could say: *I have been crucified with Christ . . . Far be it from me to glory except in the cross of our Lord Jesus Christ.*

It is evident then that Saint Francis was chosen by God. Let us ask God to hear our prayers.

Sg 4:9

LMj XIII 3

LMj XV 2

LMj XIV 4

Gal 2:20; 6:14

The Evening Sermon on Saint Francis
Preached at Paris, October 4, 1267

Behold my servant whom I uphold . . .

Earlier today we said in praise of Saint Francis that he was perfect and holy. He is commended in the text we began with for the root, loftiness, and radiance of his perfect holiness. The root of perfect holiness lies in deep humility, its loftiness in well tried virtue, and its radiance in consummate love. For these three graces Saint Francis is worthy of the highest praise. He was sustained by God because of his deep humility, pleasing to God for his well tried virtue, and through his consummate love he opened his heart to his neighbor. I showed how his deep humility is commended in this text: *Behold my servant whom I uphold. . . .* This servant was humble because of his reverence for God; humbler still in caring for his neighbor; and humblest of all in despising himself. Thus he was sustained by God's forgiving mercy because he despised himself; by his protecting mercy because of his care for his neighbor; and by his liberating mercy because of the reverence he bore him. I pointed out, further, that he was chosen by God on three accounts: his perfect observance of the Law and Gospel, his indomitable zeal for the Christian faith, and his deep love of the Crucified Christ. Now it remains for me to explain how he was pleasing to God, how God put his *spirit upon him* and how Saint Francis brought *forth justice to the nations.* _{Is 42:1}

Let us ask God, then, that in the remainder of this sermon he may grant me to say something worthwhile and you to draw inspiration from it, to his honor and glory. Amen.

Behold my servant whom I uphold . . .

As we said earlier, deep humility is the condition of our being sustained by God. Likewise, well tried virtue is the chief condition of our being pleasing to God. When God utters those words to a person: *My chosen, in which my soul delights,* how lovely they are in the hearing. It pleases God's gracious will to guide our souls. The divine will is drawn toward the Son in whom God delights uniquely, for in him is found the perfection of every virtue. Therefore, it is through well tried virtue that a person is made pleasing to God, the Lord of all virtues. The leader of an army delights in none other than a valiant soldier.

To speak now of Saint Francis, we should take note that he was pleasing to God because of his unquestioning obedience, his passion for righteousness, and the refinement of his devotion to God. Among the virtues these three are especially efficacious to make us pleasing to God. And if we are endowed with them God will delight in us.

First of all, we will be pleasing to God by unquestioning obedience. Thus Isaiah says: *You shall no more be termed Forsaken, and your land shall be no more termed Desolate; but you shall be called My delight is in her . . . for the Lord delights in you.*

Our land will never be deserted by the Lord through his abandoning it; most surely not, but only through our abandoning him. When God is far from us, then we must become as desolate land. In uttering those words: *You shall be called My delight is in her,* the Lord is speaking to the obedient soul, that is, to one who does nothing other than what pleases God, one utterly obedient to the divine will. Saint Francis strove with all his powers to imitate Christ and in truth he could say: "I will not forsake you; I will not forsake him who sent me, for *I do what is pleasing to him.* And if I am sick, then I freely will that I be sick."

The Lord showed his delight in Saint Francis by choosing to speak to him not as a stranger, but as an intimate friend, for the crucifix spoke to him, which is now preserved by the Sisters at San Damiano.

Perhaps you may ask: "What really happened there?" Then I in turn will ask you: "What took place when the angel said to the Virgin Mary: *'Hail Mary, full of grace?'* " or "What did Zechariah experience when the angel, *standing on the right side of the altar of incense,* spoke to him?"

If we are ready to do what pleases God He will make His will known to us. As the Apostle Paul says: *Do not be conformed to this world, but be transformed by the renewal of your mind, that you may prove what is the will of God, what is good and acceptable and perfect.* God, who is Creator, Sanctifier, and Glorifier, wills only what is good.

Saint Francis was once in doubt whether he should give himself to a life of prayer or to a life of preaching. For a whole week he brooded over the matter because it was not entirely clear to him what he ought to do. When at last he recognized that he should devote himself to preaching, he girded himself and went for six miles around preaching to the people. He came upon a field full of birds and the birds listened to him.

Second, Saint Francis was pleasing to God because of his passion for righteousness. We read in Scripture that *Phinehas in the goodness*

Is 62:4

Jn 8:29

LMj II 1

Lk 1: 28

Lk 1:11

Rom 12:2

LMj XI 1-9

Sir 45:23; Nm 25:8

and readiness of his soul appeased God for Israel when he pierced with his spear both the fornicator and his mistress. No sacrifice is more pleasing to God than zeal for souls. This zeal brought Christ down to earth and led him to endure many sufferings; it caused Enoch and Elijah to be taken up into heaven. The Lord will save the just and condemn the wicked.

As a result of this same zeal Saint Francis became rapt in ecstasy and was raised to the heights. Brother Pacifico had a vision in which he saw Saint Francis marked with the sign of the cross formed by two radiant swords, the one stretching from his head to his feet, the other from hand to hand across his chest. Likewise, because of his zeal, he was found worthy to be rapt in ecstacy in the church of San Rufino, where later he was to preach. His brothers were in a little shelter, about a mile away, that is, according to the measurements in this country, about half a league away.[a] Saint Francis appeared to them in a fiery chariot, and their minds were so filled with light that each could see into the consciences of the others. Saint Francis was taken up with Elijah and made pleasing to God. God's delight was in him because of his passion for righteousness. Few people nowadays worry about the wickedness the devil causes. Saint Francis, however, wept daily over his own sins and those of others.

Third, he was pleasing to God because of the refinement of his devotion. As the Psalm says: *I will praise the name of the Lord,* and continues: *this will please the Lord more than an ox or a bull with horns and hoofs* and as another Psalm tells us: *He who brings thanksgiving as his sacrifice honors me.*

Saint Francis was so carried away with the praise of God that he went into ecstasy while reciting the Divine Office, as his companion related. As he felt the ecstasy coming over him, he said to the brother: "Leave me." The brother suggested: "Wouldn't it be better to recite the Office first?" Saint Francis replied: "I cannot experience this kind of visitation at any time just as I decide, for that is not in my power; but I can begin the Divine Office whenever I like. I prefer to say the office later rather than forfeit this visitation." One day a Cistercian abbot met Saint Francis and asked him to pray for him. When Saint Francis did so, the abbot experienced a consolation he had never known before.

We see, then, Saint Francis is commended in this text for his deep humility and well tried virtue.

Margin references:
LMj IV 9
LMj IV 4
LMj X 5
Sir 44:16; 2 Kgs 2:11
1 Kgs 8:23
Ps 69:30-31
Ps 50:23

---

a. No doubt it was the cosmopolitan character of his listeners that prompted Bonaventure to give this explanation.

III

Finally, he is commended for his consummate love as the text concludes: *I have put my spirit upon him, he will bring forth justice to the nations.* Saint Paul writes to the Romans: *God's love has been poured into our hearts through the Holy Spirit who has been given to us.* When we receive grace, we receive the Holy Spirit. The Lord put his *Spirit* into Saint Francis, and afterwards *he brought forth justice.* Thus we read in the Gospel of Saint Matthew: *For it is not you who speak, but the Spirit of your Father speaking through you.* Our text asserts that God *put* his *spirit upon him.* What spirit is this? It is the spirit who is enabled to teach others, that is to say, God put the hierarchical spirit upon him.[a] Scripture says: *By his Spirit the heavens were made fair,* and Saint Gregory writes: "The virtues of preachers are the adornment of heaven."[b] I maintain, then, that God gave him the spirit of purification, enlightenment, and perfection, because the Spirit of the Lord first purified him, then enlightened him, and finally brought him to perfection.[c]

First, the Lord endowed him with the spirit of purification of which Ezechiel speaks: *The Spirit also lifted me and took me up, and I went away in bitterness in the heat of my spirit; for the hand of the Lord was with me, strengthening me.*

Our spirit is purified when it has lost the desire for earthly things. As light makes the air purer, so the soul becomes pure when it is united with the Eternal God. When the soul is united by love to a creature, it takes on that creature's likeness. Ezechiel's text says: *The Spirit lifted me,* and Job writes: *My soul would choose to be suspended.* When the soul is lifted up to God it must needs experience bitterness and conceive a distaste for created things past, present and future. As King Hezekiah lamented: *All my sleep has fled because of the bitterness of my soul.*

Saint Francis was raised on high by this purifying, strengthening, and uplifting spirit. When he went to Rome a priest saw him lifted a few feet from the ground into the air to about the height of a barrel, and the brothers often saw him lifted from the ground. All this happened because of his utmost purity. The angels lifted him into the air;

Rom 5:5

Mt 10:20

Jb 26:13

Ez 3:14

Ez 3:12

Jb 7:15

Is 38:15

LMj III 8

---

a. "Hierarchical spirit" is clumsy, but it is so technical that the editors could find no other expression, cf. supra, 44 a.

b. Gregory, *Homiliarum in evangelia* II, hom. 30, n. 7, (PL 76, 1224); *Gregory the Great: Forty Gospel Homilies,* Cistercian Studies Series 123, translated by David Hurst (Kalamazoo: Cistercian Publications, 1990), 243.

c. Pseudo-Dionysius, *The Celestial Hierarchy,* c. 3, n. 2, in *Pseudo-Dionysius: The Complete Works,* translated by Colm Luibheid and Paul Rorem, The Classics of Western Spirituality (New York: Paulist Press, 1987), 154; Saint Bonaventure is referring here to the classical three ways: *via purgativa, illuminativa, unitiva*; See *De triplici via* (VIII, 3-23).

as it is recorded, they lifted Saint Mary Magdalene while she was at prayer.[a] Such graces are given only to those who have set themselves above worldly desires.

Second, the Lord endowed Saint Francis with the spirit of enlightenment. Therefore the text of Sirach may be said of him: *In the midst of the church wisdom shall open his mouth and fill him with the spirit of wisdom and understanding.* Saint Francis was not an educated man, nor did he have a teacher. Yet he preached without ever uttering a word deserving of rebuke. The same is true of Saint Anthony.[b] The Apostles themselves were uneducated men, yet they were filled with wisdom; they preached, and they taught others.

Saint Francis once had to preach in the presence of Pope Honorius. With guidance from Pope Gregory, who was then cardinal bishop of Ostia, he prepared his sermon. When the time came to deliver it, his mind went blank, so he explained: "Someone, namely Pope Gregory IX, drew up for me a very learned sermon which I was going to preach, but now I've forgotten it completely. Wait a while and I'll ask the Lord to give me something to say." And after he had prayed, he preached a splendid sermon. We can apply to him the words of the Psalm: *I understand more than the aged.* He was a great teacher. He spoke accurately about creation and the simplicity of eternal truths. But he did not have the required competence from himself, he was enlightened entirely from on high. He unraveled hidden mysteries and he appeared to those absent. He possessed the spirit of enlightenment. If we want to receive the light of this wisdom, we must not rest content with earthly things.

Third, the Lord endowed Saint Francis with the spirit of perfection, which makes a person firm and unshakeable and brings completion and fulfillment. Of this spirit Sirach says: *Come over to me all you that desire me, and be filled with my fruits. For my spirit is sweet above honey and my inheritance above honey and the honeycomb.* The Lord filled him with this spirit and gave him its savor and solid food, as Hebrews says: *Solid food is for the perfect.* This spirit leads a person to perform humble tasks which are of the essence of perfect virtue. As Saint Augustine remarks: "Love has the right to flourish so that flourishing it

---

a. Surius in *Vita B. Mariae Magdalenae,* secund. Silvestr. Prierat., par. 10; *De probatis sanctorum historiis ab A. Lipomano conscriptis nunc primum a Laurent. Surio emandatis et auctis,* 6 vols. (Coloniae Agrippinae, 1570-1577).

b. That is, Saint Anthony the Abbot. He had no schooling, yet he was able to instruct the wise: Athanasius, *The Life of St. Antony and the Letter to Marcellinus,* The Classics of Western Spirituality, translated with introduction by Robert Gregg (New York: Paulist Press, 1980), 30.

may reach fulfillment."[a] With the Apostle Paul Saint Francis could
say: *My desire is to depart and be with Christ.* On the spirit of perfection
the Psalmist says: *Restore to me the joy of your salvation and strengthen me
with a perfect spirit.* The Lord said to the Apostles: *You shall receive the
power of the Holy Spirit coming upon you.*

Being endowed with this threefold spirit Saint Francis brought
forth justice as a model of God-like virtue, by the utter certainty of all
he foretold and by the awe-inspiring nature of the miracles he performed.

First, *he brought forth justice* as a model of God-like virtue. When we
come across someone in whom there is nothing blameworthy, who is
without anger and deceit, we account such a person upright and an
ambassador of God. According to Job, *the Lord does not save the wicked,
he gives judgment to the poor.* Saint Francis proclaimed the commands
of God, his promises, and his judgments. Job's text says: *He gives judgment to the poor,* and so the Lord told his Apostles: *Truly I say to you, in
the new world, when the Son of Man shall sit on his glorious throne, you who
have left all things and followed me will also sit on twelve thrones, judging the
twelve tribes of Israel.* According to the text quoted at the beginning of
the sermon, God's chosen servants *will bring forth justice.* To each
shepherd of his Church God has said: *I have made you a watchman.*
You, therefore, ought to live in a way that your very life is a sermon to
everyone. Saint Gregory writes: "To speak virtuously and to live
wickedly is to condemn oneself out of one's own mouth."[b] And another writer says: "Those who live in sin and preach virtue, give God
instructions on how he ought to punish them."[c] We read in the Book
of Revelation: *I saw another angel ascend from the rising of the sun; he
sealed out of every tribe of the sons of Israel the servants of God.* Those
sealed by the angel are in heaven living a life conformed to Christ.

Second, Saint Francis *brought forth justice* by the utter certainty of
everything he foretold. There was a hunchback who lived in de-
bauchery and greed, and some people asked Saint Francis to pay him
a visit. He replied: "Because you ask I will do so willingly. But this
man should know that *if he goes back to his vomit,* it will be all the worse
for him." So Saint Francis touched him, and with a creaking of his
bones, the man who had previously been bent over, now stood

Margin references: Phil 1:23 · Ps 51:12 · Acts 1:8 · Jb 36:6 · Mt 19:28 · Ez 3:17 · Rv 7:2, 4 · LMj XI 5 · Prv 26:11

---

a. Augustine, *Epistola 186*, c.3, n. 10, (PL 33, 819); *Saint Augustine: Letters*, vol. 4, The Fathers of the
Church, vol. 30, translated by Wilfrid Parsons (New York: Fathers of the Church, 1955), 198; also,
Tractatus Decem in Epistolam Iohannis ad Parthos, tr. 5, n. 4, SC 75, 353; *Tractates on the First
Epistle of John*, The Fathers of the Church, vol. 92, translated by John Retting (Washington: The
Catholic University of America Press, 1995), 188.

b. Gregory, *Moralia in Job* XV, c. 14, n. 17, CCSL 143 A, 757.

c. *Opus imperfectum in Matthaeum* (once attributed to Saint John Chrysostom), hom. 43, (PG 56, 876).

upright on his limbs. After some time he began to forget the warning Saint Francis had given and he went back to his vomit. Then one day while at a meal with some canons, the house fell in and they all escaped but him.

Finally, Saint Francis brought forth justice by the awe-inspiring nature of the miracles he performed. The Apostles had the power of working miracles: *As in their life they did wonders, so in death they wrought* Sir 48:14 *miracles.* Likewise, Saint Francis worked miracles both during his life and after his death.

You should recall, then, how Saint Francis cultivated profound humility, well tried virtue, and consummate love, so that you may arrive at eternal life, to which may He lead us Who lives and reigns with the Father and the Holy Spirit for ever. Amen.

Also Available from New City Press

FRANCIS OF ASSISI
Early Documents

General Editors: Regis J. Armstrong
William J. Short, and J. A. Wayne Hellmann

"Although its painstaking introductions and annotations are intended for scholars, the readings themselves are as vibrant, accessible, instructive and charming as Saint Francis himself must have been."

America

"*Francis of Assisi: Early Documents* provides new and updated resources to help forge the human Francis from the struggles of his time and from our misunderstanding about his call and charism. The scholarly presentation of the writings and primitive biographies in this volume focus on the earliest writings about Francis as *The Saint*, unveiling the person of Francis and his first followers in their medieval context. In this volume we are given a new song of Francis for our time."

Ingrid Peterson, O.S.F.
Author of *Praying with Clare of Assisi*

"I am told that Francis of Assisi has the longest single bibliography of any person in history. This magnificent collection, both scholarly and complete, will show you why 'the whole world runs after him.' It might start you running too."

Richard Rohr, O.F.M.
Center for Action and Contemplation
Albuquerque, New Mexico

THE SAINT
4th printing
ISBN 978-1-56548-110-7
paper, 640 pages

THE FOUNDER
2d printing
ISBN 978-1-56548-112-1
paper, 848 pages

THE PROPHET
2d printing
ISBN 978-1-56548-114-5
paper, 880 pages

INDEX
ISBN 978-1-56548-171-8
paper, 240 pages

ISBN 978-1-56548-199-2
6 x 9, paper, 280 pages

FRANCIS OF ASSISI
History, Hagiography and Hermeneutics
in the Early Documents

Jay M. Hammond (ed.)
Foreword by Joseph Chinnici, O.F.M.

The four volume publication of *Francis of Assisi*: *Early Documents — The Saint, The Founder, The Prophet*, and *Index* (1999-2002) is an indispensable resource for all who study St. Francis and the religious communities and traditions he engendered. To facilitate this study among scholars, students and those simply interested in learning more about St. Francis, the collection of essays in *Francis of Assisi*: *History, Hagiography and Hermeneutics in the Early Documents* serves as an invaluable guide for the fertile theological and spiritual terrain of the Franciscan early documents. To read these essays is to gain a deeper appreciation of Saint Francis, his medieval context, and the numerous stories written about this "poor and humble man of God."

Contributors:
Regis J. Armstrong, Margaret Carney, Lawrence S. Cunningham, Michael Cusato, Jay Hammond, Marilyn Hammond, Wayne Hellmann, Timothy J. Johnson, Daniel Michaels, Ingrid Peterson, William Short

FRANCIS TRILOGY

The Life of Saint Francis, The Remembrance
of the Desire of a Soul, The Treatise on the
Miracles of Saint Francis

Thomas of Celano
Foreword by Regis Armstrong, O.F.M. Cap.

Within two years after the death of Francis of Assisi,
Thomas of Celano composed *The Life of Saint
Francis of Assisi*, a portrait of the newly canonized
Umbrian. Less than twenty years later, Thomas
added *The Remembrance of the Desire of a Soul*, and
shortly afterwards his comprehensive *Treatise on the
Miracles of Saint Francis*. The three classic works
appear here for the first time in one volume.

ISBN 978-1-56548-204-3
6 x 9, paper, 392 pages

"Thomas of Celano's early literary portraits of Francis
brings us into intimate contact with the Poor Man of
Assisi. These works exhibit that rare combination of
charm and profundity. Every lover of Francis will
treasure this volume."

Lawrence S. Cunningham
John A. O'Brien Professor of Theology
The University of Notre Dame

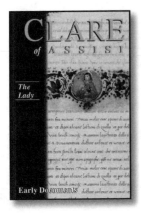

ISBN 978-1-56548-221-0
paper, 480 pages

ISBN 978-1-56548-220-3
hardcover, 480 pages

CLARE OF ASSISI: The Lady
Early Documents

Editor and Translator: Regis J. Armstrong

Provides new translations of Clare's writings and related primary sources, revised and new introductions from earlier editions, as well as previously unpublished documents to chronicle her life.

"This volume takes a big step toward making Clare and her story accessible to a wide audience. General readers and those meeting Clare for the first time will be able to see her story unfold in its chronological sequence beginning with the voice of Clare in her writings. Poor Clares will want this edition especially for its revised translations of Clare's Letters and *Form of Life*."

Ingrid Peterson, O.S.F.
Author of *Clare of Assisi: A Biographical Study*

"If Francis was the external manifestation of a new Gospel spirituality, Clare was its perfect internal manifestation. She lived secretely what he lived openly. Now some of the secrets are being revealed in this wonderful collection. What a gift to history!"

Richard Rohr
Center for Action and Contemplation
Albuquerque, New Mexico